Digital Electronics

Digital Electronics

Hilary. D. Brewster

Oxford Book Company
Jaipur ▪ New Delhi

Published By

Oxford Book Company

Regd. Off. "Bony Residency", Gate No. 2
Opp. Tilak Public School, Vishweswariya Nagar,
Gopalpura Road, Jaipur - 302018, India
Ph: 0141 - 2761280, Telefax: 2761381
email - oxfordbookjpr@gmail.com
website - oxfordbookcompany.com

Delhi Office: 102, 1st Floor, Satyam House,
4327/3, Ansari Road, Darya Ganj,
New Delhi - 110002, India
Ph: 011-45652440

Published in India, 2025

ISBN : 9788189473976

Price : ₹ 2295/-

Typeset by Shivangi Computers, Jaipur

Printed and bound in India by Thomson Press Ltd.,
New Delhi

Preface

Analog and digital electronic are one of the core course sequences in the electrical, electronics and computer engineering . As a gateway to the exciting and rapidly growing field of microelectronics, it is essential that these courses be taught well, both for future specialists and for those concentrating in other areas of electrical engineering or computer science. This book is for everyone who wants to design and study of real digital circuits.

It is based on the idea that, in order to do this, you have to grasp the fundamentals, but at the same time you need to understand how things work in the real world. In the past, when digital designers were building systems with thousands or at most tens of thousands of gates and flip-flops, academic courses emphasized minimization and efficient use of chip and board-level resources. Today, a single chip can contain tens of millions of transistors and can be programmed to create a system-on-a-chip that, using the technology of the past, would have required hundreds of discrete chips containing millions of individual.

This book must provide a solid foundation in the fundamentals of electronics rather than a sampling of the most popular current topics. Finally, circuit design, as its name implies, is a subject that should be well-suited for honing students' skills as engineering designers. All of these factors have forced a re-examination of the electronics sequence and opened the door to fresh approaches that are better adapted to the needs of students.

Hilary. D. Brewster

Contents

Chapter 1

Numeration Systems

NUMBERS AND SYMBOLS

The expression of numerical quantities is something we tend to take for granted. This is both a good and a bad thing in the study of electronics. It is good, in that we're accustomed to the use and manipulation of numbers for the many calculations used in analyzing electronic circuits. On the other hand, the particular system of notation we've been taught from grade school onward is not the system used internally in modern electronic computing devices, and learning any different system of notation requires some re–examination of deeply ingrained assumptions.

First, we have to distinguish the difference between numbers and the symbols we use to represent numbers. A number is a mathematical quantity, usually correlated in electronics to a physical quantity such as voltage, current, or resistance. There are many different types of numbers. Here are just a few types, for example

WHOLE NUMBERS:

1, 2, 3, 4, 5, 6, 7, 8, 9...

INTEGERS:

–4, –3, –2, –1, 0, 1, 2, 3, 4...

IRRATIONAL NUMBERS:

π (approx. 3.1415927), e (approx. 2.718281828),
square root of any prime

REAL NUMBERS:

(All one–dimensional numerical values, negative and positive, including zero, whole, integer, and irrational numbers)

COMPLEX NUMBERS:

$3 - 4i$, $34 + 5i$

Different types of numbers find different application in the physical world. Whole numbers work well for counting discrete objects, such as the number of resistors in a circuit. Integers are needed when negative equivalents of whole numbers are required. Irrational numbers are numbers that cannot be exactly expressed as the ratio of two integers, and the ratio of a perfect circle's circumference to its diameter ($2\pi r/d$) is a good physical example of this.

The non–integer quantities of voltage, current, and resistance that we're used to dealing with in DC circuits can be expressed as real numbers, in either fractional or decimal form. For AC circuit analysis, however, real numbers fail to capture the dual essence of magnitude and phase angle, and so we turn to the use of complex numbers in either rectangular or polar form.

If we are to use numbers to understand processes in the physical world, make scientific predictions, or balance our checkbooks, we must have a way of symbolically denoting them.

In other words, we may know how much money we have in our checking account, but to keep record of it we need to have some system worked out to symbolize that quantity on paper, or in some other kind of form for record–keeping and tracking. There are two basic ways we can do this analog and digital. With analog representation, the quantity is symbolized in a way that is infinitely divisible. With digital representation, the quantity is symbolized in a way that is discretely packaged.

You're probably already familiar with an analog representation of money, and didn't realize it for what it was. Have you ever seen a fund–raising poster made with a picture of a thermometer on it, where the height of the red column indicated the amount of money collected for the cause? The more money collected, the taller the column of red ink on the poster.

An analog representation of a numerical quantity

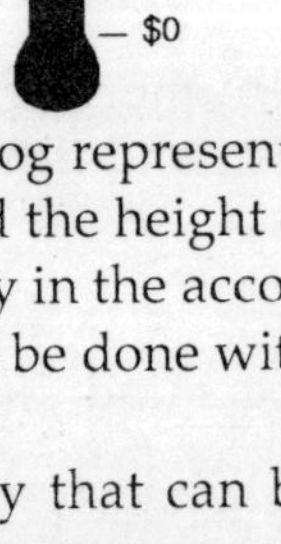

This is an example of an analog representation of a number. There is no real limit to how finely divided the height of that column can be made to symbolize the amount of money in the account. Changing the height of that column is something that can be done without changing the essential nature of what it is.

Length is a physical quantity that can be divided as small as you would like, with no practical limit. The slide rule is a mechanical device that uses the very same physical quantity—length—to represent numbers, and to help perform arithmetical operations with two or more numbers at a time. It, too, is an analog device.

On the other hand, a digital representation of that same monetary figure, written with standard symbols (sometimes called ciphers), looks like this.

$35,955.38

Unlike the "thermometer" poster with its red column, those symbolic characters above cannot be finely divided that particular combination of ciphers stand for one quantity and one quantity only. If more money is added to the account (+.$40.12), different symbols must be used to represent the new balance ($35,995.50), or at least the same symbols arranged in different patterns. This is an example of digital representation. The counterpart to the slide rule (analog) is also a digital device the abacus, with beads that are moved back and forth on rods to symbolize numerical quantities

Slide rule *(an analog device)*

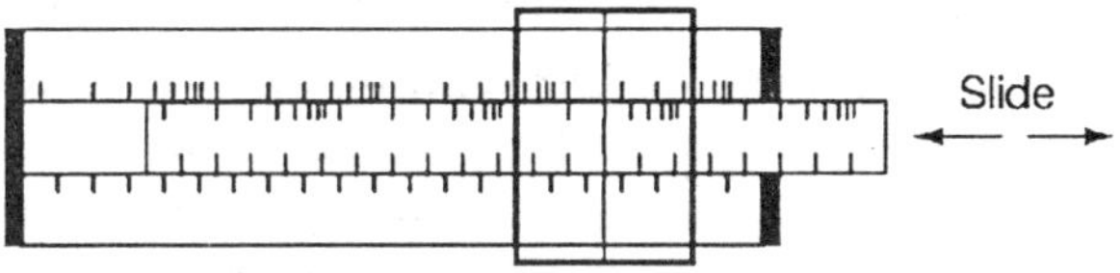

Numerical quantities are represented by the positioning of the slide.

Abacus *(a digital device)*

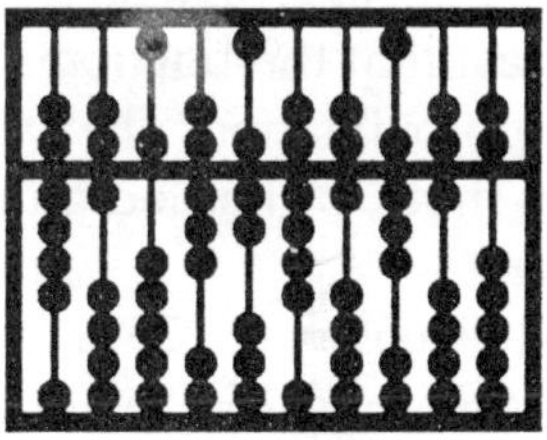

Numerical quantities are represented by the discrete positions of the beads.

Lets contrast these two methods of numerical representation .

Analog	*Digital*
Intuitively understood	Requires training to interpret
Infinitely divisible	Discrete
Prone to errors of precision	Absolute precision

Interpretation of numerical symbols is something we tend to take for granted, because it has been taught to us for many years. However, if you were to try to communicate a quantity of something to a person ignorant of decimal numerals, that person could still understand the simple thermometer chart!

The infinitely divisible vs. discrete and precision comparisons are really flip–sides of the same coin. The fact that digital representation is composed of individual, discrete symbols (decimal digits and abacus beads) necessarily means that it will be able to symbolize quantities in precise steps.

On the other hand, an analog representation (such as a slide rule's length) is not composed of individual steps, but rather a continuous range of motion.

The ability for a slide rule to characterize a numerical quantity to infinite resolution is a trade–off for imprecision. If a slide rule is bumped, an error will be introduced into the representation of the number that was "entered" into it. However, an abacus must be bumped much harder before its beads are completely dislodged from their places (sufficient to represent a different number).

Please don't misunderstand this difference in precision by thinking that digital representation is necessarily more accurate than analog. Just because a clock is digital doesn't mean that it will always read time more accurately than an analog clock, it just means that the interpretation of its display is less ambiguous.

Divisibility of analog versus digital representation can be further illuminated by talking about the representation of irrational numbers. Numbers such as? are called irrational, because they cannot be exactly expressed as the fraction of integers, or whole numbers. Although you might have learned in the past that the fraction 22/7 can be used for π in calculations, this is just an approximation. The actual number "pi" cannot be exactly expressed by any finite, or limited, number of decimal places. The digits of π go on forever

3.1415926535897932384.....

It is possible, at least theoretically, to set a slide rule (or even a thermometer column) so as to perfectly represent the number, because analog symbols have no minimum limit to the degree that they can be increased or decreased.

An abacus with 10 rods simply cannot represent any more than 10 digits worth of the number. An abacus would have to have an infinite number of beads and rods!

The tradeoff, of course, is the practical limitation to adjusting, and reading, analog symbols.

Practically speaking, one cannot read a slide rule's scale to the 10th digit of precision, because the marks on the scale are too coarse and human vision is too limited. An abacus, on the other hand, can be set and read with no interpretational errors at all.

Furthermore, analog symbols require some kind of standard by which they can be compared for precise interpretation. Slide rules have markings printed along the length of the slides to translate length into standard quantities. Even the thermometer chart has numerals written along its height to show how much money (in dollars) the red column represents for any given amount of height. Imagine if we all tried to communicate simple numbers to each other by spacing our hands apart varying distances.

The number 1 might be signified by holding our hands 1 inch apart, the number 2 with 2 inches, and so on. If someone held their hands 17 inches apart to represent the number 17, would everyone around them be able to immediately and accurately interpret that distance as 17? Probably not.

Some would guess short (15 or 16) and some would guess long (18 or 19). Of course, fishermen who brag about their catches don't mind overestimations in quantity!

Perhaps this is why people have generally settled upon digital symbols for representing numbers, especially whole numbers and integers, which find the most application in everyday life. Using the fingers on our hands, we have a ready means of symbolizing integers from 0 to 10. We can make hash marks on paper, wood, or stone to represent the same quantities quite easily

5 + 5 + 3 = 13

For large numbers, though, the "hash mark" numeration system is too inefficient.

SYSTEMS OF NUMERATION

The Romans devised a system that was a substantial improvement over hash marks, because it used a variety of symbols (or ciphers) to represent increasingly large quantities. The notation for 1 is the capital letter I. The notation for 5 is the capital letter V. Other ciphers possess increasing values

X = 10
L = 50
C = 100
D = 500
M = 1000

If a cipher is accompanied by another cipher of equal or lesser value to the immediate right of it, with no ciphers greater than that other cipher to the right of that other cipher, that other cipher's value is added to the total quantity. Thus, VIII symbolizes the number 8, and CLVII symbolizes the number 157. On the other hand, if a cipher is accompanied by another cipher of lesser value to the immediate left, that other cipher's value is subtracted from the first.

Therefore, IV symbolizes the number 4 (V minus I), and CM symbolizes the number 900 (M minus C). You might have noticed that ending credit sequences for most motion pictures contain a notice for the date of production, in Roman numerals. For the year 1987, it would read .MCMLXXXVII. Let's break this numeral down into its constituent parts, from left to right:

M = 1000

+

CM = 900

+

L = 50

+

XXX = 30

+

V = 5

+

II = 2

Aren't you glad we don't use this system of numeration? Large numbers are very difficult to denote this way, and the left vs. right/ subtraction vs. addition of values can be very confusing, too. Another major problem with this system is that there is no provision for representing the number zero or negative numbers, both very important concepts in mathematics.

Roman culture, however, was more pragmatic with respect to mathematics than most, choosing only to develop their numeration system as far as it was necessary for use in daily life.

We owe one of the most important ideas in numeration to the ancient Babylonians, who were the first (as far as we know) to develop the concept of cipher position, or place value, in representing larger numbers. Instead of inventing new ciphers to represent larger numbers, as the Romans did, they re–used the same ciphers, placing them in different positions from right to left.

Our own decimal numeration system uses this concept, with only ten ciphers (0, 1, 2, 3, 4, 5, 6, 7, 8, and 9) used in "weighted" positions to represent very large and very small numbers.

Each cipher represents an integer quantity, and each place from right to left in the notation represents a multiplying constant, or weight, for each integer quantity. For example, if we see the decimal notation "1206", we known that this may be broken down into its constituent weight–products as such .

$$1206 = 1000 + 200 + 6$$
$$1206 = (1 \times 1000) + (2 \times 100) + (0 \times 10) + (6 \times 1)$$

Each cipher is called a digit in the decimal numeration system, and each weight, or place value, is ten times that of the one to the immediate right. So, we have a ones place, a tens place, a hundreds place, a thousands place, and so on, working from right to left.

Right about now, you're probably wondering why I'm laboring to describe the obvious.

Who needs to be told how decimal numeration works, after you've studied math as advanced as algebra and trigonometry? The reason is to better understand other numeration systems, by first knowing the how's and why's of the one you're already used to. The decimal numeration system uses ten ciphers, and place–weights that are multiples of ten. What if we made a numeration system with the same strategy of weighted places, except with fewer or more ciphers?

The binary numeration system is such a system. Instead of ten different cipher symbols, with each weight constant being ten times the one before it, we only have two cipher symbols, and each weight constant is twice as much as the one before it.

The two allowable cipher symbols for the binary system of numeration are "1" and "0," and these ciphers are arranged right–to–left in doubling values of weight.

The rightmost place is the ones place, just as with decimal notation. Proceeding to the left, we have the twos place, the fours place, the eights place, the sixteens place, and so on. For example, the following binary number can be expressed, just like the decimal number 1206, as a sum of each cipher value times its respective weight constant .

$$11010 = 2 + 8 + 16 = 26$$
$$11010 = (1 \times 16) + (1 \times 8) + (0 \times 4) + (1 \times 2) + (0 \times 1)$$

This can get quite confusing, as I've written a number with binary numeration (11010), and then shown its place values and total in standard, decimal numeration form (16 + 8 + 2 = 26). In the above example, we're mixing two different kinds of numerical notation. To avoid unnecessary confusion, we have to denote which form of numeration we're using when we write (or type!).

Typically, this is done in subscript form, with a "2" for binary and a "10" for decimal, so the binary number 110102 is equal to the decimal number 2610. The subscripts are not mathematical operation symbols like superscripts (exponents) are.

All they do is indicate what system of numeration we're using when we write these symbols for other people to read. If you see "310", all this means is the number three written using decimal numeration. However, if you see "310", this means something completely different three to the tenth power (59,049).

As usual, if no subscript is shown, the cipher(s) are assumed to be representing a decimal number.

Commonly, the number of cipher types (and therefore, the place–value multiplier) used in a numeration system is called that system's base. Binary is referred to as "base two" numeration, and decimal as "base ten." Additionally, we refer to each cipher position in binary as a bit rather than the familiar word digit used in the decimal system.

Now, why would anyone use binary numeration? The decimal system, with its ten ciphers, makes a lot of sense, being that we have ten fingers on which to count between our two hands. (It is interesting that some ancient central American cultures used numeration systems with a base of twenty.

Presumably, they used both fingers and toes to count!!). But the primary reason that the binary numeration system is used in modern electronic computers is because of the ease of representing two cipher states (0 and 1) electronically. With relatively simple circuitry, we can perform mathematical operations on binary numbers by representing each bit of the numbers by a circuit which is either on (current) or off (no current).

Just like the abacus with each rod representing another decimal digit, we simply add more circuits to give us more bits to symbolize larger numbers.

Binary numeration also lends itself well to the storage and retrieval of numerical information on magnetic tape (spots of iron oxide on the tape either being magnetized for a binary "1" or demagnetized for a binary "0"), optical disks (a laser–burned pit in the aluminum foil representing a binary "1" and an unburned spot representing a binary "0"), or a variety of other media types.

Before we go on to learning exactly how all this is done in digital circuitry, we need to become more familiar with binary and other associated systems of numeration.

DECIMAL VERSUS BINARY NUMERATION

Let's count from zero to twenty using four different kinds of numeration systems hash marks, Roman numerals, decimal, and binary.

<table>
<tr><th>System:</th><th>HashMarks</th><th>Roman</th><th>Decimal</th><th>Binary</th></tr>
<tr><td>Zero</td><td>n/a</td><td>n/a</td><td>0</td><td>0</td></tr>
<tr><td>One</td><td>|</td><td>I</td><td>1</td><td>1</td></tr>
<tr><td>Two</td><td>||</td><td>II</td><td>2</td><td>10</td></tr>
<tr><td>Three</td><td>|||</td><td>III</td><td>3</td><td>11</td></tr>
<tr><td>Four</td><td>||||</td><td>IV</td><td>4</td><td>100</td></tr>
<tr><td>Five</td><td>/|||/</td><td>V</td><td>5</td><td>101</td></tr>
<tr><td>Six</td><td>/|||/|</td><td>VI</td><td>6</td><td>110</td></tr>
<tr><td>Seven</td><td>/|||/||</td><td>VII</td><td>7</td><td>111</td></tr>
<tr><td>Eight</td><td>/|||/|||</td><td>VIII</td><td>8</td><td>1000</td></tr>
<tr><td>Nine</td><td>/|||/||||</td><td>IX</td><td>9</td><td>1001</td></tr>
<tr><td>Ten</td><td>/|||//|||/</td><td>X</td><td>10</td><td>1010</td></tr>
<tr><td>Eleven</td><td>/|||//|||/|</td><td>XI</td><td>11</td><td>1011</td></tr>
<tr><td>Twelve</td><td>/|||//|||/||</td><td>XII</td><td>12</td><td>1100</td></tr>
<tr><td>Thirteen</td><td>/|||//|||/|||</td><td>XIII</td><td>13</td><td>1101</td></tr>
<tr><td>Fourteen</td><td>/|||//|||/||||</td><td>XIV</td><td>14</td><td>1110</td></tr>
<tr><td>Fifteen</td><td>/|||//|||//|||/</td><td>XV</td><td>15</td><td>1111</td></tr>
<tr><td>Sixteen</td><td>/|||//|||//|||/|</td><td>XVI</td><td>16</td><td>10000</td></tr>
<tr><td>Seventeen</td><td>/|||//|||//|||/||</td><td>XVII</td><td>17</td><td>10001</td></tr>
<tr><td>Eighteen</td><td>/|||//|||//|||/|||</td><td>XVIII</td><td>18</td><td>10010</td></tr>
<tr><td>Nineteen</td><td>/|||//|||//|||/||||</td><td>XIX</td><td>19</td><td>10011</td></tr>
<tr><td>Twenty</td><td>/|||//|||//|||//|||/</td><td>XX</td><td>20</td><td>10100</td></tr>
</table>

Neither hash marks nor the Roman system are very practical for symbolizing large numbers. Obviously, place–weighted systems such as decimal and binary are more efficient for the task. Notice, though, how much shorter decimal notation is over binary notation, for the same number of quantities. What takes five bits in binary notation only takes two digits in decimal notation.

This raises an interesting question regarding different numeration systems how large of a number can be represented with a limited number of cipher positions, or places? With the crude hash–mark system, the number of places is the largest number that can be represented, since one hash mark "place" is required for every integer step. For place–weighted systems of numeration, however, the answer is found by taking base of the numeration system (10 for decimal, 2 for binary) and raising it to the power of the number of places.

For example, 5 digits in a decimal numeration system can represent 100,000 different integer number values, from 0 to 99,999 (10 to the 5th power = 100,000). 8 bits in a binary numeration system can represent 256 different integer number values, from 0 to 11111111 (binary), or 0 to 255 (decimal), because 2 to the 8th power equals 256. With each additional place position to the number field, the capacity for representing numbers increases by a factor of the base (10 for decimal, 2 for binary).

An interesting footnote for this topic is the one of the first electronic digital computers, the Eniac. The designers of the Eniac chose to represent numbers in decimal form, digitally, using a series of circuits called "ring counters" instead of just going with the binary numeration system, in an effort to minimize the number of circuits required to represent and calculate very large numbers. This approach turned out to be counter–productive, and virtually all digital computers since then have been purely binary in design.

To convert a number in binary numeration to its equivalent in decimal form, all you have to do is calculate the sum of all the products of bits with their respective place–weight constants. To illustrate

Convert 110011012 to decimal form:

bits	=	1	1	0	0	1	1	0	1
weight = (in decimal notation)	— 128	— 64	— 32	— 16	— 8	— 4	— 2	— 1	

The bit on the far right side is called the Least Significant Bit (LSB), because it stands in the place of the lowest weight (the one's place). The bit on the far left side is called the Most Significant Bit (MSB), because it stands in the place of the highest weight (the one hundred twenty–eight's place). Remember, a bit value of "1" means that the respective place weight gets added to the total value, and a bit value of "0" means that the respective place weight does not get added to the total value. With the above example, we have

12810 + 6410 + 810 + 410 + 110 = 20510

If we encounter a binary number with a dot (.), called a "binary point" instead of a decimal point, we follow the same procedure, realizing that each place weight to the right of the point is one–half the value of the one to the left of it (just as each place weight to the right of a decimal point is one–tenth the weight of the one to the left of it).

OCTAL AND HEXADECIMAL NUMERATION

Because binary numeration requires so many bits to represent relatively small numbers compared to the economy of the decimal system, analyzing the numerical states inside of digital electronic circuitry can be a tedious task. Computer programmers who design sequences of number codes instructing a computer what to do would have a very difficult task if they were forced to work with nothing but long strings of 1's and 0's, the "native language" of any digital circuit.

To make it easier for human engineers, technicians, and programmers to "speak" this language of the digital world, other systems of place–weighted numeration have been made which are very easy to convert to and from binary.

One of those numeration systems is called octal, because it is a place–weighted system with a base of eight. Valid ciphers include the symbols 0, 1, 2, 3, 4, 5, 6, and 7. Each place weight differs from the one next to it by a factor of eight. Another system is called hexadecimal, because it is a place–weighted system with a base of sixteen.

Valid ciphers include the normal decimal symbols 0, 1, 2, 3, 4, 5, 6, 7, 8, and 9, plus six alphabetical characters A, B, C, D, E, and F, to make a total of sixteen. As you might have guessed already, each place weight differs from the one before it by a factor of sixteen. Let's count again from zero to twenty using decimal, binary, octal, and hexadecimal to contrast these systems of numeration:

Number	*Decimal*	*Binary*	*Octal*	*Hexadecimal*
Zero	0	0	0	0
One	1	1	1	1
Two	2	10	2	2
Three	3	11	3	3
Four	4	100	4	4
Five	5	101	5	5
Six	6	110	6	6
Seven	7	111	7	7
Eight	8	1000	10	8
Nine	9	1001	11	9
Ten	10	1010	12	A
Eleven	11	1011	13	B
Twelve	12	1100	14	C
Thirteen	13	1101	15	D
Fourteen	14	1110	16	E
Fifteen	15	1111	17	F
Sixteen	16	10000	20	10
Seventeen	17	10001	21	11
Eighteen	18	10010	22	12
Nineteen	19	10011	23	13
Twenty	20	10100	24	14

Octal and hexadecimal numeration systems would be pointless if not for their ability to be easily converted to and from binary notation. Their primary purpose in being is to serve as a "shorthand" method of denoting a number represented electronically in binary form. Because the bases of octal (eight) and hexadecimal (sixteen) are even multiples of binary's base (two), binary. Bits can be grouped together and directly converted to or from their respective octal or hexadecimal digits. With octal, the binary bits are grouped in three's (because 23 = 8), and with hexadecimal, the binary bits are grouped in four's (because 24 = 16).

Binary to Octalconversion
Convert 10110111.12 to octal:

	implied zero			implied zeros
	|			||
	010	110	111	100
Convert each group of bits to its octal equivalent:	2	6	7	4

Answer: 10110111.12 = 267.48

We had to group the bits in three's, from the binary point left, and from the binary point right, adding (implied) zeros as necessary to make complete 3–bit groups. Each octal digit was translated from the 3–bit binary groups. Binary–to–Hexadecimal conversion is much the same

---

Binary to Hexadecimal Conversion
Convert 10110111.12 to hexadecimal:

			implied zeros
			|||
	1011	0111	1000
Convert each group of bits to its hexadecimal equivalent	B	7	8

Answer: 10110111.12 = B7.816

Here we had to group the bits in four's, from the binary point left, and from the binary point right, adding (implied) zeros as necessary to make complete 4–bit groups.

Likewise, the conversion from either octal or hexadecimal to binary is done by taking each octal or hexadecimal digit and converting it to its equivalent binary (3 or 4 bit) group, then putting all the binary bit groups together. Incidentally, hexadecimal notation is more popular, because binary bit groupings in digital equipment are commonly multiples of eight (8, 16, 32, 64, and 128 bit), which are also multiples of 4. Octal, being based on binary bit groups of 3, doesn't work out evenly with those common bit group sizings.

OCTAL AND HEXADECIMAL TO DECIMAL CONVERSION

Although the prime intent of octal and hexadecimal numeration systems is for the "shorthand" representation of binary numbers in digital electronics, we sometimes have the need to convert from either of those systems to decimal form. Of course, we could simply convert the hexadecimal or octal format to binary, then convert from binary to decimal, since we already know how to do both, but we can also convert directly.

Because octal is a base–eight numeration system, each place–weight value differs from either adjacent place by a factor of eight. For example, the octal number 245.37 can be broken down into place values as such.

octal digits =	2	4	5		3	7
	–	–	–	–	–	–
weight =	6	8	1		1	1
(in decimal	4				/	/
notation)					8	6

The decimal value of each octal place–weight times its respective cipher multiplier can be determined as follows.

(2 × 6410) + (4 × 810) + (5 × 110) + (3 × 0.12510) +
(7 × 0.01562510) = 165.48437510

The technique for converting hexadecimal notation to decimal is the same, except that each successive place–weight changes by a factor of sixteen. Simply denote each digit's weight, multiply each hexadecimal digit value by its respective weight (in decimal form), then add up all the decimal values to get a total. For example, the hexadecimal number 30F.A916 can be converted like this.

hexadecimal digits =	3	0	F		A	9
–	–	–	–	–	–	
weight =	2	1	1		1	1
(in decimal	5	6			/	/
notation)	6				1	2
					6	5
					6	

(3 × 25610) + (0 × 1610) + (15 × 110) + (10 × 0.062510) +
(9 × 0.0039062510) = 783.660156251O

These basic techniques may be used to convert a numerical notation of any base into decimal form, if you know the value of that numeration system's base.

CONVERSION FROM DECIMAL NUMERATION

Because octal and hexadecimal numeration systems have bases that are multiples of binary (base 2), conversion back and forth between either hexadecimal or octal and binary is very easy. Also, because we are so familiar with the decimal system, converting binary, octal, or hexadecimal to decimal form is relatively easy (simply add up the products of cipher values and place–weights).

However, conversion from decimal to any of these "strange" numeration systems is a different matter. The method which will probably make the most sense is the "trial–and–fit" method, where you try to "fit" the binary, octal, or hexadecimal notation to the desired value as represented in decimal form.

For example, let's say that the decimal value of 87 in binary form. Let's start by drawing a binary number field, complete with place–weight values.

	_	_	_	_	_	_	_	_
weight =	1	6	3	1	8	4	2	1
(in decimal	2	4	2	6				
notation)	8							

Well, we know that we won't have a "1" bit in the 128's place, because that would immediately give us a value greater than 87. However, since the next weight to the right (64) is less than 87, we know that we must have a "1" there.

	1							
	_	_	_	_	_	_	_	Decimal value so far=64_{10}
weight =	6	3	1	8	4	2	1	
(in decimal	4	2	6					
notation)								

If we were to make the next place to the right a "1" as well, our total value would be 6410 + 3210, or 9610. This is greater than 8710, so we know that this bit must be a "0".

If we make the next (16's) place bit equal to "1," this brings our total value to 6410 + 1610, or 8010, which is closer to our desired value (8710) without exceeding it.

	1	0	1					
	_	_	_	_	_	_	_	Decimal value so far = 80_{10}
weight =	6	3	1	8	4	2	1	
(in decimal	4	2	6					
notation)								

By continuing in this progression, setting each lesser–weight bit as we need to come up to our desired total value without exceeding it, we will eventually arrive at the correct figure.

	1	0	1	0	1	1	1	
	_	_	_	_	_	_	_	Decimal value so far = 87_{10}
weight=	6	3	1	8	4	2	1	
(in decimal	4	2	6					
notation)								

This trial–and–fit strategy will work with octal and hexadecimal conversions, too. Let's take the same decimal figure, 8710, and convert it to octal numeration.

	_	_	_
weight = (in decimal notation)	64	8	1

If we put a cipher of "1" in the 64's place, we would have a total value of 6410 (less than 8710).

If we put a cipher of "2" in the 64's place, we would have a total value of 12810 (greater than 8710). This tells us that our octal numeration must start with a "1" in the 64's place.

	1			
	_	_	_	Decimalvalueso far = 64_{10}
weight = (in decimal notation)	64	8	1	

Now, we need to experiment with cipher values in the 8's place to try and get a total (decimal) value as close to 87 as possible without exceeding it. Trying the first few cipher options, we get.

"1" = 6410 + 810 = 7210

"2" = 6410 + 1610 = 8010

"3" = 6410 + 2410 = 8810

A cipher value of "3" in the 8's place would put us over the desired total of 8710, so "2" it is!

	1	2		
	_	_	_	Decimalvalue so far = 80_{10}
weight = (in decimal notation)	64	8	1	

Now, all we Need to Make a total of 87 is a Cipher of "7" in the 1's Place.

Conversion from decimal numeration: Because octal and hexadecimal numeration systems have bases that are multiples of binary (base 2), conversion back and forth between either hexadecimal or octal and binary is very easy.

Also, because we are so familiar with the decimal system, converting binary, octal, or hexadecimal to decimal form is relatively easy (simply add up the products of cipher values and place-weights). However, conversion from decimal to any of these "strange" numeration systems is a different matter.

The method which will probably make the most sense is the "trial-and-fit" method, where you try to "fit" the binary, octal, or hexadecimal notation to the desired value as represented in decimal form. For example, let's say that the decimal value of 87 in binary form.

Let's start by drawing a binary number field, complete with place-weight values.

weight = 1 6 3 1 8 4 2 1

(in decimal 2 4 2 6 notation) 8

Well, we know that we won't have a "1" bit in the 128's place, because that would immediately give us a value greater than 87. However, since the next weight to the right (64) is less than 87, we know that we must have a "1" there.

1 - - - - - - - Decimal value so far = 64_{10}

weight = 6 3 1 8 4 2 1

(in decimal 4 2 6 notation)

If we were to make the next place to the right a "1" as well, our total value would be 64_{10} + 32_{10}, or 96_{10}. This is greater than 87_{10}, so we know that this bit must be a "0".

If we make the next (16's) place bit equal to "1," this brings our total value to 64_{10} + 16_{10}, or 80_{10}, which is closer to our desired value (87_{10}) without exceeding it.

1 0 1. - - - - - - - Decimal value so far = 80_{10}

weight = 6 3 1 8 4 2 1

(in decimal 4 2 6 notation)

By continuing in this progression, setting each lesser-weight bit as we need to come up to our desired total value without exceeding it, we will eventually arrive at the correct figure.

1 0 1 0 1 1 1 - - - - - - - Decimal value so far = 87_{10}

weight = 6 3 1 8 4 2 1

(in decimal 4 2 6 notation)

This trial-and-fit strategy will work with octal and hexadecimal conversions, too. Let's take the same decimal figure, 87_{10}, and convert it to octal numeration.

weight= 6 8 1 in decimal 4 notation)

If we put a cipher of "1" in the 64's place, we would have a total value of 64_{10} (less than 87_{10}).

If we put a cipher of "2" in the 64's place, we would have a total value of 128_{10} (greater than 87_{10}). This tells us that our octal numeration must start with a "1" in the 64's place.

1 - - - Decimal value so far = 64_{10} weight = 6 8 1

(in decimal 4 notation)

Now, we need to experiment with cipher values in the 8's place to try and get a total (decimal) value as close to 87 as possible without exceeding it. Trying the first few cipher options, we get.

"1" = $64_{10} + 8_{10} = 72_{10}$

"2" = $64_{10} + 16_{10} = 80_{10}$

"3" = $64_{10} + 24_{10} = 88_{10}$

A cipher value of "3" in the 8's place would put us over the desired total of 87_{10}, so "2" it is!

12 - - - Decimal value so far = 80_{10}

weight= 6 8 1

(in decimal 4

notation)

Now, all we need to make a total of 87 is a cipher of "7" in the 1's place.

1 2 7 - - - Decimal value so far = 87_{10}

weight = 6 8 1

(in decimal 4 notation)

Of course, if you were paying attention during the last section on octal/binary conversions, you will realize that we can take the binary representation of (decimal) 87_{10}, which we previously determined to be 1010111_2, and easily convert from that to octal to check our work.

Implied zeros

| |

001 010 111 Binary

1 2 7 Octal

Answer: $1010111_2 = 127_8$

Can we do decimal-to-hexadecimal conversion the same way? Sure, but who would want to? This method is simple to understand, but laborious to carry out.

There is another way to do these conversions, which is essentially the same (mathematically), but easier to accomplish.

This other method uses repeated cycles of division (using decimal notation) to break the decimal numeration down into multiples of binary, octal, or hexadecimal place-weight values. In the first cycle of division, we take the original decimal number and divide it by the base of the numeration system that we're converting to (binary=2 octal=8, hex=16). Then, we take the whole-number portion of division result (quotient) and divide it by the base value again, and so on, until we end up with a quotient of less than 1.

The binary, octal, or hexadecimal digits are determined by the "remainders" left over by each division step. Let's see how this works for binary, with the decimal example of 87_{10}.

87/2 = 43.5

Divide 87 by 2, to get a quotient of 43.5

Division "remainder" = 1, or the < 1 portion of the quotient times the divisor (0.5 × 2).

43/2 = 21.5

Take the whole-number portion of 43.5 (43) and divide it by 2 to get 21.5, or 21 with a remainder of 1.

21/2 = 10.5

And so on... remainder = 1 (0.5 × 2)

10/2 = 5.0

And so on... remainder = 0

5/2 = 2.5

And so on... remainder = 1 (0.5 × 2)

2/2 = 1.0

And so on... remainder = 0

1/2 = 0.5

... until we get a quotient of less than 1 remainder = 1 (0.5 × 2)

The binary bits are assembled from the remainders of the successive division steps, beginning with the LSB and proceeding to the MSB. In this case, we arrive at a binary notation of 1010111_2. When we divide by 2, we will always get a quotient ending with either ".0" or ".5", i.e. a remainder of either 0 or 1.

As was said before, this repeat-division technique for conversion will work for numeration systems other than binary. If we were to perform successive divisions using a different number, such as 8 for conversion to octal, we will necessarily get remainders between 0 and 7. Let's try this with the same decimal number, 87_{10}.

87/8 = 10.875

Divide 87 by 8, to get a quotient of 10.875 Division "remainder" = 7, or the < 1 portion of the quotient times the divisor (.875 × 8)

10/8 = 1.25

Remainder = 2

1/8 = 0.125

Quotient is less than 1, so we'll stop here.

Remainder = 1

Result: $87_{10} = 127_8$

We can use a similar technique for converting numeration systems dealing with quantities less than 1, as well. For converting a decimal number less than 1 into binary, octal, or hexadecimal, we use repeated multiplication, taking the integer portion of the product in each step as the next digit of our converted number. Let's use the decimal number 0.8125_{10} as an example, converting to binary.

$0.8125 \times 2 = 1.625$ Integer portion of product = 1

$0.625 \times 2 = 1.25$ Take < 1 portion of product and remultiply

Integer portion of product = 1

$0.25 \times 2 = 0.5$ Integer portion of product = 0

$0.5 \times 2 = 1.0$ Integer portion of product = 1

Stop when product is a pure integer (ends with.0)

Result : $0.8125_{10} = 0.1101_2$

As with the repeat-division process for integers, each step gives us the next digit (or bit) further away from the "point." With integer (division), we worked from the LSB to the MSB (right-to-left), but with repeated multiplication, we worked from the left to the right. To convert a decimal number greater than 1, with a < 1 component, we must use *both* techniques, one at a time. Take the decimal example of 54.40625_{10}, converting to binary.

Repeated Division for the integer portion:

54/2 = 27.0	Remainder = 0
27/2 = 13.5	Remainder = 1 (0.5 × 2)
13/2 = 6.5	Remainder = 1 (0.5 × 2)
6/2 = 3.0	Remainder = 0
3/2 = 1.5	Remainder = 1 (0.5 × 2)
1/2 = 0.5	Remainder = 1 (0.5 × 2)

Partial Answer: $54_{10} = 110110_2$

Repeated Multiplication For The < 1 Portion:

$0.40625 \times 2 = 0.8125$ Integer portion of product = 0

$0.8125 \times 2 = 1.625$ Integer portion of product = 1

$0.625 \times 2 = 1.25$ Integer portion of product = 1

$0.25 \times 2 = 0.5$ Integer portion of product = 0

$0.5 \times 2 = 1.0$ Integer portion of product = 1

Partial Answer: $0.40625_{10} = 0.01101_2$

Complete Answer: $54_{10} + 0.40625_{10} = 54.40625_{10}$

$110110_2 + 0.01101_2 = 110110.01101_2$

Chapter 2

Binary Arithmetic and Boolean Algebra

NUMBERS VERSUS NUMERATION

It is imperative to understand that the type of numeration system used to represent numbers has no impact upon the outcome of any arithmetical function (addition, subtraction, multiplication, division, roots, powers, or logarithms). A number is a number is a number; one plus one will always equal two (so long as we're dealing with real numbers), no matter how you symbolize one, one, and two. A prime number in decimal form is still prime if its shown in binary form, or octal, or hexadecimal. π is still the ratio between the circumference and diameter of a circle, no matter what symbol(s) you use to denote its value.

The essential functions and interrelations of mathematics are unaffected by the particular system of symbols we might choose to represent quantities. This distinction between numbers and systems of numeration is critical to understand. The essential distinction between the two is much like that between an object and the spoken word(s) we associate with it. A house is still a house regardless of whether we call it by its English name house or its Spanish name casa. The first is the actual thing, while the second is merely the symbol for the thing.

That being said, performing a simple arithmetic operation such as addition (longhand) in binary form can be confusing to a person accustomed to working with decimal numeration only. In this lesson, we'll explore the techniques used to perform simple arithmetic functions on binary numbers, since these techniques will be employed in the design of electronic circuits to do the same. You might take longhand addition and subtraction for granted, having used a calculator for so long, but deep inside that calculator's circuitry all those operations are performed "longhand," using binary numeration. To understand how that's accomplished, we need to review to the basics of arithmetic.

BINARY ADDITION

Adding binary numbers is a very simple task, and very similar to the longhand addition of decimal numbers. As with decimal numbers, you start by adding the bits (digits) one column, or place weight, at a time, from right to left. Unlike decimal addition, there is little to memorize in the way of rules for the addition of binary bits.

$$0 + 0 = 0$$
$$1 + 0 = 1$$
$$0 + 1 = 1$$
$$1 + 1 = 10$$
$$1 + 1 + 1 = 11$$

Just as with decimal addition, when the sum in one column is a two–bit (two–digit) number, the least significant figure is written as part of the total sum and the most significant figure is "carried" to the next left column. Consider the following examples.

	11 1	← Carry bits →	11
1001101	1001001		1000111
+ 0010010	+ 0011001		+ 0010110
1011111	1100010		1011101

The addition problem on the left did not require any bits to be carried, since the sum of bits in each column was either 1 or 0, not 10 or 11. In the other two problems, there definitely were bits to be carried, but the process of addition is still quite simple.

As we'll see later, there are ways that electronic circuits can be built to perform this very task of addition, by representing each bit of each binary number as a voltage signal (either "high," for a 1; or "low" for a 0). This is the very foundation of all the arithmetic which modern digital computers perform.

NEGATIVE BINARY NUMBERS

With addition being easily accomplished, we can perform the operation of subtraction with the same technique simply by making one of the numbers negative. For example, the subtraction problem of 7 – 5 is essentially the same as the addition problem 7 + (–5). Since we already know how to represent positive numbers in binary, all we need to know now is how to represent their negative counterparts and we'll be able to subtract.

Usually we represent a negative decimal number by placing a minus sign directly to the left of the most significant digit, just as in the example above, with –5. However, the whole purpose of using binary notation is for constructing on/off circuits that can represent bit values in terms of voltage (2 alternative values either "high" or "low"). In this context, we don't have the luxury of a third symbol such as a "minus" sign, since these circuits can only be on or off (two possible states). One solution is to reserve a bit (circuit) that does nothing but represent the mathematical sign.

1012 = 510 (positive)
Extra bit, representing sign (0=positive, 1=negative)
|
01012 = 510 (positive)
Extra bit, representing sign (0=positive, 1=negative)
|
11012 = –510 (negative)

As you can see, we have to be careful when we start using bits for any purpose other than standard place–weighted values. Otherwise, 11012 could be misinterpreted as the number thirteen when in fact we mean to represent negative five. To keep things straight here, we must first decide how many bits are going to be needed to represent the largest numbers we'll be dealing with, and then be sure not to exceed that bit field length in our arithmetic operations.

For the above example, I've limited myself to the representation of numbers from negative seven (11112) to positive seven (01112), and no more, by making the fourth bit the "sign" bit. Only by first establishing these limits can avoid confusion of a negative number with a larger, positive number.

Representing negative five as 11012 is an example of the sign–magnitude system of negative binary numeration.

There's another method for representing negative numbers which works with our familiar technique of longhand addition, and also happens to make more sense from a place–weighted numeration point of view, called complementation. With this strategy, we assign the leftmost bit to serve a special purpose, just as we did with the sign–magnitude approach, defining our number limits just as before. However, this time, the leftmost bit is more than just a sign bit; rather, it possesses a negative place–weight value. For example, a value of negative five would be represented as such.

Extra bit, place weight = negative eight
|
10112 = 510 (negative)
(1 × –810) + (0 × 410) + (1 × 210) + (1 × 110) = –510

With the right three bits being able to represent a magnitude from zero through seven, and the leftmost bit representing either zero or negative eight, we can successfully represent any integer number from negative seven (10012 = –810 + 110 = –110) to positive seven (01112 = 010 + 710 = 710).

Representing positive numbers in this scheme (with the fourth bit designated as the negative weight) is no different from that of ordinary binary notation. However, representing negative numbers is not quite as straightforward.

Zero	0000		
Positive one	0001	Negative one	1111
Positive two	0010	Negative two	1110
Positive three	0011	Negative three	1101
Positive four	0100	Negative four	1100
Positive five	0101	Negative five	1011
Positive six	0110	Negative six	1010
Positive seven	0111	Negative seven	1001
		Negative eight	1000

Note that the negative binary numbers in the right column, being the sum of the right three bits' total plus the negative eight of the leftmost bit, don't "count" in the same progression as the positive binary numbers in the left column. Rather, the right three bits have to be set at the proper value to equal the desired (negative) total when summed with the negative eight place value of the leftmost bit.

Those right three bits are referred to as the two's complement of the corresponding positive number. Consider the following comparison.

Positive Number	*Two's Complement*
001	111
010	110
011	101
100	100
101	011
110	010
111	001

In this case, with the negative weight bit being the fourth bit (place value of negative eight), the two's complement for any positive number will be whatever value is needed to add to negative eight to make that positive value's negative equivalent. Thankfully, there's an easy way to figure out the two's complement for any binary number simply invert all the bits of that number, changing all 1's to 0's and vice versa (to arrive at what is called the one's complement) and then add one! For example, to obtain the two's complement of five (1012), we would first invert all the bits to obtain 0102 (the "one's complement"), then add one to obtain 0112, or –510 in three–bit, two's complement form.

Interestingly enough, generating the two's complement of a binary number works the same if you manipulate all the bits, including the leftmost (sign) bit at the same time as the magnitude bits. Let's try this with the former example, converting a positive five to a negative five, but performing the complementation process on all four bits. We must be sure to include the 0 (positive) sign bit on the original number, five (01012). First, inverting all bits to obtain the one's complement: 10102. Then, adding one, we obtain the final answer: 10112, or –510 expressed in four–bit, two's complement form.

It is critically important to remember that the place of the negative–weight bit must be already determined before any two's complement conversions can be done. If our binary numeration field were such that the eighth bit was designated as the negative–weight bit (100000002), we'd have to determine the two's complement based on all seven of the other bits. Here, the two's complement of five (00001012) would be 11110112. A positive five in this system would be represented as 000001012, and a negative five as 111110112.

SUBTRACTION

We can subtract one binary number from another by using the standard techniques adapted for decimal numbers (subtraction of each bit pair, right to left, "borrowing" as needed from bits to the left). However, if we can leverage the already familiar (and easier) technique of binary addition to subtract, that would be better. We can represent negative binary numbers by using the "two's complement" method and a negative place–weight bit. Here, we'll use those negative binary numbers to subtract through addition. Here's a sample problem.

Subtraction: 710 – 510 Addition equivalent: 710 + (–510)

If all we need to do is represent seven and negative five in binary (two's complemented) form, all we need is three bits plus the negative–weight bit.

positive seven = 01112

negative five = 10112

Now, let's add them together:

```
                1111 ←—Carry bits
                0111
              + 1011
              ------
               10010
               |
   Discard extra bit
     Answer = 00102
```

Since we've already defined our number bit field as three bits plus the negative–weight bit, the fifth bit in the answer (1) will be discarded to give us a result of 00102, or positive two, which is the correct answer.

Another way to understand why we discard that extra bit is to remember that the leftmost bit of the lower number possesses a negative weight, in this case equal to negative eight. When we add these two binary numbers together, what we're actually doing with the MSBs is subtracting the lower number's MSB from the upper number's MSB. In subtraction, one never "carries" a digit or bit on to the next left place–weight.

Let's try another example, this time with larger numbers. If we want to add –2510 to 1810, we must first decide how large our binary bit field must be. To represent the largest (absolute value) number in our problem, which is twenty–five, we need at least five bits, plus a sixth bit for the negative–weight bit. Let's start by representing positive twenty–five, then finding the two's complement and putting it all together into one numeration:

+2510 = 0110012 (showing all six bits)
One's complement of 110012 = 1001102
One's complement + 1 = two's complement = 1001112
–2510 = 1001112

Essentially, we're representing negative twenty–five by using the negative–weight (sixth) bit with a value of negative thirty–two, plus positive seven (binary 1112).

Now, let's represent positive eighteen in binary form, showing all six bits.

1810 = 0100102

Now, let's add them together and see what we get:

```
  11 ←—Carry bits
 100111
+ 010010
 ———————
 111001
```

Since there were no "extra" bits on the left, there are no bits to discard. The leftmost bit on the answer is a 1, which means that the answer is negative, in two's complement form, as it should be. Converting the answer to decimal form by summing all the bits times their respective weight values, we get:

(1 × –3210) + (1 × 1610) + (1 × 810) + (1 × 110) = –710
Indeed –710 is the proper sum of –2510 and 1810.

OVERFLOW

One caveat with signed binary numbers is that of overflow, where the answer to an addition or subtraction problem exceeds the magnitude which can be represented with the alloted number of bits. Remember that the place of the sign bit is fixed from the beginning of the problem. With the last example problem, we used five binary bits to represent the magnitude of the number, and the left–most (sixth) bit as the negative–weight, or sign, bit.

With five bits to represent magnitude, we have a representation range of 25, or thirty–two integer steps from 0 to maximum. This means that we can represent a number as high as +3110 (0111112), or as low as –3210 (1000002). If we set up an addition problem with two binary numbers, the sixth bit used for sign, and the result either exceeds +3110 or is less than –3210, our answer will be incorrect. Let's try adding 1710 and 1910 to see how this overflow condition works for excessive positive numbers.

17_{10} = 100012 19_{10} = 100112

1 11 ⟵ Carry bits

(Showing sign bits) 010001

\+ 010011

100100

The answer (1001002), interpreted with the sixth bit as the –3210 place, is actually equal to –2810, not +3610 as we should get with +1710 and +1910 added together! Obviously, this is not correct. What went wrong? The answer lies in the restrictions of the six–bit number field within which we're working Since the magnitude of the true and proper sum (3610) exceeds the allowable limit for our designated bit field, we have an overflow error. Simply put, six places doesn't give enough bits to represent the correct sum, so whatever figure we obtain using the strategy of discarding the left–most "carry" bit will be incorrect.

A similar error will occur if we add two negative numbers together to produce a sum that is too low for our six–bit binary field. Let's try adding –1710 and –1910 together to see how this works (or doesn't work, as the case may be!).

–1710 = 1011112 -19_{10} = 1011012

1 1111 ⟵ Carry bits

(Showing sign bits) 101111

\+ 101101

1011100

|

Discard extra bit

FINAL ANSWER: 0111002 = +2810

The (incorrect) answer is a positive twenty–eight. The fact that the real sum of negative seventeen and negative nineteen was too low to be properly represented with a five bit magnitude field and a sixth sign bit is the root cause of this difficulty.

Let's try these two problems again, except this time using the seventh bit for a sign bit, and allowing the use of 6 bits for representing the magnitude.

1710 + 1910	(–1710) + (–1910)
1 11	11 1111
0010001	1101111
+ 0010011	+ 1101101
01001002	110111002
	|
	Discard extra bit

ANSWERS: 01001002 = +3610
10111002 = –3610

By using bit fields sufficiently large to handle the magnitude of the sums, we arrive at the correct answers.

In these sample problems we've been able to detect overflow errors by performing the addition problems in decimal form and comparing the results with the binary answers. For example, when adding +1710 and +1910 together, we knew that the answer was supposed to be +3610, so when the binary sum checked out to be –2810, we knew that something had to be wrong. Although this is a valid way of detecting overflow, it is not very efficient.

After all, the whole idea of complementation is to be able to reliably add binary numbers together and not have to double–check the result by adding the same numbers together in decimal form! This is especially true for the purpose of building electronic circuits to add binary quantities together the circuit has to be able to check itself for overflow without the supervision of a human being who already knows what the correct answer is.

What we need is a simple error–detection method that doesn't require any additional arithmetic. Perhaps the most elegant solution is to check for the sign of the sum and compare it against the signs of the numbers added. Obviously, two positive numbers added together should give a positive result, and two negative numbers added together should give a negative result. Notice that whenever we had a condition of overflow in the example problems, the sign of the sum was always opposite of the two added numbers: +1710 plus +1910 giving –2810, or –1710 plus –1910 giving +2810. By checking the signs alone we are able to tell that something is wrong.

But what about cases where a positive number is added to a negative number? What sign should the sum be in order to be correct. Or, more precisely, what sign of sum would necessarily indicate an overflow error? The answer to this is equally elegant there will never be an overflow error when two numbers of opposite signs are added together! The reason for this is apparent when the nature of overflow is considered. Overflow occurs when the magnitude of a number exceeds the range allowed by the size of the bit field.

he sum of two identically–signed numbers may very well exceed the range of the bit field of those two numbers, and so in this case overflow is a possibility. However, if a positive number is added to a negative number, the sum will always be closer to zero than either of the two added numbers its magnitude must be less than the magnitude of either original number, and so overflow is impossible.

Fortunately, this technique of overflow detection is easily implemented in electronic circuitry, and it is a standard feature in digital adder circuits a subject for a later chapter.

BIT GROUPINGS

The singular reason for learning and using the binary numeration system in electronics is to understand how to design, build, and troubleshoot circuits that represent and process numerical quantities in digital form. Since the bivalent (two–valued) system of binary bit numeration lends itself so easily to representation by "on" and "off" transistor states (saturation and cutoff, respectively), it makes sense to design and build circuits leveraging this principle to perform binary calculations.

If we were to build a circuit to represent a binary number, we would have to allocate enough transistor circuits to represent as many bits as we desire. In other words, in designing a digital circuit, we must first decide how many bits (maximum) we would like to be able to represent, since each bit requires one on/off circuit to represent it. This is analogous to designing an abacus to digitally represent decimal numbers we must decide how many digits we wish to handle in this primitive "calculator" device, for each digit requires a separate rod with its own beads.

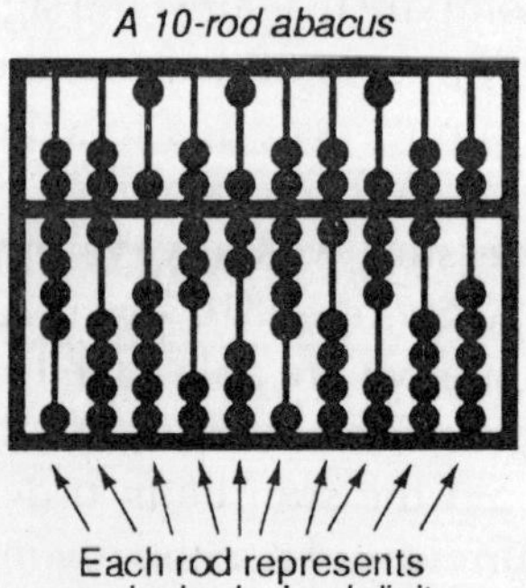

A ten–rod abacus would be able to represent a ten–digit decimal number, or a maxmium value of 9,999,999,999. If we wished to represent a larger number on this abacus, we would be unable to, unless additional rods could be added to it.

In digital, electronic computer design, it is common to design the system for a common "bit width:" a maximum number of bits allocated to represent numerical quantities. Early digital computers handled bits in groups of four or eight. More modern systems handle numbers in clusters of 32 bits or more. To more conveniently express the "bit width" of such clusters in a digital computer, specific labels were applied to the more common groupings.

Eight bits, grouped together to form a single binary quantity, is known as a byte. Four bits, grouped together as one binary number, is known by the humorous title of nibble, often spelled as nybble.

A multitude of terms have followed byte and nibble for labeling specfiic groupings of binary bits. Most of the terms shown here are informal, and have not been made "authoritative" by any standards group or other sanctioning body. However, their inclusion into this chapter is warranted by their occasional appearance in technical literature, as well as the levity they add to an otherwise dry subject:

- *Bit:* A single, bivalent unit of binary notation. Equivalent to a decimal "digit."
- Crumb, Tydbit, or Tayste: Two bits.
- Nibble, or Nybble: Four bits.
- *Nickle:* Five bits.
- Byte: Eight bits.
- *Deckle:* Ten bits.
- *Playte:* Sixteen bits.
- *Dynner:* Thirty–two bits.
- *Word:* (system dependent).

The most ambiguous term by far is word, referring to the standard bit–grouping within a particular digital system. For a computer system using a 32 bit–wide "data path," a "word" would mean 32 bits. If the system used 16 bits as the standard grouping for binary quantities, a "word" would mean 16 bits. The terms playte and dynner, by contrast, always refer to 16 and 32 bits, respectively, regardless of the system context in which they are used.

Context dependence is likewise true for derivative terms of word, such as double word and longword (both meaning twice the standard bit–width), half–word (half the standard bit–width), and quad (meaning four times the standard bit–width). One humorous addition to this somewhat boring collection of word–derivatives is the term chawmp, which means the same as half–word. For example, a chawmp would be 16 bits in the context of a 32–bit digital system, and 18 bits in the context of a 36–bit system. Also, the term gawble is sometimes synonymous with word.

Definitions for bit grouping terms were taken from Eric S. Raymond's "Jargon Lexicon," an indexed collection of terms—both common and obscure—germane to the world of computer programming.

BOOLEAN ALGEBRA

Mathematical rules are based on the defining limits we place on the particular numerical quantities dealt with. When we say that 1 + 1 = 2 or 3 + 4 = 7, we are implying the use of integer quantities the same types of numbers we all learned to count in elementary education. What most people assume to be self–evident rules of arithmetic — valid at all times and for all purposes — actually depend on what we define a number to be.

For instance, when calculating quantities in AC circuits, we find that the "real" number quantities which served us so well in DC circuit analysis are inadequate for the task of representing AC quantities. We know that voltages add when connected in series, but we also know that it is possible to connect a 3–volt AC source in series with a 4–volt AC source and end up with 5 volts total voltage (3 + 4 = 5)! Does this mean the inviolable and self–evident rules of arithmetic have been violated? No, it just means that the rules of "real" numbers do not apply to the kinds of quantities encountered in AC circuits, where every variable has both a magnitude and a phase.

Consequently, we must use a different kind of numerical quantity, or object, for AC circuits (complex numbers, rather than real numbers), and along with this different system of numbers comes a different set of rules telling us how they relate to one another.

An expression such as "3 + 4 = 5" is nonsense within the scope and definition of real numbers, but it fits nicely within the scope and definition of complex numbers (think of a right triangle with opposite and adjacent sides of 3 and 4, with a hypotenuse of 5). Because complex numbers are two–dimensional, they are able to "add" with one another trigonometrically as single–dimension "real" numbers cannot.

Logic is much like mathematics in this respect the so–called "Laws" of logic depend on how we define what a proposition is. The Greek philosopher Aristotle founded a system of logic based on only two types of propositions true and false. His bivalent (two–mode) definition of truth led to the four foundational laws of logic the Law of Identity (A is A); the Law of Non–contradiction (A is not non–A); the Law of the Excluded

Middle (either A or non–A); and the Law of Rational Inference. These so–called Laws function within the scope of logic where a proposition is limited to one of two possible values, but may not apply in cases where propositions can hold values other than "true" or "false."

In fact, much work has been done and continues to be done on "multivalued," or fuzzy logic, where propositions may be true or false to a limited degree. In such a system of logic, "Laws" such as the Law of the Excluded Middle simply do not apply, because they are founded on the assumption of bivalence.

Likewise, many premises which would violate the Law of Non–contradiction in Aristotelian logic have validity in "fuzzy" logic. Again, the defining limits of propositional values determine the Laws describing their functions and relations.

The English mathematician George Boole (1815–1864) sought to give symbolic form to Aristotle's system of logic. Boole wrote a treatise on the subject in 1854, titled An Investigation of the Laws of Thought, on Which Are Founded the Mathematical Theories of Logic and Probabilities, which codified several rules of relationship between mathematical quantities limited to one of two possible values true or false, 1 or 0. His mathematical system became known as Boolean algebra.

All arithmetic operations performed with Boolean quantities have but one of two possible outcomes either 1 or 0. There is no such thing as "2" or "–1" or "1/2" in the Boolean world. It is a world in which all other possibilities are invalid by fiat. As one might guess, this is not the kind of math you want to use when balancing a checkbook or calculating current through a resistor. However, Claude Shannon of MIT fame recognized how Boolean algebra could be applied to on–and–off circuits, where all signals are characterized as either "high" (1) or "low" (0).

His 1938 thesis, titled A Symbolic Analysis of Relay and Switching Circuits, put Boole's theoretical work to use in a way Boole never could have imagined, giving us a powerful mathematical tool for designing and analyzing digital circuits.

In this chapter, you will find a lot of similarities between Boolean algebra and "normal" algebra, the kind of algebra involving so–called real numbers. Just bear in mind that the system of numbers defining Boolean algebra is severely limited in terms of scope, and that there can only be one of two possible values for any Boolean variable 1 or 0. Consequently, the "Laws" of Boolean algebra often differ from the "Laws" of real–number algebra, making possible such statements as 1 + 1 = 1, which would normally be considered absurd.

Once you comprehend the premise of all quantities in Boolean algebra being limited to the two possibilities of 1 and 0, and the general philosophical principle of Laws depending on quantitative definitions, the "nonsense" of Boolean algebra disappears.

It should be clearly understood that Boolean numbers are not the same as binary numbers. Whereas Boolean numbers represent an entirely different system of mathematics from real numbers, binary is nothing more than an alternative notation for real numbers. The two are often confused because both Boolean math and binary notation use the same two ciphers 1 and 0.

The difference is that Boolean quantities are restricted to a single bit (either 1 or 0), whereas binary numbers may be composed of many bits adding up in place–weighted form to a value of any finite size. The binary number 100112 ("nineteen") has no more place in the Boolean world than the decimal number 210 ("two") or the octal number 328 ("twenty–six").

BOOLEAN ARITHMETIC

Let us begin our exploration of Boolean algebra by adding numbers together.

The first three sums make perfect sense to anyone familiar with elementary addition. The last sum, though, is quite possibly responsible for more confusion than any other single statement in digital electronics, because it seems to run contrary to the basic principles of mathematics. Well, it does contradict principles of addition for real numbers, but not for Boolean numbers. Remember that in the world of Boolean algebra, there are only two possible values for any quantity and for any arithmetic operation 1 or 0. There is no such thing as "2" within the scope of Boolean values. Since the sum "1 + 1" certainly isn't 0, it must be 1 by process of elimination.

It does not matter how many or few terms we add together, either. Consider the following sums.

Take a close look at the two–term sums in the first set of equations. Does that pattern look familiar to you? It should! It is the same pattern of 1's and 0's as seen in the truth table for an OR gate. In other words, Boolean addition corresponds to the logical function of an "OR" gate, as well as to parallel switch contacts.

There is no such thing as subtraction in the realm of Boolean mathematics. Subtraction implies the existence of negative numbers 5 – 3 is the same thing as 5 + (–3), and in Boolean algebra negative quantities are forbidden. There is no such thing as division in Boolean mathematics, either, since division is really nothing more than compounded subtraction, in the same way that multiplication is compounded addition.

Multiplication is valid in Boolean algebra, and thankfully it is the same as in real–number algebra anything multiplied by 0 is 0, and anything multiplied by 1 remains unchanged. This set of equations should also look familiar to you: it is the same pattern found in the truth table for an AND gate. In other words, Boolean multiplication corresponds to the logical function of an "AND" gate, as well as to series switch contacts:

Like "normal" algebra, Boolean algebra uses alphabetical letters to denote variables. Unlike "normal" algebra, though, Boolean variables are always CAPITAL letters, never lower–case. Because they are allowed to possess only one of two possible values, either 1 or 0, each and every variable has a complement: the opposite of its value. For example, if variable "A" has a value of 0, then the complement of A has a value of 1. Boolean notation uses a bar above the variable character to denote complementation, like this:

In written form, the complement of "A" denoted as "A–not" or "A–bar". Sometimes a "prime" symbol is used to represent complementation. For example, A' would be the complement of A, much the same as using a prime symbol to denote differentiation in calculus rather than the fractional notation d/dt. Usually, though, the "bar" symbol finds more widespread use than the "prime" symbol, for reasons that will become more apparent later in this chapter.

Boolean complementation finds equivalency in the form of the NOT gate, or a normally–closed switch or relay contact:

The basic definition of Boolean quantities has led to the simple rules of addition and multiplication, and has excluded both subtraction and division as valid arithmetic operations. We have a symbology for denoting Boolean variables, and their complements. In the next section we will proceed to develop Boolean identities.

BOOLEAN ALGEBRAIC IDENTITIES

In mathematics, an identity is a statement true for all possible values of its variable or variables. The algebraic identity of $x + 0 = x$ tells us that anything (x) added to zero equals the original "anything," no matter what value that "anything" (x) may be. Like ordinary algebra, Boolean algebra has its own unique identities based on the bivalent states of Boolean variables. The first Boolean identity is that the sum of anything and zero is the same as the original "anything." This identity is no different from its real–number algebraic equivalent:

No matter what the value of A, the output will always be the same: when A=1, the output will also be 1; when A=0, the output will also be 0.

The next identity is most definitely different from any seen in normal algebra. Here we discover that the sum of anything and one is one:

No matter what the value of A, the sum of A and 1 will always be 1. In a sense, the "1" signal overrides the effect of A on the logic circuit, leaving the output fixed at a logic level of 1. Next, we examine the effect of adding A and A together, which is the same as connecting both inputs of an OR gate to each other and activating them with the same signal:

In real–number algebra, the sum of two identical variables is twice the original variable's value (x + x = 2x), but remember that there is no concept of "2" in the world of Boolean math, only 1 and 0, so we cannot say that A + A = 2A. Thus, when we add a Boolean quantity to itself, the sum is equal to the original quantity: 0 + 0 = 0, and 1 + 1 = 1.

Introducing the uniquely Boolean concept of complementation into an additive identity, we find an interesting effect. Since there must be one "1" value between any variable and its complement, and since the sum of any Boolean quantity and 1 is 1, the sum of a variable and its complement must be 1.

Just as there are four Boolean additive identities (A+0, A+1, A+A, and A+A'), so there are also four multiplicative identities: Ax0, Ax1, AxA, and AxA'. Of these, the first two are no different from their equivalent expressions in regular algebra:

The third multiplicative identity expresses the result of a Boolean quantity multiplied by itself. In normal algebra, the product of a variable and itself is the square of that variable (3 × 3 = 32 = 9). However, the concept of "square" implies a quantity of 2, which has no meaning in Boolean algebra, so we cannot say that A × A = A2. Instead, we find that the product of a Boolean quantity and itself is the original quantity, since 0 × 0 = 0 and 1 × 1 = 1.

The fourth multiplicative identity has no equivalent in regular algebra because it uses the complement of a variable, a concept unique to Boolean mathematics. Since there must be one "0" value between any variable and its complement, and since the product of any Boolean quantity and 0 is 0, the product of a variable and its complement must be 0:

To summarize, then, we have four basic Boolean identities for addition and four for multiplication.

Another identity having to do with complementation is that of the double complement: a variable inverted twice. Complementing a variable twice (or any even number of times) results in the original Boolean value. This is analogous to negating (multiplying by –1) in real–number algebra: an even number of negations cancel to leave the original value.

BOOLEAN ALGEBRAIC PROPERTIES

Another type of mathematical identity, called a "property" or a "law," describes how differing variables relate to each other in a system of numbers. One of these properties is known as the commutative property, and it applies equally to addition and multiplication. In essence, the commutative property tells us we can reverse the order of variables that are either added together or multiplied together without changing the truth of the expression.

Along with the commutative properties of addition and multiplication, we have the associative property, again applying equally well to addition and multiplication. This property tells us we can associate groups of added or multiplied variables together with parentheses without altering the truth of the equations.

Lastly, we have the distributive property, illustrating how to expand a Boolean expression formed by the product of a sum, and in reverse shows us how terms may be factored out of Boolean sums–of–products.

To summarize, here are the three basic properties: commutative, associative, and distributive.

Boolean Rules for Simplification

Boolean algebra finds its most practical use in the simplification of logic circuits. If we translate a logic circuit's function into symbolic (Boolean) form, and apply certain algebraic rules to the resulting equation to reduce the number of terms and/or arithmetic operations, the simplified equation may be translated back into circuit form for a logic circuit performing the same function with fewer components. If equivalent function may be achieved with fewer components, the result will be increased reliability and decreased cost of manufacture.

To this end, there are several rules of Boolean algebra presented in this section for use in reducing expressions to their simplest forms. The identities and properties already reviewed in this chapter are very useful in Boolean simplification, and for the most part bear similarity to many identities and properties of "normal" algebra. However, the rules shown in this section are all unique to Boolean mathematics.

This rule may be proven symbolically by factoring an "A" out of the two terms, then applying the rules of A + 1 = 1 and 1A = A to achieve the final result.

Please note how the rule A + 1 = 1 was used to reduce the (B + 1) term to 1. When a rule like "A + 1 = 1" is expressed using the letter "A", it doesn't mean it only applies to expressions containing "A". What the "A" stands for in a rule like A + 1 = 1 is any Boolean variable or collection of variables. This is perhaps the most difficult concept for new students to master in Boolean simplification: applying standardized identities, properties, and rules to expressions not in standard form.

For instance, the Boolean expression ABC + 1 also reduces to 1 by means of the "A + 1 = 1" identity. In this case, we recognize that the "A" term in the identity's standard form can represent the entire "ABC" term in the original expression. The next rule looks similar to the first on shown in this section, but is actually quite different and requires a more clever proof.

Note how the last rule (A + AB = A) is used to "un–simplify" the first "A" term in the expression, changing the "A" into an "A + AB". While this may seem like a backward step, it certainly helped to reduce the expression to something simpler! Sometimes in mathematics we must take "backward" steps to achieve the most elegant solution. Knowing when to take such a step and when not to is part of the art–form of algebra, just as a victory in a game of chess almost always requires calculated sacrifices.

Circuit Simplification Examples

Let's begin with a semiconductor gate circuit in need of simplification. The "A," "B," and "C" input signals are assumed to be provided from switches, sensors, or perhaps other gate circuits. Where these signals originate is of no concern in the task of gate reduction.

Our first step in simplification must be to write a Boolean expression for this circuit. This task is easily performed step by step if we start by writing sub–expressions at the output of each gate, corresponding to the respective input signals for each gate. Remember that OR gates are equivalent to Boolean addition, while AND gates are equivalent to Boolean multiplication. For example, I'll write sub–expressions at the outputs of the first three gates.

... then another sub–expression for the next gate.

Finally, the output ("Q") is seen to be equal to the expression AB + BC(B + C).

Now that we have a Boolean expression to work with, we need to apply the rules of Boolean algebra to reduce the expression to its simplest form (simplest defined as requiring the fewest gates to implement).

The final expression, B(A + C), is much simpler than the original, yet performs the same function. If you would like to verify this, you may generate a truth table for both expressions and determine Q's status (the circuits' output) for all eight logic–state combinations of A, B, and C, for both circuits. The two truth tables should be identical.

Now, we must generate a schematic diagram from this Boolean expression. To do this, evaluate the expression, following proper mathematical order of operations (multiplication before addition, operations inside parentheses before anything else), and draw gates for each step.

Remember again that OR gates are equivalent to Boolean addition, while AND gates are equivalent to Boolean multiplication. In this case, we would begin with the sub–expression "A + C", which is an OR gate:

The next step in evaluating the expression "B(A + C)" is to multiply (AND gate) the signal B by the output of the previous gate (A + C).

Obviously, this circuit is much simpler than the original, having only two logic gates instead of five. Such component reduction results in higher operating speed (less delay time from input signal transition to output signal transition), less power consumption, less cost, and greater reliability. Electromechanical relay circuits, typically being slower, consuming more electrical power to operate, costing more, and having a shorter average life than their semiconductor counterparts, benefit dramatically from Boolean simplification. Let's consider an example circuit.

As before, our first step in reducing this circuit to its simplest form must be to develop a Boolean expression from the schematic. The easiest way I've found to do this is to follow the same steps I'd normally follow to reduce a series–parallel resistor network to a single, total resistance. For example, examine the following resistor network with its resistors arranged in the same connection pattern as the relay contacts in the former circuit, and corresponding total resistance formula.

Remember that parallel contacts are equivalent to Boolean addition, while series contacts are equivalent to Boolean multiplication. Write a Boolean expression for this relay contact circuit, following the same order of precedence that you would follow in reducing a series–parallel resistor network to a total resistance. It may be helpful to write a Boolean sub–expression to the left of each ladder "rung," to help organize your expression–writing.

Now that we have a Boolean expression to work with, we need to apply the rules of Boolean algebra to reduce the expression to its simplest form (simplest defined as requiring the fewest relay contacts to implement).

The more mathematically inclined should be able to see that the two steps employing the rule "A + AB = A" may be combined into a single step, the rule being expandable to: "A + AB + AC + AD +... = A"

As you can see, the reduced circuit is much simpler than the original, yet performs the same logical function.

THE EXCLUSIVE–OR FUNCTION

One element conspicuously missing from the set of Boolean operations is that of Exclusive–OR. Whereas the OR function is equivalent to Boolean addition, the AND function to Boolean multiplication, and the NOT function (inverter) to Boolean complementation, there is no direct Boolean equivalent for Exclusive–OR. This hasn't stopped people from developing a symbol to represent it, though.

This symbol is seldom used in Boolean expressions because the identities, laws, and rules of simplification involving addition, multiplication, and complementation do not apply to it. However, there is a way to represent the Exclusive–OR function in terms of OR and AND, as has been shown in previous chapters: AB' + A'B.

As a Boolean equivalency, this rule may be helpful in simplifying some Boolean expressions. Any expression following the AB' + A'B form (two AND gates and an OR gate) may be replaced by a single Exclusive–OR gate.

DEMORGAN'S THEOREMS

A mathematician named DeMorgan developed a pair of important rules regarding group complementation in Boolean algebra. By group complementation, I'm referring to the complement of a group of terms, represented by a long bar over more than one variable.

You should recall from the chapter on logic gates that inverting all inputs to a gate reverses that gate's essential function from AND to OR, or vice versa, and also inverts the output. So, an OR gate with all inputs inverted (a Negative–OR gate) behaves the same as a NAND gate, and an AND gate with all inputs inverted (a Negative–AND gate) behaves the same as a NOR gate. DeMorgan's theorems state the same equivalence in "backward" form: that inverting the output of any gate results in the same function as the opposite type of gate (AND vs. OR) with inverted inputs.

A long bar extending over the term AB acts as a grouping symbol, and as such is entirely different from the product of A and B independently inverted. In other words, (AB)' is not equal to A'B'. Because the "prime" symbol (') cannot be stretched over two variables like a bar can, we are forced to use parentheses to make it apply to the whole term AB in the previous sentence. A bar, however, acts as its own grouping symbol when stretched over more than one variable. This has profound impact on how Boolean expressions are evaluated and reduced, as we shall see.

DeMorgan's theorem may be thought of in terms of breaking a long bar symbol. When a long bar is broken, the operation directly underneath the break changes from addition to multiplication, or vice versa, and the broken bar pieces remain over the individual variables. To illustrate.

When multiple "layers" of bars exist in an expression, you may only break one bar at a time, and it is generally easier to begin simplification by breaking the longest (uppermost) bar first. To illustrate, let's take the expression (A + (BC)')' and reduce it using DeMorgan's Theorems.

Following the advice of breaking the longest (uppermost) bar first, I'll begin by breaking the bar covering the entire expression as a first step: As a result, the original circuit is reduced to a three–input AND gate with the A input inverted: You should never break more than one bar in a single step, as illustrated here.

As tempting as it may be to conserve steps and break more than one bar at a time, it often leads to an incorrect result, so don't do it! It is possible to properly reduce this expression by breaking the short bar first, rather than the long bar first.

The end result is the same, but more steps are required compared to using the first method, where the longest bar was broken first. Note how in the third step we broke the long bar in two places. This is a legitimate mathematical operation, and not the same as breaking two bars in one step! The prohibition against breaking more than one bar in one step is not a prohibition against breaking a bar in more than one place. Breaking in more than one place in a single step is okay; breaking more than one bar in a single step is not.

You might be wondering why parentheses were placed around the sub–expression B' + C', considering the fact that we just removed them in the next step. we did this to emphasize an important but easily neglected aspect of DeMorgan's theorem.

Since a long bar functions as a grouping symbol, the variables formerly grouped by a broken bar must remain grouped lest proper precedence (order of operation) be lost. In this example, it really wouldn't matter if we forgot to put parentheses in after breaking the short bar, but in other cases it might. Consider this example, starting with a different expression.

As you can see, maintaining the grouping implied by the complementation bars for this expression is crucial to obtaining the correct answer. Let's apply the principles of DeMorgan's theorems to the simplification of a gate circuit.

As always, our first step in simplifying this circuit must be to generate an equivalent Boolean expression. We can do this by placing a sub–expression label at the output of each gate, as the inputs become known. Here's the first step in this process.

Next, we can label the outputs of the first NOR gate and the NAND gate. When dealing with inverted–output gates, we find it easier to write an expression for the gate's output without the final inversion, with an arrow pointing to just before the inversion bubble. Then, at the wire leading out of the gate (after the bubble), complemented expression. This helps ensure we don't forget a complementing bar in the sub–expression, by forcing myself to split the expression–writing task into two steps.

Finally, we write an expression (or pair of expressions) for the last NOR gate: Now, we reduce this expression using the identities, properties, rules, and theorems (DeMorgan's) of Boolean algebra.

CONVERTING TRUTH TABLES INTO BOOLEAN EXPRESSIONS

In designing digital circuits, the designer often begins with a truth table describing what the circuit should do. The design task is largely to determine what type of circuit will perform the function described in the truth table. While some people seem to have a natural ability to look at a truth table and immediately envision the necessary logic gate or relay logic circuitry for the task, there are procedural techniques available for the rest of us. Here, Boolean algebra proves its utility in a most dramatic way.

To illustrate this procedural method, we should begin with a realistic design problem. Suppose we were given the task of designing a flame detection circuit for a toxic waste incinerator. The intense heat of the fire is intended to neutralize the toxicity of the waste introduced into the incinerator. Such combustion–based techniques are commonly used to neutralize medical waste, which may be infected with deadly viruses or bacteria.

So long as a flame is maintained in the incinerator, it is safe to inject waste into it to be neutralized. If the flame were to be extinguished, however, it would be unsafe to continue to inject waste into the combustion chamber, as it would exit the exhaust un–neutralized, and pose a health threat to anyone in close proximity to the exhaust. What we need in this system is a sure way of detecting the presence of a flame, and permitting waste to be injected only if a flame is "proven" by the flame detection system.

Several different flame–detection technologies exist: optical (detection of light), thermal (detection of high temperature), and electrical conduction (detection of ionized particles in the flame path), each one with its unique advantages and disadvantages.

Suppose that due to the high degree of hazard involved with potentially passing un–neutralized waste out the exhaust of this incinerator, it is decided that the flame detection system be made redundant (multiple sensors), so that failure of a single sensor does not lead to an emission of toxins out the exhaust. Each sensor comes equipped with a normally–open contact (open if no flame, closed if flame detected) which we will use to activate the inputs of a logic system.

Our task, now, is to design the circuitry of the logic system to open the waste valve if and only if there is good flame proven by the sensors. First, though, we must decide what the logical behaviour of this control system should be. Do we want the valve to be opened if only one out of the three sensors detects flame? Probably not, because this would defeat the purpose of having multiple sensors.

If any one of the sensors were to fail in such a way as to falsely indicate the presence of flame when there was none, a logic system based on the principle of "any one out of three sensors showing flame" would give the same output that a single–sensor system would with the same failure. A far better solution would be to design the system so that the valve is commanded to open if any only if all three sensors detect a good flame. This way, any single, failed sensor falsely showing flame could not keep the valve in the open position; rather, it would require all three sensors to be failed in the same manner — a highly improbable scenario — for this dangerous condition to occur.

Thus, our truth table would look like this: It does not require much insight to realize that this functionality could be generated with a three–input AND gate: the output of the circuit will be "high" if and only if input A AND input B AND input C are all "high:" If using relay circuitry, we could create this AND function by wiring three relay contacts in series, or simply by wiring the three sensor contacts in series, so that the only way electrical power could be sent to open the waste valve is if all three sensors indicate flame.

While this design strategy maximizes safety, it makes the system very susceptible to sensor failures of the opposite kind. Suppose that one of the three sensors were to fail in such a way that it indicated no flame when there really was a good flame in the incinerator's combustion chamber. That single failure would shut off the waste valve unnecessarily, resulting in lost production time and wasted fuel (feeding a fire that wasn't being used to incinerate waste).

It would be nice to have a logic system that allowed for this kind of failure without shutting the system down unnecessarily, yet still provide sensor redundancy so as to maintain safety in the event that any single sensor failed "high" (showing flame at all times, whether or not there was one to detect).

A strategy that would meet both needs would be a "two out of three" sensor logic, whereby the waste valve is opened if at least two out of the three sensors show good flame. The truth table for such a system would look like this: Here, it is not necessarily obvious what kind of logic circuit would satisfy the truth table. However, a simple method for designing such a circuit is found in a standard form of Boolean expression called the Sum–Of–Products, or SOP, form.

As you might suspect, a Sum–Of–Products Boolean expression is literally a set of Boolean terms added (summed) together, each term being a multiplicative (product) combination of Boolean variables. An example of an SOP expression would be something like this: ABC + BC + DF, the sum of products "ABC," "BC," and "DF." Sum–Of–Products expressions are easy to generate from truth tables.

All we have to do is examine the truth table for any rows where the output is "high" (1), and write a Boolean product term that would equal a value of 1 given those input conditions. For instance, in the fourth row down in the truth table for our two–out–of–three logic system, where A=0, B=1, and C=1, the product term would be A'BC, since that term would have a value of 1 if and only if A=0, B=1, and C=1:

Three other rows of the truth table have an output value of 1, so those rows also need Boolean product expressions to represent them:

Finally, we join these four Boolean product expressions together by addition, to create a single Boolean expression describing the truth table as a whole:

Now that we have a Boolean Sum–Of–Products expression for the truth table's function, we can easily design a logic gate or relay logic circuit based on that expression:

Unfortunately, both of these circuits are quite complex, and could benefit from simplification. Using Boolean algebra techniques, the expression may be significantly simplified:

As a result of the simplification, we can now build much simpler logic circuits performing the same function, in either gate or relay form:

Either one of these circuits will adequately perform the task of operating the incinerator waste valve based on a flame verification from two out of the three flame sensors. At minimum, this is what we need to have a safe incinerator system. We can, however, extend the functionality of the system by adding to it logic circuitry designed to detect if any one of the sensors does not agree with the other two.

If all three sensors are operating properly, they should detect flame with equal accuracy. Thus, they should either all register "low" (000: no flame) or all register "high" (111: good flame). Any other output combination (001, 010, 011, 100, 101, or 110) constitutes a disagreement between sensors, and may therefore serve as an indicator of a potential sensor failure. If we added circuitry to detect any one of the six "sensor disagreement" conditions, we could use the output of that circuitry to activate an alarm.

Whoever is monitoring the incinerator would then exercise judgment in either continuing to operate with a possible failed sensor (inputs: 011, 101, or 110), or shut the incinerator down to be absolutely safe. Also, if the incinerator is shut down (no flame), and one or more of the sensors still indicates flame (001, 010, 011, 100, 101, or 110) while the other(s) indicate(s) no flame, it will be known that a definite sensor problem exists.

The first step in designing this "sensor disagreement" detection circuit is to write a truth table describing its behaviour. Since we already have a truth table describing the output of the "good flame" logic circuit, we can simply add another output column to the table to represent the second circuit, and make a table representing the entire logic system:

While it is possible to generate a Sum–Of–Products expression for this new truth table column, it would require six terms, of three variables each! Such a Boolean expression would require many steps to simplify, with a large potential for making algebraic errors:

An alternative to generating a Sum–Of–Products expression to account for all the "high" (1) output conditions in the truth table is to generate a Product–Of–Sums, or POS, expression, to account for all the "low" (0) output conditions instead.

Being that there are much fewer instances of a "low" output in the last truth table column, the resulting Product–Of–Sums expression should contain fewer terms.

As its name suggests, a Product–Of–Sums expression is a set of added terms (sums), which are multiplied (product) together. An example of a POS expression would be (A + B)(C + D), the product of the sums "A + B" and "C + D".

To begin, we identify which rows in the last truth-table column have "low" (0) outputs, and write a Boolean sum term that would equal 0 for that row's input conditions. For instance, in the first row of the truth table, where A=0, B=0, and C=0, the sum term would be (A + B + C), since that term would have a value of 0 if and only if A=0, B=0, and C=0:

Only one other row in the last truth table column has a "low" (0) output, so all we need is one more sum term to complete our Product–Of–Sums expression. This last sum term represents a 0 output for an input condition of A=1, B=1 and C=1. Therefore, the term must be written as (A' + B'+ C'), because only the sum of the complemented input variables would equal 0 for that condition only:

The completed Product–Of–Sums expression, of course, is the multiplicative combination of these two sum terms:

Whereas a Sum–Of–Products expression could be implemented in the form of a set of AND gates with their outputs connecting to a single OR gate, a Product–Of–Sums expression can be implemented as a set of OR gates feeding into a single AND gate:

Correspondingly, whereas a Sum–Of–Products expression could be implemented as a parallel collection of series–connected relay contacts, a Product–Of–Sums expression can be implemented as a series collection of parallel-connected relay contacts: The previous two circuits represent different versions of the "sensor disagreement" logic circuit only, not the "good flame" detection circuit(s). The entire logic system would be the combination of both "good flame" and "sensor disagreement" circuits.

Implemented in a Programmable Logic Controller (PLC), the entire logic system might resemble something like this. As you can see, both the Sum–Of–Products and Products–Of–Sums standard Boolean forms are powerful tools when applied to truth tables. They allow us to derive a Boolean expression — and ultimately, an actual logic circuit — from nothing but a truth table, which is a written specification for what we want a logic circuit to do.

To be able to go from a written specification to an actual circuit using simple, deterministic procedures means that it is possible to automate the design process for a digital circuit. In other words, a computer could be programmed to design a custom logic circuit from a truth table specification!

The steps to take from a truth table to the final circuit are so unambiguous and direct that it requires little, if any, creativity or other original thought to execute them.

Chapter 3

Digital Signals and Logic Gates

While the binary numeration system is an interesting mathematical abstraction, we haven't yet seen its practical application to electronics. This chapter is devoted to just that: practically applying the concept of binary bits to circuits. What makes binary numeration so important to the application of digital electronics is the ease in which bits may be represented in physical terms.

Because a binary bit can only have one of two different values, either 0 or 1, any physical medium capable of switching between two saturated states may be used to represent a bit.

Consequently, any physical system capable of representing binary bits is able to represent numerical quantities, and potentially has the ability to manipulate those numbers. This is the basic concept underlying digital computing.

Electronic circuits are physical systems that lend themselves well to the representation of binary numbers. Transistors, when operated at their bias limits, may be in one of two different states: either cutoff (no controlled current) or saturation (maximum controlled current).

If a transistor circuit is designed to maximize the probability of falling into either one of these states (and not operating in the linear, or active, mode), it can serve as a physical representation of a binary bit. A voltage signal measured at the output of such a circuit may also serve as a representation of a single bit, a low voltage representing a binary "0" and a (relatively) high voltage representing a binary "1." Note the following transistor circuit:

In this circuit, the transistor is in a state of saturation by virtue of the applied input voltage (5 volts) through the two–position switch. Because its saturated, the transistor drops very little voltage between collector and emitter, resulting in an output voltage of (practically) 0 volts. If we were using this circuit to represent binary bits, we would say that the input signal is a binary "1" and that the output signal is a binary "0."

Any voltage close to full supply voltage (measured in reference to ground, of course) is considered a "1" and a lack of voltage is considered a "0." Alternative terms for these voltage levels are high (same as a binary "1") and low (same as a binary "0"). A general term for the representation of a binary bit by a circuit voltage is logic level.

Transistor in saturation

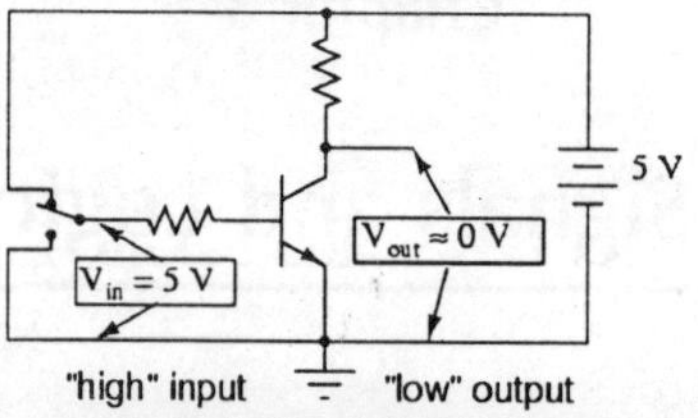

0 V = "low" logic level (0)
5 V = "high" logic level (1)

Moving the switch to the other position, we apply a binary "0" to the input and receive a binary "1" at the output:

Transistor in cutoff

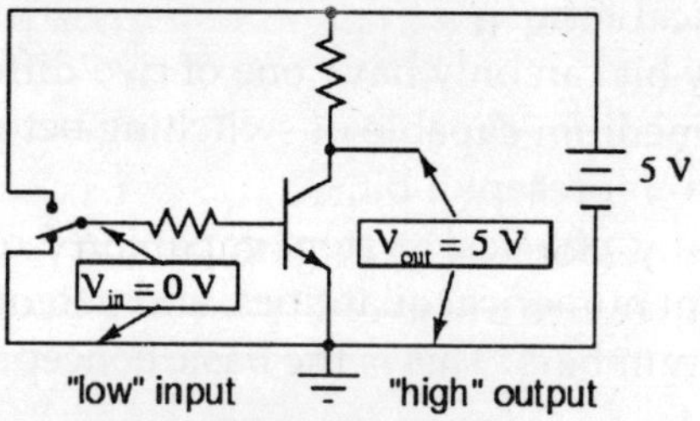

0 V = "low" logic level (0)
5 V = "high" logic level (1)

What we've created here with a single transistor is a circuit generally known as a logic gate, or simply gate. A gate is a special type of amplifier circuit designed to accept and generate voltage signals corresponding to binary 1's and 0's.

As such, gates are not intended to be used for amplifying analog signals (voltage signals between 0 and full voltage). Used together, multiple gates may be applied to the task of binary number storage (memory circuits) or manipulation (computing circuits), each gate's output representing one bit of a multi–bit binary number. Just how this is done is a subject for a later chapter. Right now it is important to focus on the operation of individual gates.

The gate shown here with the single transistor is known as an inverter, or NOT gate, because it outputs the exact opposite digital signal as what is input.

For convenience, gate circuits are generally represented by their own symbols rather than by their constituent transistors and resistors. The following is the symbol for an inverter:

Inverter, or NOT gate

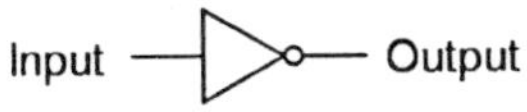

An alternative symbol for an inverter is shown here:

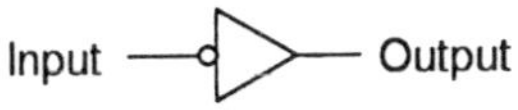

Notice the triangular shape of the gate symbol, much like that of an operational amplifier. As was stated before, gate circuits actually are amplifiers. The small circle, or "bubble" shown on either the input or output terminal is standard for representing the inversion function. As you might suspect, if we were to remove the bubble from the gate symbol, leaving only a triangle, the resulting symbol would no longer indicate inversion, but merely direct amplification. Such a symbol and such a gate actually do exist, and it is called a buffer, the subject of the next section.

Like an operational amplifier symbol, input and output connections are shown as single wires, the implied reference point for each voltage signal being "ground."

In digital gate circuits, ground is almost always the negative connection of a single voltage source (power supply). Dual, or "split," power supplies are seldom used in gate circuitry. Because gate circuits are amplifiers, they require a source of power to operate. Like operational amplifiers, the power supply connections for digital gates are often omitted from the symbol for simplicity's sake. If we were to show all the necessary connections needed for operating this gate, the schematic would look something like this: Power supply conductors are rarely shown in gate circuit schematics, even if the power supply connections at each gate are. Minimizing lines in our schematic, we get this:

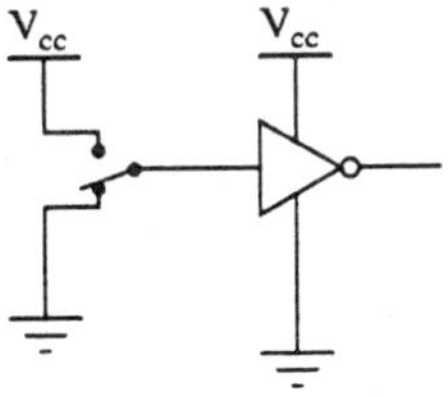

"V_{cc}" stands for the constant voltage supplied to the collector of a bipolar junction transistor circuit, in reference to ground. Those points in a gate circuit marked by the label "V_{cc}" are all connected to the same point, and that point is the positive terminal of a DC voltage source, usually 5 volts.

As we will see in other sections of this chapter, there are quite a few different types of logic gates, most of which have multiple input terminals for accepting more than one signal. The output of any gate is dependent on the state of its input(s) and its logical function.

One common way to express the particular function of a gate circuit is called a truth table. Truth tables show all combinations of input conditions in terms of logic level states (either "high" or "low," "1" or "0," for each input terminal of the gate), along with the corresponding output logic level, either "high" or "low." For the inverter, or NOT, circuit just illustrated, the truth table is very simple indeed:

NOT gate truth table

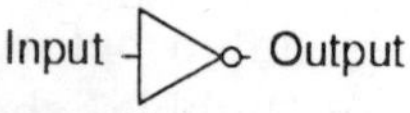

Input	Output
0	1
1	0

Truth tables for more complex gates are, of course, larger than the one shown for the NOT gate. A gate's truth table must have as many rows as there are possibilities for unique input combinations. For a single–input gate like the NOT gate, there are only two possibilities, 0 and 1. For a two input gate, there are four possibilities (00, 01, 10, and 11), and thus four rows to the corresponding truth table. For a three–input gate, there are eight possibilities (000, 001, 010, 011, 100, 101, 110, and 111), and thus a truth table with eight rows are needed. The mathematically inclined will realize that the number of truth table rows needed for a gate is equal to 2 raised to the power of the number of input terminals.

THE NOT GATE

The single–transistor inverter circuit illustrated earlier is actually too crude to be of practical use as a gate. Real inverter circuits contain more than one transistor to maximize voltage gain (so as to ensure that the final output transistor is either in full cutoff or full saturation), and other components designed to reduce the chance of accidental damage.

Practical inverter (NOT) circuit

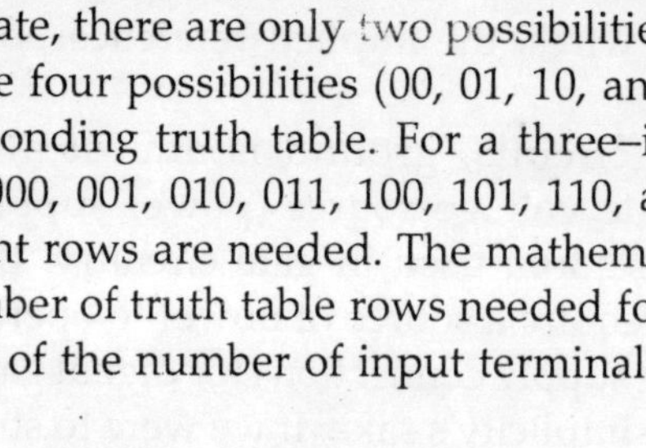

Shown here is a schematic diagram for a real inverter circuit, complete with all necessary components for efficient and reliable operation:

This circuit is composed exclusively of resistors and bipolar transistors. Bear in mind that other circuit designs are capable of performing the NOT gate function, including designs substituting field–effect transistors for bipolar (discussed later in this chapter).

Let's analyse this circuit for the condition where the input is "high," or in a binary "1" state. We can simulate this by showing the input terminal connected to Vcc through a switch:

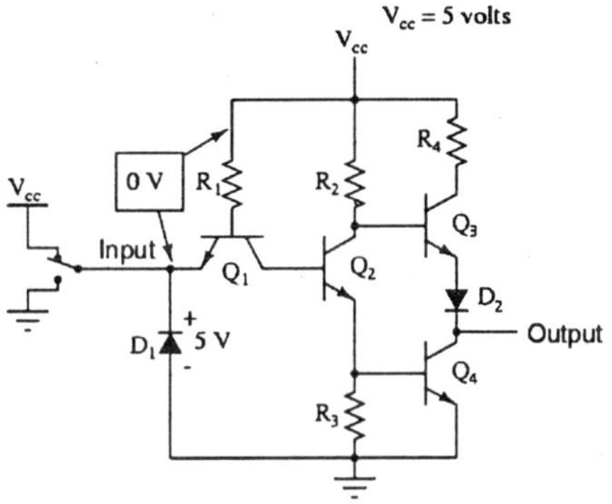

In this case, diode D_1 will be reverse–biased, and therefore not conduct any current. In fact, the only purpose for having D_1 in the circuit is to prevent transistor damage in the case of a negative voltage being impressed on the input (a voltage that is negative, rather than positive, with respect to ground).

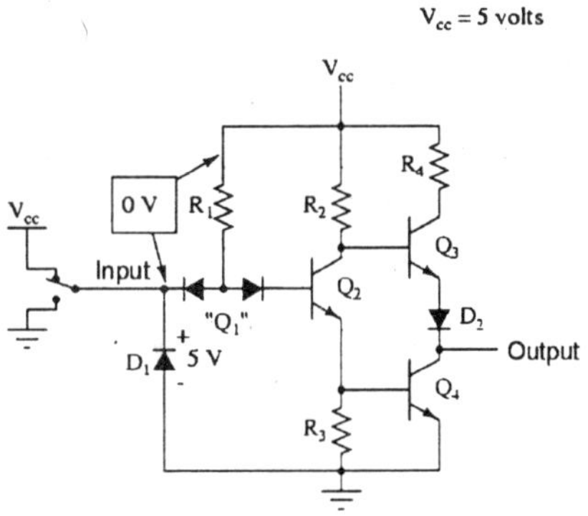

With no voltage between the base and emitter of transistor Q_1, we would expect no current through it, either. However, as strange as it may seem, transistor Q_1 is not being used as is customary for a transistor. In reality, Q_1 is being used in this circuit as nothing more than a back–to–back pair of diodes.

The following schematic shows the real function of Q_1: The purpose of these diodes is to "steer" current to or away from the base of transistor Q_2, depending on the logic level of the input.

Exactly how these two diodes are able to "steer" current isn't exactly obvious at first inspection, so a short example may be necessary for understanding. Suppose we had the following diode/resistor circuit, representing the base–emitter junctions of transistors Q_2 and Q_4 as single diodes, stripping away all other portions of the circuit so that we can concentrate on the current "steered" through the two back–to–back diodes:

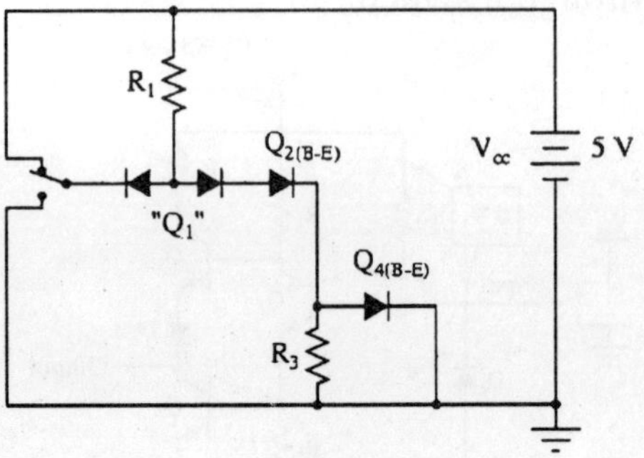

With the input switch in the "up" position (connected to Vcc), it should be obvious that there will be no current through the left steering diode of Q_1, because there isn't any voltage in the switch–diode–R1–switch loop to motivate electrons to flow.

However, there will be current through the right steering diode of Q_1, as well as through Q_2's base–emitter diode junction and Q_4's base–emitter diode junction:

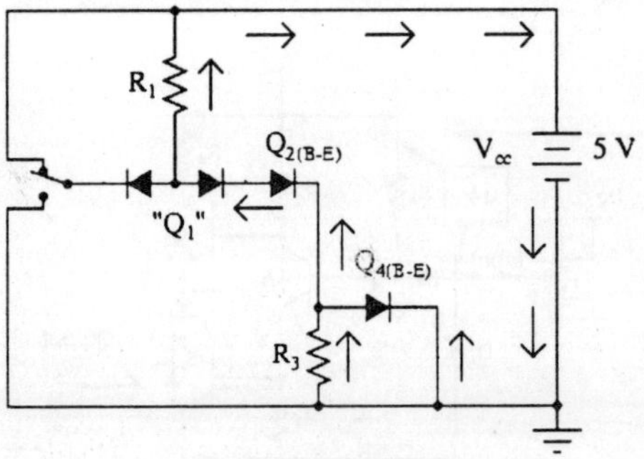

This tells us that in the real gate circuit, transistors Q_2 and Q_4 will have base current, which will turn them on to conduct collector current. The total voltage dropped between the base of Q_1 (the node joining the two back–to–back steering diodes) and ground will be about 2.1 volts, equal to the combined voltage drops of three PN junctions: the right steering diode, Q2's base–emitter diode, and Q_4's base–emitter diode.

Now, let's move the input switch to the "down" position and see what happens: If we were to measure current in this circuit, we would find that all of the current goes through the left steering diode of Q_1 and none of it through the right diode. Why is this? It still appears as though there is a complete path for current through Q4's diode, Q2's diode, the right diode of the pair, and R1, so why will there be no current through that path?

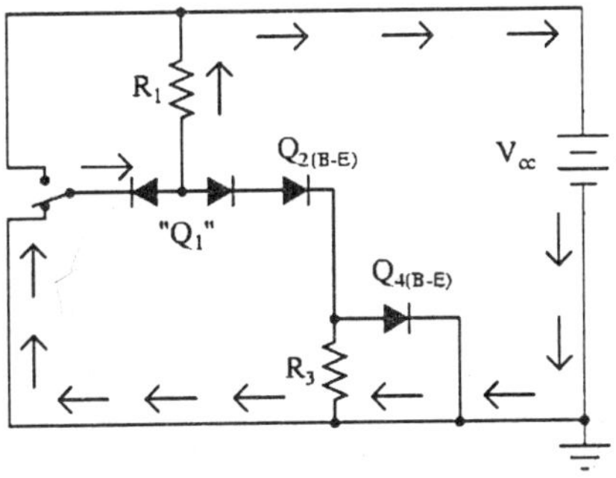

Remember that PN junction diodes are very nonlinear devices: they do not even begin to conduct current until the forward voltage applied across them reaches a certain minimum quantity, approximately 0.7 volts for silicon and 0.3 volts for germanium. And then when they begin to conduct current, they will not drop substantially more than 0.7 volts. When the switch in this circuit is in the "down" position, the left diode of the steering diode pair is fully conducting, and so it drops about 0.7 volts across it and no more.

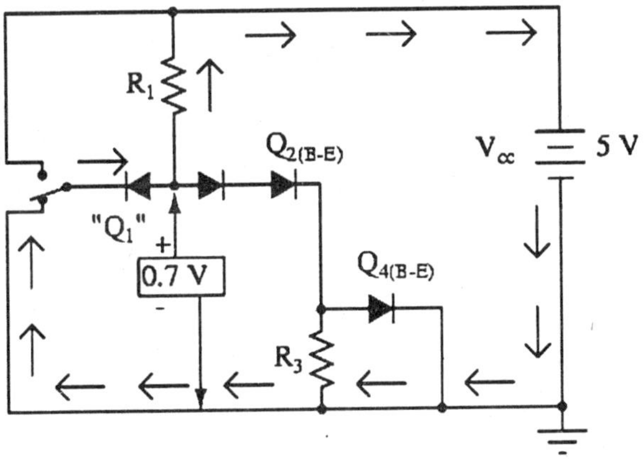

Recall that with the switch in the "up" position (transistors Q2 and Q4 conducting), there was about 2.1 volts dropped between those same two points (Q1's base and ground), which also happens to be the minimum voltage necessary to forward–bias three series–connected silicon PN junctions into a state of conduction. The 0.7 volts provided by the left diode's forward voltage drop is simply insufficient to allow any electron flow through the series string of the right diode, Q2's diode, and the R3/ /Q4 diode parallel subcircuit, and so no electrons flow through that path.

With no current through the bases of either transistor Q2 or Q4, neither one will be able to conduct collector current: transistors Q2 and Q4 will both be in a state of cutoff.

Consequently, this circuit configuration allows 100 per cent switching of Q2 base current (and therefore control over the rest of the gate circuit, including voltage at the output) by diversion of current through the left steering diode. In the case of our example gate circuit, the input is held "high" by the switch (connected to Vcc), making the left steering diode (zero voltage dropped across it). However, the right steering diode is conducting current through the base of Q2, through resistor R1:

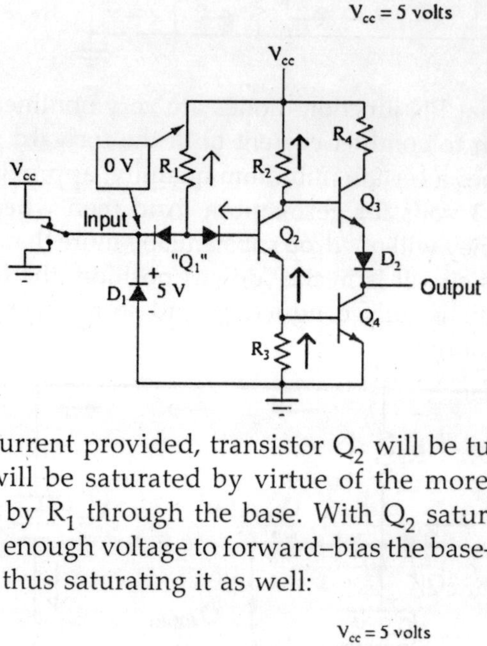

With base current provided, transistor Q_2 will be turned "on." More specifically, it will be saturated by virtue of the more–than–adequate current allowed by R_1 through the base. With Q_2 saturated, resistor R_3 will be dropping enough voltage to forward–bias the base–emitter junction of transistor Q_4, thus saturating it as well:

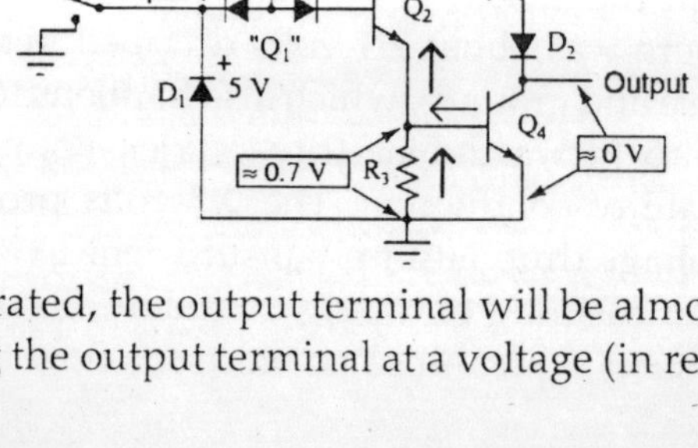

With Q4 saturated, the output terminal will be almost directly shorted to ground, leaving the output terminal at a voltage (in reference to ground)

of almost 0 volts, or a binary "0" ("low") logic level. Due to the presence of diode D2, there will not be enough voltage between the base of Q3 and its emitter to turn it on, so it remains in cutoff.

Let's see now what happens if we reverse the input's logic level to a binary "0" by actuating the input switch:

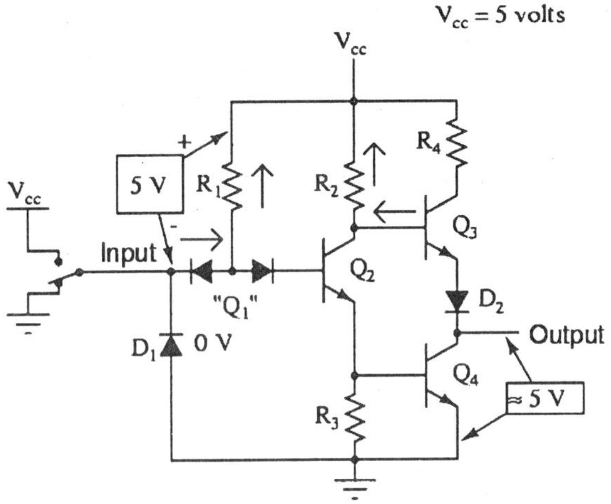

Now there will be current through the left steering diode of Q_1 and no current through the right steering diode. This eliminates current through the base of Q_2, thus turning it off. With Q_2 off, there is no longer a path for Q_4 base current, so Q_4 goes into cutoff as well. Q_3, on the other hand, now has sufficient voltage dropped between its base and ground to forward–bias its base–emitter junction and saturate it, thus raising the output terminal voltage to a "high" state. In actuality, the output voltage will be somewhere around 4 volts depending on the degree of saturation and any load current, but still high enough to be considered a "high" (1) logic level.

With this, our simulation of the inverter circuit is complete: a "1" in gives a "0" out, and vice versa. The astute observer will note that this inverter circuit's input will assume a "high" state of left floating (not connected to either Vcc or ground). With the input terminal left unconnected, there will be no current through the left steering diode of Q1, leaving all of R1's current to go through Q2's base, thus saturating Q2 and driving the circuit output to a "low" state:

The tendency for such a circuit to assume a high input state if left floating is one shared by all gate circuits based on this type of design, known as Transistor–to–Transistor Logic, or TTL.

This characteristic may be taken advantage of in simplifying the design of a gate's output circuitry, knowing that the outputs of gates typically drive the inputs of other gates. If the input of a TTL gate circuit assumes a high state when floating, then the output of any gate driving a TTL input need only provide a path to ground for a low state and be floating for a high state.

This concept may require further elaboration for full understanding.

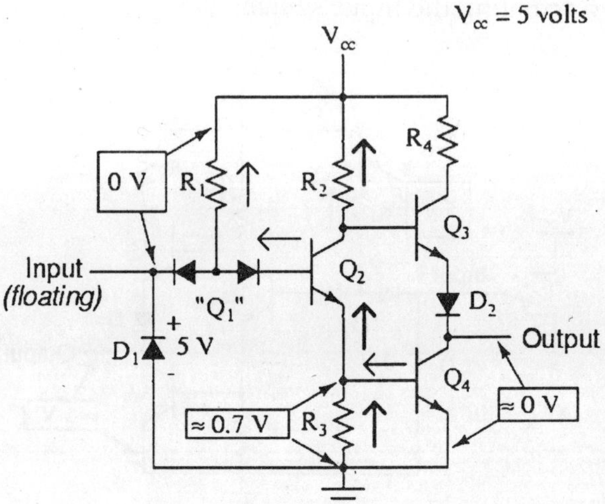

A gate circuit as we have just analyzed has the ability to handle output current in two directions: in and out. Technically, this is known as sourcing and sinking current, respectively.

When the gate output is high, there is continuity from the output terminal to Vcc through the top output transistor (Q_3), allowing electrons to flow from ground, through a load, into the gate's output terminal, through the emitter of Q_3, and eventually up to the Vcc power terminal (positive side of the DC power supply).

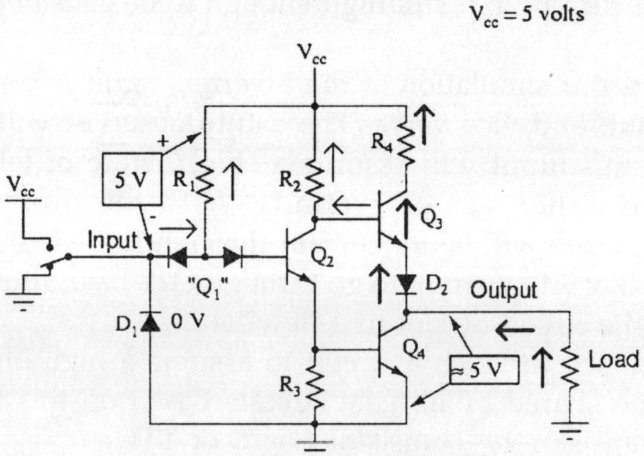

Inverter gate ***sourcing*** *current*

To simplify this concept, we may show the output of a gate circuit as being a double–throw switch, capable of connecting the output terminal either to Vcc or ground, depending on its state. For a gate outputting a "high" logic level. The combination of Q3 saturated and Q4 cutoff is analogous to a double-throw switch in the "Vcc" position, providing a path for current through a grounded load:

Simplified gate circuit ***sourcing*** *current*

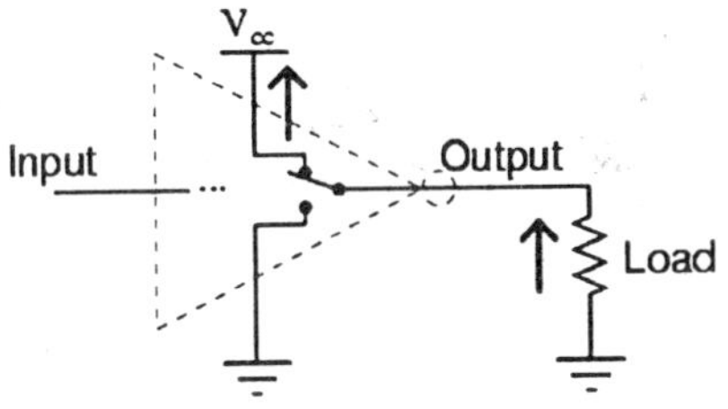

Please note that this two-position switch shown inside the gate symbol is representative of transistors Q3 and Q4 alternately connecting the output terminal to Vcc or ground, not of the switch previously shown sending an input signal to the gate!

Conversely, when a gate circuit is outputting a "low" logic level to a load, it is analogous to the double-throw switch being set in the "ground" position. Current will then be going the other way if the load resistance connects to Vcc: from ground, through the emitter of Q_4, out the output terminal, through the load resistance, and back to Vcc. In this condition, the gate is said to be sinking current:

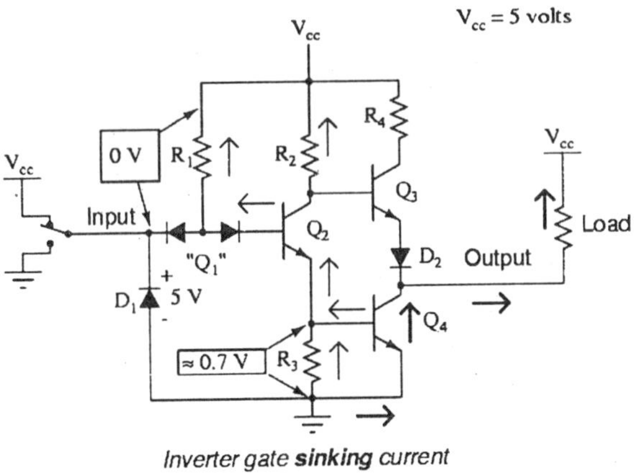

Inverter gate ***sinking*** *current*

The combination of Q_3 and Q_4 working as a "push–pull" transistor pair (otherwise known as a totem pole output) has the ability to either source current (draw in current to Vcc) or sink current (output current from ground) to a load.

However, a standard TTL gate input never needs current to be sourced, only sunk. That is, since a TTL gate input naturally assumes a high state if left floating, any gate output driving a TTL input need only sink current to provide a "0" or "low" input, and need not source current to provide a "1" or a "high" logic level at the input of the receiving gate:

*Simplified gate circuit **sinking** current*

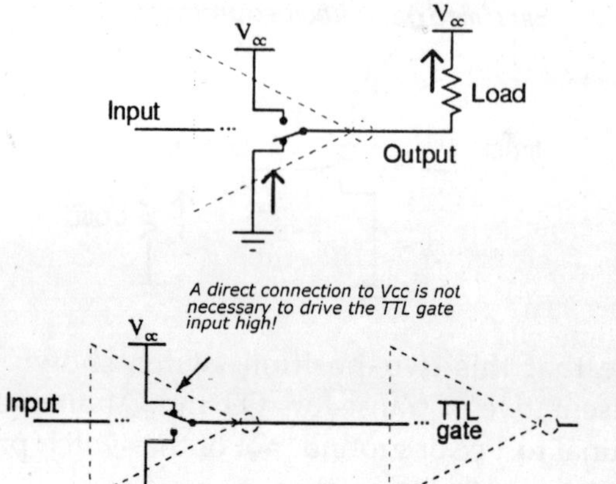

This means we have the option of simplifying the output stage of a gate circuit so as to eliminate Q_3 altogether.

The result is known as an open–collector output: To designate open–collector output circuitry within a standard gate symbol, a special marker is used. Shown here is the symbol for an inverter gate with open–collector output:

Inverter with open-collector output

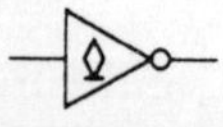

Please keep in mind that the "high" default condition of a floating gate input is only true for TTL circuitry, and not necessarily for other types, especially for logic gates constructed of field–effect transistors.

Inverter circuit with open-collector output

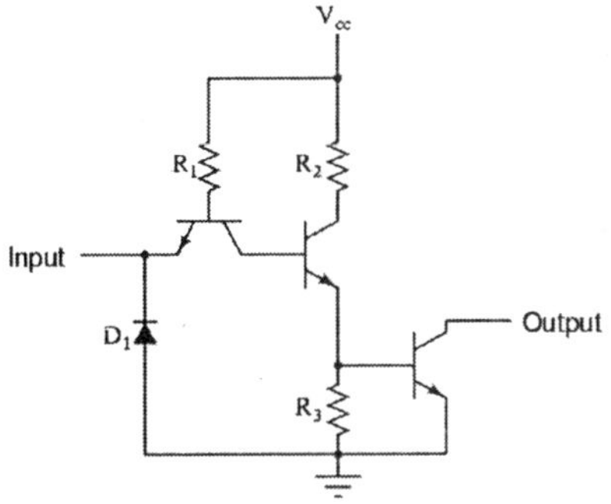

THE "BUFFER" GATE

If we were to connect two inverter gates together so that the output of one fed into the input of another, the two inversion functions would "cancel" each other out so that there would be no inversion from input to final output:

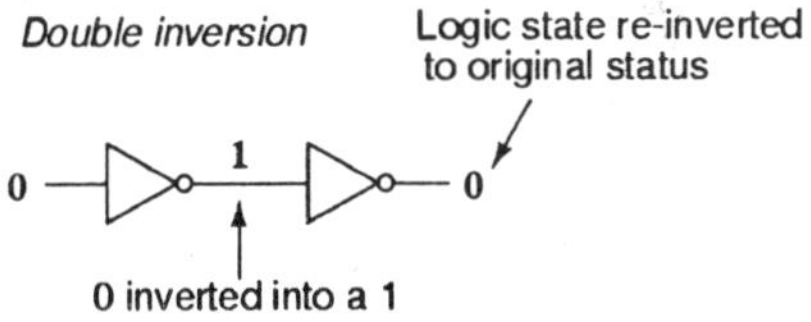

While this may seem like a pointless thing to do, it does have practical application. Remember that gate circuits are signal amplifiers, regardless of what logic function they may perform. A weak signal source (one that is not capable of sourcing or sinking very much current to a load) may be boosted by means of two inverters like the pair shown in the previous illustration. The logic level is unchanged, but the full current–sourcing or –sinking capabilities of the final inverter are available to drive a load resistance if needed.

For this purpose, a special logic gate called a buffer is manufactured to perform the same function as two inverters. Its symbol is simply a triangle, with no inverting "bubble" on the output terminal:

"Buffer" gate

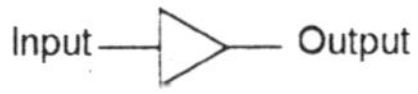

Input	Output
0	0
1	1

The internal schematic diagram for a typical open–collector buffer is not much different from that of a simple inverter: only one more common–emitter transistor stage is added to re–invert the output signal.

Buffer circuit with open-collector output

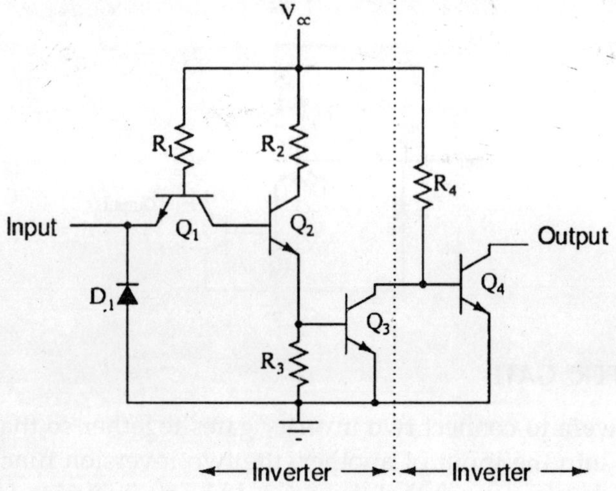

Let's analyse this circuit for two conditions: an input logic level of "1" and an input logic level of "0." First, a "high" (1) input:

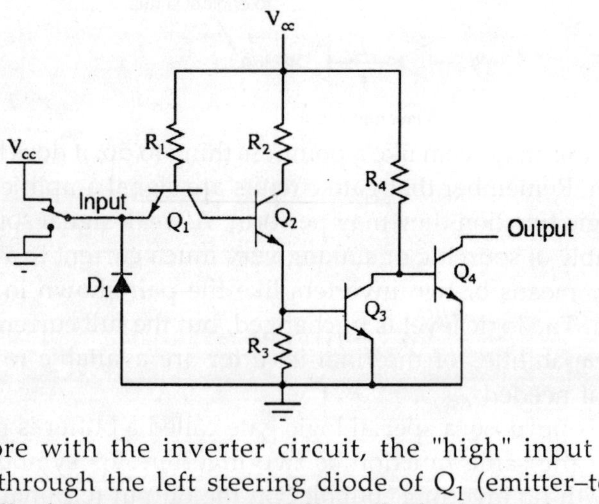

As before with the inverter circuit, the "high" input causes no conduction through the left steering diode of Q_1 (emitter–to–base PN junction). All of R1's current goes through the base of transistor Q_2, saturating it:

Having Q_2 saturated causes Q_3 to be saturated as well, resulting in very little voltage dropped between the base and emitter of the final output transistor Q_4.

Thus, Q_4 will be in cutoff mode, conducting no current. The output terminal will be floating (neither connected to ground nor Vcc), and this will be equivalent to a "high" state on the input of the next TTL gate that this one feeds in to.

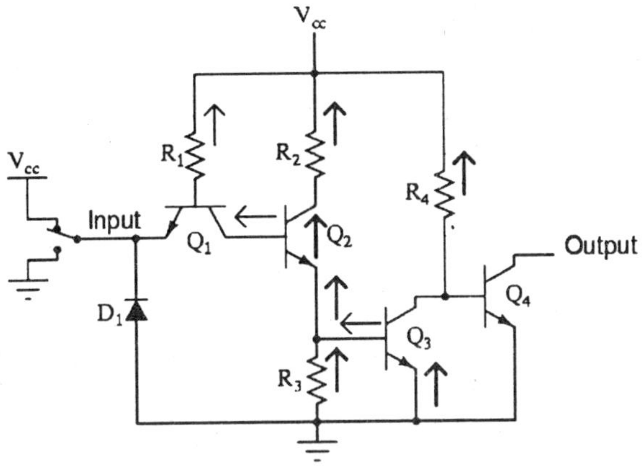

Thus, a "high" input gives a "high" output. With a "low" input signal (input terminal grounded), the analysis looks something like this:

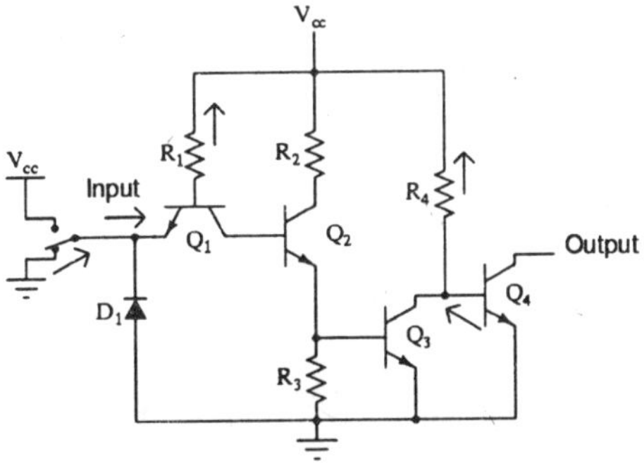

All of R1's current is now diverted through the input switch, thus eliminating base current through Q2.

Buffer circuit with totem pole output

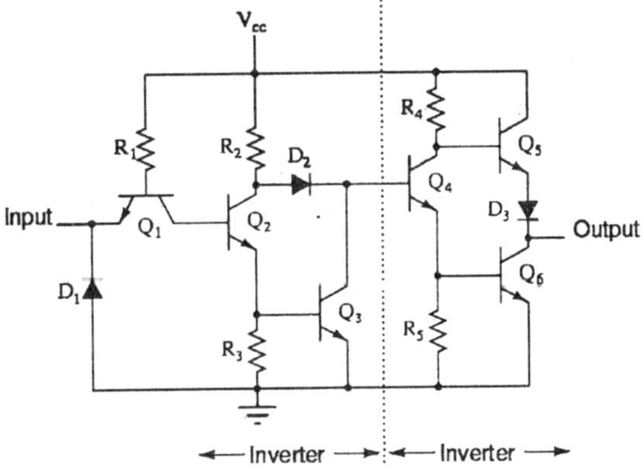

This forces transistor Q2 into cutoff so that no base current goes through Q3 either. With Q3 cutoff as well, Q4 is will be saturated by the current through resistor R4, thus connecting the output terminal to ground, making it a "low" logic level. Thus, a "low" input gives a "low" output. The schematic diagram for a buffer circuit with totem pole output transistors is a bit more complex, but the basic principles, and certainly the truth table, are the same as for the open–collector circuit:

MULTIPLE–INPUT GATES

Inverters and buffers exhaust the possibilities for single–input gate circuits. What more can be done with a single logic signal but to buffer it or invert it? To explore more logic gate possibilities, we must add more input terminals to the circuit(s).

Adding more input terminals to a logic gate increases the number of input state possibilities. With a single–input gate such as the inverter or buffer, there can only be two possible input states: either the input is "high" (1) or it is "low" (0). As was mentioned previously in this chapter, a two input gate has four possibilities (00, 01, 10, and 11). A three–input gate has eight possibilities (000, 001, 010, 011, 100, 101, 110, and 111) for input states. The number of possible input states is equal to two to the power of the number of inputs:

Number of possible input states = $2n$

Where,

n = Number of inputs

This increase in the number of possible input states obviously allows for more complex gate behaviour. Now, instead of merely inverting or amplifying (buffering) a single "high" or "low" logic level, the output of the gate will be determined by whatever combination of 1's and 0's is present at the input terminals.

Since so many combinations are possible with just a few input terminals, there are many different types of multiple–input gates, unlike single–input gates which can only be inverters or buffers. Each basic gate type will be presented in this section, showing its standard symbol, truth table, and practical operation. The actual TTL circuitry of these different gates will be explored in subsequent sections.

The AND Gate

One of the easiest multiple–input gates to understand is the AND gate, so–called because the output of this gate will be "high" (1) if and only if all inputs (first input and the second input and...) are "high" (1). If any input(s) are "low" (0), the output is guaranteed to be in a "low" state as well.

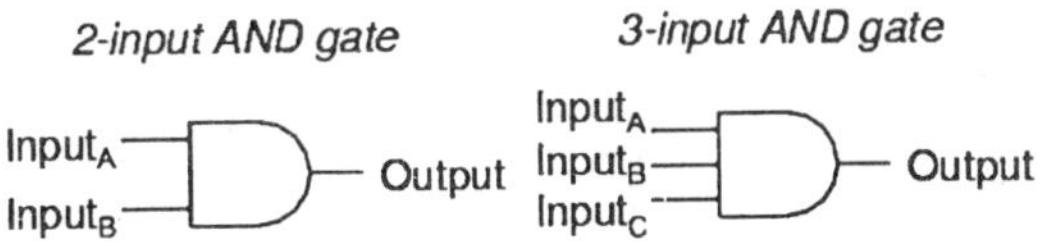

In case you might have been wondering, AND gates are made with more than three inputs, but this is less common than the simple two-input variety.

A two-input AND gate's truth table looks like this:

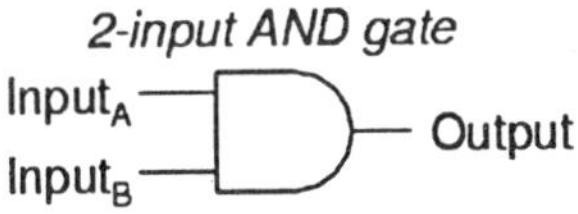

A	B	Output
0	0	0
0	1	0
1	0	0
1	1	1

What this truth table means in practical terms is shown in the following sequence of illustrations, with the 2-input AND gate subjected to all possibilities of input logic levels. An LED (Light-Emitting Diode) provides visual indication of the output logic level:

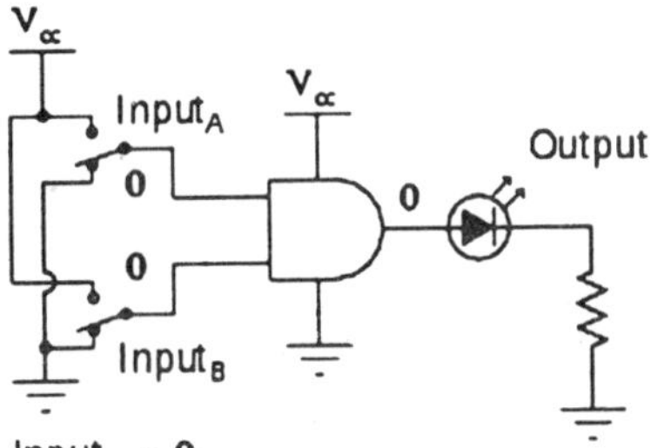

$Input_A = 0$

$Input_B = 0$

Output = 0 *(no light)*

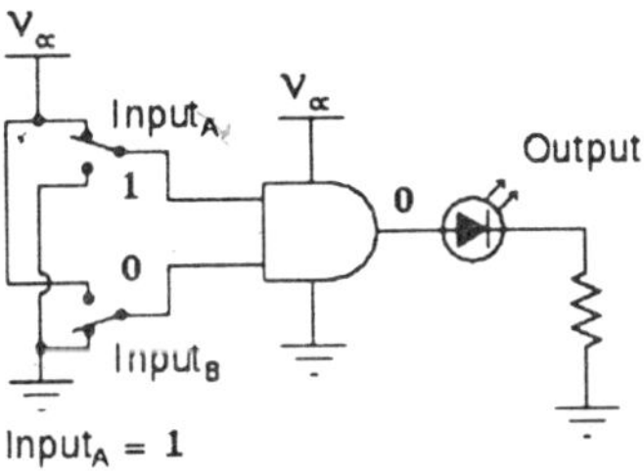

$Input_A = 1$

$Input_B = 0$

Output = 0 *(no light)*

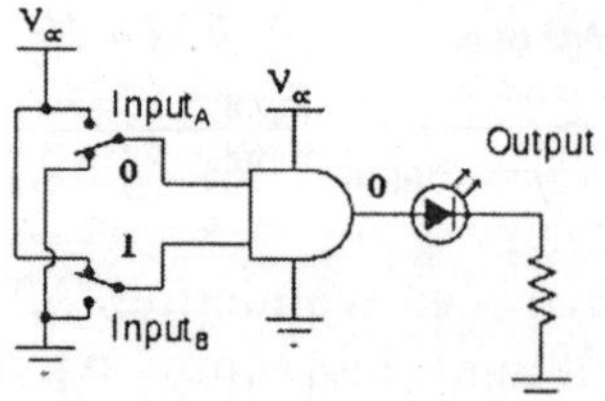

$Input_A = 0$
$Input_B = 1$
Output = 0 *(no light)*

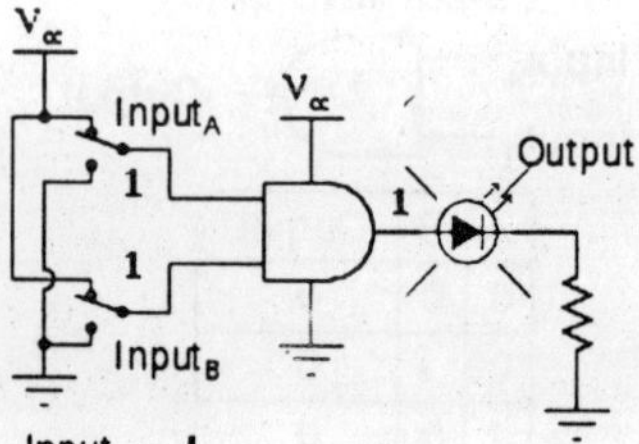

$Input_A = 1$
$Input_B = 1$
Output = 1 *(light!)*

It is only with all inputs raised to "high" logic levels that the AND gate's output goes "high," thus energizing the LED for only one out of the four input combination states.

The NAND Gate

A variation on the idea of the AND gate is called the NAND gate. The word "NAND" is a verbal contraction of the words NOT and AND. Essentially, a NAND gate behaves the same as an AND gate with a NOT (inverter) gate.

Connected to the output terminal. To symbolize this output signal inversion, the NAND gate symbol has a bubble on the output line. The truth table for a NAND gate is as one might expect, exactly opposite as that of an AND gate:

2-input NAND gate

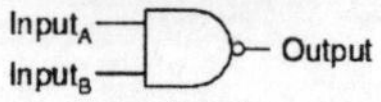

A	B	Output
0	0	1
0	1	1
1	0	1
1	1	0

Equivalent gate circuit

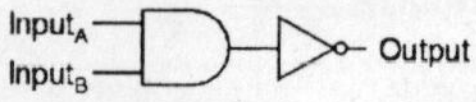

As with AND gates, NAND gates are made with more than two inputs. In such cases, the same general principle applies: the output will be "low" (0) if and only if all inputs are "high" (1). If any input is "low" (0), the output will go "high" (1).

The OR Gate

Our next gate to investigate is the OR gate, so–called because the output of this gate will be "high" (1) if any of the inputs (first input or the second input or...) are "high" (1). The output of an OR gate goes "low" (0) if and only if all inputs are "low" (0).

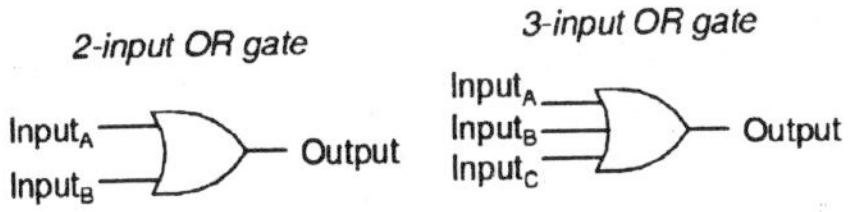

A two–input OR gate's truth table looks like this:

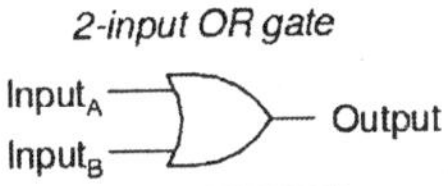

A	B	Output
0	0	0
0	1	1
1	0	1
1	1	1

The following sequence of illustrations demonstrates the OR gate's function, with the 2–inputs experiencing all possible logic levels. An LED (Light–Emitting Diode) provides visual indication of the gate's output logic level:

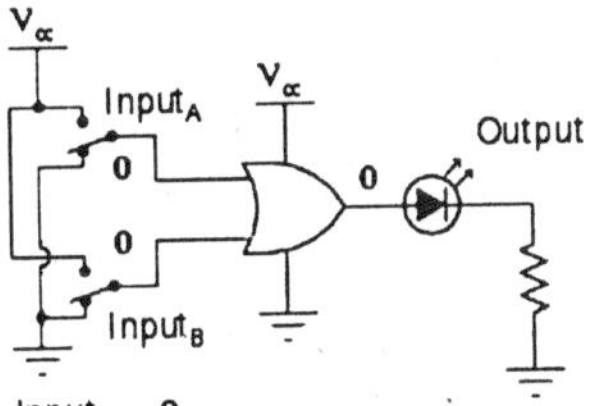

$Input_A = 0$

$Input_B = 0$

Output = 0 *(no light)*

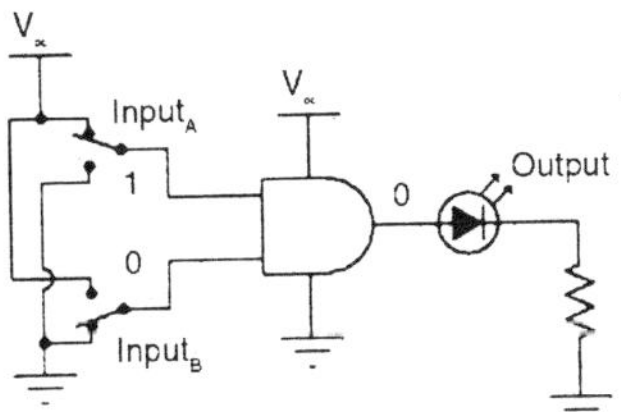

$Input_A = 1$

$Input_B = 0$

Output = 0 (no light)

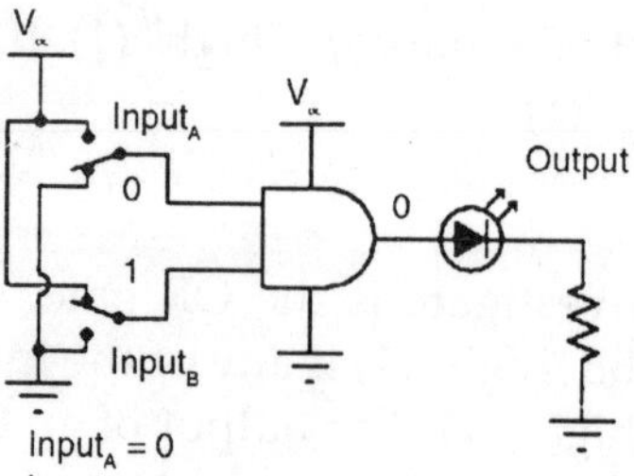

$Input_A = 0$
$Input_B = 0$
Output = 0 (no light)

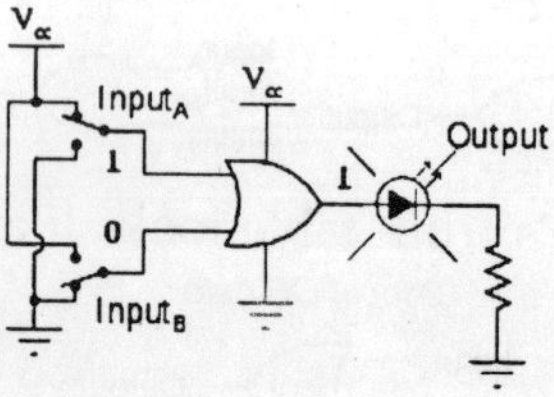

$Input_A = 1$
$Input_B = 0$
Output = 1 *(light!)*

A condition of any input being raised to a "high" logic level makes the OR gate's output go "high," thus energizing the LED for three out of the four input combination states.

The NOR Gate

As you might have suspected, the NOR gate is an OR gate with its output inverted, just like a NAND gate is an AND gate with an inverted output.

2-input NOR gate

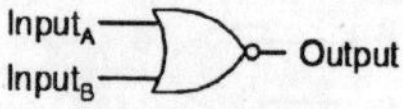

A	B	Output
0	0	1
0	1	0
1	0	0
1	1	0

Equivalent gate circuit

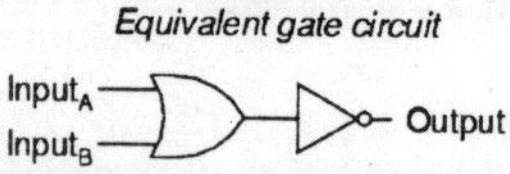

NOR gates, like all the other multiple–input gates seen thus far, can be manufactured with more than two inputs. Still, the same logical principle applies: the output goes "low" (0) if any of the inputs are made "high" (1). The output is "high" (1) only when all inputs are "low" (0).

The Negative–AND Gate

A Negative–AND gate functions the same as an AND gate with all its inputs inverted (connected through NOT gates). In keeping with standard gate symbol convention, these inverted inputs are signified by bubbles. Contrary to most peoples' first instinct, the logical behaviour of a Negative–AND gate is not the same as a NAND gate. Its truth table, actually, is identical to a NOR gate:

2-input Negative-AND gate

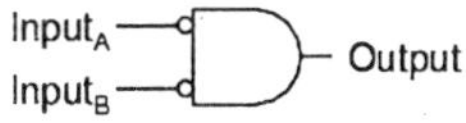

A	B	Output
0	0	1
0	1	0
1	0	0
1	1	0

Equivalent gate circuits

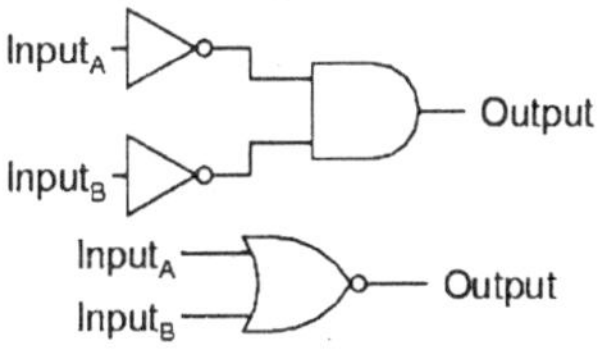

The Negative–Or Gate

Following the same pattern, a Negative–OR gate functions the same as an OR gate with all its inputs inverted. In keeping with standard gate symbol convention, these inverted inputs are signified by bubbles. The behaviour and truth table of a Negative–OR gate is the same as for a NAND

2-input Negative-OR gate

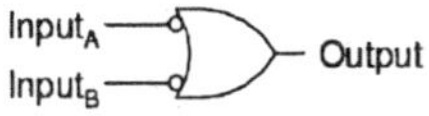

A	B	Output
0	0	1
0	1	1
1	0	1
1	1	0

Equivalent gate circuits

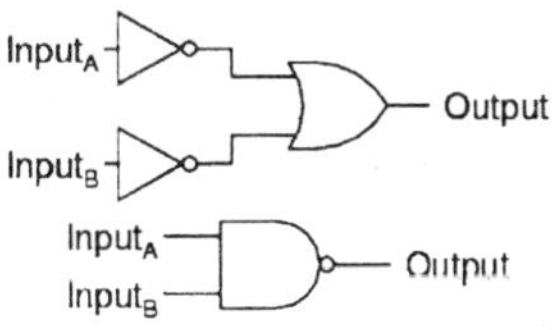

The Exclusive–Or Gate

The last six gate types are all fairly direct variations on three basic functions: AND, OR, and NOT. The Exclusive–OR gate, however, is something quite different.

Exclusive–OR gates output a "high" (1) logic level if the inputs are at different logic levels, either 0 and 1 or 1 and 0. Conversely, they output a "low" (0) logic level if the inputs are at the same logic levels. The Exclusive–OR (sometimes called XOR) gate has both a symbol and a truth table pattern that is unique:

Exclusive-OR gate

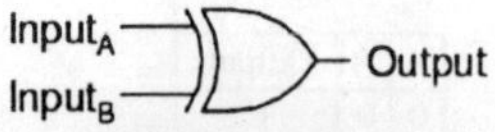

A	B	Output
0	0	0
0	1	1
1	0	1
1	1	0

There are equivalent circuits for an Exclusive–OR gate made up of AND, OR, and NOT gates, just as there were for NAND, NOR, and the negative–input gates. A rather direct approach to simulating an Exclusive–OR gate is to start with a regular OR gate, then add additional gates to inhibit the output from going "high" (1) when both inputs are "high" (1).

Exclusive-OR equivalent circuit

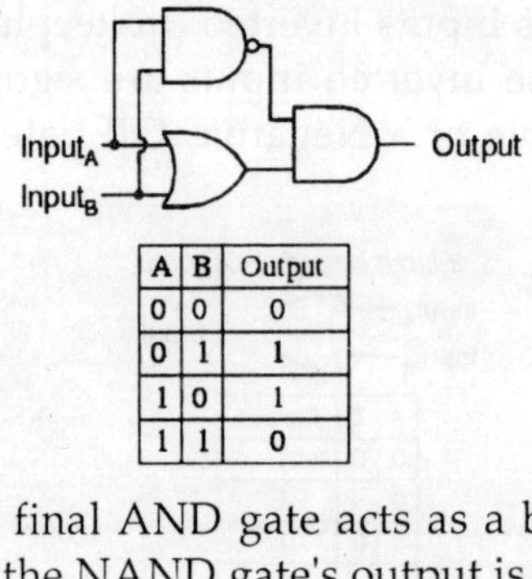

A	B	Output
0	0	0
0	1	1
1	0	1
1	1	0

In this circuit, the final AND gate acts as a buffer for the output of the OR gate whenever the NAND gate's output is high, which it is for the first three input state combinations (00, 01, and 10). However, when both inputs are "high" (1), the NAND gate outputs a "low" (0) logic level, which forces the final AND gate to produce a "low" (0) output. Another equivalent circuit for the Exclusive–OR gate uses a strategy of two AND gates with inverters, set up to generate "high" (1) outputs for input conditions 01 and 10.

A final OR gate then allows either of the AND gates' "high" outputs to create a final "high" output:

Exclusive–OR gates are very useful for circuits where two or more binary numbers are to be compared bit–for–bit, and also for error detection (parity check) and code conversion (binary to Grey and vice versa).

Exclusive-OR equivalent circuit

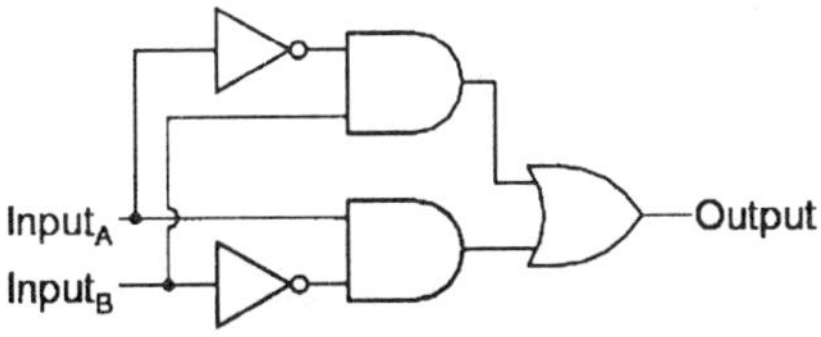

A	B	Output
0	0	0
0	1	1
1	0	1
1	1	0

The Exclusive–Nor Gate

Finally, our last gate for analysis is the Exclusive–NOR gate, otherwise known as the XNOR gate. It is equivalent to an Exclusive–OR gate with an inverted output. The truth table for this gate is exactly opposite as for the Exclusive–OR gate:

Exclusive-NOR gate

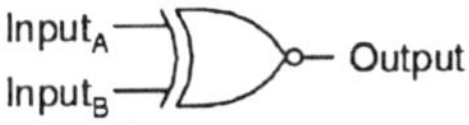

A	B	Output
0	0	1
0	1	0
1	0	0
1	1	1

Equivalent gate circuit

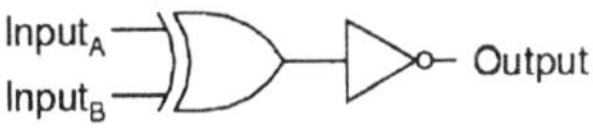

As indicated by the truth table, the purpose of an Exclusive–NOR gate is to output a "high" (1) logic level whenever both inputs are at the same logic levels (either 00 or 11).

TTL NAND AND AND GATES

Suppose we altered our basic open–collector inverter circuit, adding a second input terminal just like the first: This schematic illustrates a real circuit, but it isn't called a "two–input inverter." Through analysis we will discover what this circuit's logic function is and correspondingly what it should be designated as. Just as in the case of the inverter and buffer, the "steering" diode cluster marked "Q1" is actually formed like a transistor, even though it isn't used in any amplifying capacity.

A two-input inverter circuit

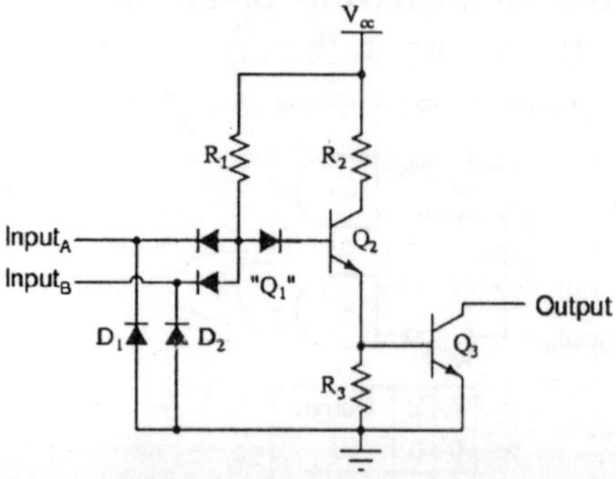

Unfortunately, a simple NPN transistor structure is inadequate to simulate the three PN junctions necessary in this diode network, so a different transistor (and symbol) is needed. This transistor has one collector, one base, and two emitters, and in the circuit it looks like this:

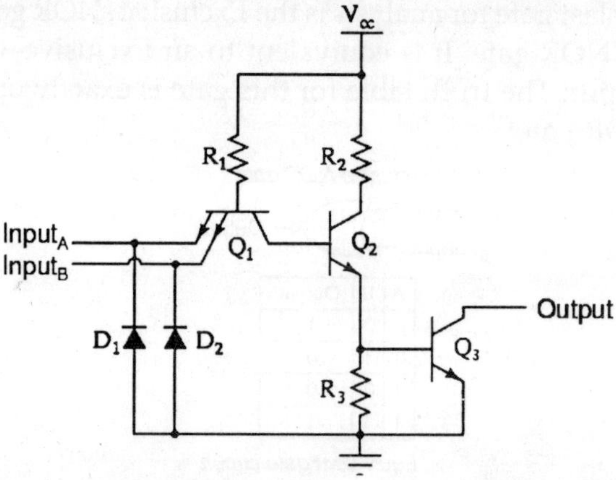

In the single–input (inverter) circuit, grounding the input resulted in an output that assumed the "high" (1) state. In the case of the open–collector output configuration, this "high" state was simply "floating." Allowing the input to float (or be connected to Vcc) resulted in the output becoming grounded, which is the "low" or 0 state. Thus, a 1 in resulted in a 0 out, and vice versa.

Since this circuit bears so much resemblance to the simple inverter circuit, the only difference being a second input terminal connected in the same way to the base of transistor Q_2, we can say that each of the inputs will have the same effect on the output. Namely, if either of the inputs are grounded, transistor Q_2 will be forced into a condition of cutoff, thus turning Q_3 off and floating the output (output goes "high"). The following series of illustrations shows this for three input states (00, 01, and 10).

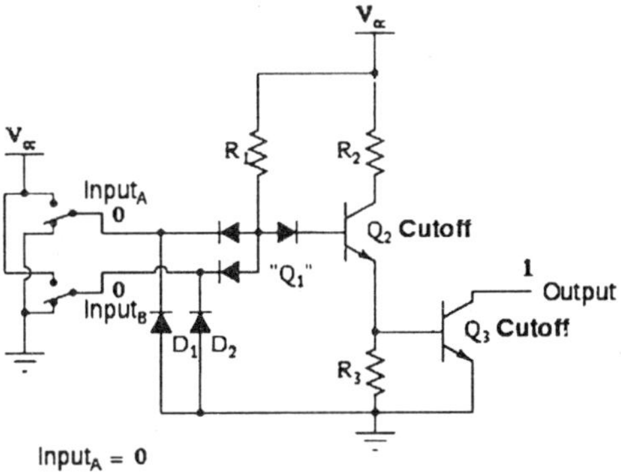

$Input_A$ = 0

$Input_B$ = 0

Output = 1

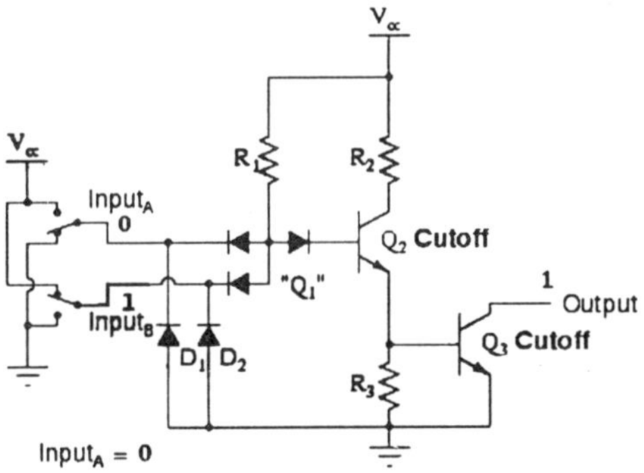

$Input_A$ = 0

$Input_B$ = 1

Output = 1

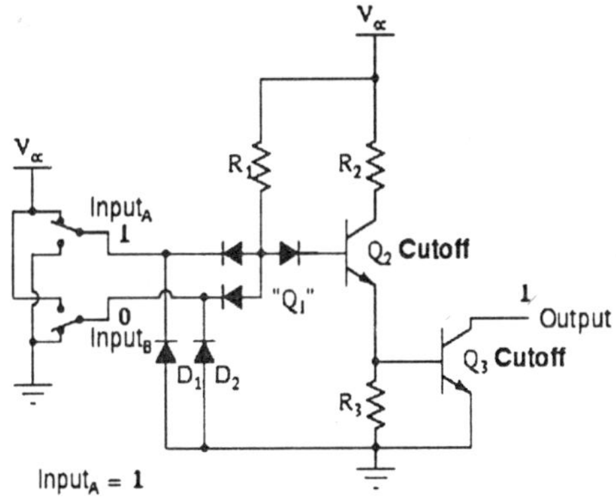

$Input_A$ = 1

$Input_B$ = 0

Output = 1

In any case where there is a grounded ("low") input, the output is guaranteed to be floating ("high"). Conversely, the only time the output will ever go "low" is if transistor Q_3 turns on, which means transistor Q_2

must be turned on (saturated), which means neither input can be diverting R_1 current away from the base of Q_2. The only condition that will satisfy this requirement is when both inputs are "high" (1).

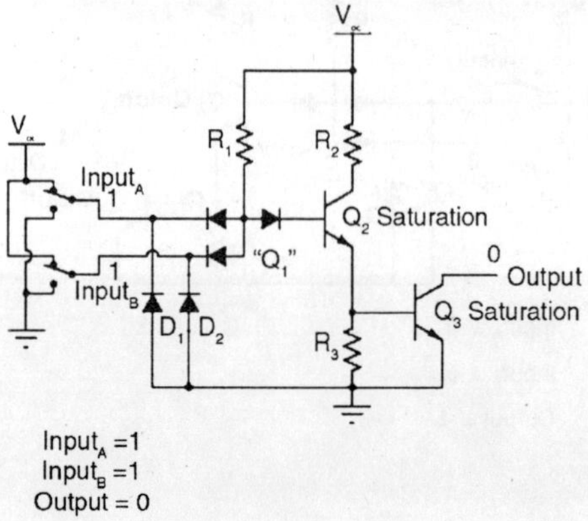

Collecting and tabulating these results into a truth table, we see that the pattern matches that of the NAND gate:

NAND gate

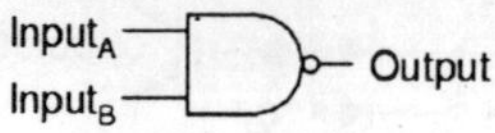

A	B	Output
0	0	1
0	1	1
1	0	1
1	1	0

In the earlier section on NAND gates, this type of gate was created by taking an AND gate and increasing its complexity by adding an inverter (NOT gate) to the output. However, when we examine this circuit, we see that the NAND function is actually the simplest, most natural mode of operation for this TTL design.

AND gate with open-collector output

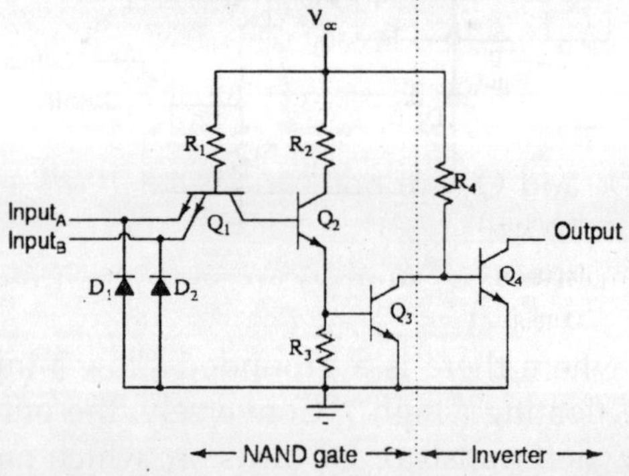

To create an AND function using TTL circuitry, we need to increase the complexity of this circuit by adding an inverter stage to the output, just like we had to add an additional transistor stage to the TTL inverter circuit to turn it into a buffer:

The truth table and equivalent gate circuit (an inverted–output NAND gate) are shown here:

AND gate

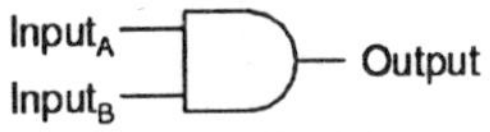

A	B	Output
0	0	0
0	1	0
1	0	0
1	1	1

Equivalent circuit

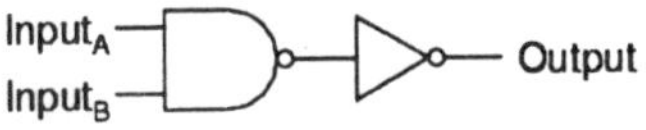

Of course, both NAND and AND gate circuits may be designed with totem–pole output stages rather than open–collector.

TTL NOR AND OR GATES

Let's examine the following TTL circuit and analyse its operation:

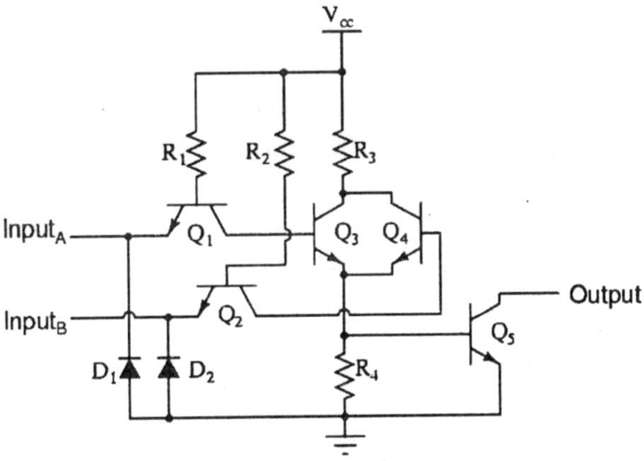

Transistors Q_1 and Q_2 are both arranged in the same manner that we've seen for transistor Q_1 in all the other TTL circuits. Rather than functioning as amplifiers, Q_1 and Q_2 are both being used as two–diode "steering" networks. We may replace Q_1 and Q_2 with diode sets to help illustrate:

If input A is left floating (or connected to Vcc), current will go through the base of transistor Q_3, saturating it.

If input A is grounded, that current is diverted away from Q3's base through the left steering diode of "Q1," thus forcing Q_3 into cutoff. The same can be said for input B and transistor Q_4: the logic level of input B determines Q4's conduction: either saturated or cutoff.

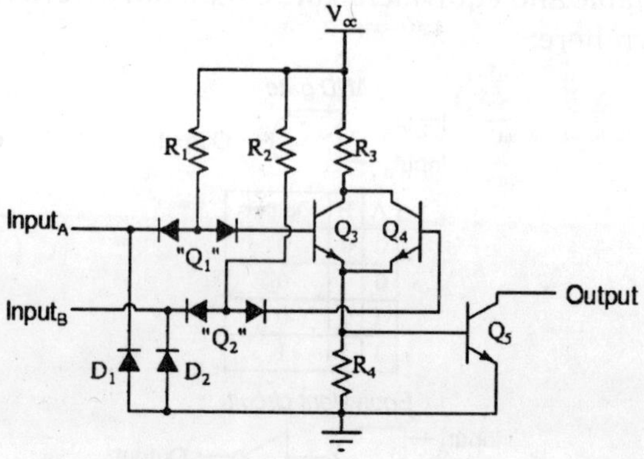

Notice how transistors Q_3 and Q_4 are paralleled at their collector and emitter terminals.

In essence, these two transistors are acting as paralleled switches, allowing current through resistors R_3 and R_4 according to the logic levels of inputs A and B.

If any input is at a "high" (1) level, then at least one of the two transistors (Q_3 and/or Q_4) will be saturated, allowing.

Current through resistors R_3 and R_4, and turning on the final output transistor Q_5 for a "low" (0) logic level output.

The only way the output of this circuit can ever assume a "high" (1) state is if both Q_3 and Q_4 are cutoff, which means both inputs would have to be grounded, or "low" (0).

This circuit's truth table, then, is equivalent to that of the NOR gate:

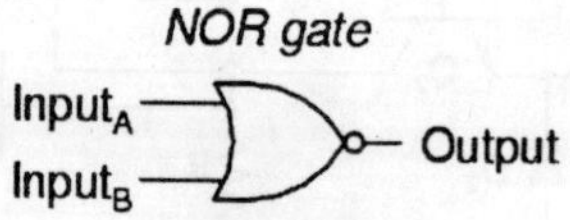

A	B	Output
0	0	1
0	1	0
1	0	0
1	1	0

In order to turn this NOR gate circuit into an OR gate, we would have to invert the output logic level with another transistor stage, just like we did with the NAND–to–AND gate example:

OR gate with open-collector output

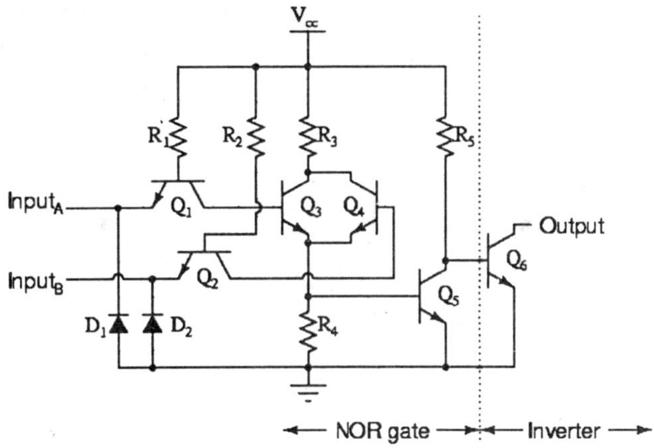

The truth table and equivalent gate circuit (an inverted–output NOR gate) are shown here:

OR gate

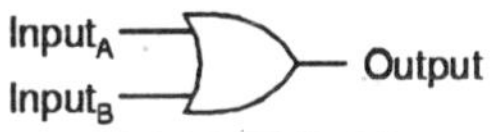

A	B	Output
0	0	0
0	1	1
1	0	1
1	1	1

Equivalent circuit

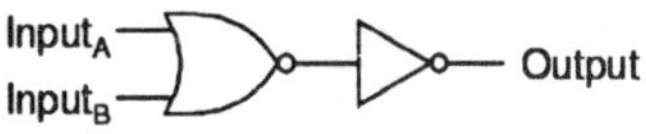

Of course, totem–pole output stages are also possible in both NOR and OR TTL logic circuits.

CMOS GATE CIRCUITRY

Up until this point, our analysis of transistor logic circuits has been limited to the TTL design paradigm, whereby bipolar transistors are used, and the general strategy of floating inputs being equivalent to "high" (connected to Vcc) inputs — and correspondingly, the allowance of "open–collector" output stages — is maintained. This, however, is not the only way we can build logic gates.

Field–effect transistors, particularly the insulated–gate variety, may be used in the design of gate circuits. Being voltage–controlled rather than current–controlled devices, IGFETs tend to allow very simple circuit designs. Take for instance, the following inverter circuit built using P– and N–channel IGFETs:

Inverter circuit using IGFETs

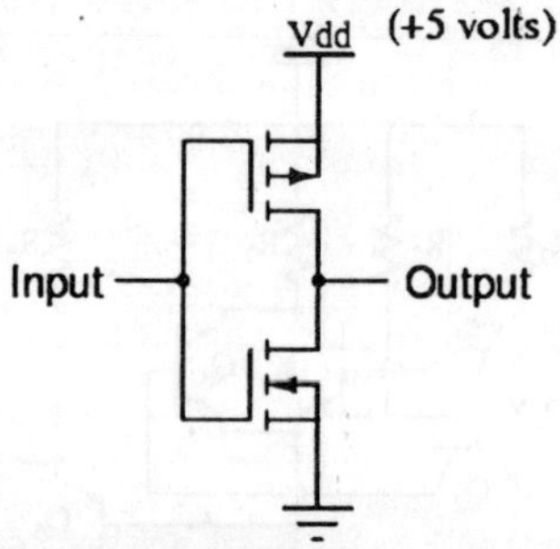

Notice the "Vdd" label on the positive power supply terminal. This label follows the same convention as "Vcc" in TTL circuits: it stands for the constant voltage applied to the drain of a field effect transistor, in reference to ground.

Let's connect this gate circuit to a power source and input switch, and examine its operation. Please note that these IGFET transistors are E–type (Enhancement–mode), and so are normally–off devices. It takes an applied voltage between gate and drain (actually, between gate and substrate) of the correct polarity to bias them on.

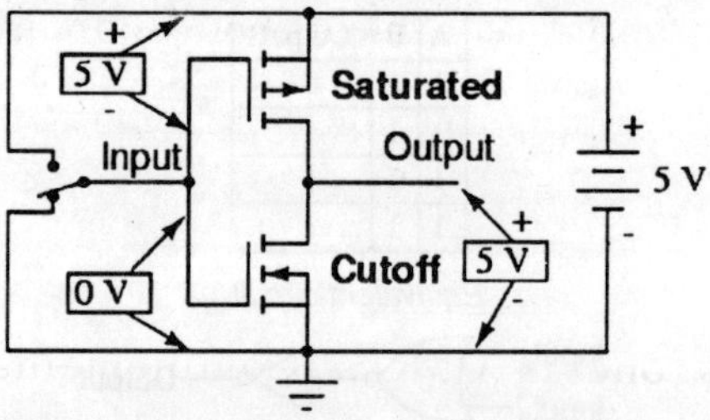

Input = "low" (0)
Output = "high" (1)

The upper transistor is a P–channel IGFET. When the channel (substrate) is made more positive than the gate (gate negative in reference to the substrate), the channel is enhanced and current is allowed between source and drain. So, in the above illustration, the top transistor is turned on.

The lower transistor, having zero voltage between gate and substrate (source), is in its normal mode: off. Thus, the action of these two transistors are such that the output terminal of the gate circuit has a solid connection to Vdd and a very high resistance connection to ground. This makes the output "high" (1) for the "low" (0) state of the input.

Next, we'll move the input switch to its other position and see what happens:

Now the lower transistor (N–channel) is saturated because it has sufficient voltage of the correct polarity applied between gate and substrate (channel) to turn it on (positive on gate, negative on the channel).

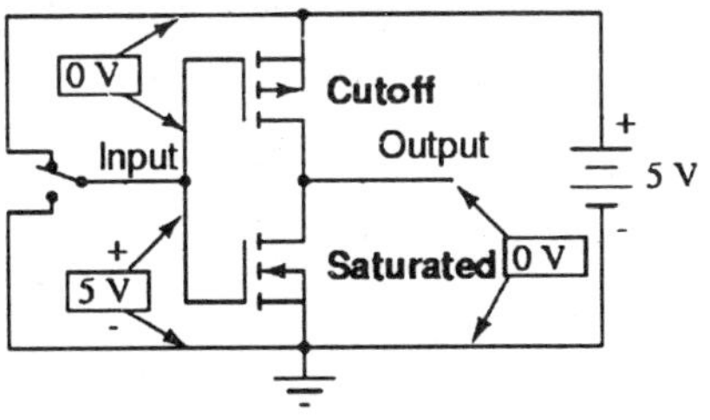

Input = "high" (1)
Output = "low" (0)

The upper transistor, having zero voltage applied between its gate and substrate, is in its normal mode: off. Thus, the output of this gate circuit is now "low" (0). Clearly, this circuit exhibits the behaviour of an inverter, or NOT gate.

Using field–effect transistors instead of bipolar transistors has greatly simplified the design of the inverter gate. Note that the output of this gate never floats as is the case with the simplest TTL circuit: it has a natural "totem–pole" configuration, capable of both sourcing and sinking load current. Key to this gate circuit's elegant design is the complementary use of both P– and N–channel IGFETs.

Since IGFETs are more commonly known as MOSFETs (Metal–Oxide–Semiconductor Field Effect Transistor), and this circuit uses both P– and N–channel transistors together, the general classification given to gate circuits like this one is CMOS: Complementary Metal Oxide Semiconductor.

CMOS circuits aren't plagued by the inherent nonlinearities of the field–effect transistors, because as digital circuits their transistors always operate in either the saturated or cutoff modes and never in the active mode.

Their inputs are, however, sensitive to high voltages generated by electrostatic (static electricity) sources, and may even be activated into "high" (1) or "low" (0) states by spurious voltage sources if left floating. For this reason, it is inadvisable to allow a CMOS logic gate input to float under any circumstances. Please note that this is very different from the behaviour of a TTL gate where a floating input was safely interpreted as a "high" (1) logic level.

This may cause a problem if the input to a CMOS logic gate is driven by a single–throw switch, where one state has the input solidly connected to either Vdd or ground and the other state has the input floating (not connected to anything).

Also, this problem arises if a CMOS gate input is being driven by an open–collector TTL gate. Because such a TTL gate's output floats when it goes "high" (1), the CMOS gate input will be left in an uncertain state:

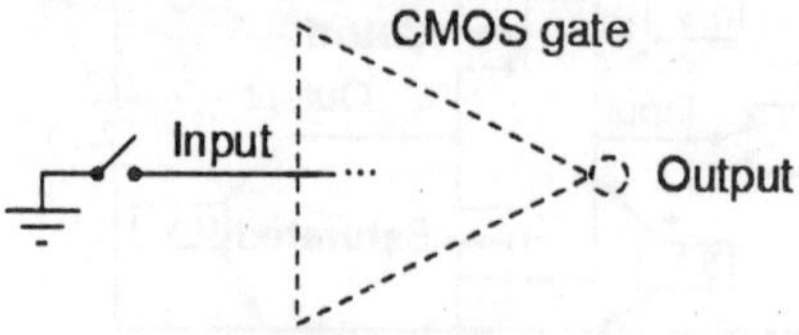

When switch is closed, the gate sees a definite "low" (0) input. However, when switch is open, the input logic level will be uncertain because it's floating.

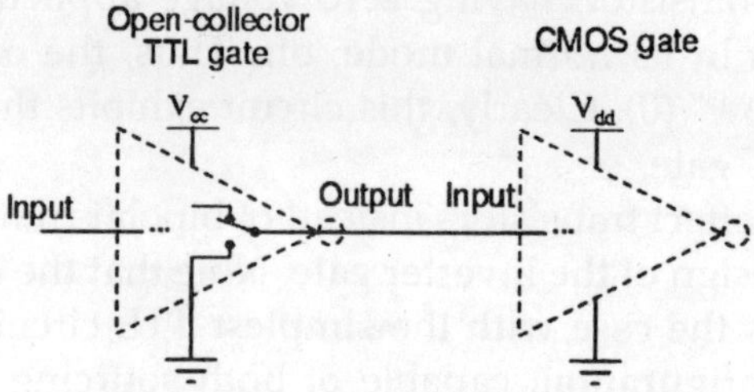

When the open-collector TTL gate's output is "high" (1), the CMOS gate's input will be left floating and in an uncertain logic state.

Fortunately, there is an easy solution to this dilemma, one that is used frequently in CMOS logic circuitry. Whenever a single–throw switch (or any other sort of gate output incapable of both sourcing and sinking current) is being used to drive a CMOS input, a resistor connected to either Vdd or ground may be used to provide a stable logic level for the state in which the driving device's output is floating. This resistor's value is not critical: 10 k? is usually sufficient. When used to provide a "high" (1) logic level in the event of a floating signal source, this resistor is known as a pullup resistor:

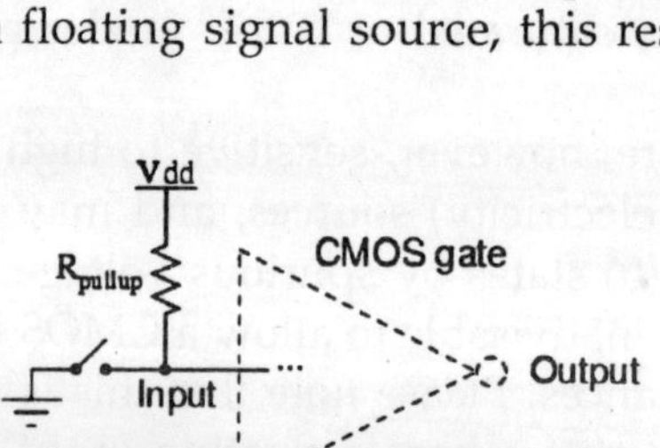

When switch is closed, the gate sees a definite "low" (0) input. When the switch is open, R_{pullup} will provide the connection to Vdd needed to secure a reliable "high" logic level for the CMOS gate input.

When such a resistor is used to provide a "low" (0) logic level in the event of a floating signal source, it is known as a pulldown resistor. Again, the value for a pulldown resistor is not critical:

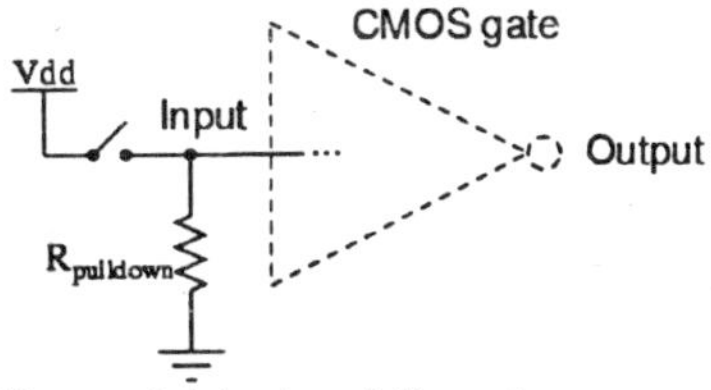

When switch is closed, the gate sees a definite "high" (1) input. When the switch is open, $R_{pulldown}$ will provide the connection to ground needed to secure a reliable "low" logic level for the CMOS gate input.

Because open-collector TTL outputs always sink, never source, current, pullup resistors are necessary when interfacing such an output to a CMOS gate input:

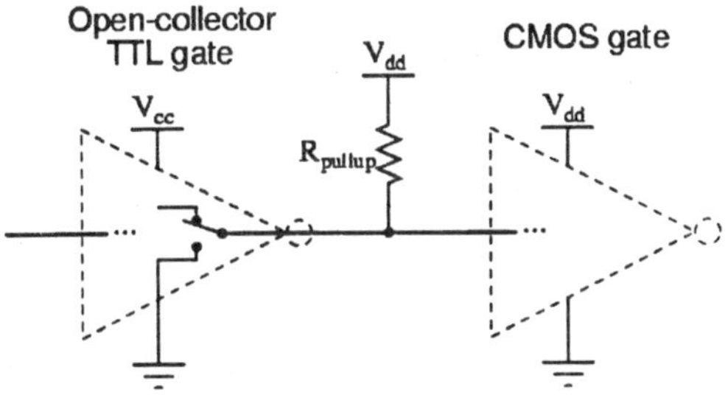

Although the CMOS gates used in the preceding examples were all inverters (single-input), the same principle of pullup and pulldown resistors applies to multiple-input CMOS gates. Of course, a separate pullup or pulldown resistor will be required for each gate input:

Pullup resistors for a 3-input CMOS AND gate

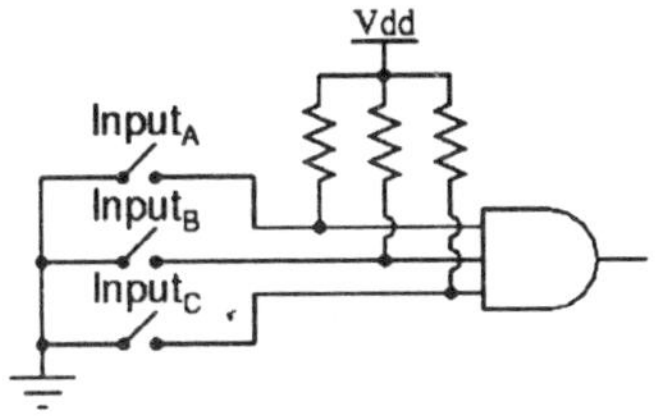

This brings us to the next question: how do we design multiple-input CMOS gates such as AND, NAND, OR, and NOR? Not surprisingly, the answer(s) to this question reveal a simplicity of design much like that of the CMOS inverter over its TTL equivalent.

For example, here is the schematic diagram for a CMOS NAND gate:

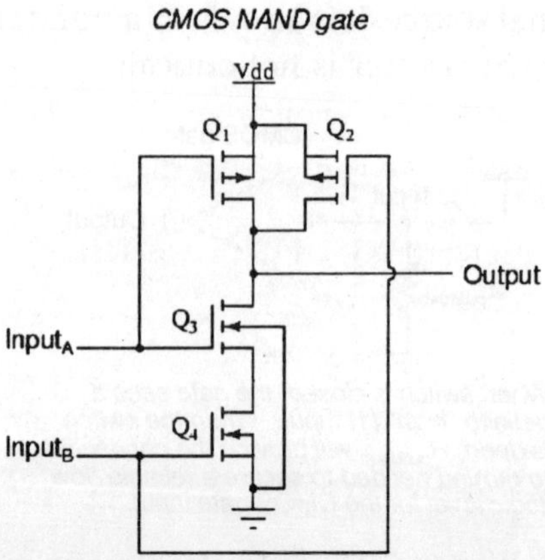

Notice how transistors Q1 and Q3 resemble the series–connected complementary pair from the inverter circuit. Both are controlled by the same input signal (input A), the upper transistor turning off and the lower transistor turning on when the input is "high" (1), and vice versa. Notice also how transistors Q2 and Q4 are similarly controlled by the same input signal (input B), and how they will also exhibit the same on/off behaviour for the same input logic levels.

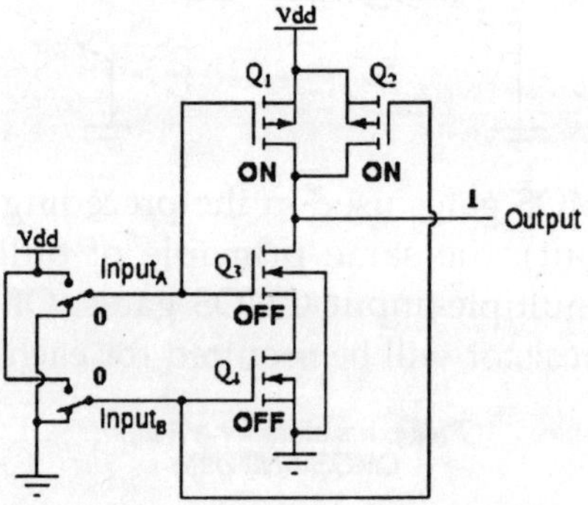

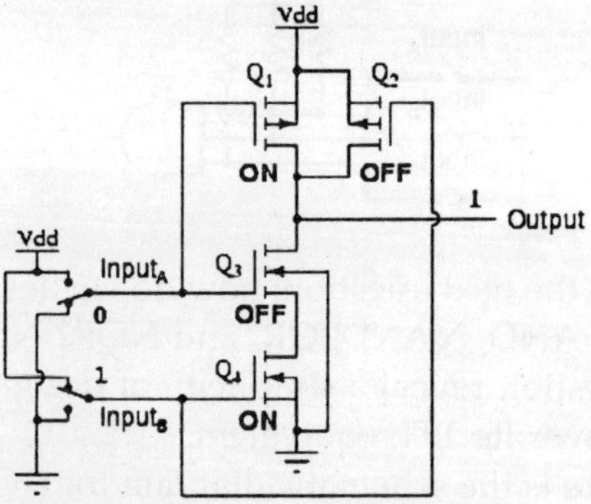

The upper transistors of both pairs (Q_1 and Q_2) have their source and drain terminals paralleled, while the lower transistors (Q_3 and Q_4) are series–connected. What this means is that the output will go "high" (1) if either top transistor saturates, and will go "low" (0) only if both lower transistors saturate. The following sequence of illustrations shows the behaviour of this NAND gate for all four possibilities of input logic levels (00, 01, 10, and 11).

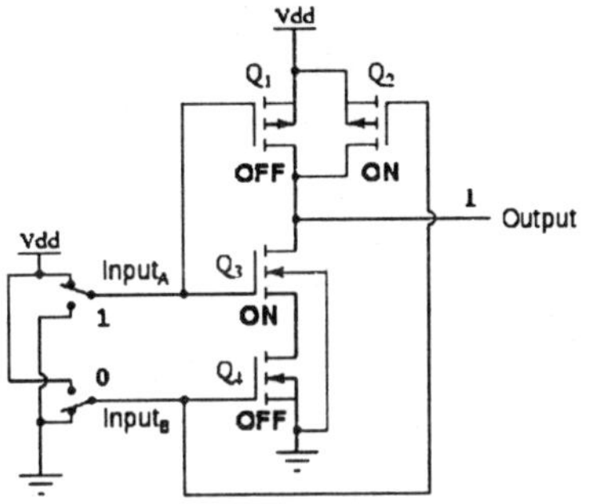

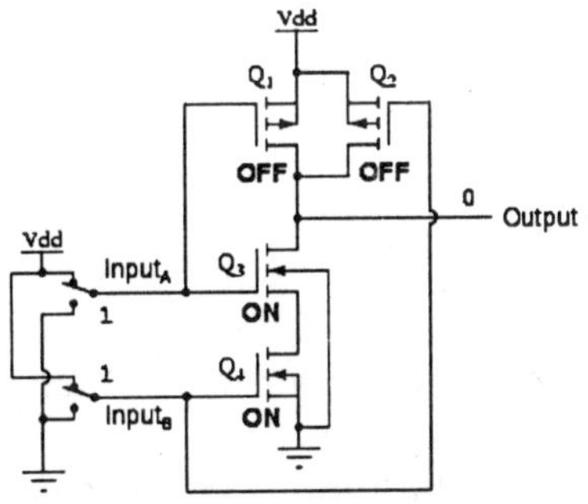

As with the TTL NAND gate, the CMOS NAND gate circuit may be used as the starting point for the creation of an AND gate. All that needs to be added is another stage of transistors to invert the output signal:

CMOS AND gate

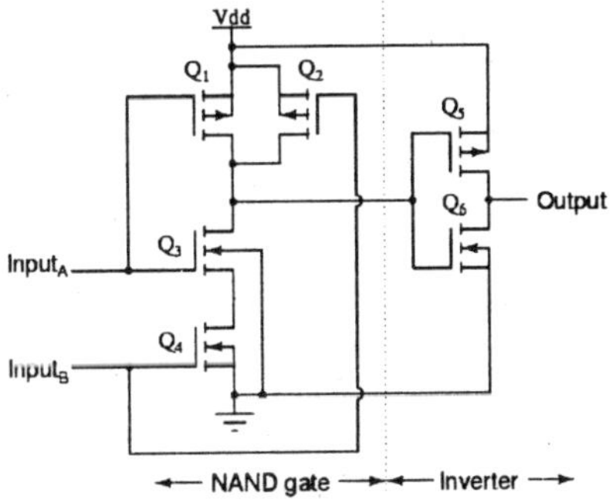

A CMOS NOR gate circuit uses four MOSFETs just like the NAND gate, except that its transistors are differently arranged. Instead of two paralleled sourcing (upper) transistors connected to Vdd and two series–connected sinking (lower) transistors connected to ground, the NOR gate uses two series–connected sourcing transistors and two parallel–connected sinking transistors like this:

CMOS NOR gate

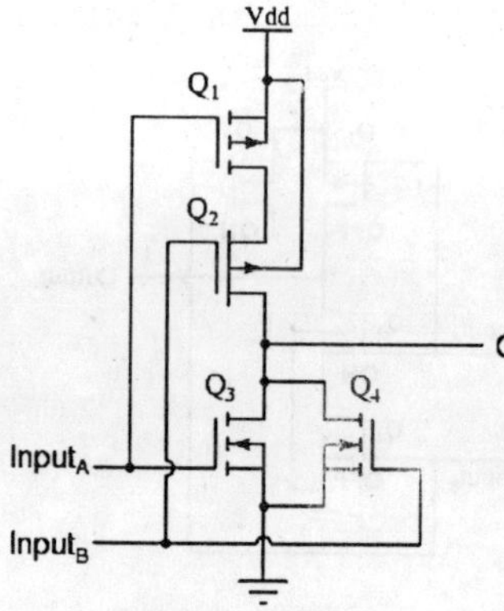

As with the NAND gate, transistors Q_1 and Q_3 work as a complementary pair, as do transistors Q_2 and Q_4. Each pair is controlled by a single input signal. If either input A or input B are "high" (1), at least one of the lower transistors (Q_3 or Q_4) will be saturated, thus making the output "low" (0). Only in the event of both inputs being "low" (0) will both lower transistors be in cutoff mode and both upper transistors be saturated, the conditions necessary for the output to go "high" (1). This behaviour, of course, defines the NOR logic function.

The OR function may be built up from the basic NOR gate with the addition of an inverter stage on the output:

CMOS OR gate

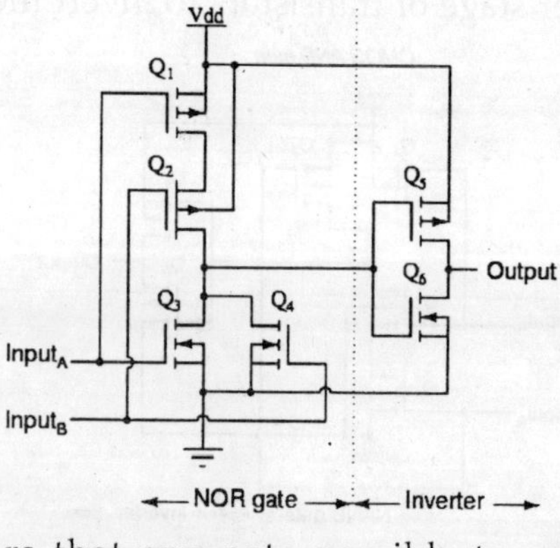

Since it appears that any gate possible to construct using TTL technology can be duplicated in CMOS, why do these two "families" of logic design still coexist? The answer is that both TTL and CMOS have their own unique advantages.

First and foremost on the list of comparisons between TTL and CMOS is the issue of power consumption. In this measure of performance, CMOS is the unchallenged victor.

Because the complementary P– and N–channel MOSFET pairs of a CMOS gate circuit are (ideally) never conducting at the same time, there is little or no current drawn by the circuit from the Vdd power supply except for what current is necessary to source current to a load. TTL, on the other hand, cannot function without some current drawn at all times, due to the biasing requirements of the bipolar transistors from which it is made.

There is a caveat to this advantage, though. While the power dissipation of a TTL gate remains rather constant regardless of its operating state(s), a CMOS gate dissipates more power as the frequency of its input signal(s) rises.

If a CMOS gate is operated in a static (unchanging) condition, it dissipates zero power (ideally). However, CMOS gate circuits draw transient current during every output state switch from "low" to "high" and vice versa. So, the more often a CMOS gate switches modes, the more often it will draw current from the Vdd supply, hence greater power dissipation at greater frequencies.

A CMOS gate also draws much less current from a driving gate output than a TTL gate because MOSFETs are voltage–controlled, not current–controlled, devices. This means that one gate can drive many more CMOS inputs than TTL inputs. The measure of how many gate inputs a single gate output can drive is called fanout.

Another advantage that CMOS gate designs enjoy over TTL is a much wider allowable range of power supply voltages. Whereas TTL gates are restricted to power supply (Vcc) voltages between 4.75 and 5.25 volts, CMOS gates are typically able to operate on any voltage between 3 and 15 volts!

The reason behind this disparity in power supply voltages is the respective bias requirements of MOSFET versus bipolar junction transistors. MOSFETs are controlled exclusively by gate voltage (with respect to substrate), whereas BJTs are current–controlled devices. TTL gate circuit resistances are precisely calculated for proper bias currents assuming a 5 volt regulated power supply.

Any significant variations in that power supply voltage will result in the transistor bias currents being incorrect, which then results in unreliable (unpredictable) operation. The only effect that variations in power supply voltage have on a CMOS gate is the voltage definition of a "high" (1) state. For a CMOS gate operating at 15 volts of power supply voltage (Vdd), an input signal must be close to 15 volts in order to be considered "high" (1). The voltage threshold for a "low" (0) signal remains the same: near 0 volts.

One decided disadvantage of CMOS is slow speed, as compared to TTL. The input capacitances of a CMOS gate are much, much greater than that of a comparable TTL gate — owing to the use of MOSFETs rather than BJTs — and so a CMOS gate will be slower to respond to a signal transition (low–to–high or vice versa) than a TTL gate, all other factors being equal. The RC time constant formed by circuit resistances and the input capacitance of the gate tend to impede the fast rise– and fall–times of a digital logic level, thereby degrading high–frequency performance.

"Unbuffered" NOR gate

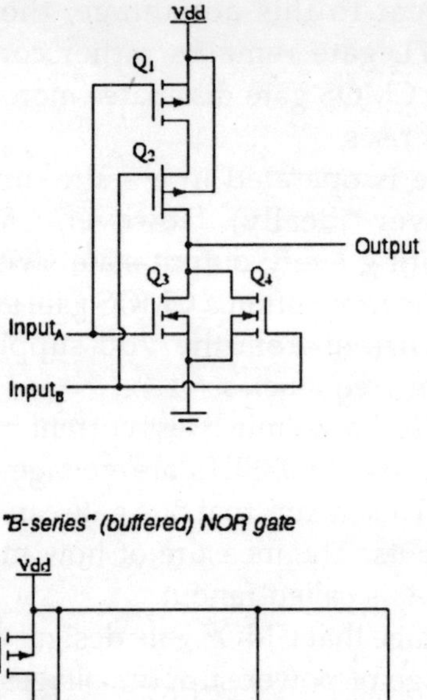

"B-series" (buffered) NOR gate

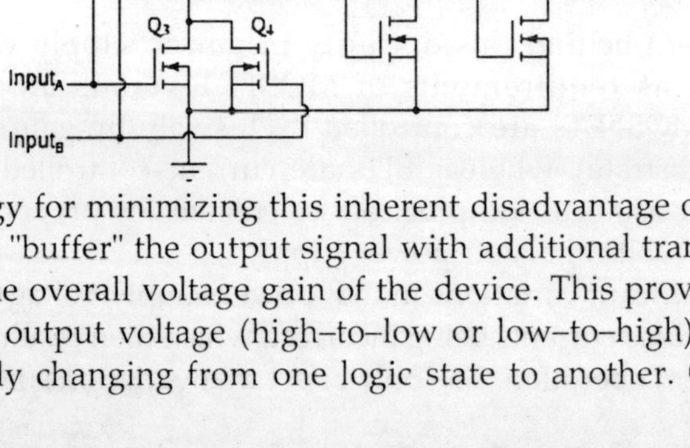

A strategy for minimizing this inherent disadvantage of CMOS gate circuitry is to "buffer" the output signal with additional transistor stages, to increase the overall voltage gain of the device. This provides a faster–transitioning output voltage (high–to–low or low–to–high) for an input voltage slowly changing from one logic state to another. Consider this example, of an "unbuffered" NOR gate versus a "buffered," or B–series, NOR gate:

In essence, the B–series design enhancement adds two inverters to the output of a simple NOR circuit. This serves no purpose as far as digital logic is concerned, since two cascaded inverters simply cancel:

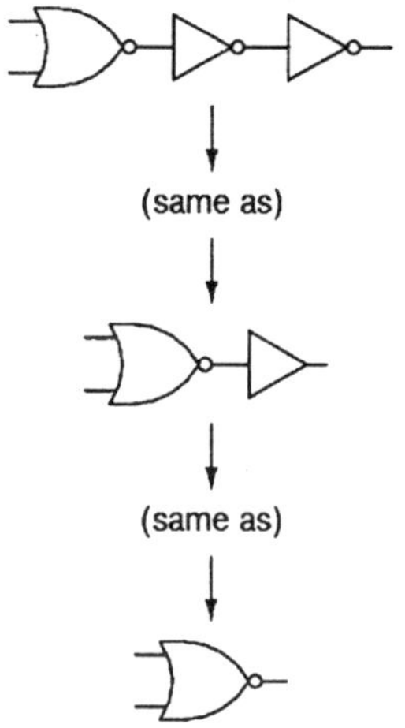

However, adding these inverter stages to the circuit does serve the purpose of increasing overall voltage gain, making the output more sensitive to changes in input state, working to overcome the inherent slowness caused by CMOS gate input capacitance.

Special–Output Gates

It is sometimes desirable to have a logic gate that provides both inverted and non–inverted outputs. For example, a single–input gate that is both a buffer and an inverter, with a separate output terminal for each function.

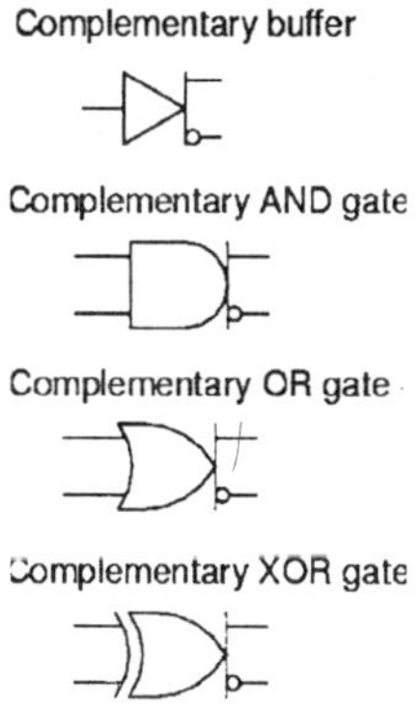

Or, a two–input gate that provides both the AND and the NAND functions in a single circuit. Such gates do exist and they are referred to as complementary output gates. The general symbology for such a gate is the basic gate figure with a bar and two output lines protruding from it. An array of complementary gate symbols is shown in the following illustration:

Complementary gates are especially useful in "crowded" circuits where there may not be enough physical room to mount the additional integrated circuit chips necessary to provide both inverted and noninverted outputs using standard gates and additional inverters. They are also useful in applications

Where a complementary output is necessary from a gate, but the addition of an inverter would introduce an unwanted time lag in the inverted output relative to the noninverted output. The internal circuitry of complemented gates is such that both inverted and noninverted outputs change state at almost exactly the same time:

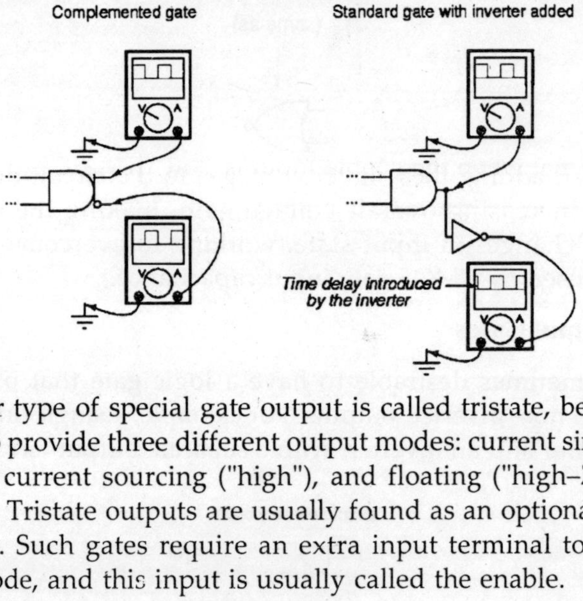

Another type of special gate output is called tristate, because it has the ability to provide three different output modes: current sinking ("low" logic level), current sourcing ("high"), and floating ("high–Z," or high–impedance). Tristate outputs are usually found as an optional feature on buffer gates. Such gates require an extra input terminal to control the "high–Z" mode, and this input is usually called the enable.

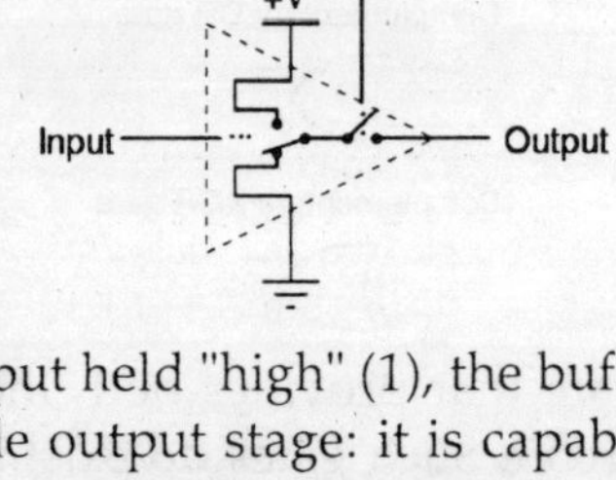

With the enable input held "high" (1), the buffer acts like an ordinary buffer with a totem pole output stage: it is capable of both sourcing and

sinking current. However, the output terminal floats (goes into "high–Z" mode) if ever the enable input is grounded ("low"), regardless of the data signal's logic level. In other words, making the enable input terminal "low" (0) effectively disconnects the gate from whatever its output is wired to so that it can no longer have any effect.

Tristate buffers are marked in schematic diagrams by a triangle character within the gate symbol like this:

Tristate buffer symbol

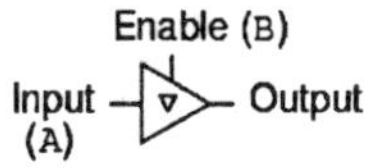

Truth table

A	B	Output
0	0	High-Z
0	1	0
1	0	High-Z
1	1	1

Tristate buffers are also made with inverted enable inputs. Such a gate acts normal when the enable input is "low" (0) and goes into high–Z output mode when the enable input is "high" (1).

Tristate buffer with inverted enable input

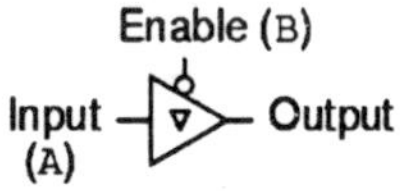

Truth table

A	B	Output
0	0	0
0	1	High-Z
1	0	1
1	1	High-Z

One special type of gate known as the bilateral switch uses gate–controlled MOSFET transistors acting as on/off switches to switch electrical signals, analog or digital.

The "on" resistance of such a switch is in the range of several hundred ohms, the "off" resistance being in the range of several hundred mega–ohms. Bilateral switches appear in schematics as SPST (Single–Pole, Single–Throw) switches inside of rectangular boxes, with a control terminal on one of the box's long sides:

CMOS bilateral switch

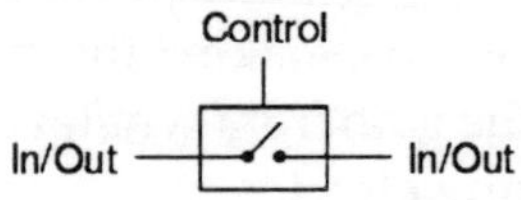

A bilateral switch might be best envisioned as a solid–state (semiconductor) version of an electromechanical relay: a signal–actuated switch contact that may be used to conduct virtually any type of electric signal.

Of course, being solid–state, the bilateral switch has none of the undesirable characteristics of electromechanical relays, such as contact "bouncing," arcing, slow speed, Or susceptibility to mechanical vibration. Conversely, though, they are rather limited in their current–carrying ability.

Additionally, the signal conducted by the "contact" must not exceed the power supply "rail" voltages powering the bilateral switch circuit. Four bilateral switches are packaged inside the popular model "4066" integrated circuit:

Quad CMOS bilateral switch
4066

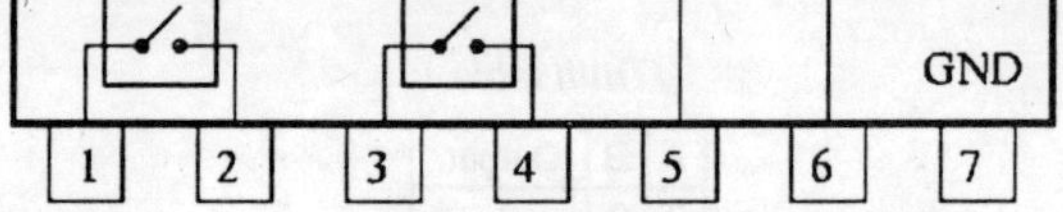

GATE UNIVERSALITY

NAND and NOR gates possess a special property: they are universal. That is, given enough gates, either type of gate is able to mimic the operation of any other gate type.

For example, it is possible to build a circuit exhibiting the OR function using three interconnected NAND gates. The ability for a single gate type to be able to mimic any other gate type is one enjoyed only by the NAND and the NOR.

In fact, digital control systems have been designed around nothing but either NAND or NOR gates, all the necessary logic functions being derived from collections of interconnected NANDs or NORs. As proof of this property, this section will be divided into subsections showing how all the basic gate types may be formed using only NANDs or only NORs.

Constructing the NOT Function

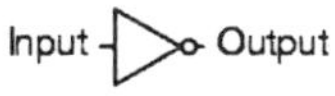

Input	Output
0	1
1	0

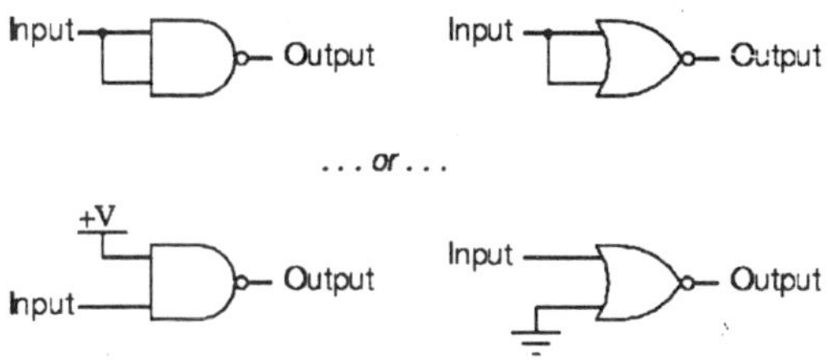

As you can see, there are two ways to use a NAND gate as an inverter, and two ways to use a NOR gate as an inverter. Either method works, although connecting TTL inputs together increases the amount of current loading to the driving gate.

For CMOS gates, common input terminals decreases the switching speed of the gate due to increased input capacitance.

Inverters are the fundamental tool for transforming one type of logic function into another, and so there will be many inverters shown in the illustrations to follow.

In those diagrams, and that will be where the unused NAND gate input is connected to +V (either Vcc or Vdd, depending on whether the circuit is TTL or CMOS) and where the unused.

Input for the NOR gate is connected to ground. Bear in mind that the other inversion method (connecting both NAND or NOR inputs together) works just as well from a logical (1's and 0's) point of view, but is undesirable from the practical perspectives of increased current loading for TTL and increased input capacitance for CMOS.

Constructing the "Buffer" Function

Being that it is quite easy to employ NAND and NOR gates to perform the inverter (NOT) function, it stands to reason that two such stages of gates will result in a buffer function, where the output is the same logical state as the input.

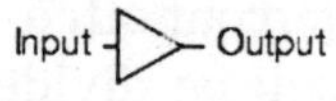

Input	Output
0	0
1	1

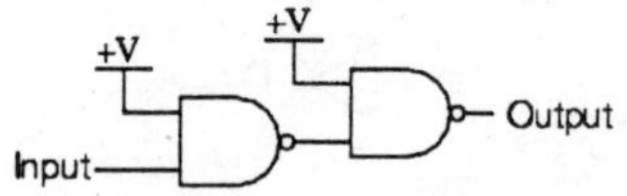

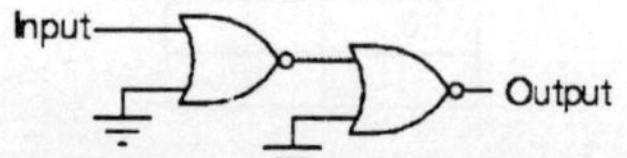

Constructing the AND Function

To make the AND function from NAND gates, all that is needed is an inverter (NOT) stage on the output of a NAND gate. This extra inversion "cancels out" the first N in NAND, leaving the AND function. It takes a little more work to wrestle the same functionality out of NOR gates, but it can be done by inverting ("NOT") all of the inputs to a NOR gate.

2-input AND gate

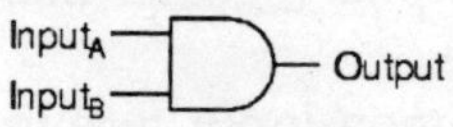

A	B	Output
0	0	0
0	1	0
1	0	0
1	1	1

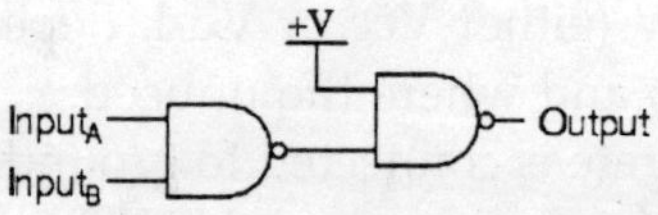

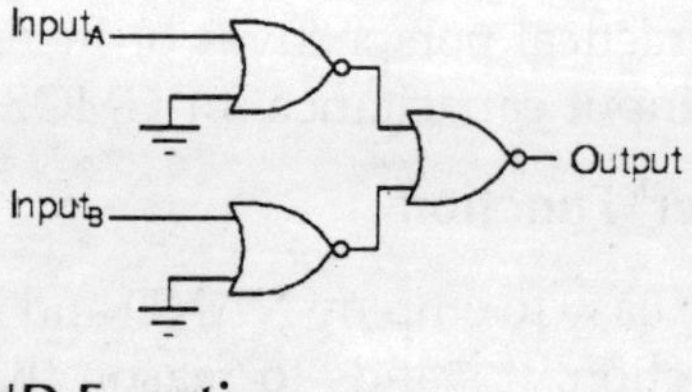

Constructing the NAND Function

It would be pointless to show you how to "construct" the NAND function using a NAND gate, since there is nothing to do. To make a NOR gate perform the NAND function, we must invert all inputs to the NOR gate as well as the NOR gate's output. For a two–input gate, this requires three more NOR gates connected as inverters.

2-input NAND gate

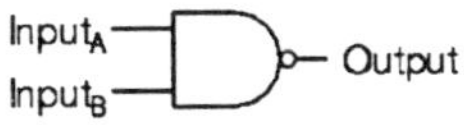

A	B	Output
0	0	1
0	1	1
1	0	1
1	1	0

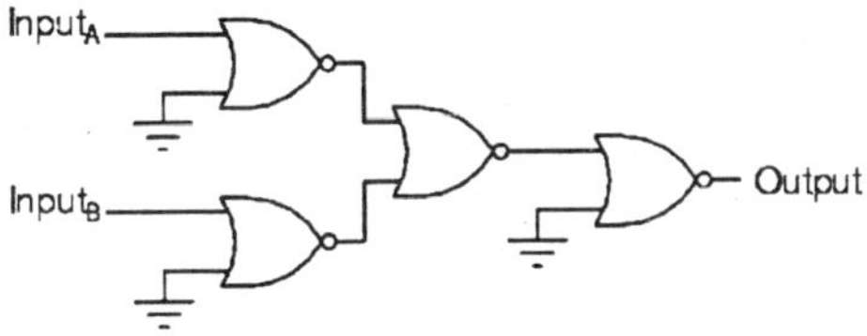

Constructing the or Function

2-input OR gate

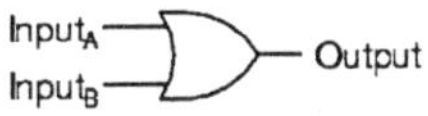

A	B	Output
0	0	0
0	1	1
1	0	1
1	1	1

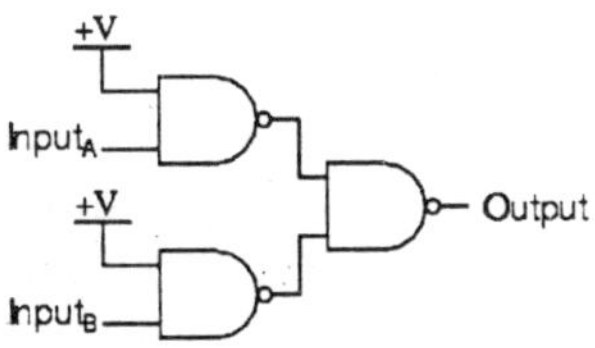

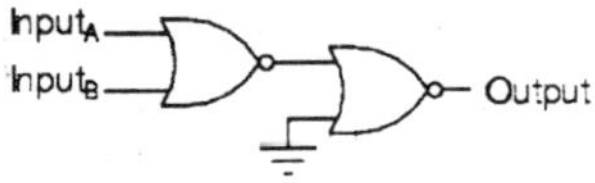

Inverting the output of a NOR gate (with another NOR gate connected as an inverter) results in the OR function. The NAND gate, on the other hand, requires inversion of all inputs to mimic the OR function, just as we needed to invert all inputs of a NOR gate to obtain the AND function. Remember that inversion of all inputs to a gate results in changing that gate's essential function from AND to OR (or vice versa), plus an inverted output. Thus, with all inputs inverted, a NAND behaves as an OR, a NOR behaves as an AND, an AND behaves as a NOR, and an OR behaves as a NAND.

Constructing the Nor Function

Much the same as the procedure for making a NOR gate behave as a NAND, we must invert all inputs and the output to make a NAND gate function as a NOR.

2-input NOR gate

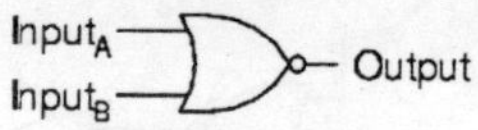

A	B	Output
0	0	1
0	1	0
1	0	0
1	1	0

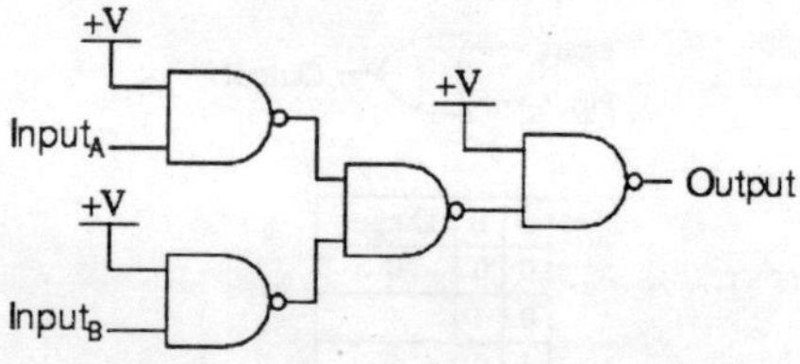

LOGIC SIGNAL VOLTAGE LEVELS

Logic gate circuits are designed to input and output only two types of signals: "high" (1) and "low" (0), as represented by a variable voltage: full power supply voltage for a "high" state and zero voltage for a "low" state. In a perfect world, all logic circuit signals would exist at these extreme voltage limits, and never deviate from them (i.e., less than full voltage for a "high," or more than zero voltage for a "low"). However, in reality, logic signal voltage levels rarely attain these perfect limits due to stray voltage drops in the transistor circuitry, and so we must understand the signal level limitations of gate circuits as they try to interpret signal voltages lying somewhere between full supply voltage and zero.

TTL gates operate on a nominal power supply voltage of 5 volts, +/– 0.25 volts. Ideally, a TTL "high" signal would be 5.00 volts exactly, and a

TTL "low" signal 0.00 volts exactly. However, real TTL gate circuits cannot output such perfect voltage levels, and are designed to accept "high" and "low" signals deviating substantially from these ideal values. "Acceptable" input signal voltages range from 0 volts to 0.8 volts for a "low" logic state, and 2 volts to 5 volts for a "high" logic state.

"Acceptable" output signal voltages (voltage levels guaranteed by the gate manufacturer over a specified range of load conditions) range from 0 volts to 0.5 volts for a "low" logic state, and 2.7 volts to 5 volts for a "high" logic state:

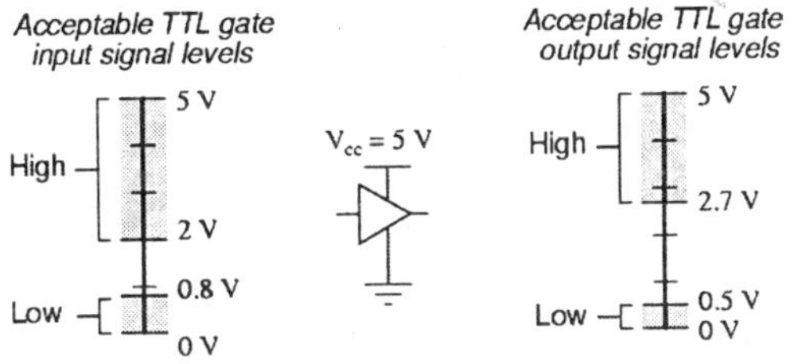

If a voltage signal ranging between 0.8 volts and 2 volts were to be sent into the input of a TTL gate, there would be no certain response from the gate. Such a signal would be considered uncertain, and no logic gate manufacturer would guarantee how their gate circuit would interpret such a signal.

As you can see, the tolerable ranges for output signal levels are narrower than for input signal levels, to ensure that any TTL gate outputting a digital signal into the input of another TTL gate will transmit voltages acceptable to the receiving gate.

The difference between the tolerable output and input ranges is called the noise margin of the gate. For TTL gates, the low–level noise margin is the difference between 0.8 volts and 0.5 volts (0.3 volts), while the high–level noise margin is the difference between 2.7 volts and 2 volts (0.7 volts). Simply put, the noise margin is the peak amount of spurious or "noise" voltage that may be superimposed on a weak gate output voltage signal before the receiving gate might interpret it wrongly:

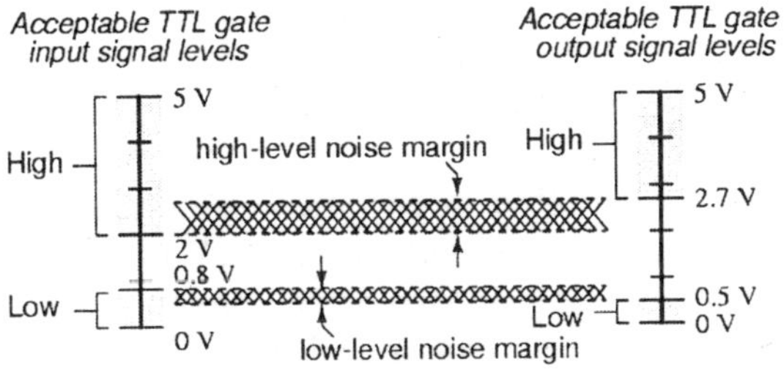

CMOS gate circuits have input and output signal specifications that are quite different from TTL. For a CMOS gate operating at a power supply voltage of 5 volts, the acceptable input signal voltages range from 0 volts to 1.5 volts for a "low" logic state, and 3.5 volts to 5 volts for a "high" logic state. "Acceptable" output signal voltages (voltage levels guaranteed by the gate manufacturer over a specified range of load conditions) range from 0 volts to 0.05 volts for a "low" logic state, and 4.95 volts to 5 volts for a "high" logic state:

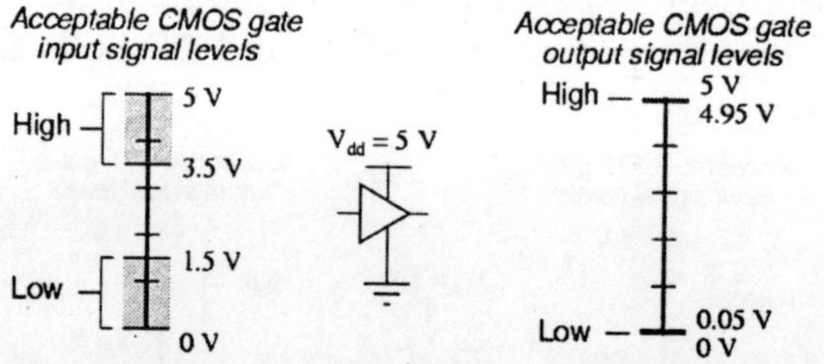

It should be obvious from these figures that CMOS gate circuits have far greater noise margins than TTL: 1.45 volts for CMOS low–level and high–level margins, versus a maximum of 0.7 volts for TTL.

In other words, CMOS circuits can tolerate over twice the amount of superimposed "noise" voltage on their input lines before signal interpretation errors will result.

CMOS noise margins widen even further with higher operating voltages. Unlike TTL, which is restricted to a power supply voltage of 5 volts, CMOS may be powered by voltages as high as 15 volts (some CMOS circuits as high as 18 volts).

Shown here are the acceptable "high" and "low" states, for both input and output, of CMOS integrated circuits operating at 10 volts and 15 volts, respectively:

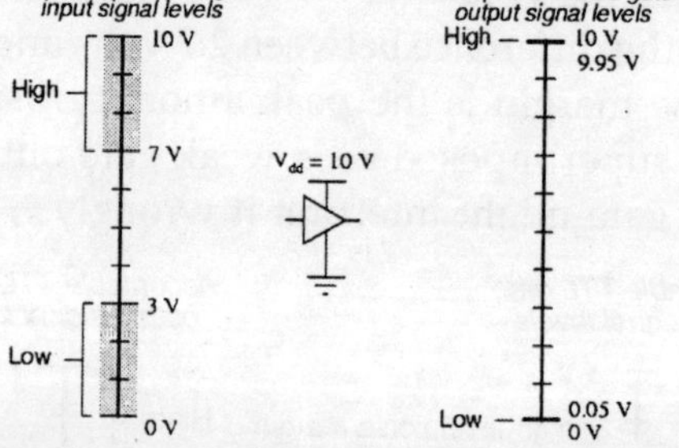

The margins for acceptable "high" and "low" signals may be greater than what is shown in the previous illustrations. What is shown represents "worst–case" input signal performance, based on manufacturer's specifications. In practice, it may be found that a gate circuit will tolerate "high" signals of considerably less voltage and "low" signals of considerably greater voltage than those specified here.

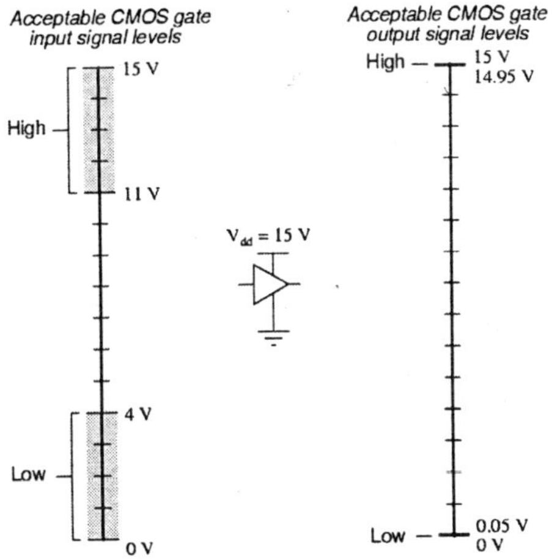

Conversely, the extremely small output margins shown -- guaranteeing output states for "high" and "low" signals to within 0.05 volts of the power supply "rails" — are optimistic.

Such "solid" output voltage levels will be true only for conditions of minimum loading. If the gate is sourcing or sinking substantial current to a load, the output voltage will not be able to maintain these optimum levels, due to internal channel resistance of the gate's final output MOSFETs.

Within the "uncertain" range for any gate input, there will be some point of demarcation dividing the gate's actual "low" input signal range from its actual "high" input signal range.

That is, somewhere between the lowest "high" signal voltage level and the highest "low" signal voltage level guaranteed by the gate manufacturer, there is a threshold voltage at which the gate will actually switch its interpretation of a signal from "low" or "high" or vice versa. For most gate circuits, this unspecified voltage is a single point:

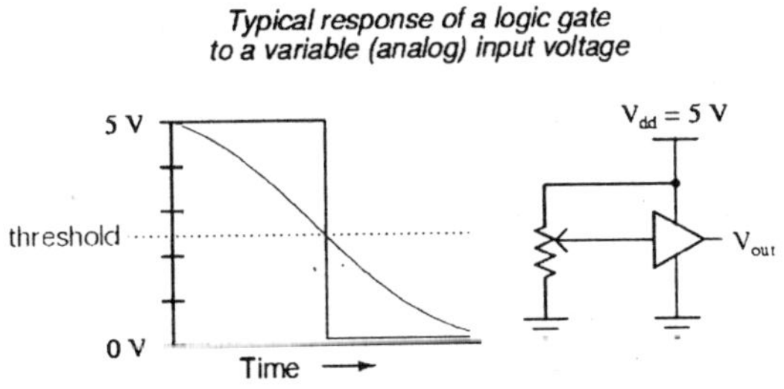

In the presence of AC "noise" voltage superimposed on the DC input signal, a single threshold point at which the gate alters its interpretation of logic level will result in an erratic output:

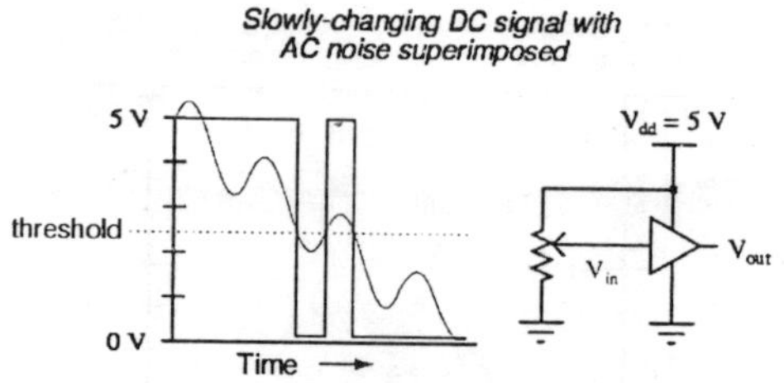

If this scenario looks familiar to you, its because you remember a similar problem with (analog) voltage comparator op–amp circuits. With a single threshold point at which an input causes the output to switch between "high" and "low" states, the presence of significant noise will cause erratic changes in the output:

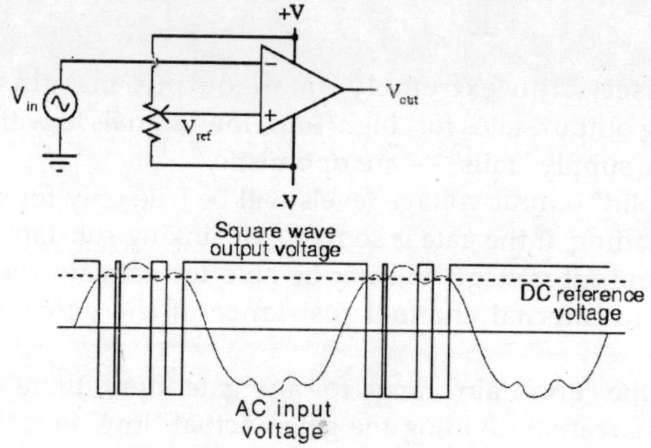

The solution to this problem is a bit of positive feedback introduced into the amplifier circuit. With an op–amp, this is done by connecting the output back around to the noninverting (+) input through a resistor. In a gate circuit, this entails redesigning the internal gate circuitry, establishing the feedback inside the gate package rather than through external connections. A gate so designed is called a Schmitt trigger. Schmitt triggers interpret varying input voltages according to two threshold voltages: a positive–going threshold (VT+), and a negative–going threshold (VT–).

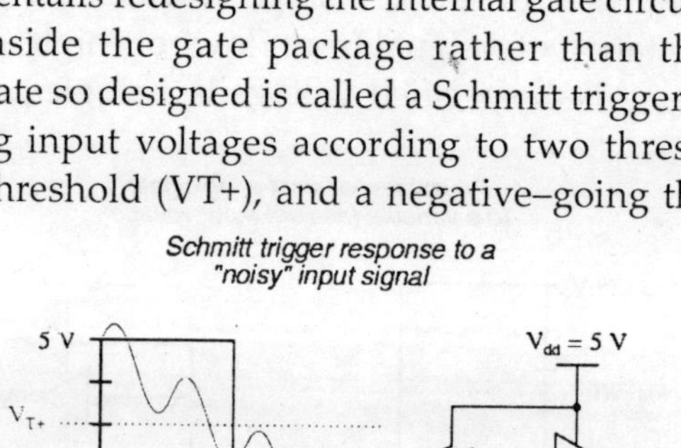

Schmitt trigger gates are distinguished in schematic diagrams by the small "hysteresis" symbol drawn within them, reminiscent of the B–H curve for a ferromagnetic material. Hysteresis engendered by positive feedback within the gate circuitry adds an additional level of noise immunity to the gate's performance.

Schmitt trigger gates are frequently used in applications where noise is expected on the input signal line(s), and/or where an erratic output would be very detrimental to system performance.

The differing voltage level requirements of TTL and CMOS technology present problems when the two types of gates are used in the same system. Although operating CMOS gates on the same 5.00 volt power supply voltage required by the TTL gates is no problem, TTL output voltage levels will not be compatible with CMOS input voltage requirements.

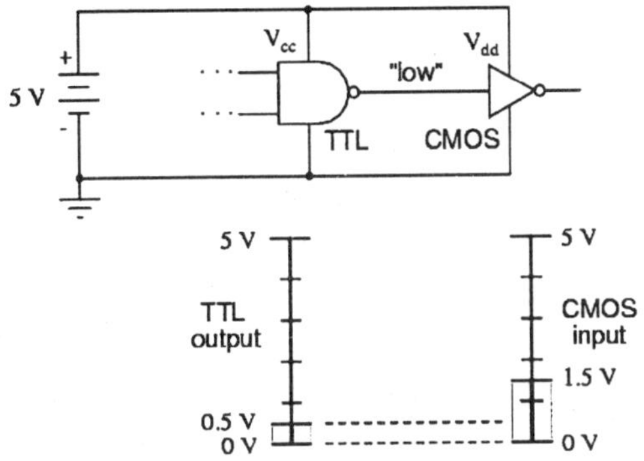

TTL output falls within acceptable limits for CMOS input

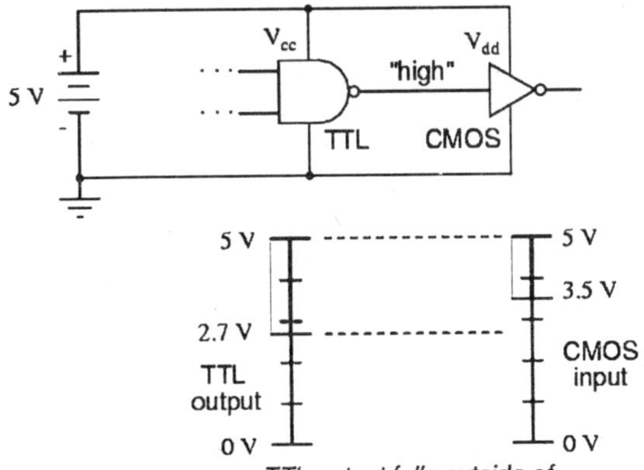

TTL output falls outside of acceptable limits for CMOS input

Take for instance a TTL NAND gate outputting a signal into the input of a CMOS inverter gate. Both gates are powered by the same 5.00 volt supply (Vcc). If the TTL gate outputs a "low" signal (guaranteed to be between 0 volts and 0.5 volts), it will be properly interpreted by the CMOS gate's input as a "low" (expecting a voltage between 0 volts and 1.5 volts).

However, if the TTL gate outputs a "high" signal (guaranteed to be between 5 volts and 2.7 volts), it might not be properly interpreted by the CMOS gate's input as "high" (expecting a voltage between 5 volts and 3.5 volts).

Given this mismatch, it is entirely possible for the TTL gate to output a valid "high" signal (valid, that is, according to the standards for TTL) that lies within the "uncertain" range for the CMOS input, and may be (falsely) interpreted as a "low" by the receiving gate. An easy "fix" for this problem is to augment the TTL gate's "high" signal voltage level by means of a pullup resistor:

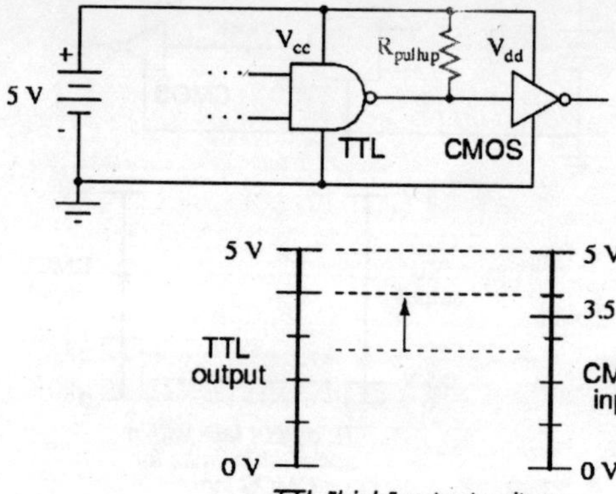

TTL "high" output voltage assisted by R_{pullup}

Something more than this, though, is required to interface a TTL output with a CMOS input, if the receiving CMOS gate is powered by a greater power supply voltage:

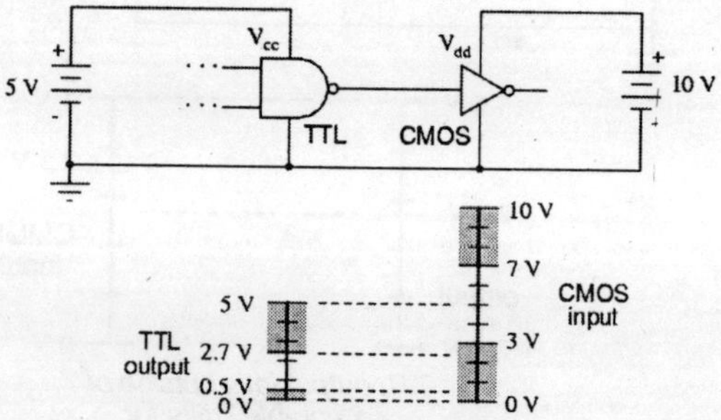

The TTL "high" signal will definitely not fall within the CMOS gate's acceptable limits

There will be no problem with the CMOS gate interpreting the TTL gate's "low" output, of course, but a "high" signal from the TTL gate is another matter entirely. The guaranteed output voltage range of 2.7 volts to 5 volts from the TTL gate output is nowhere near the CMOS gate's acceptable range of 7 volts to 10 volts for a "high" signal. If we use an open–collector TTL gate instead of a totem–pole output gate, though, a pullup resistor to the 10 volt Vdd supply rail will raise the TTL gate's "high" output voltage to the full power supply voltage supplying the CMOS gate. Since an open–collector gate can only sink current, not source current, the "high" state voltage level is entirely determined by the power supply to which the pullup resistor is attached, thus neatly solving the mismatch problem:

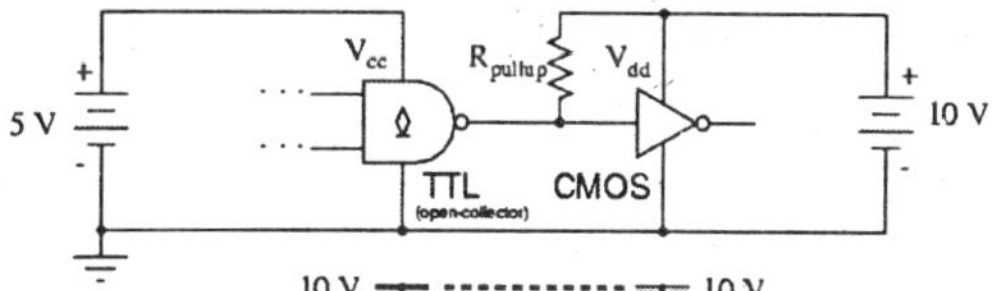

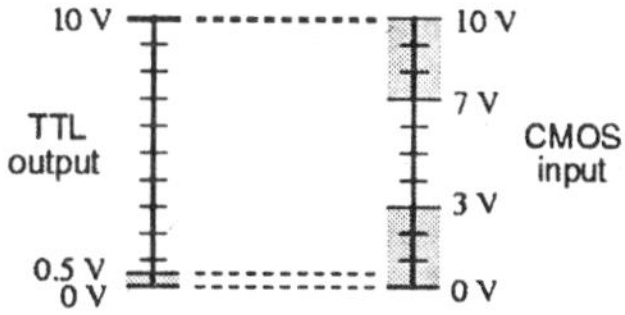

Now, both "low" and "high" TTL signals are acceptable to the CMOS gate input

Due to the excellent output voltage characteristics of CMOS gates, there is typically no problem connecting a CMOS output to a TTL input. The only significant issue is the current loading presented by the TTL inputs, since the CMOS output must sink current for each of the TTL inputs while in the "low" state.

When the CMOS gate in question is powered by a voltage source in excess of 5 volts (Vcc), though, a problem will result. The "high" output state of the CMOS gate, being greater than 5 volts, will exceed the TTL gate's acceptable input limits for a "high" signal. A solution to this problem is to create an "open–collector" inverter circuit using a discrete NPN transistor, and use it to interface the two gates together:

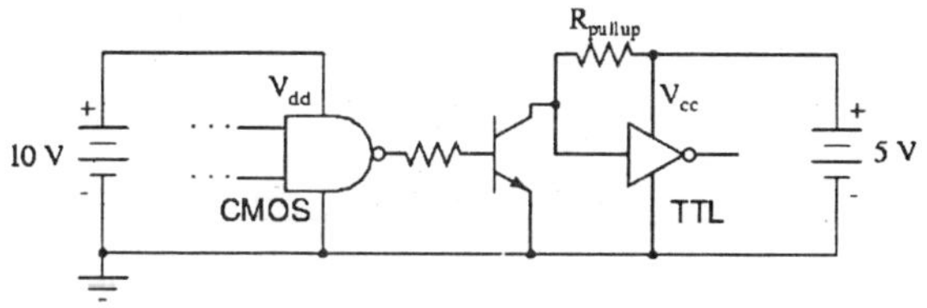

The "Rpullup" resistor is optional, since TTL inputs automatically assume a "high" state when left floating, which is what will happen when the CMOS gate output is "low" and the transistor cuts off. Of course, one very important consequence of implementing this solution is the logical inversion created by the transistor: when the CMOS gate outputs a "low" signal, the TTL gate sees a "high" input; and when the CMOS gate outputs a "high" signal, the transistor saturates and the TTL gate sees a "low" input. So long as this inversion is accounted for in the logical scheme of the system, all will be well.

DIP GATE PACKAGING

Digital logic gate circuits are manufactured as integrated circuits: all the constituent transistors and resistors built on a single piece of semiconductor material. The engineer, technician, or hobbyist using small numbers of gates will likely find what he or she needs enclosed in a DIP (Dual Inline Package) housing. DIP–enclosed integrated circuits are available with even numbers of pins, located at 0.100 inch intervals from each other for standard circuit board layout compatibility. Pin counts of 8, 14, 16, 18, and 24 are common for DIP "chips."

5400/7400
Quad NAND gate

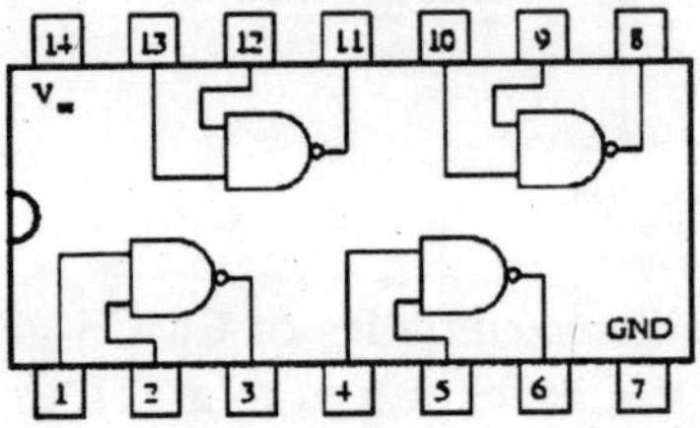

5402/7402
Quad NOR gate

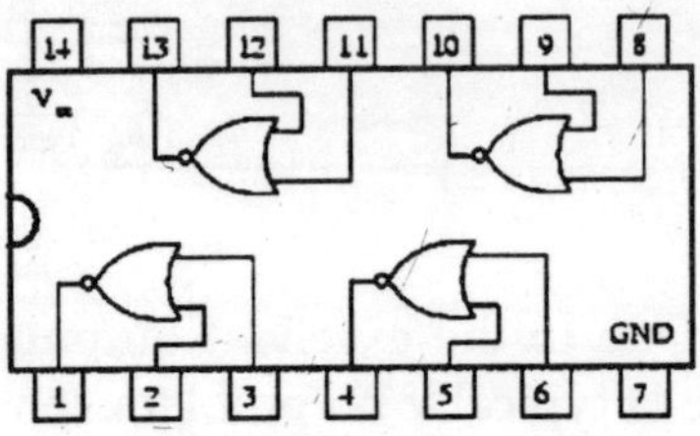

5408/7408
Quad AND gate

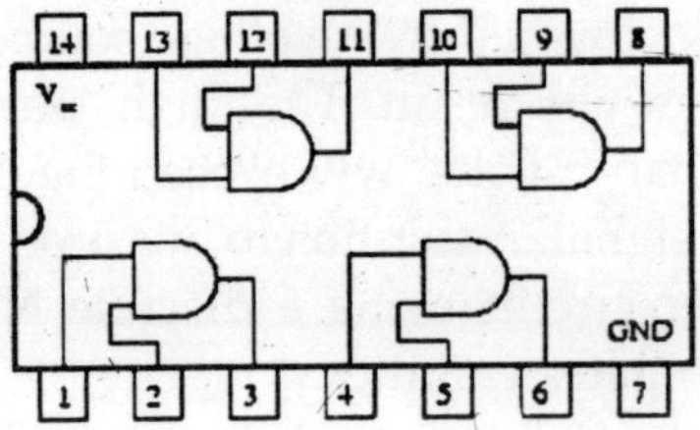

5432/7432
Quad OR gate

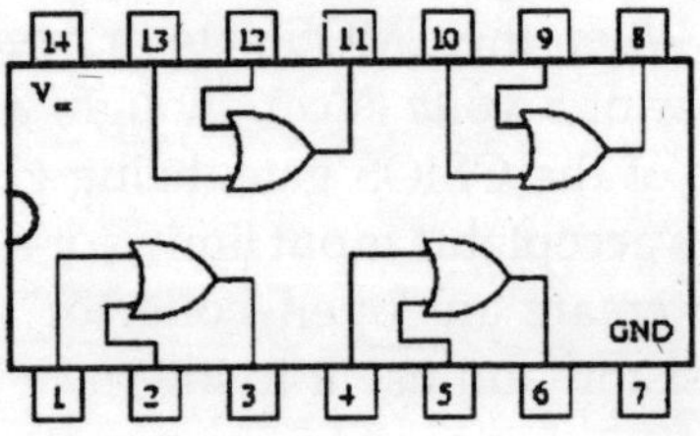

5486/7486
Quad XOR gate

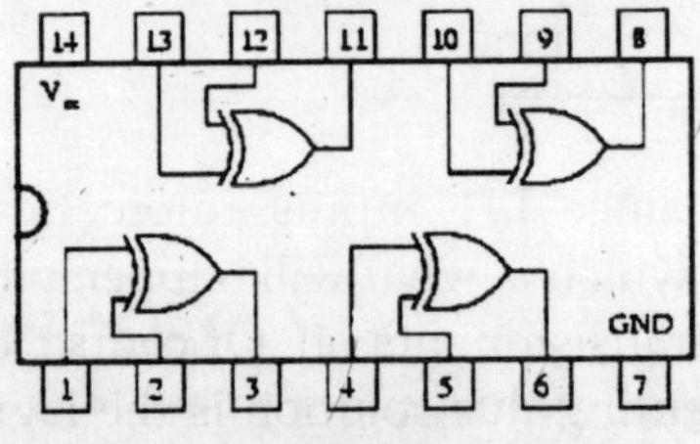

5404/7404
Hex inverter

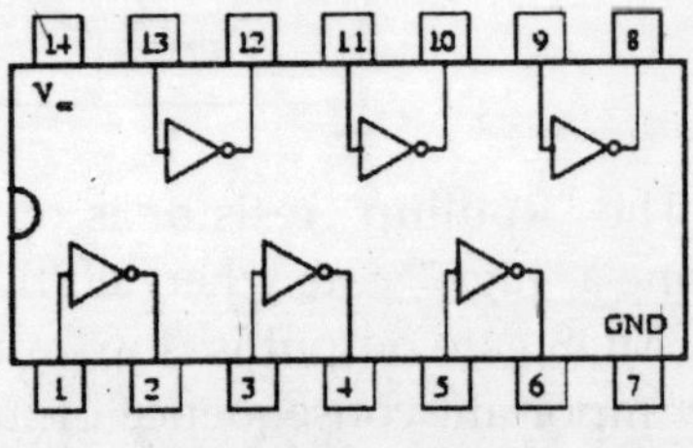

Part numbers given to these DIP packages specify what type of gates are enclosed, and how many.

These part numbers are industry standards, meaning that a "74LS02" manufactured by Motorola will be identical in function to a "74LS02" manufactured by Fairchild or by any other manufacturer. Letter codes prepended to the part number are unique to the manufacturer, and are not industry–standard codes.

4011
Quad NAND gate

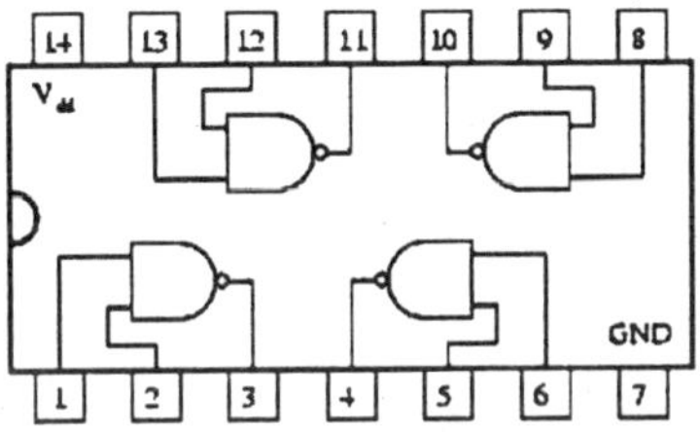

4001
Quad NOR gate

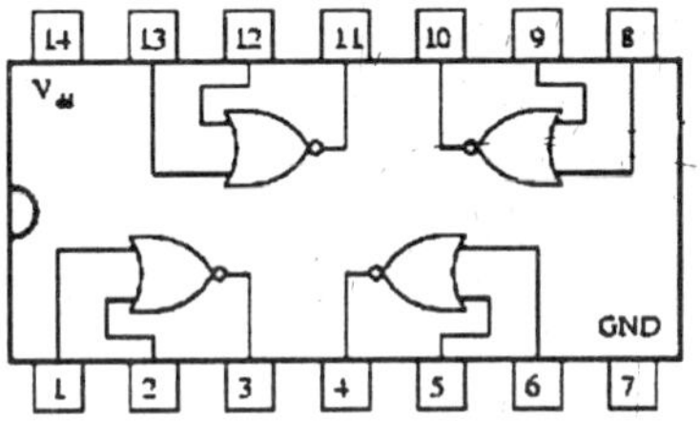

4081
Quad AND gate

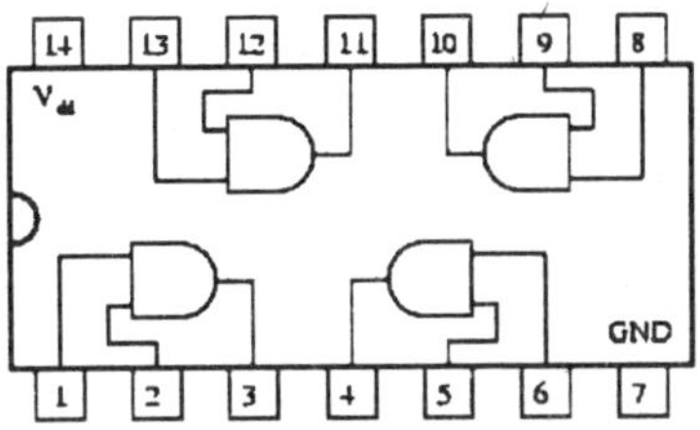

4071
Quad OR gate

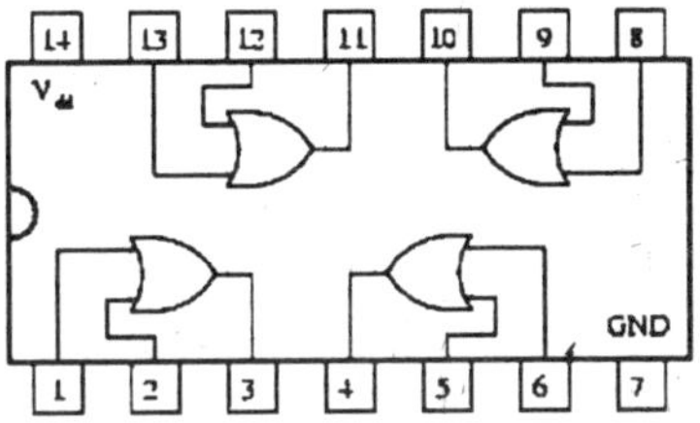

4070
Quad XOR gate

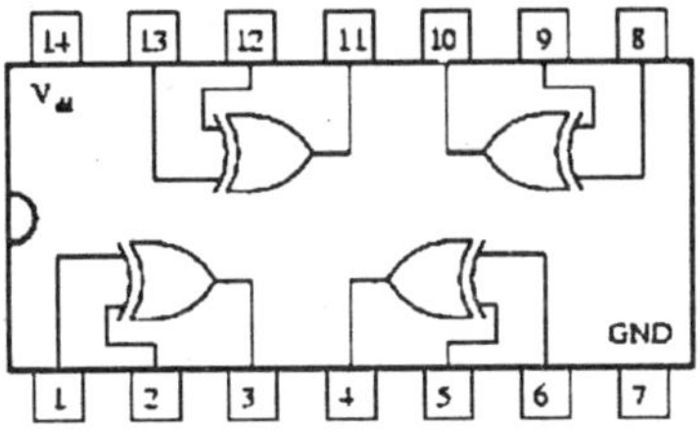

4069
Hex inverter

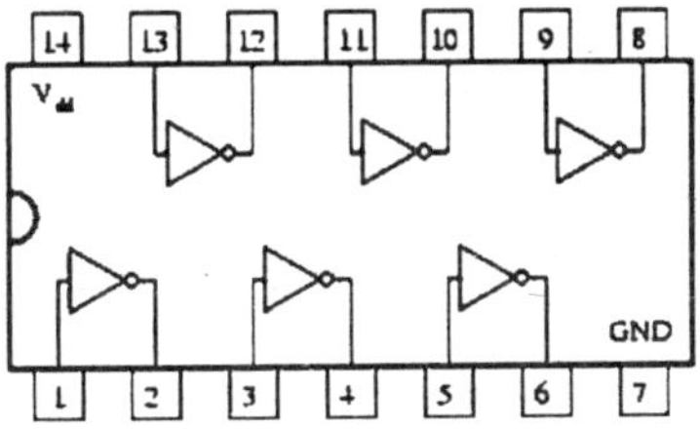

For instance, a SN74LS02 is a quad 2–input TTL NOR gate manufactured by Motorola, while a DM74LS02 is the exact same circuit manufactured by Fairchild. Logic circuit part numbers beginning with "74" are commercial–grade TTL. If the part number begins with the number "54", the chip is a military–grade unit: having a greater operating temperature range, and typically more robust in regard to allowable power supply and signal voltage levels.

The letters "LS" immediately following the 74/54 prefix indicate "Low–power Schottky" circuitry, using Schottky–barrier diodes and transistors throughout, to decrease power dissipation. Non–Schottky gate circuits consume more power, but are able to operate at higher frequencies due to their faster switching times.

A few of the more common TTL "DIP" circuit packages are shown here for reference:

SWITCHES

Switch Types

An electrical switch is any device used to interrupt the flow of electrons in a circuit. Switches are essentially binary devices: they are either completely on ("closed") or completely off ("open").

Explore an older realm of digital technology based on mechanical switch contacts rather than solid–state gate circuits, and a thorough understanding of switch types is necessary for the undertaking. Learning the function of switch–based circuits at the same time that you learn about solid–state logic gates makes both topics easier to grasp, and sets the stage for an enhanced learning experience in Boolean algebra, the mathematics behind digital logic circuits.

The simplest type of switch is one where two electrical conductors are brought in contact with each other by the motion of an actuating mechanism.

Other switches are more complex, containing electronic circuits able to turn on or off depending on some physical stimulus (such as light or magnetic field) sensed. In any case, the final output of any switch will be (at least) a pair of wire–connection terminals that will either be connected together by the switch's internal contact mechanism ("closed"), or not connected together ("open").

Any switch designed to be operated by a person is generally called a hand switch, and they are manufactured in several varieties:

Toggle switch

Toggle switches are actuated by a lever angled in one of two or more positions. The common light switch used in household wiring is an example of a toggle switch.

Most toggle switches will come to rest in any of their lever positions, while others have an internal spring mechanism returning the lever to a certain normal position, allowing for what is called "momentary" operation.

Pushbutton switch

Pushbutton switches are two–position devices actuated with a button that is pressed and released. Most pushbutton switches have an internal spring mechanism returning the button to its "out," or "unpressed," position, for momentary operation. Some pushbutton switches will latch alternately on or off with every push of the button. Other pushbutton switches will stay in their "in," or "pressed," position until the button is pulled back out. This last type of pushbutton switches usually have a mushroom–shaped button for easy push–pull action.

Selector switch

Selector switches are actuated with a rotary knob or lever of some sort to select one of two or more positions. Like the toggle switch, selector switches can either rest in any of their positions or contain spring–return mechanisms for momentary operation.

Joystick switch

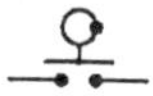

A joystick switch is actuated by a lever free to move in more than one axis of motion. One or more of several switch contact mechanisms are actuated depending on which way the lever is pushed, and sometimes by how far it is pushed. The circle–and–dot notation on the switch symbol represents the direction of joystick lever motion required to actuate the contact. Joystick hand switches are commonly used for crane and robot control.

Some switches are specifically designed to be operated by the motion of a machine rather than by the hand of a human operator. These motion–operated switches are commonly called limit switches, because they are often used to limit the motion of a machine by turning off the actuating power to a component if it moves too far. As with hand switches, limit switches come in several varieties:

Lever actuator limit switch

These limit switches closely resemble rugged toggle or selector hand switches fitted with a lever pushed by the machine part. Often, the levers are tipped with a small roller bearing, preventing the lever from being worn off by repeated contact with the machine part.

Proximity switch

Proximity switches sense the approach of a metallic machine part either by a magnetic or high–frequency electromagnetic field. Simple proximity switches use a permanent magnet to actuate a sealed switch mechanism whenever the machine part gets close (typically 1 inch or less). More complex proximity switches work like a metal detector, energizing a coil of wire with a high–frequency current, and electronically monitoring the magnitude of that current.

If a metallic part (not necessarily magnetic) gets close enough to the coil, the current will increase, and trip the monitoring circuit. The symbol shown here for the proximity switch is of the electronic variety, as indicated by the diamond–shaped box surrounding the switch. A non–electronic proximity switch would use the same symbol as the lever–actuated limit switch.

Another form of proximity switch is the optical switch, comprised of a light source and photocell. Machine position is detected by either the interruption or reflection of a light beam. Optical switches are also useful in safety applications, where beams of light can be used to detect personnel entry into a dangerous area.

In many industrial processes, it is necessary to monitor various physical quantities with switches. Such switches can be used to sound alarms, indicating that a process variable has exceeded normal parameters, or they can be used to shut down processes or equipment if those variables have reached dangerous or destructive levels. There are many different types of process switches:

Speed switch

These switches sense the rotary speed of a shaft either by a centrifugal weight mechanism mounted on the shaft, or by some kind of non–contact detection of shaft motion such as optical or magnetic.

Pressure switch

Gas or liquid pressure can be used to actuate a switch mechanism if that pressure is applied to a piston, diaphragm, or bellows, which converts pressure to mechanical force.

Temperature switch

An inexpensive temperature–sensing mechanism is the "bimetallic strip:" a thin strip of two metals, joined back–to–back, each metal having a different rate of thermal expansion. When the strip heats or cools, differing rates of thermal expansion between the two metals causes it to bend. The bending of the strip can then be used to actuate a switch contact mechanism. Other temperature switches use a brass bulb filled with either a liquid or gas, with a tiny tube connecting the bulb to a pressure–sensing switch. As the bulb is heated, the gas or liquid expands, generating a pressure increase which then actuates the switch mechanism.

Liquid level switch

A floating object can be used to actuate a switch mechanism when the liquid level in an tank rises past a certain point. If the liquid is electrically conductive, the liquid itself can be used as a conductor to bridge between two metal probes inserted into the tank at the required depth. The conductivity technique is usually implemented with a special design of relay triggered by a small amount of current through the conductive liquid. In most cases it is impractical and dangerous to switch the full load current of the circuit through a liquid.

Level switches can also be designed to detect the level of solid materials such as wood chips, grain, coal, or animal feed in a storage silo, bin, or hopper. A common design for this application is a small paddle wheel, inserted into the bin at the desired height, which is slowly turned by a small electric motor. When the solid material fills the bin to that height, the material prevents the paddle wheel from turning. The torque response of the small motor than trips the switch mechanism. Another design uses a "tuning fork" shaped metal prong, inserted into the bin from the outside at the desired height. The fork is vibrated at its resonant frequency by an electronic circuit and magnet/electromagnet coil assembly. When the bin fills to that height, the solid material dampens the vibration of the fork, the change in vibration amplitude and/or frequency detected by the electronic circuit.

Liquid flow switch

Inserted into a pipe, a flow switch will detect any gas or liquid flow rate in excess of a certain threshold, usually with a small paddle or vane which is pushed by the flow. Other flow switches are constructed as differential pressure switches, measuring the pressure drop across a restriction built into the pipe.

Another type of level switch, suitable for liquid or solid material detection, is the nuclear switch. Composed of a radioactive source material and a radiation detector, the two are mounted across the diameter of a storage vessel for either solid or liquid material.

Any height of material beyond the level of the source/detector arrangement will attenuate the strength of radiation reaching the detector. This decrease in radiation at the detector can be used to trigger a relay mechanism to provide a switch contact for measurement, alarm point, or even control of the vessel level.

Nuclear level switch
(for soild or liquid material)

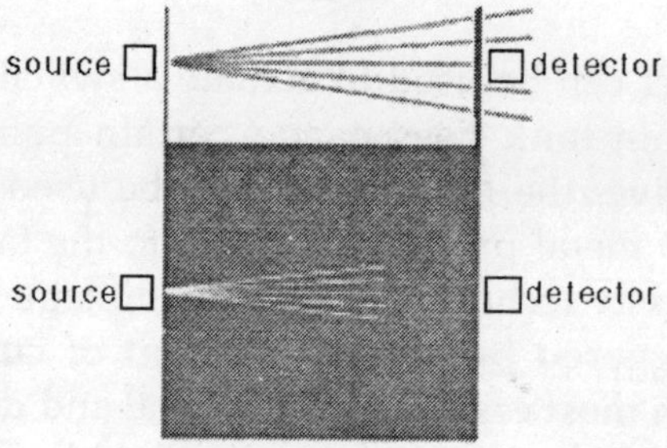

Both source and detector are outside of the vessel, with no intrusion at all except the radiation flux itself. The radioactive sources used are fairly weak and pose no immediate health threat to operations or maintenance personnel.

As usual, there is usually more than one way to implement a switch to monitor a physical process or serve as an operator control. There is usually no single "perfect" switch for any application, although some obviously exhibit certain advantages over others. Switches must be intelligently matched to the task for efficient and reliable operation.

SWITCH CONTACT DESIGN

A switch can be constructed with any mechanism bringing two conductors into contact with each other in a controlled manner. This can be as simple as allowing two copper wires to touch each other by the motion of a lever, or by directly pushing two metal strips into contact. However, a good switch design must be rugged and reliable, and avoid presenting the operator with the possibility of electric shock. Therefore, industrial switch designs are rarely this crude.

The conductive parts in a switch used to make and break the electrical connection are called contacts. Contacts are typically made of silver or silver–cadmium alloy, whose conductive properties are not significantly compromised by surface corrosion or oxidation. Gold contacts exhibit the best corrosion resistance, but are limited in current–carrying capacity and may "cold weld" if brought together with high mechanical force. Whatever the choice of metal, the switch contacts are guided by a mechanism ensuring square and even contact, for maximum reliability and minimum resistance.

Contacts such as these can be constructed to handle extremely large amounts of electric current, up to thousands of amps in some cases. The limiting factors for switch contact ampacity are as follows:

- Heat generated by current through metal contacts (while closed).
- Sparking caused when contacts are opened or closed.
- The voltage across open switch contacts (potential of current jumping across the gap).

One major disadvantage of standard switch contacts is the exposure of the contacts to the surrounding atmosphere. In a nice, clean, control–room environment, this is generally not a problem. However, most industrial environments are not this benign. The presence of corrosive chemicals in the air can cause contacts to deteriorate and fail prematurely. Even more troublesome is the possibility of regular contact sparking causing flammable or explosive chemicals to ignite.

When such environmental concerns exist, other types of contacts can be considered for small switches. These other types of contacts are sealed from contact with the outside air, and therefore do not suffer the same exposure problems that standard contacts do.

A common type of sealed–contact switch is the mercury switch. Mercury is a metallic element, liquid at room temperature. Being a metal, it possesses excellent conductive properties. Being a liquid, it can be brought into contact with metal probes (to close a circuit) inside of a sealed chamber simply by tilting the chamber so that the probes are on the bottom.

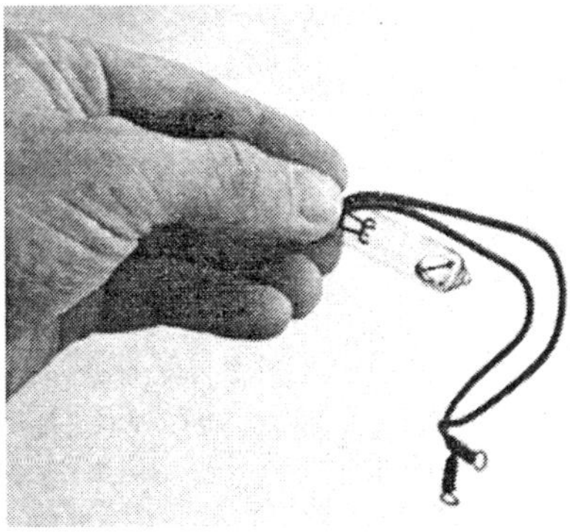

Many industrial switches use small glass tubes containing mercury which are tilted one way to close the contact, and tilted another way to open. Aside from the problems of tube breakage and spilling mercury (which is a toxic material), and susceptibility to vibration, these devices are an excellent alternative to open–air switch contacts wherever environmental exposure problems are a concern.

Here, a mercury switch (often called a tilt switch) is shown in the open position, where the mercury is out of contact with the two metal contacts at the other end of the glass bulb:

Here, the same switch is shown in the closed position. Gravity now holds the liquid mercury in contact with the two metal contacts, providing electrical continuity from one to the other:

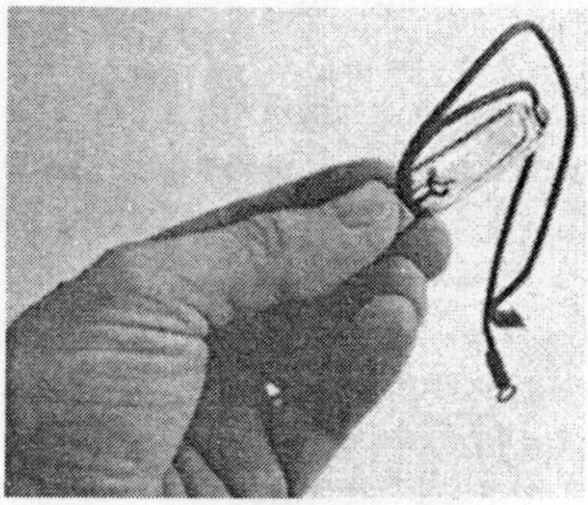

Mercury switch contacts are impractical to build in large sizes, and so you will typically find such contacts rated at no more than a few amps, and no more than 120 volts. There are exceptions, of course, but these are common limits.

Another sealed–contact type of switch is the magnetic reed switch. Like the mercury switch, a reed switch's contacts are located inside a sealed tube. Unlike the mercury switch which uses liquid metal as the contact medium, the reed switch is simply a pair of very thin, magnetic, metal strips (hence the name "reed") which are brought into contact with each other by applying a strong magnetic field outside the sealed tube. The source of the magnetic field in this type of switch is usually a permanent magnet, moved closer to or further away from the tube by the actuating mechanism.

Due to the small size of the reeds, this type of contact is typically rated at lower currents and voltages than the average mercury switch. However, reed switches typically handle vibration better than mercury contacts, because there is no liquid inside the tube to splash around.

It is common to find general–purpose switch contact voltage and current ratings to be greater on any given switch or relay if the electric power being switched is AC instead of DC. The reason for this is the self–extinguishing tendency of an alternating–current arc across an air gap. Because 60 Hz power line current actually stops and reverses direction

120 times per second, there are many opportunities for the ionized air of an arc to lose enough temperature to stop conducting current, to the point where the arc will not re–start on the next voltage peak. DC, on the other hand, is a continuous, uninterrupted flow of electrons which tends to maintain an arc across an air gap much better.

Therefore, switch contacts of any kind incur more wear when switching a given value of direct current than for the same value of alternating current. The problem of switching DC is exaggerated when the load has a significant amount of inductance, as there will be very high voltages generated across the switch's contacts when the circuit is opened (the inductor doing its best to maintain circuit current at the same magnitude as when the switch was closed).

With both AC and DC, contact arcing can be minimized with the addition of a "snubber" circuit (a capacitor and resistor wired in series) in parallel with the contact, like this:

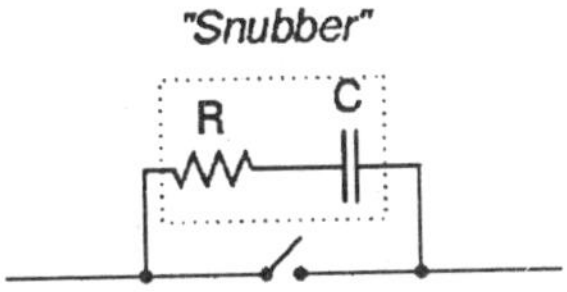

A sudden rise in voltage across the switch contact caused by the contact opening will be tempered by the capacitor's charging action (the capacitor opposing the increase in voltage by drawing current). The resistor limits the amount of current that the capacitor will discharge through the contact when it closes again.

If the resistor were not there, the capacitor might actually make the arcing during contact closure worse than the arcing during contact opening without a capacitor! While this addition to the circuit helps mitigate contact arcing, it is not without disadvantage: a prime consideration is the possibility of a failed (shorted) capacitor/resistor combination providing a path for electrons to flow through the circuit at all times, even when the contact is open and current is not desired. The risk of this failure, and the severity of the resulting consequences must be considered against the increased contact wear (and inevitable contact failure) without the snubber circuit.

The use of snubbers in DC switch circuits is nothing new: automobile manufacturers have been doing this for years on engine ignition systems, minimizing the arcing across the switch contact "points" in the distributor with a small capacitor called a condenser. As any mechanic can tell you, the service life of the distributor's "points" is directly related to how well the condenser is functioning.

With all this discussion concerning the reduction of switch contact arcing, one might be led to think that less current is always better for a mechanical switch. This, however, is not necessarily so. It has been found that a small amount of periodic arcing can actually be good for the switch contacts, because it keeps the contact faces free from small amounts of dirt and corrosion.

If a mechanical switch contact is operated with too little current, the contacts will tend to accumulate excessive resistance and may fail prematurely! This minimum amount of electric current necessary to keep a mechanical switch contact in good health is called the wetting current.

Normally, a switch's wetting current rating is far below its maximum current rating, and well below its normal operating current load in a properly designed system. However, there are applications where a mechanical switch contact may be required to routinely handle currents below normal wetting current limits (for instance, if a mechanical selector switch needs to open or close a digital logic or analog electronic circuit where the current value is extremely small).

In these applications, is it highly recommended that gold–plated switch contacts be specified. Gold is a "noble" metal and does not corrode as other metals will. Such contacts have extremely low wetting current requirements as a result. Normal silver or copper alloy contacts will not provide reliable operation if used in such low–current service!

CONTACT "NORMAL" STATE AND MAKE/BREAK SEQUENCE

Any kind of switch contact can be designed so that the contacts "close" (establish continuity) when actuated, or "open" (interrupt continuity) when actuated. For switches that have a spring–return mechanism in them, the direction that the spring returns it to with no applied force is called the normal position. Therefore, contacts that are open in this position are called normally open and contacts that are closed in this position are called normally closed.

For process switches, the normal position, or state, is that which the switch is in when there is no process influence on it. An easy way to figure out the normal condition of a process switch is to consider the state of the switch as it sits on a storage shelf, uninstalled. Here are some examples of "normal" process switch conditions:

- Speed switch: Shaft not turning
- Pressure switch: Zero applied pressure
- Temperature switch: Ambient (room) temperature
- Level switch: Empty tank or bin
- Flow switch: Zero liquid flow

It is important to differentiate between a switch's "normal" condition and its "normal" use in an operating process. Consider the example of a liquid flow switch that serves as a low–flow alarm in a cooling water system. The normal, or properly–operating, condition of the cooling water system is to have fairly constant coolant flow going through this pipe. If we want the flow switch's contact to close in the event of a loss of coolant flow (to complete an electric circuit which activates an alarm siren, for example), we would want to use a flow switch with normally–closed rather than normally–open contacts.

When there's adequate flow through the pipe, the switch's contacts are forced open; when the flow rate drops to an abnormally low level, the contacts return to their normal (closed) state. This is confusing if you think of "normal" as being the regular state of the process, so be sure to always think of a switch's "normal" state as that which its in as it sits on a shelf.

The schematic symbology for switches vary according to the switch's purpose and actuation. A normally–open switch contact is drawn in such a way as to signify an open connection, ready to close when actuated. Conversely, a normally–closed switch is drawn as a closed connection which will be opened when actuated. Note the following symbols:

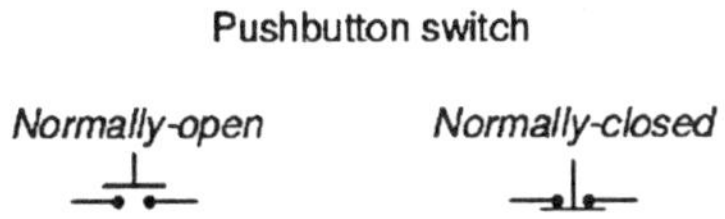

There is also a generic symbology for any switch contact, using a pair of vertical lines to represent the contact points in a switch. Normally–open contacts are designated by the lines not touching, while normally–closed contacts are designated with a diagonal line bridging between the two lines. Compare the two:

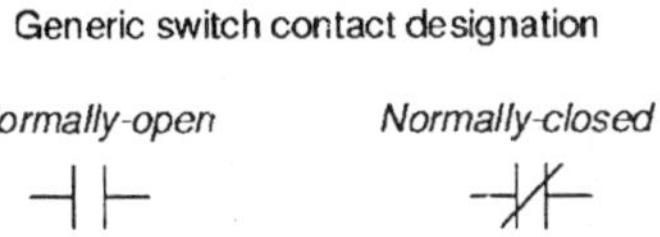

The switch on the left will close when actuated, and will be open while in the "normal" (unactuated) position. The switch on the right will open when actuated, and is closed in the "normal" (unactuated) position. If switches are designated with these generic symbols, the type of switch usually will be noted in text immediately beside the symbol. Please note that the symbol on the left is not to be confused with that of a capacitor. If a capacitor needs to be represented in a control logic schematic, it will be shown like this: In standard electronic symbology, the figure shown above is reserved for polarity–sensitive capacitors.

In control logic symbology, this capacitor symbol is used for any type of capacitor, even when the capacitor is not polarity sensitive, so as to clearly distinguish it from a normally–open switch contact. With multiple–

position selector switches, another design factor must be considered: that is, the sequence of breaking old connections and making new connections as the switch is moved from position to position, the moving contact touching several stationary contacts in sequence.

The selector switch shown above switches a common contact lever to one of five different positions, to contact wires numbered 1 through 5. The most common configuration of a multi–position switch like this is one where the contact with one position is broken before the contact with the next position is made. This configuration is called break–before–make. To give an example, if the switch were set at position number 3 and slowly turned clockwise, the contact lever would move off of the number 3 position, opening that circuit, move to a position between number 3 and number 4 (both circuit paths open), and then touch position number 4, closing that circuit.

There are applications where it is unacceptable to completely open the circuit attached to the "common" wire at any point in time. For such an application, a make–before–break switch design can be built, in which the movable contact lever actually bridges between two positions of contact (between number 3 and number 4, in the above scenario) as it travels between positions. The compromise here is that the circuit must be able to tolerate switch closures between adjacent position contacts (1 and 2, 2 and 3, 3 and 4, 4 and 5) as the selector knob is turned from position to position. Such a switch is shown here:

When movable contact(s) can be brought into one of several positions with stationary contacts, those positions are sometimes called throws. The number of movable contacts is sometimes called poles. Both selector switches shown above with one moving contact and five stationary contacts would be designated as "single–pole, five–throw" switches.

If two identical single–pole, five–throw switches were mechanically ganged together so that they were actuated by the same mechanism, the whole assembly would be called a "double–pole, five–throw" switch: Here are a few common switch configurations and their abbreviated designations:

- Multiposition switches can be either break–before–make (most common) or make–before–break.
- The "poles" of a switch refers to the number of moving contacts, while the "throws" of a switch refers to the number of stationary contacts per moving contact.

CONTACT "BOUNCE"

When a switch is actuated and contacts touch one another under the force of actuation, they are supposed to establish continuity in a single, crisp moment. Unfortunately, though, switches do not exactly achieve this goal. Due to the mass of the moving contact and any elasticity inherent in the mechanism and/or contact materials, contacts will "bounce" upon closure for a period of milliseconds before coming to a full rest and providing unbroken contact.

In many applications, switch bounce is of no consequence: it matters little if a switch controlling an incandescent lamp "bounces" for a few cycles every time it is actuated. Since the lamp's warm–up time greatly exceeds the bounce period, no irregularity in lamp operation will result.

However, if the switch is used to send a signal to an electronic amplifier or some other circuit with a fast response time, contact bounce may produce very noticeable and undesired effects: A closer look at the oscilloscope display reveals a rather ugly set of makes and breaks when the switch is actuated a single time:

If, for example, this switch is used to provide a "clock" signal to a digital counter circuit, so that each actuation of the pushbutton switch is supposed to increment the counter by a value of 1, what will happen instead is the counter will increment by several counts each time the switch is actuated.

Since mechanical switches often interface with digital electronic circuits in modern systems, switch contact bounce is a frequent design consideration. Somehow, the "chattering" produced by bouncing contacts must be eliminated so that the receiving circuit sees a clean, crisp off/on transition: Switch contacts may be debounced several different ways. The most direct means is to address the problem at its source: the switch itself. Here are some suggestions for designing switch mechanisms for minimum bounce:

- Reduce the kinetic energy of the moving contact. This will reduce the force of impact as it comes to rest on the stationary contact, thus minimizing bounce.
- Use "buffer springs" on the stationary contact(s) so that they are free to recoil and gently absorb the force of impact from the moving contact.
- Design the switch for "wiping" or "sliding" contact rather than direct impact. "Knife" switch designs use sliding contacts.
- Dampen the switch mechanism's movement using an air or oil "shock absorber" mechanism.
- Use sets of contacts in parallel with each other, each slightly different in mass or contact gap, so that when one is rebounding off the stationary contact, at least one of the others will still be in firm contact.
- "Wet" the contacts with liquid mercury in a sealed environment.

After initial contact is made, the surface tension of the mercury will maintain circuit continuity even though the moving contact may bounce off the stationary contact several times.

Each one of these suggestions sacrifices some aspect of switch performance for limited bounce, and so it is impractical to design all switches with limited contact bounce in mind. Alterations made to reduce the kinetic energy of the contact may result in a small open–contact gap or a slow–moving contact, which limits the amount of voltage the switch may handle and the amount of current it may interrupt.

Sliding contacts, while non–bouncing, still produce "noise" (irregular current caused by irregular contact resistance when moving), and suffer from more mechanical wear than normal contacts.

Multiple, parallel contacts give less bounce, but only at greater switch complexity and cost. Using mercury to "wet" the contacts is a very effective means of bounce mitigation, but it is unfortunately limited to switch contacts of low ampacity. Also, mercury–wetted contacts are usually limited in mounting position, as gravity may cause the contacts to "bridge" accidently if oriented the wrong way.

If re–designing the switch mechanism is not an option, mechanical switch contacts may be debounced externally, using other circuit components to condition the signal. A low–pass filter circuit attached to the output of the switch, for example, will reduce the voltage/current fluctuations generated by contact bounce:

Switch contacts may be debounced electronically, using hysteretic transistor circuits (circuits that "latch" in either a high or a low state) with built–in time delays (called "one–shot" circuits), or two inputs controlled by a double–throw switch.

Chapter 4

Electromechanical Relays

RELAY CONSTRUCTION

An electric current through a conductor will produce a magnetic field at right angles to the direction of electron flow. If that conductor is wrapped into a coil shape, the magnetic field produced will be oriented along the length of the coil. The greater the current, the greater the strength of the magnetic field, all other factors being equal:

Inductors react against changes in current because of the energy stored in this magnetic field. When we construct a transformer from two inductor coils around a common iron core, we use this field to transfer energy from one coil to the other.

However, there are simpler and more direct uses for electromagnetic fields than the applications we've seen with inductors and transformers. The magnetic field produced by a coil of current–carrying wire can be used to exert a mechanical force on any magnetic object, just as we can use a permanent magnet to attract magnetic objects, except that this magnet (formed by the coil) can be turned on or off by switching the current on or off through the coil.

If we place a magnetic object near such a coil for the purpose of making that object move when we energize the coil with electric current, we have what is called a solenoid. The movable magnetic object is called an armature, and most armatures can be moved with either direct current (DC) or alternating current (AC) energizing the coil. The polarity of the magnetic field is irrelevant for the purpose of attracting an iron armature. Solenoids can be used to electrically open door latches, open or shut valves, move robotic limbs, and even actuate electric switch mechanisms. However, if a solenoid is used to actuate a set of switch contacts, we have a device so useful it deserves its own name: the relay.

Relays are extremely useful when we have a need to control a large amount of current and/or voltage with a small electrical signal. The relay coil which produces the magnetic field may only consume fractions of a watt of power, while the contacts closed or opened by that magnetic field may be able to conduct hundreds of times that amount of power to a load. In effect, a relay acts as a binary (on or off) amplifier.

Just as with transistors, the relay's ability to control one electrical signal with another finds application in the construction of logic functions. This topic will be covered in greater detail in another lesson. For now, the relay's "amplifying" ability will be explored.

In the above schematic, the relay's coil is energized by the low–voltage (12 VDC) source, while the single–pole, single–throw (SPST) contact interrupts the high–voltage (480 VAC) circuit. It is quite likely that the current required to energize the relay coil will be hundreds of times less than the current rating of the contact. Typical relay coil currents are well below 1 amp, while typical contact ratings for industrial relays are at least 10 amps.

One relay coil/armature assembly may be used to actuate more than one set of contacts. Those contacts may be normally–open, normally–closed, or any combination of the two. As with switches, the "normal" state of a relay's contacts is that state when the coil is de–energized, just as you would find the relay sitting on a shelf, not connected to any circuit.

Relay contacts may be open–air pads of metal alloy, mercury tubes, or even magnetic reeds, just as with other types of switches. The choice of contacts in a relay depends on the same factors which dictate contact choice in other types of switches. Open–air contacts are the best for high–current applications, but their tendency to corrode and spark may cause problems in some industrial environments. Mercury and reed contacts are sparkless and won't corrode, but they tend to be limited in current–carrying capacity.

Shown here are three small relays (about two inches in height, each), installed on a panel as part of an electrical control system at a municipal water treatment plant:

The relay units shown here are called "octal–base," because they plug into matching sockets, the electrical connections secured via eight metal pins on the relay bottom. The screw terminal connections you see in the photograph where wires connect to the relays are actually part of the socket assembly, into which each relay is plugged. This type of construction facilitates easy removal and replacement of the relay(s) in the event of failure.

Aside from the ability to allow a relatively small electric signal to switch a relatively large electric signal, relays also offer electrical isolation between coil and contact circuits. This means that the coil circuit and contact circuit(s) are electrically insulated from one another. One circuit may be DC and the other AC (such as in the example circuit shown earlier), and/or they may be at completely different voltage levels, across the connections or from connections to ground.

While relays are essentially binary devices, either being completely on or completely off, there are operating conditions where their state may be indeterminate, just as with semiconductor logic gates. In order for a relay to positively "pull in" the armature to actuate the contact(s), there must be a certain minimum amount of current through the coil.

This minimum amount is called the pull–in current, and it is analogous to the minimum input voltage that a logic gate requires to guarantee a "high" state (typically 2 Volts for TTL, 3.5 Volts for CMOS). Once the armature is pulled closer to the coil's centre, however, it takes less magnetic field flux (less coil current) to hold it there. Therefore, the coil current must drop below a value significantly lower than the pull–in current before the armature "drops out" to its spring–loaded position and the contacts resume their normal state. This current level is called the drop–out current, and it is analogous to the maximum input voltage that a logic gate input will allow to guarantee a "low" state (typically 0.8 Volts for TTL, 1.5 Volts for CMOS).

The hysteresis, or difference between pull–in and drop–out currents, results in operation that is similar to a Schmitt trigger logic gate. Pull–in and drop–out currents (and voltages) vary widely from relay to relay, and are specified by the manufacturer.

CONTACTORS

When a relay is used to switch a large amount of electrical power through its contacts, it is designated by a special name: contactor. Contactors typically have multiple contacts, and those contacts are usually (but not always) normally–open, so that power to the load is shut off when the coil is de–energized. Perhaps the most common industrial use for contactors is the control of electric motors.

The top three contacts switch the respective phases of the incoming 3–phase AC power, typically at least 480 Volts for motors 1 horsepower or greater. The lowest contact is an "auxiliary" contact which has a current rating much lower than that of the large motor power contacts, but is actuated by the same armature as the power contacts. The auxiliary contact is often used in a relay logic circuit, or for some other part of the motor control scheme, typically switching 120 Volt AC power instead of the motor voltage. One contactor may have several auxiliary contacts, either normally–open or normally–closed, if required.

The three "opposed–question–mark" shaped devices in series with each phase going to the motor are called overload heaters. Each "heater" element is a low–resistance strip of metal intended to heat up as the motor draws current. If the temperature of any of these heater elements reaches a critical point (equivalent to a moderate overloading of the motor), a normally–closed switch contact will spring open. This normally–closed contact is usually connected in series with the relay coil, so that when it opens the relay will automatically de–energize, thereby shutting off power to the motor. We will see more of this overload protection wiring in the next chapter. Overload heaters are intended to provide overcurrent protection for large electric motors, unlike circuit breakers and fuses which serve the primary purpose of providing overcurrent protection for power conductors.

Overload heater function is often misunderstood. They are not fuses; that is, it is not their function to burn open and directly break the circuit as a fuse is designed to do. Rather, overload heaters are designed to thermally mimic the heating characteristic of the particular electric motor to be protected. All motors have thermal characteristics, including the amount of heat energy generated by resistive dissipation (I2R), the thermal transfer characteristics of heat "conducted" to the cooling medium through the metal frame of the motor, the physical mass and specific heat of the materials constituting the motor, etc.

These characteristics are mimicked by the overload heater on a miniature scale: when the motor heats up toward its critical temperature, so will the heater toward its critical temperature, ideally at the same rate and approach curve.

Thus, the overload contact, in sensing heater temperature with a thermo–mechanical mechanism, will sense an analogue of the real motor. If the overload contact trips due to excessive heater temperature, it will be an indication that the real motor has reached its critical temperature (or, would have done so in a short while). After tripping, the heaters are supposed to cool down at the same rate and approach curve as the real motor, so that they indicate an accurate proportion of the motor's thermal condition, and will not allow power to be re–applied until the motor is truly ready for start–up again.

Shown here is a contactor for a three–phase electric motor, installed on a panel as part of an electrical control system at a municipal water treatment plant:

Three–phase, 480 volt AC power comes in to the three normally–open contacts at the top of the contactor via screw terminals labeled "L1," "L2," and "L3" (The "L2" terminal is hidden behind a square–shaped "snubber" circuit connected across the contactor's coil terminals). Power to the motor exits the overload heater assembly at the bottom of this device via screw terminals labeled "T1," "T2," and "T3."

The overload heater units themselves are black, square–shaped blocks with the label "W34," indicating a particular thermal response for a certain horsepower and temperature rating of electric motor. If an electric motor of differing power and/or temperature ratings were to be substituted for the one presently in service, the overload heater units would have to be replaced with units having a thermal response suitable for the new motor. The motor manufacturer can provide information on the appropriate heater units to use.

A white pushbutton located between the "T1" and "T2" line heaters serves as a way to manually re–set the normally–closed switch contact back to its normal state after having been tripped by excessive heater temperature. Wire connections to the "overload" switch contact may be seen at the lower–right of the photograph, near a label reading "NC" (normally–closed). On this particular overload unit, a small "window" with the label "Tripped" indicates a tripped condition by means of a colored flag. In this photograph, there is no "tripped" condition, and the indicator appears clear.

As a footnote, heater elements may be used as a crude current shunt resistor for determining whether or not a motor is drawing current when the contactor is closed. There may be times when you're working on a motor control circuit, where the contactor is located far away from the motor itself. How do you know if the motor is consuming power when the contactor coil is energized and the armature has been pulled in?

If the motor's windings are burnt open, you could be sending voltage to the motor through the contactor contacts, but still have zero current, and thus no motion from the motor shaft. If a clamp–on ammeter isn't available to measure line current, you can take your multimeter and measure millivoltage across each heater element: if the current is zero, the voltage across the heater will be zero (unless the heater element itself is open, in which case the voltage across it will be large); if there is current going to the motor through that phase of the contactor, you will read a definite millivoltage across that heater:

This is an especially useful trick to use for troubleshooting 3–phase AC motors, to see if one phase winding is burnt open or disconnected, which will result in a rapidly destructive condition known as "single–phasing." If one of the lines carrying power to the motor is open, it will not have any current through it (as indicated by a 0.00 mV reading across its heater), although the other two lines will (as indicated by small amounts of voltage dropped across the respective heaters).

TIME–DELAY RELAYS

Some relays are constructed with a kind of "shock absorber" mechanism attached to the armature which prevents immediate, full motion when the coil is either energized or de–energized. This addition gives the relay the property of time–delay actuation. Time–delay relays can be constructed to delay armature motion on coil energization, de-energization, or both.

Time–delay relay contacts must be specified not only as either normally–open or normally–closed, but whether the delay operates in the direction of closing or in the direction of opening. The following is a description of the four basic types of time–delay relay contacts.

First we have the normally–open, timed–closed (NOTC) contact. This type of contact is normally open when the coil is unpowered (de-energized). The contact is closed by the application of power to the relay coil, but only after the coil has been continuously powered for the specified amount of time. In other words, the direction of the contact's motion (either to close or to open) is identical to a regular NO contact, but there is a delay in closing direction. Because the delay occurs in the direction of coil energization, this type of contact is alternatively known as a normally–open, on–delay:

The following is a timing diagram of this relay contact's operation:

Next we have the normally–open, timed–open (NOTO) contact. Like the NOTC contact, this type of contact is normally open when the coil is unpowered (de–energized), and closed by the application of power to the relay coil. However, unlike the NOTC contact, the timing action occurs upon de–energization of the coil rather than upon energization. Because the delay occurs in the direction of coil de–energization, this type of contact is alternatively known as a normally–open, off–delay:

The following is a timing diagram of this relay contact's operation:

Next we have the normally–closed, timed–open (NCTO) contact. This type of contact is normally closed when the coil is unpowered (de-energized). The contact is opened with the application of power to the relay coil, but only after the coil has been continuously powered for the specified amount of time. In other words, the direction of the contact's motion (either to close or to open) is identical to a regular NC contact, but there is a delay in the opening direction. Because the delay occurs in the direction of coil energization, this type of contact is alternatively known as a normally–closed, on–delay:

The following is a timing diagram of this relay contact's operation:

Finally we have the normally–closed, timed–closed (NCTC) contact. Like the NCTO contact, this type of contact is normally closed when the coil is unpowered (de–energized), and opened by the application of power to the relay coil. However, unlike the NCTO contact, the timing action occurs upon de–energization of the coil rather than upon energization. Because the delay occurs in the direction of coil de–energization, this type of contact is alternatively known as a normally–closed, off–delay:

The following is a timing diagram of this relay contact's operation:

Time–delay relays are very important for use in industrial control logic circuits. Some examples of their use include:

"Flashing light control (time on, time off): two time–delay relays are used in conjunction with one another to provide a constant–frequency on/off pulsing of contacts for sending intermittent power to a lamp.

"Engine autostart control: Engines that are used to power emergency generators are often equipped with "autostart" controls that allow for automatic start–up if the main electric power fails. To properly start a large engine, certain auxiliary devices must be started first and allowed some brief time to stabilize (fuel pumps, pre–lubrication oil pumps) before the engine's starter motor is energized. Time–delay relays help sequence these events for proper start–up of the engine.

"Furnace safety purge control: Before a combustion–type furnace can be safely lit, the air fan must be run for a specified amount of time to "purge" the furnace chamber of any potentially flammable or explosive vapors. A time–delay relay provides the furnace control logic with this necessary time element.

"Motor soft–start delay control: Instead of starting large electric motors by switching full power from a dead stop condition, reduced voltage can be switched for a "softer" start and less inrush current. After a prescribed time delay (provided by a time–delay relay), full power is applied.

"Conveyor belt sequence delay: when multiple conveyor belts are arranged to transport material, the conveyor belts must be started in reverse sequence (the last one first and the first one last) so that material doesn't get piled on to a stopped or slow–moving conveyor. In order to get large belts up to full speed, some time may be needed (especially if soft–start motor controls are used). For this reason, there is usually a time–delay circuit arranged on each conveyor to give it adequate time to attain full belt speed before the next conveyor belt feeding it is started.

The older, mechanical time–delay relays used pneumatic dashpots or fluid–filled piston/cylinder arrangements to provide the "shock absorbing" needed to delay the motion of the armature. Newer designs of time–delay relays use electronic circuits with resistor–capacitor (RC) networks to generate a time delay, then energize a normal (instantaneous) electromechanical relay coil with the electronic circuit's output. The electronic–timer relays are more versatile than the older, mechanical models, and less prone to failure.

Many models provide advanced timer features such as "one–shot" (one measured output pulse for every transition of the input from de–energized to energized), "recycle" (repeated on/off output cycles for as long as the input connection is energized) and "watchdog" (changes state if the input signal does not repeatedly cycle on and off). The "watchdog" timer is especially useful for monitoring of computer systems. If a computer is being used to control a critical process, it is usually recommended to have an automatic alarm to detect computer "lockup" (an abnormal halting of programme execution due to any number of causes). An easy way to set up such a monitoring system is to have the computer regularly energize and de–energize the coil of a watchdog timer relay (similar to the output of the "recycle" timer). If the computer execution halts for any reason, the signal it outputs to the watchdog relay coil will stop cycling and freeze in one or the other state. A short time thereafter, the watchdog relay will "time out" and signal a problem.

Protective Relays

A special type of relay is one which monitors the current, voltage, frequency, or any other type of electric power measurement either from a generating source or to a load for the purpose of triggering a circuit breaker to open in the event of an abnormal condition. These relays are referred to in the electrical power industry as protective relays.

The circuit breakers which are used to switch large quantities of electric power on and off are actually electromechanical relays, themselves. Unlike the circuit breakers found in residential and commercial use which determine when to trip (open) by means of a bimetallic strip inside that bends when it gets too hot from overcurrent, large industrial circuit breakers must be "told" by an external device when to open. Such breakers have two electromagnetic coils inside: one to close the breaker contacts and one to open them.

The "trip" coil can be energized by one or more protective relays, as well as by hand switches, connected to switch 125 Volt DC power. DC power is used because it allows for a battery bank to supply close/trip power to the breaker control circuits in the event of a complete (AC) power failure.

Protective relays can monitor large AC currents by means of current transformers (CT's), which encircle the current–carrying conductors exiting a large circuit breaker, transformer, generator, or other device. Current transformers step down the monitored current to a secondary (output) range of 0 to 5 amps AC to power the protective relay. The current relay uses this 0–5 amp signal to power its internal mechanism, closing a contact to switch 125 Volt DC power to the breaker's trip coil if the monitored current becomes excessive.

Likewise, (protective) voltage relays can monitor high AC voltages by means of voltage, or potential, transformers (PT's) which step down the monitored voltage to a secondary range of 0 to 120 Volts AC, typically.

Like (protective) current relays, this voltage signal powers the internal mechanism of the relay, closing a contact to switch 125 Volt DC power to the breaker's trip coil is the monitored voltage becomes excessive.

There are many types of protective relays, some with highly specialized functions. Not all monitor voltage or current, either. They all, however, share the common feature of outputting a contact closure signal which can be used to switch power to a breaker trip coil, close coil, or operator alarm panel. Most protective relay functions have been categorized into an ANSI standard number code. Here are a few examples from that code list:

ANSI protective relay designation numbers
12 = Overspeed
24 = Overexcitation
25 = Syncrocheck
27 = Bus/Line undervoltage
32 = Reverse power (anti–motoring)
38 = Stator overtemp (RTD)
39 = Bearing vibration
40 = Loss of excitation
46 = Negative sequence undercurrent (phase current imbalance)
47 = Negative sequence undervoltage (phase voltage imbalance)
49 = Bearing overtemp (RTD)
50 = Instantaneous overcurrent
51 = Time overcurrent
51V = Time overcurrent — voltage restrained
55 = Power factor
59 = Bus overvoltage
60FL = Voltage transformer fuse failure
67 = Phase/Ground directional current
79 = Autoreclose
81 = Bus over/underfrequency

Solid–State Relays

As versatile as electromechanical relays can be, they do suffer many limitations. They can be expensive to build, have a limited contact cycle life, take up a lot of room, and switch slowly, compared to modern semiconductor devices. These limitations are especially true for large power contactor relays.

To address these limitations, many relay manufacturers offer "solid–state" relays, which use an SCR, TRIAC, or transistor output instead of mechanical contacts to switch the controlled power. The output device (SCR, TRIAC, or transistor) is optically–coupled to an LED light source inside the relay. The relay is turned on by energizing this LED, usually with low–voltage DC power. This optical isolation between input to output rivals the best that electromechanical relays can offer.

Being solid–state devices, there are no moving parts to wear out, and they are able to switch on and off much faster than any mechanical relay armature can move. There is no sparking between contacts, and no problems with contact corrosion. However, solid–state relays are still too expensive to build in very high current ratings, and so electromechanical contactors continue to dominate that application in industry today.

One significant advantage of a solid–state SCR or TRIAC relay over an electromechanical device is its natural tendency to open the AC circuit only at a point of zero load current. Because SCR's and TRIAC's are thyristors, their inherent hysteresis maintains circuit continuity after the LED is de–energized until the AC current falls below a threshold value (the holding current).

In practical terms what this means is the circuit will never be interrupted in the middle of a sine wave peak. Such untimely interruptions in a circuit containing substantial inductance would normally produce large voltage spikes due to the sudden magnetic field collapse around the inductance. This will not happen in a circuit broken by an SCR or TRIAC. This feature is called zero–crossover switching.

One disadvantage of solid state relays is their tendency to fail "shorted" on their outputs, while electromechanical relay contacts tend to fail "open." In either case, it is possible for a relay to fail in the other mode, but these are the most common failures. Because a "fail–open" state is generally considered safer than a "fail–closed" state, electromechanical relays are still favored over their solid–state counterparts in many applications.

LADDER LOGIC

"LADDER" DIAGRAMS

Ladder diagrams are specialized schematics commonly used to document industrial control logic systems. They are called "ladder" diagrams because they resemble a ladder, with two vertical rails (supply power) and as many "rungs" (horizontal lines) as there are control circuits to represent. If we wanted to draw a simple ladder diagram showing a lamp that is controlled by a hand switch, it would look like this:

The "L1" and "L2" designations refer to the two poles of a 120 VAC supply, unless otherwise noted. L1 is the "hot" conductor, and L2 is the grounded ("neutral") conductor. These designations have nothing to do with inductors, just to make things confusing. The actual transformer or generator supplying power to this circuit is omitted for simplicity. In reality, the circuit looks something like this:

Typically in industrial relay logic circuits, but not always, the operating voltage for the switch contacts and relay coils will be 120 volts AC. Lower voltage AC and even DC systems are sometimes built and documented according to "ladder" diagrams:

So long as the switch contacts and relay coils are all adequately rated, it really doesn't matter what level of voltage is chosen for the system to operate with.

Note the number "1" on the wire between the switch and the lamp. In the real world, that wire would be labeled with that number, using heat–shrink or adhesive tags, wherever it was convenient to identify. Wires leading to the switch would be labeled "L1" and "1," respectively. Wires leading to the lamp would be labeled "1" and "L2," respectively. These wire numbers make assembly and maintenance very easy.

Each conductor has its own unique wire number for the control system that its used in. Wire numbers do not change at any junction or node, even if wire size, colour, or length changes going into or out of a connection point. Of course, it is preferable to maintain consistent wire colors, but this is not always practical.

What matters is that any one, electrically continuous point in a control circuit possesses the same wire number. Take this circuit section, for example, with wire #25 as a single, electrically continuous point threading to many different devices:

In ladder diagrams, the load device (lamp, relay coil, solenoid coil, etc.) is almost always drawn at the right–hand side of the rung. While it doesn't matter electrically where the relay coil is located within the rung, it does matter which end of the ladder's power supply is grounded, for reliable operation.

Take for instance this circuit: Here, the lamp (load) is located on the right–hand side of the rung, and so is the ground connection for the power source. This is no accident or coincidence; rather, it is a purposeful element of good design practice. Suppose that wire #1 were to accidently come in contact with ground, the insulation of that wire having been rubbed off so that the bare conductor came in contact with grounded, metal conduit. Our circuit would now function like this:

With both sides of the lamp connected to ground, the lamp will be "shorted out" and unable to receive power to light up. If the switch were to close, there would be a short–circuit, immediately blowing the fuse.

However, consider what would happen to the circuit with the same fault (wire #1 coming in contact with ground), except this time we'll swap the positions of switch and fuse (L2 is still grounded).

This time the accidental grounding of wire #1 will force power to the lamp while the switch will have no effect. It is much safer to have a system that blows a fuse in the event of a ground fault than to have a system that uncontrollably energizes lamps, relays, or solenoids in the event of the same fault. For this reason, the load(s) must always be located nearest the grounded power conductor in the ladder diagram.

DIGITAL LOGIC FUNCTIONS

We can construct simply logic functions for our hypothetical lamp circuit, using multiple contacts, and document these circuits quite easily and understandably with additional rungs to our original "ladder." If we use standard binary notation for the status of the switches and lamp (0 for unactuated or de–energized; 1 for actuated or energized), a truth table can be made to show how the logic works:

Now, the lamp will come on if either contact A or contact B is actuated, because all it takes for the lamp to be energized is to have at least one path for current from wire L1 to wire 1. What we have is a simple OR logic function, implemented with nothing more than contacts and a lamp.

We can mimic the AND logic function by wiring the two contacts in series instead of parallel:

Now, the lamp energizes only if contact A and contact B are simultaneously actuated. A path exists for current from wire L1 to the lamp (wire 2) if and only if both switch contacts are closed.

The logical inversion, or NOT, function can be performed on a contact input simply by using a normally–closed contact instead of a normally–open contact: Now, the lamp energizes if the contact is not actuated, and de–energizes when the contact is actuated.

If we take our OR function and invert each "input" through the use of normally–closed contacts, we will end up with a NAND function. In a special branch of mathematics known as Boolean algebra, this effect of gate function identity changing with the inversion of input signals is described by DeMorgan's Theorem, a subject to be explored in more detail in a later chapter.

The lamp will be energized if either contact is unactuated. It will go out only if both contacts are actuated simultaneously.

Likewise, if we take our AND function and invert each "input" through the use of normally–closed contacts, we will end up with a NOR function:

A pattern quickly reveals itself when ladder circuits are compared with their logic gate counterparts:

- Parallel contacts are equivalent to an OR gate.
- Series contacts are equivalent to an AND gate.

- Normally–closed contacts are equivalent to a NOT gate (inverter).

We can build combinational logic functions by grouping contacts in series–parallel arrangements, as well. In the following example, we have an Exclusive–OR function built from a combination of AND, OR, and inverter (NOT) gates:

The top rung (NC contact A in series with NO contact B) is the equivalent of the top NOT/AND gate combination. The bottom rung (NO contact A in series with NC contact B) is the equivalent of the bottom NOT/AND gate combination. The parallel connection between the two rungs at wire number 2 forms the equivalent of the OR gate, in allowing either rung 1 or rung 2 to energize the lamp.

To make the Exclusive–OR function, we had to use two contacts per input: one for direct input and the other for "inverted" input. The two "A" contacts are physically actuated by the same mechanism, as are the two "B" contacts. The common association between contacts is denoted by the label of the contact.

There is no limit to how many contacts per switch can be represented in a ladder diagram, as each new contact on any switch or relay (either normally–open or normally–closed) used in the diagram is simply marked with the same label.

Sometimes, multiple contacts on a single switch (or relay) are designated by a compound labels, such as "A–1" and "A–2" instead of two "A" labels. This may be especially useful if you want to specifically designate which set of contacts on each switch or relay is being used for which part of a circuit.

For simplicity's sake, I'll refrain from such elaborate labeling in this lesson. If you see a common label for multiple contacts, you know those contacts are all actuated by the same mechanism.

If we wish to invert the output of any switch–generated logic function, we must use a relay with a normally–closed contact. For instance, if we want to energize a load based on the inverse, or NOT, of a normally–open contact, we could do this:

We will call the relay, "control relay 1," or CR1. When the coil of CR1 (symbolized with the pair of parentheses on the first rung) is energized, the contact on the second rung opens, thus de–energizing the lamp. From switch A to the coil of CR1, the logic function is noninverted. The normally–closed contact actuated by relay coil CR1 provides a logical inverter function to drive the lamp opposite that of the switch's actuation status. Applying this inversion strategy to one of our inverted–input functions created earlier, such as the OR–to–NAND, we can invert the output with a relay to create a noninverted function:

From the switches to the coil of CR1, the logical function is that of a NAND gate. CR1's normally–closed contact provides one final inversion to turn the NAND function into an AND function.

PERMISSIVE AND INTERLOCK CIRCUITS

A practical application of switch and relay logic is in control systems where several process conditions have to be met before a piece of equipment is allowed to start. A good example of this is burner control for large combustion furnaces. In order for the burners in a large furnace to be started safely, the control system requests "permission" from several process switches, including high and low fuel pressure, air fan flow check, exhaust stack damper position, access door position, etc. Each process condition is called a permissive, and each permissive switch contact is wired in series, so that if any one of them detects an unsafe condition, the circuit will be opened.

If all permissive conditions are met, CR1 will energize and the green lamp will be lit. In real life, more than just a green lamp would be energized: usually a control relay or fuel valve solenoid would be placed in that rung of the circuit to be energized when all the permissive contacts were "good:" that is, all closed. If any one of the permissive conditions are not met, the series string of switch contacts will be broken, CR2 will de–energize, and the red lamp will light.

Note that the high fuel pressure contact is normally–closed. This is because we want the switch contact to open if the fuel pressure gets too high. Since the "normal" condition of any pressure switch is when zero (low) pressure is being applied to it, and we want this switch to open with excessive (high) pressure, we must choose a switch that is closed in its normal state.

Another practical application of relay logic is in control systems where we want to ensure two incompatible events cannot occur at the same time. An example of this is in reversible motor control, where two motor contactors are wired to switch polarity (or phase sequence) to an electric motor, and we don't want the forward and reverse contactors energized simultaneously.

When contactor M1 is energized, the 3 phases (A, B, and C) are connected directly to terminals 1, 2, and 3 of the motor, respectively. However, when contactor M2 is energized, phases A and B are reversed, A going to motor terminal 2 and B going to motor terminal 1. This reversal of phase wires results in the motor spinning the opposite direction. Let's examine the control circuit for these two contactors.

Take note of the normally–closed "OL" contact, which is the thermal overload contact activated by the "heater" elements wired in series with each phase of the AC motor. If the heaters get too hot, the contact will change from its normal (closed) state to being open, which will prevent either contactor from energizing.

This control system will work fine, so long as no one pushes both buttons at the same time. If someone were to do that, phases A and B would be short–circuited together by virtue of the fact that contactor M1 sends phases A and B straight to the motor and contactor M2 reverses them; phase A would be shorted to phase B and vice versa. Obviously, this is a bad control system design!

To prevent this occurrence from happening, we can design the circuit so that the energization of one contactor prevents the energization of the other. This is called interlocking, and it is accomplished through the use of auxiliary contacts on each contactor, as such.

Now, when M1 is energized, the normally–closed auxiliary contact on the second rung will be open, thus preventing M2 from being energized, even if the "Reverse" pushbutton is actuated. Likewise, M1's energization is prevented when M2 is energized. Note, as well, how additional wire numbers (4 and 5) were added to reflect the wiring changes.

It should be noted that this is not the only way to interlock contactors to prevent a short–circuit condition. Some contactors come equipped with the option of a mechanical interlock: a lever joining the armatures of two contactors together so that they are physically prevented from simultaneous closure. For additional safety, electrical interlocks may still be used, and due to the simplicity of the circuit there is no good reason not to employ them in addition to mechanical interlocks.

MOTOR CONTROL CIRCUITS

The interlock contacts installed in the previous section's motor control circuit work fine, but the motor will run only as long as each pushbutton switch is held down. If we wanted to keep the motor running even after the operator takes his or her hand off the control switch(es), we could change the circuit in a couple of different ways: we could replace the pushbutton switches with toggle switches, or we could add some more relay logic to "latch" the control circuit with a single, momentary actuation of either switch. Let's see how the second approach is implemented, since it is commonly used in industry.

When the "Forward" pushbutton is actuated, M1 will energize, closing the normally–open auxiliary contact in parallel with that switch. When the pushbutton is released, the closed M1 auxiliary contact will maintain current to the coil of M1, thus latching the "Forward" circuit in the "on" state. The same sort of thing will happen when the "Reverse" pushbutton is pressed. These parallel auxiliary contacts are sometimes referred to as seal–in contacts, the word "seal" meaning essentially the same thing as the word latch.

However, this creates a new problem: how to stop the motor! As the circuit exists right now, the motor will run either forward or backward once the corresponding pushbutton switch is pressed, and will continue to run as long as there is power. To stop either circuit (forward or backward), we require some means for the operator to interrupt power to the motor contactors. We'll call this new switch, Stop.

Now, if either forward or reverse circuits are latched, they may be "unlatched" by momentarily pressing the "Stop" pushbutton, which will open either forward or reverse circuit, de–energizing the energized contactor, and returning the seal–in contact to its normal (open) state. The "Stop" switch, having normally–closed contacts, will conduct power to either forward or reverse circuits when released.

So far, so good. Let's consider another practical aspect of our motor control scheme before we quit adding to it. If our hypothetical motor turned a mechanical load with a lot of momentum, such as a large air fan, the motor might continue to coast for a substantial amount of time after the stop button had been pressed. This could be problematic if an operator were to try to reverse the motor direction without waiting for the fan to stop turning. If the fan was still coasting forward and the "Reverse" pushbutton was pressed, the motor would struggle to overcome that inertia of the large fan as it tried to begin turning in reverse, drawing excessive current and potentially reducing the life of the motor, drive mechanisms, and fan. What we might like to have is some kind of a time–delay function in this motor control system to prevent such a premature startup from happening.

Let's begin by adding a couple of time–delay relay coils, one in parallel with each motor contactor coil. If we use contacts that delay returning to their normal state, these relays will provide us a "memory" of which direction the motor was last powered to turn. What we want each time–delay contact to do is to open the starting–switch leg of the opposite rotation circuit for several seconds, while the fan coasts to a halt.

If the motor has been running in the forward direction, both M1 and TD1 will have been energized. This being the case, the normally–closed, timed–closed contact of TD1 between wires 8 and 5 will have immediately opened the moment TD1 was energized.

When the stop button is pressed, contact TD1 waits for the specified amount of time before returning to its normally–closed state, thus holding the reverse pushbutton circuit open for the duration so M2 can't be energized. When TD1 times out, the contact will close and the circuit will allow M2 to be energized, if the reverse pushbutton is pressed. In like manner, TD2 will prevent the "Forward" pushbutton from energizing M1 until the prescribed time delay after M2 (and TD2) have been de-energized.

The careful observer will notice that the time–interlocking functions of TD1 and TD2 render the M1 and M2 interlocking contacts redundant. We can get rid of auxiliary contacts M1 and M2 for interlocks and just use TD1 and TD2's contacts, since they immediately open when their respective relay coils are energized, thus "locking out" one contactor if the other is energized. Each time delay relay will serve a dual purpose: preventing the other contactor from energizing while the motor is running, and preventing the same contactor from energizing until a prescribed time after motor shutdown. The resulting circuit has the advantage of being simpler than the previous example:

Fail–Safe Design

Logic circuits, whether comprised of electromechanical relays or solid–state gates, can be built in many different ways to perform the same functions. There is usually no one "correct" way to design a complex logic circuit, but there are usually ways that are better than others.

In control systems, safety is (or at least should be) an important design priority. If there are multiple ways in which a digital control circuit can be designed to perform a task, and one of those ways happens to hold certain advantages in safety over the others, then that design is the better one to choose.

Let's take a look at a simple system and consider how it might be implemented in relay logic. Suppose that a large laboratory or industrial building is to be equipped with a fire alarm system, activated by any one of several latching switches installed throughout the facility. The system should work so that the alarm siren will energize if any one of the switches is actuated. At first glance it seems as though the relay logic should be incredibly simple: just use normally–open switch contacts and connect them all in parallel with each other.

Essentially, this is the OR logic function implemented with four switch inputs. We could expand this circuit to include any number of switch inputs, each new switch being added to the parallel network, but I'll limit it to four in this example to keep things simple. At any rate, it is an elementary system and there seems to be little possibility of trouble.

Except in the event of a wiring failure, that is. The nature of electric circuits is such that "open" failures (open switch contacts, broken wire connections, open relay coils, blown fuses, etc.) are statistically more likely to occur than any other type of failure. With that in mind, it makes sense to engineer a circuit to be as tolerant as possible to such a failure. Let's suppose that a wire connection for Switch #2 were to fail open: If this failure were to occur, the result would be that Switch #2 would no longer energize the siren if actuated. This, obviously, is not good in a fire alarm system. Unless the system were regularly tested (a good idea anyway), no one would know there was a problem until someone tried to use that switch in an emergency.

What if the system were re–engineered so as to sound the alarm in the event of an open failure? That way, a failure in the wiring would result in a false alarm, a scenario much more preferable than that of having a switch silently fail and not function when needed. In order to achieve this design goal, we would have to re–wire the switches so that an open contact sounded the alarm, rather than a closed contact. That being the case, the switches will have to be normally–closed and in series with each other, powering a relay coil which then activates a normally–closed contact for the siren.

When all switches are unactuated (the regular operating state of this system), relay CR1 will be energized, thus keeping contact CR1 open, preventing the siren from being powered. However, if any of the switches are actuated, relay CR1 will de–energize, closing contact CR1 and sounding the alarm.

Also, if there is a break in the wiring anywhere in the top rung of the circuit, the alarm will sound. When it is discovered that the alarm is false, the workers in the facility will know that something failed in the alarm system and that it needs to be repaired.

Granted, the circuit is more complex than it was before the addition of the control relay, and the system could still fail in the "silent" mode with a broken connection in the bottom rung, but its still a safer design than the original circuit, and thus preferable from the standpoint of safety.

This design of circuit is referred to as fail–safe, due to its intended design to default to the safest mode in the event of a common failure such as a broken connection in the switch wiring. Fail–safe design always starts with an assumption as to the most likely kind of wiring or component failure, and then tries to configure things so that such a failure will cause the circuit to act in the safest way, the "safest way" being determined by the physical characteristics of the process.

Take for example an electrically–actuated (solenoid) valve for turning on cooling water to a machine. Energizing the solenoid coil will move an armature which then either opens or closes the valve mechanism, depending on what kind of valve we specify. A spring will return the valve to its "normal" position when the solenoid is de–energized. We already know that an open failure in the wiring or solenoid coil is more likely than a short or any other type of failure, so we should design this system to be in its safest mode with the solenoid de–energized. If its cooling water we're controlling with this valve, chances are it is safer to have the cooling water turn on in the event of a failure than to shut off, the consequences of a machine running without coolant usually being severe. This means we should specify a valve that turns on (opens up) when de–energized and turns off (closes down) when energized. This may seem "backwards" to have the valve set up this way, but it will make for a safer system in the end.

One interesting application of fail–safe design is in the power generation and distribution industry, where large circuit breakers need to be opened and closed by electrical control signals from protective relays. If a 50/51 relay (instantaneous and time overcurrent) is going to command a circuit breaker to trip (open) in the event of excessive current, should we design it so that the relay closes a switch contact to send a "trip" signal to the breaker, or opens a switch contact to interrupt a regularly "on" signal to initiate a breaker trip? We know that an open connection will be the most likely to occur, but what is the safest state of the system: breaker open or breaker closed?

At first, it would seem that it would be safer to have a large circuit breaker trip (open up and shut off power) in the event of an open fault in the protective relay control circuit, just like we had the fire alarm system default to an alarm state with any switch or wiring failure. However, things are not so simple in the world of high power. To have a large circuit breaker indiscriminately trip open is no small matter, especially when customers are depending on the continued supply of electric power to supply hospitals, telecommunications systems, water treatment systems, and other important infrastructures.

For this reason, power system engineers have generally agreed to design protective relay circuits to output a closed contact signal (power applied) to open large circuit breakers, meaning that any open failure in the control wiring will go unnoticed, simply leaving the breaker in the status quo position.

Is this an ideal situation? Of course not. If a protective relay detects an overcurrent condition while the control wiring is failed open, it will not be able to trip open the circuit breaker. Like the first fire alarm system design, the "silent" failure will be evident only when the system is needed. However, to engineer the control circuitry the other way — so that any open failure would immediately shut the circuit breaker off, potentially blacking out large potions of the power grid — really isn't a better alternative.

An entire book could be written on the principles and practices of good fail–safe system design. At least here, you know a couple of the fundamentals: that wiring tends to fail open more often than shorted, and that an electrical control system's (open) failure mode should be such that it indicates and/or actuates the real–life process in the safest alternative mode. These fundamental principles extend to non–electrical systems as well: identify the most common mode of failure, then engineer the system so that the probable failure mode places the system in the safest condition.

PROGRAMMABLE LOGIC CONTROLLERS

Before the advent of solid–state logic circuits, logical control systems were designed and built exclusively around electromechanical relays. Relays are far from obsolete in modern design, but have been replaced in many of their former roles as logic–level control devices, relegated most often to those applications demanding high current and/or high voltage switching.

Systems and processes requiring "on/off" control abound in modern commerce and industry, but such control systems are rarely built from either electromechanical relays or discrete logic gates. Instead, digital computers fill the need, which may be programmed to do a variety of logical functions.

In the late 1960's an American company named Bedford Associates released a computing device they called the MODICON. As an acronym, it meant Modular Digital Controller, and later became the name of a company division devoted to the design, manufacture, and sale of these special–purpose control computers. Other engineering firms developed their own versions of this device, and it eventually came to be known in non–proprietary terms as a PLC, or Programmable Logic Controller. The purpose of a PLC was to directly replace electromechanical relays as logic elements, substituting instead a solid–state digital computer with a stored programme, able to emulate the interconnection of many relays to perform certain logical tasks.

A PLC has many "input" terminals, through which it interprets "high" and "low" logical states from sensors and switches. It also has many output terminals, through which it outputs "high" and "low" signals to power lights, solenoids, contactors, small motors, and other devices lending themselves to on/off control. In an effort to make PLCs easy to programme, their programming language was designed to resemble ladder logic diagrams.

Thus, an industrial electrician or electrical engineer accustomed to reading ladder logic schematics would feel comfortable programming a PLC to perform the same control functions.

PLCs are industrial computers, and as such their input and output signals are typically 120 volts AC, just like the electromechanical control relays they were designed to replace. Although some PLCs have the ability to input and output low–level DC voltage signals of the magnitude used in logic gate circuits, this is the exception and not the rule.

Signal connection and programming standards vary somewhat between different models of PLC, but they are similar enough to allow a "generic" introduction to PLC programming here. The following illustration shows a simple PLC, as it might appear from a front view. Two screw terminals provide connection to 120 volts AC for powering the PLC's internal circuitry, labeled L1 and L2.

Six screw terminals on the left–hand side provide connection to input devices, each terminal representing a different input "channel" with its own "X" label. The lower–left screw terminal is a "Common" connection, which is generally connected to L2 (neutral) of the 120 VAC power source.

Inside the PLC housing, connected between each input terminal and the Common terminal, is an opto–isolator device (Light–Emitting Diode) that provides an electrically isolated "high" logic signal to the computer's circuitry (a photo–transistor interprets the LED's light) when there is 120 VAC power applied between the respective input terminal and the Common terminal. An indicating LED on the front panel of the PLC gives visual indication of an "energized" input:

Output signals are generated by the PLC's computer circuitry activating a switching device (transistor, TRIAC, or even an electromechanical relay), connecting the "Source" terminal to any of the "Y–" labeled output terminals. The "Source" terminal, correspondingly, is usually connected to the L1 side of the 120 VAC power source. As with each input, an indicating LED on the front panel of the PLC gives visual indication of an "energized" output.

In this way, the PLC is able to interface with real–world devices such as switches and solenoids.

The actual logic of the control system is established inside the PLC by means of a computer programme. This programme dictates which output gets energized under which input conditions. Although the programme itself appears to be a ladder logic diagram, with switch and relay symbols, there are no actual switch contacts or relay coils operating inside the PLC to create the logical relationships between input and output. These are imaginary contacts and coils, if you will. The programme is entered and viewed via a personal computer connected to the PLC's programming port.

Consider the following circuit and PLC programme: When the pushbutton switch is unactuated (unpressed), no power is sent to the X1 input of the PLC. Following the programme, which shows a normally–open X1 contact in series with a Y1 coil, no "power" will be sent to the Y1 coil. Thus, the

PLC's Y1 output remains de–energized, and the indicator lamp connected to it remains dark. If the pushbutton switch is pressed, however, power will be sent to the PLC's X1 input. Any and all X1 contacts appearing in the programme will assume the actuated (non–normal) state, as though they were relay contacts actuated by the energizing of a relay coil named "X1". In this case, energizing the X1 input will cause the normally–open X1 contact will "close," sending "power" to the Y1 coil. When the Y1 coil of the programme "energizes," the real Y1 output will become energized, lighting up the lamp connected to it.

It must be understood that the X1 contact, Y1 coil, connecting wires, and "power" appearing in the personal computer's display are all virtual. They do not exist as real electrical components. They exist as commands in a computer programme — a piece of software only — that just happens to resemble a real relay schematic diagram.

Equally important to understand is that the personal computer used to display and edit the PLC's programme is not necessary for the PLC's continued operation. Once a programme has been loaded to the PLC from the personal computer, the personal computer may be unplugged from the PLC, and the PLC will continue to follow the programmed commands.

The personal computer display in these illustrations for your sake only, in aiding to understand the relationship between real–life conditions (switch closure and lamp status) and the program's status ("power" through virtual contacts and virtual coils).

The true power and versatility of a PLC is revealed when we want to alter the behaviour of a control system. Since the PLC is a programmable device, we can alter its behaviour by changing the commands we give it, without having to reconfigure the electrical components connected to it. For example, suppose we wanted to make this switch–and–lamp circuit function in an inverted fashion: push the button to make the lamp turn off, and release it to make it turn on.

The "hardware" solution would require that a normally–closed pushbutton switch be substituted for the normally–open switch currently in place. The "software" solution is much easier: just alter the programme so that contact X1 is normally–closed rather than normally–open.

In the following illustration, we have the altered system shown in the state where the pushbutton is unactuated (not being pressed).

In this next illustration, the switch is shown actuated (pressed): One of the advantages of implementing logical control in software rather than in hardware is that input signals can be re–used as many times in the programme as is necessary. For example, take the following circuit and programme, designed to energize the lamp if at least two of the three pushbutton switches are simultaneously actuated: To build an equivalent circuit using electromechanical relays, three relays with two normally–open contacts each would have to be used, to provide two contacts per input switch.

Using a PLC, however, we can programme as many contacts as we wish for each "X" input without adding additional hardware, since each input and each output is nothing more than a single bit in the PLC's digital memory (either 0 or 1), and can be recalled as many times as necessary.

Furthermore, since each output in the PLC is nothing more than a bit in its memory as well, we can assign contacts in a PLC programme "actuated" by an output (Y) status. Take for instance this next system, a motor start–stop control circuit.

The pushbutton switch connected to input X1 serves as the "Start" switch, while the switch connected to input X2 serves as the "Stop." Another contact in the programme, named Y1, uses the output coil status as a seal–in contact, directly, so that the motor contactor will continue to be energized after the "Start" pushbutton switch is released. You can see the normally–closed contact X2 appear in a colored block, showing that it is in a closed ("electrically conducting") state.

If we were to press the "Start" button, input X1 would energize, thus "closing" the X1 contact in the programme, sending "power" to the Y1 "coil," energizing the Y1 output and applying 120 volt AC power to the real motor contactor coil. The parallel Y1 contact will also "close," thus latching the "circuit" in an energized state.

Now, if we release the "Start" pushbutton, the normally–open X1 "contact" will return to its "open" state, but the motor will continue to run because the Y1 seal–in "contact" continues to provide "continuity" to "power" coil Y1, thus keeping the Y1 output energized.

To stop the motor, we must momentarily press the "Stop" pushbutton, which will energize the X2 input and "open" the normally–closed "contact," breaking continuity to the Y1 "coil".

When the "Stop" pushbutton is released, input X2 will de–energize, returning "contact" X2 to its normal, "closed" state. The motor, however, will not start again until the "Start" pushbutton is actuated, because the "seal–in" of Y1 has been lost.

An important point to make here is that fail–safe design is just as important in PLC–controlled systems as it is in electromechanical relay–controlled systems. One should always consider the effects of failed (open) wiring on the device or devices being controlled. In this motor control circuit example, we have a problem: if the input wiring for X2 (the "Stop" switch) were to fail open, there would be no way to stop the motor!

The solution to this problem is a reversal of logic between the X2 "contact" inside the PLC programme and the actual "Stop" pushbutton switch: When the normally–closed "Stop" pushbutton switch is unactuated (not pressed), the PLC's X2 input will be energized, thus "closing" the X2 "contact" inside the programme.

This allows the motor to be started when input X1 is energized, and allows it to continue to run when the "Start" pushbutton is no longer pressed. When the "Stop" pushbutton is actuated, input X2 will de–energize, thus "opening" the X2 "contact" inside the PLC programme and shutting off the motor. So, we see there is no operational difference between this new design and the previous design.

However, if the input wiring on input X2 were to fail open, X2 input would de–energize in the same manner as when the "Stop" pushbutton is pressed.

The result, then, for a wiring failure on the X2 input is that the motor will immediately shut off. This is a safer design than the one previously shown, where a "Stop" switch wiring failure would have resulted in an inability to turn off the motor.

In addition to input (X) and output (Y) programme elements, PLCs provide "internal" coils and contacts with no intrinsic connection to the outside world. These are used much the same as "control relays" (CR1, CR2, etc.) are used in standard relay circuits: to provide logic signal inversion when necessary.

To demonstrate how one of these "internal" relays might be used, consider the following example circuit and programme, designed to emulate the function of a three–input NAND gate. Since PLC programme elements are typically designed by single letters, we will call the internal control relay "C1" rather than "CR1" as would be customary in a relay control circuit:

In this circuit, the lamp will remain lit so long as any of the pushbuttons remain unactuated (unpressed). To make the lamp turn off, we will have to actuate (press) all three switches, like this.

This section on programmable logic controllers illustrates just a small sample of their capabilities. As computers, PLCs can perform timing functions (for the equivalent of time–delay relays), drum sequencing, and other advanced functions with far greater accuracy and reliability than what is possible using electromechanical logic devices. Most PLCs have the capacity for far more than six inputs and six outputs. The following photograph shows several input and output modules of a single Allen–Bradley PLC.

With each module having sixteen "points" of either input or output, this PLC has the ability to monitor and control dozens of devices. Fit into a control cabinet, a PLC takes up little room, especially considering the equivalent space that would be needed by electromechanical relays to perform the same functions: One advantage of PLCs that simply cannot be duplicated by electromechanical relays is remote monitoring and control via digital computer networks.

Because a PLC is nothing more than a special–purpose digital computer, it has the ability to communicate with other computers rather easily. The following photograph shows a personal computer displaying a graphic image of a real liquid–level process (a pumping, or "lift," station for a municipal wastewater treatment system) controlled by a PLC.

The actual pumping station is located miles away from the personal computer display:

Chapter 5

Karnaugh Mapping

The Karnaugh map, like Boolean algebra, is a simplification tool applicable to digital logic. See the "Toxic waste incinerator" in the Boolean algebra chapter for an example of Boolean simplification of digital logic. The Karnaugh Map will simplify logic faster and more easily in most cases.

Boolean simplification is actually faster than the Karnaugh map for a task involving two or fewer Boolean variables. It is still quite usable at three variables, but a bit slower.

At four input variables, Boolean algebra becomes tedious. Karnaugh maps are both faster and easier. Karnaugh maps work well for up to six input variables, are usable for up to eight variables. For more than six to eight variables, simplification should be by CAD (computer automated design). In theory any of the three methods will work.

However, as a practical matter, the above guidelines work well. We would not normally resort to computer automation to simplify a three input logic block. We could sooner solve the problem with pencil and paper. However, if we had seven of these problems to solve, say for a BCD (Binary Coded Decimal) to seven segment decoder, we might want to automate the process. A BCD to seven segment decoder generates the logic signals to drive a seven segment LED (light emitting diode) display.

Examples of computer automated design languages for simplification of logic are PALASM, ABEL, CUPL, Verilog, and VHDL. These programs accept a hardware descriptor language input file which is based on Boolean equations and produce an output file describing a reduced (or simplified) Boolean solution. We will not require such tools. Let's move on to Venn diagrams as an introduction to Karnaugh maps.

KARNAUGH MAPS, TRUTH TABLES, AND BOOLEAN EXPRESSIONS

Maurice Karnaugh, a telecommunications engineer, developed the Karnaugh map at Bell Labs in 1953 while designing digital logic based telephone switching circuits.

Now that we have developed the Karnaugh map with the aid of Venn diagrams, let's put it to use. Karnaugh maps reduce logic functions more quickly and easily compared to Boolean algebra. By reduce we mean simplify, reducing the number of gates and inputs. We like to simplify logic to a lowest cost form to save costs by elimination of components. We define lowest cost as being the lowest number of gates with the lowest number of inputs per gate.

Given a choice, most students do logic simplification with Karnaugh maps rather than Boolean algebra once they learn this tool.

We show five individual items above, which are just different ways of representing the same thing: an arbitrary 2–input digital logic function. First is relay ladder logic, then logic gates, a truth table, a Karnaugh map, and a Boolean equation. The point is that any of these are equivalent. Two inputs A and B can take on values of either 0 or 1, high or low, open or closed, True or False, as the case may be. There are 22 = 4 combinations of inputs producing an output. This is applicable to all five examples.

These four outputs may be observed on a lamp in the relay ladder logic, on a logic probe on the gate diagram. These outputs may be recorded in the truth table, or in the Karnaugh map. Look at the Karnaugh map as being a rearranged truth table. The Output of the Boolean equation may be computed by the laws of Boolean algebra and transfered to the truth table or Karnaugh map. Which of the five equivalent logic descriptions should we use? The one which is most useful for the task to be accomplished.

The outputs of a truth table correspond on a one–to–one basis to Karnaugh map entries. Starting at the top of the truth table, the A=0, B=0 inputs produce an output. Note that this same output is found in the Karnaugh map at the A=0, B=0 cell address, upper left corner of K–map where the A=0 row and B=0 column intersect.

The adjacent 2–cell regions in the 2–variable K–map with the aid of previous rectangular Venn diagram like Boolean regions.

The K–map as ellipses in the left most K–map below. Referring to the previous truth table, this is not the case. There is another truth table entry between them. Which brings us to the whole point of the organizing the K–map into a square array, cells with any Boolean variables in common need to be close to one another so as to present a pattern that jumps out at us.They have the Boolean variable B' in common. We know this because B=0 (same as B') for the column. Compare this to the square Venn diagram above the K–map. Boolean B (B=1) in common. Then, 0 and 1 have Boolean A' (A=0) in common. Finally, Boolean A (A=1) in common. Compare the last two maps to the middle square Venn diagram.

To summarize, we are looking for commonality of Boolean variables among cells. The Karnaugh map is organized so that we may see that commonality. Let's try some examples.

Example: Transfer the contents of the truth table to the Karnaugh map above.

Solution: The truth table contains two 1s. the K– map must have both of them. locate the first 1 in the 2nd row of the truth table above.

- Note the truth table AB address
- Locate the cell in the K–map having the same address
- Place a 1 in that cell

Repeat the process for the 1 in the last line of the truth table.

Example: For the Karnaugh map in the above problem, write the Boolean expression. Solution is below.

Solution: Look for adjacent cells, that is, above or to the side of a cell. Diagonal cells are not adjacent. Adjacent cells will have one or more Boolean variables in common.

- Group (circle) the two 1s in the column
- Find the variable(s) top and/or side which are the same for the group, Write this as the Boolean result. It is B in our case.
- Ignore variable(s) which are not the same for a cell group. In our case A varies, is both 1 and 0, ignore Boolean A.
- Ignore any variable not associated with cells containing 1s. B' has no ones under it. Ignore B'
- Result Out = B

This might be easier to see by comparing to the Venn diagrams to the right, specifically the B column.

Example: Write the Boolean expression for the Karnaugh map below.
Solution: (above)

- Group (circle) the two 1's in the row
- Find the variable(s) which are the same for the group,Out A'

Example: For the Truth table below, transfer the outputs to the Karnaugh, then write the Boolean expression for the result.

Solution: Transfer the 1s from the locations in the Truth table to the corresponding locations in the K–map.

- Group (circle) the two 1's in the column under B=1
- Group (circle) the two 1's in the row right of A=1
- Write product term for first group = B
- Write product term for second group = A
- Write Sum–Of–Products of above two terms Output = A+B

The solution of the K–map in the middle is the simplest or lowest cost solution.

A less desirable solution is at far right. After grouping the two 1s, we make the mistake of forming a group of 1–cell. The reason that this is not desirable is that:

- The single cell has a product term of AB'

- The corresponding solution is Output = AB' + B
- This is not the simplest solution

The way to pick up this single 1 is to form a group of two with the 1 to the right of it as shown in the lower line of the middle K–map, even though this 1 has already been included in the column group (B). We are allowed to re–use cells in order to form larger groups. In fact, it is desirable because it leads to a simpler result.

We need to point out that either of the above solutions, Output or Wrong Output, are logically correct. Both circuits yield the same output. It is a matter of the former circuit being the lowest cost solution.

Example: Fill in the Karnaugh map for the Boolean expression below, then write the Boolean expression for the result.

Solution: The Boolean expression has three product terms. There will be a 1 entered for each product term. Though, in general, the number of 1s per product term varies with the number of variables in the product term compared to the size of the K–map. The product term is the address of the cell where the 1 is entered. The first product term, A'B, corresponds to the 01 cell in the map.

A 1 is entered in this cell. The other two P–terms are entered for a total of three 1s

Next, proceed with grouping and extracting the simplified result as in the previous truth table problem.

Example: Simplify the logic diagram below.

Solution: (Figure below)

- Write the Boolean expression for the original logic
- Transfer the product terms to the Karnaugh map
- Form groups of cells as in previous examples
- Write Boolean expression for groups as in previous examples
- Draw simplified logic diagram

Example: Simplify the logic diagram below.

Solution:

- Write the Boolean expression for the original logic diagram shown above
- Transfer the product terms to the Karnaugh map.
- It is not possible to form groups.
- No simplification is possible; leave it as it is.

No logic simplification is possible for the above diagram. This sometimes happens. Neither the methods of Karnaugh maps nor Boolean algebra can simplify this logic further.

We show an Exclusive–OR schematic symbol above; however, this is not a logical simplification.

It just makes a schematic diagram look nicer. Since it is not possible to simplify the Exclusive–OR logic and it is widely used, it is provided by manufacturers as a basic integrated circuit (7486).

LOGIC SIMPLIFICATION WITH KARNAUGH MAPS

The logic simplification examples that we have done so could have been performed with Boolean algebra about as quickly. Real world logic simplification problems call for larger Karnaugh maps so that we may do serious work. We will work some contrived examples in this section, leaving most of the real world applications for the Combinatorial Logic chapter. By contrived, we mean examples which illustrate techniques. This approach will develop the tools we need to transition to the more complex applications in the Combinatorial Logic chapter.

We show our previously developed Karnaugh map. We will use the form on the right.

Note the sequence of numbers across the top of the map. It is not in binary sequence which would be 00, 01, 10, 11. It is 00, 01, 11 10, which is Gray code sequence. Gray code sequence only changes one binary bit as we go from one number to the next in the sequence, unlike binary. That means that adjacent cells will only vary by one bit, or Boolean variable.

This is what we need to organize the outputs of a logic function so that we may view commonality. Moreover, the column and row headings must be in Gray code order, or the map will not work as a Karnaugh map. Cells sharing common Boolean variables would no longer be adjacent, nor show visual patterns. Adjacent cells vary by only one bit because a Gray code sequence varies by only one bit.

If we sketch our own Karnaugh maps, we need to generate Gray code for any size map that we may use. This is how we generate Gray code of any size.

Note that the Gray code sequence, above right, only varies by one bit as we go down the list, or bottom to top up the list. This property of Gray code is often useful in digital electronics in general. In particular, it is applicable to Karnaugh maps.

Let us move on to some examples of simplification with 3–variable Karnaugh maps. We show how to map the product terms of the unsimplified logic to the K–map. We illustrate how to identify groups of adjacent cells which leads to a Sum–of–Products simplification of the digital logic.

Above we, place the 1's in the K–map for each of the product terms, identify a group of two, then write a p–term (product term) for the sole group as our simplified result.

Mapping the four product terms above yields a group of four covered by Boolean A' Mapping the four p–terms yields a group of four, which is covered by one variable C. After mapping the six p–terms above, identify the upper group of four, pick up the lower two cells as a group of four by sharing the two with two more from the other group. Covering these two with a group of four gives a simpler result. Since there are two groups, there will be two p–terms in the Sum–of–Products result A'+B The two product terms above form one group of two and simplifies to BC

Mapping the four p–terms yields a single group of four, which is B visualize the group of four by rolling up the ends of the map to form a cylinder, then the cells are adjacent. We normally mark the group of four as above left. Out of the variables A, B, C, there is a common variable: C'. C' is a 0 over all four cells. Final result is C'.

The six cells above from the unsimplified equation can be organized into two groups of four. These two groups should give us two p–terms in our simplified result of A' + C'.

Below, we revisit the Toxic Waste Incinerator from the Boolean algebra chapter. See Boolean algebra chapter for details on this example. We will simplify the logic using a Karnaugh map.

The Boolean equation for the output has four product terms. Map four 1's corresponding to the p–terms. Forming groups of cells, we have three groups of two. There will be three p–terms in the simplified result, one for each group. See, "Toxic Waste Incinerator", Boolean algebra chapter for a gate diagram of the result, which is reproduced below. Below we repeat the Boolean algebra simplification of Toxic waste incinerator for comparison.

Below we repeat the Toxic waste incinerator Karnaugh map solution for comparison to the above Boolean algebra simplification. This case illustrates why the Karnaugh map is widely used for logic simplification.

LARGER 4–VARIABLE KARNAUGH MAPS

Knowing how to generate Gray code should allow us to build larger maps. Actually, all we need to do is look at the left to right sequence across the top of the 3–variable map, and copy it down the left side of the 4–variable map. See below.

The following four variable Karnaugh maps illustrate reduction of Boolean expressions too tedious for Boolean algebra. Reductions could be done with Boolean algebra. However, the Karnaugh map is faster and easier, especially if there are many logic reductions to do.

The above Boolean expression has seven product terms. They are mapped top to bottom and left to right on the K–map above. For example, the first P–term A'B'CD is first row 3rd cell, corresponding to map location A=0, B=0, C=1, D=1. The other product terms are placed in a similar manner. Encircling the largest groups possible, two groups of four are shown above. The dashed horizontal group corresponds the the simplified product term AB. The vertical group corresponds to Boolean CD. Since there are two groups, there will be two product terms in the Sum–Of–Products result of Out=AB+CD.

Fold up the corners of the map below like it is a napkin to make the four cells physically adjacent.

The four cells above are a group of four because they all have the Boolean variables B' and D' in common. In other words, B = 0 for the four cells, and D = 0 for the four cells. The other variables (A, B) are 0 in some cases, 1 in other cases with respect to the four corner cells. Thus, these variables (A, B) are not involved with this group of four. This single group comes out of the map as one product term for the simplified result: Out = B'C'. For the K–map below, roll the top and bottom edges into a cylinder forming eight adjacent cells.

The above group of eight has one Boolean variable in common: B=0. Therefore, the one group of eight is covered by one p–term: B'. The original eight term Boolean expression simplifies to Out=B'

The Boolean expression below has nine p–terms, three of which have three Booleans instead of four. The difference is that while four Boolean variable product terms cover one cell, the three Boolean p–terms cover a pair of cells each.

The six product terms of four Boolean variables map in the usual manner above as single cells. The three Boolean variable terms (three each) map as cell pairs, which is shown above. Note that we are mapping p–terms into the K–map, not pulling them out at this point.

For the simplification, we form two groups of eight. Cells in the corners are shared with both groups. This is fine. In fact, this leads to a better solution than forming a group of eight and a group of four without sharing any cells. Final Solution is Out=B'+D'

Below we map the unsimplified Boolean expression to the Karnaugh map. Above, three of the cells form into a groups of two cells. A fourth cell cannot be combined with anything, which often happens in "real world" problems. In this case, the Boolean p–term ABCD is unchanged in the simplification process. Result: Out= B'C'D'+A'B'D'+ABCD

Often times there is more than one minimum cost solution to a simplification problem. Such is the case illustrated below.

Both results above have four product terms of three Boolean variable each. Both are equally valid minimal cost solutions. The difference in the final solution is due to how the cells are grouped. A minimal cost solution is a valid logic design with the minimum number of gates with the minimum number of inputs.

Below we map the unsimplified Boolean equation as usual and form a group of four as a first simplification step. It may not be obvious how to pick up the remaining cells. Pick up three more cells in a group of four, centre above. There are still two cells remaining. the minimal cost method to pick up those is to group them with neighboring cells as groups of four as at above right.

On a cautionary note, do not attempt to form groups of three. Groupings must be powers of 2, that is, 1, 2, 4, 8...

Below we have another example of two possible minimal cost solutions. Start by forming a couple of groups of four after mapping the cells. The two solutions depend on whether the single remaining cell is grouped with the first or the second group of four as a group of two cells. That cell either comes out as either ABC' or ABD, your choice. Either way, this cell is covered by either Boolean product term. Final results are shown above.

Below we have an example of a simplification using the Karnaugh map at left or Boolean algebra at right. Plot C' on the map as the area of all cells covered by address C=0, the 8–cells on the left of the map. Then, plot the single ABCD cell. That single cell forms a group of 2–cell as shown, which simplifies to P–term ABD, for an end result of Out = C' + ABD.

This (above) is a rare example of a four variable problem that can be reduced with Boolean algebra without a lot of work, assuming that you remember the theorems.

MINTERM VS MAXTERM SOLUTION

So far we have been finding Sum–Of–Product (SOP) solutions to logic reduction problems. For each of these SOP solutions, there is also a Product–Of–Sums solution (POS), which could be more useful, depending on the application. Before working a Product–Of–Sums solution, we need to introduce some new terminology. The procedure below for mapping product terms is not new to this chapter. We just want to establish a formal procedure for minterms for comparison to the new procedure for maxterms.

A minterm is a Boolean expression resulting in 1 for the output of a single cell, and 0s for all other cells in a Karnaugh map, or truth table. If a minterm has a single 1 and the remaining cells as 0s, it would appear to cover a minimum area of 1s. The illustration above left shows the minterm ABC, a single product term, as a single 1 in a map that is otherwise 0s. We have not shown the 0s in our Karnaugh maps up to this point, as it is customary to omit them unless specifically needed. Another minterm A'BC' is shown above right.

The point to review is that the address of the cell corresponds directly to the minterm being mapped. That is, the cell 111 corresponds to the minterm ABC above left. Above right we see that the minterm A'BC' corresponds directly to the cell 010. A Boolean expression or map may have multiple minterms.

Referring to the above figure, Let's summarize the procedure for placing a minterm in a K–map.

- Identify the minterm (product term) term to be mapped.
- Write the corresponding binary numeric value.
- Use binary value as an address to place a 1 in the K–map
- Repeat steps for other minterms (P–terms within a Sum–Of–Products).

A Boolean expression will more often than not consist of multiple minterms corresponding to multiple cells in a Karnaugh map. The point we review for reference is that the 1s come out of the K–map as a binary cell address which converts directly to one or more product terms. By directly we mean that a 0 corresponds to a complemented variable, and a 1 corresponds to a true variable. Example: 010 converts directly to A'BC'. There was no reduction in this example. Though, we do have a Sum–Of–Products result from the minterms.

Referring to the above figure, Let's summarize the procedure for writing the Sum–Of–Products reduced Boolean equation from a K–map:

- Form largest groups of 1s possible covering all minterms. Groups must be a power of 2.
- Write binary numeric value for groups.
- Convert binary value to a product term.
- Repeat steps for other groups. Each group yields a p–terms within a Sum–Of–Products.

Nothing new so far, a formal procedure has been written down for dealing with minterms. This serves as a pattern for dealing with maxterms. Next we attack the Boolean function which is 0 for a single cell and 1s for all others. A maxterm is a Boolean expression resulting in a 0 for the output of a single cell expression, and 1s for all other cells in the Karnaugh map, or truth table. The illustration above left shows the maxterm (A+B+C), a single sum term, as a single 0 in a map that is otherwise 1s. If a maxterm has a single 0 and the remaining cells as 1s, it would appear to cover a maximum area of 1s.

There are some differences now that we are dealing with something new, maxterms. The maxterm is a 0, not a 1 in the Karnaugh map. A maxterm is a sum term, (A+B+C) in our example, not a product term.

It also looks strange that (A+B+C) is mapped into the cell 000. For the equation Out=(A+B+C)=0, all three variables (A, B, C) must individually be equal to 0. Only (0+0+0)=0 will equal 0. Thus we place our sole 0 for minterm (A+B+C) in cell A,B,C=000 in the K–map, where the inputs are all0. This is the only case which will give us a 0 for our maxterm. All other cells contain 1s because any input values other than ((0,0,0) for (A+B+C) yields 1s upon evaluation.

Referring to the above figure, the procedure for placing a maxterm in the K–map is:

- Identify the Sum term to be mapped.
- Write corresponding binary numeric value.
- Form the complement
- Use the complement as an address to place a 0 in the K–map
- Repeat for other maxterms (Sum terms within Product–Of–Sums expression).

Another maxterm A'+B'+C' is shown above. Numeric 000 corresponds to A'+B'+C'. The complement is 111. Place a 0 for maxterm (A'+B'+C') in this cell (1,1,1) of the K–map.

Why should (A'+B'+C') cause a 0 to be in cell 111? When A'+B'+C' is (1'+1'+1'), all 1s in, which is (0+0+0) after taking complements, we have the only condition that will give us a 0. All the 1s are complemented to all 0s, which is 0.

A Boolean Product–Of–Sums expression or map may have multiple maxterms. Maxterm (A+B+C) yields numeric 111 which complements to 000, placing a 0 in cell (0,0,0). Maxterm (A+B+C') yields numeric 110 which complements to 001, placing a 0 in cell (0,0,1).

Now that we have the k–map setup, what we are really interested in is showing how to write a Product–Of–Sums reduction. Form the 0s into groups. That would be a group of two below. Write the binary value corresponding to the sum–term which is (0,0,X). Both A and B are 0 for the group.

But, C is both 0 and 1 so we write an X as a place holder for C. Form the complement (1,1,X). Write the Sum–term (A+B) discarding the C and the X which held its' place. In general, expect to have more sum–terms multiplied together in the Product–Of–Sums result. Though, we have a simple example here.

Let's summarize the procedure for writing the Product–Of–Sums Boolean reduction for a K–map:

- Form largest groups of 0s possible, covering all maxterms. Groups must be a power of 2.
- Write binary numeric value for group.
- Complement binary numeric value for group.
- Convert complement value to a sum–term.
- Repeat steps for other groups. Each group yields a sum–term within a Product–Of–Sums result.

Example: Simplify the Product–Of–Sums Boolean expression below, providing a result in POS form.

Solution: Transfer the seven maxterms to the map below as 0s. Be sure to complement the input variables in finding the proper cell location.

We map the 0s as they appear left to right top to bottom on the map above. We locate the last three maxterms with leader lines..

Larger groups will give a sum–term with fewer inputs. Fewer groups will yield fewer sum–terms in the result.

We have three groups, so we expect to have three sum–terms in our POS result above. The group of 4–cells yields a 2–variable sum–term. The two groups of 2–cells give us two 3–variable sum–terms. Details are shown for how we arrived at the Sum–terms above. For a group, write the binary group input address, then complement it, converting that to the Boolean sum–term. The final result is product of the three sums.

Example: Simplify the Product–Of–Sums Boolean expression below, providing a result in SOP form.

Solution: This looks like a repeat of the last problem. It is except that we ask for a Sum–Of–Products Solution instead of the Product–Of–Sums which we just finished. Map the maxterm 0s from the Product–Of–Sums given as in the previous problem, below left. Then fill in the implied 1s in the remaining cells of the map above right. Form groups of 1s to cover all 1s. Then write the Sum–Of–Products simplified result as in the previous section of this chapter. This is identical to a previous problem.

Above we show both the Product–Of–Sums solution, from the previous example, and the Sum–Of–Products solution from the current problem for comparison. Which is the simpler solution? The POS uses 3–OR gates and 1–AND gate, while the SOP uses 3–AND gates and 1–OR gate. Both use four gates each. Taking a closer look, we count the number of gate inputs. The POS uses 8–inputs; the SOP uses 7–inputs. By the definition of minimal cost solution, the SOP solution is simpler. This is an example of a technically correct answer that is of little use in the real world.

The better solution depends on complexity and the logic family being used. The SOP solution is usually better if using the TTL logic family, as NAND gates are the basic building block, which works well with SOP implementations. On the other hand, A POS solution would be acceptable when using the CMOS logic family since all sizes of NOR gates are available. The gate diagrams for both cases are shown above, Product–Of–Sums left, and Sum–Of–Products right. Below, we take a closer look at the Sum–Of–Products version of our example logic, which is repeated at left.

Above all AND gates at left have been replaced by NAND gates at right. The OR gate at the output is replaced by a NAND gate. To prove that AND–OR logic is equivalent to NAND–NAND logic, move the inverter invert bubbles at the output of the 3–NAND gates to the input of the final NAND.

Above right we see that the output NAND gate with inverted inputs is logically equivalent to an OR gate by DeMorgan's theorem and double negation. This information is useful in building digital logic in a laboratory setting where TTL logic family NAND gates are more readily available in a wide variety of configurations than other types.

The Procedure for constructing NAND–NAND logic, in place of AND–OR logic is as follows:

- Produce a reduced Sum–Of–Products logic design.
- When drawing the wiring diagram of the SOP, replace all gates (both AND and OR) with NAND gates.
- Unused inputs should be tied to logic High.
- In case of troubleshooting, internal nodes at the first level of

NAND gate outputs do NOT match AND–OR diagram logic levels, but are inverted. Use the NAND–NAND logic diagram. Inputs and final output are identical, though.

- Label any multiple packages U1, U2,.. etc.
- Use data sheet to assign pin numbers to inputs and outputs of all gates.

Example: Let us revisit a previous problem involving an SOP minimization. Produce a Product–Of–Sums solution. Compare the POS solution to the previous SOP.

Solution: Above left we have the original problem starting with a 9–minterm Boolean unsimplified expression. Reviewing, we formed four groups of 4–cells to yield a 4–product–term SOP result, lower left.

In the middle figure, above, we fill in the empty spaces with the implied 0s. The 0s form two groups of 4–cells. The solid red group is (A'+B), the dashed red group is (C'+D). This yields two sum–terms in the Product–Of–Sums result, above right Out = (A'+B)(C'+D).

Comparing the previous SOP simplification, left, to the POS simplification, right, shows that the POS is the least cost solution. The SOP uses 5–gates total, the POS uses only 3–gates. This POS solution even looks attractive when using TTL logic due to simplicity of the result. We can find AND gates and an OR gate with 2–inputs.

The SOP and POS gate diagrams are shown above for our comparison problem. Given the pin–outs for the TTL logic family integrated circuit gates below, label the maxterm diagram above right with Circuit designators (U1–a, U1–b, U2–a, etc), and pin numbers.

Each integrated circuit package that we use will receive a circuit designator: U1, U2, U3. To distinguish between the individual gates within the package, they are identified as a, b, c, d, etc. The 7404 hex–inverter package is U1. The individual inverters in it are are U1–a, U1–b, U1–c, etc. U2 is assigned to the 7432 quad OR gate. U3 is assigned to the 7408 quad AND gate. With reference to the pin numbers on the package diagram above, we assign pin numbers to all gate inputs and outputs on the schematic diagram below.

We can now build this circuit in a laboratory setting. Or, we could design a printed circuit board for it. A printed circuit board contains copper foil "wiring" backed by a non conductive substrate of phenolic, or epoxy–fiberglass. Printed circuit boards are used to mass produce electronic circuits. Ground the inputs of unused gates.

Label the previous POS solution diagram above left (third figure back) with Circuit designators and pin numbers. This will be similar to what we just did. We can find 2–input AND gates, 7408 in the previous example. However, we have trouble finding a 4–input OR gate in our TTL catalog. The only kind of gate with 4–inputs is the 7420 NAND gate shown above right. We can make the 4–input NAND gate into a 4–input OR gate by inverting the inputs to the NAND gate. So we will use the 7420 4–input NAND gate as an OR gate by inverting the inputs.

We will not use discrete inverters to invert the inputs to the 7420 4–input NAND gate, but will drive it with 2–input NAND gates in place of the AND gates called for in the SOP, minterm, solution. The inversion at the output of the 2–input NAND gates supply the inversion for the 4–input OR gate. The result is shown above. It is the only practical way to actually build it with TTL gates by using NAND–NAND logic replacing AND–OR logic.

(SUM) AND (PRODUCT) NOTATION

For reference, this section introduces the terminology used in some texts to describe the minterms and maxterms assigned to a Karnaugh map. Otherwise, there is no new material here. (sigma) indicates sum and lower case "m" indicates minterms. m indicates sum of minterms. The following example is revisited to illustrate our point. Instead of a Boolean equation description of unsimplified logic, we list the minterms.

f(A,B,C,D) = m(1, 2, 3, 4, 5, 7, 8, 9, 11, 12, 13, 15)

or

f(A,B,C,D) = (m1,m2,m3,m4,m5,m7,m8,m9,m11,m12, m13,m15)

The numbers indicate cell location, or address, within a Karnaugh map. This is certainly a compact means of describing a list of minterms or cells in a K–map.

The Sum–Of–Products solution is not affected by the new

terminology. The minterms, 1s, in the map have been grouped as usual and a Sum–OF–Products solution written.

Below, we show the terminology for describing a list of maxterms. Product is indicated by the Greek (pi), and upper case "M" indicates maxterms. M indicates product of maxterms. The same example illustrates our point. The Boolean equation description of unsimplified logic, is replaced by a list of maxterms.

$$f(A,B,C,D) = M(2, 6, 8, 9, 10, 11, 14)$$

or

$$f(A,B,C,D) = (M2, M6, M8, M9, M10, M11, M14)$$

Once again, the numbers indicate K–map cell address locations. For maxterms this is the location of 0s. A Product–OF–Sums solution is completed in the usual manner.

CELLS IN THE KARNAUGH MAP

Up to this point we have considered logic reduction problems where the input conditions were completely specified. That is, a 3–variable truth table or Karnaugh map had 2n = 23 or 8–entries, a full table or map. It is not always necessary to fill in the complete truth table for some real–world problems. We may have a choice to not fill in the complete table.

For example, when dealing with BCD (Binary Coded Decimal) numbers encoded as four bits, we may not care about any codes above the BCD range of (0, 1, 2...9). The 4–bit binary codes for the hexadecimal numbers (Ah, Bh, Ch, Eh, Fh) are not valid BCD codes.

Thus, we do not have to fill in those codes at the end of a truth table, or K–map, if we do not care to. We would not normally care to fill in those codes because those codes (1010, 1011, 1100, 1101, 1110, 1111) will never exist as long as we are dealing only with BCD encoded numbers. These six invalid codes are don't cares as far as we are concerned. That is, we do not care what output our logic circuit produces for these don't cares. Don't cares in a Karnaugh map, or truth table, may be either 1s or 0s, as long as we don't care what the output is for an input condition we never expect to see. We plot these cells with an asterisk, *, among the normal 1s and 0s. When forming groups of cells, treat the don't care cell as either a 1 or a 0, or ignore the don't cares.

This is helpful if it allows us to form a larger group than would otherwise be possible without the don't cares. There is no requirement to group all or any of the don't cares. Only use them in a group if it simplifies the logic.

Above is an example of a logic function where the desired output is 1 for input ABC = 101 over the range from 000 to 101. We do not care what the output is for the other possible inputs (110, 111). Map those two as don't cares. We show two solutions. The solution on the right Out = AB'C is the more complex solution since we did not use the don't care cells.

The solution in the middle, Out=AC, is less complex because we grouped a don't care cell with the single 1 to form a group of two. The third solution, a Product–Of–Sums on the right, results from grouping a don't care with three zeros forming a group of four 0s. This is the same, less complex, Out=AC. We have illustrated that the don't care cells may be used as either 1s or 0s, whichever is useful.

The electronics class of Lightning State College has been asked to build the lamp logic for a stationary bicycle exhibit at the local science museum. As a rider increases his pedaling speed. No lamps will light for no motion. As speed increases, the lower lamp, L1 lights, then L1 and L2, then, L1, L2, and L3, until all lamps light at the highest speed. Once all the lamps illuminate, no further increase in speed will have any effect on the display.

A small DC generator coupled to the bicycle tire outputs a voltage proportional to speed. It drives a tachometer board which limits the voltage at the high end of speed where all lamps light. No further increase in speed can increase the voltage beyond this level. This is crucial because the downstream A to D (Analog to Digital) converter puts out a 3–bit code, ABC, 23 or 8–codes, but we only have five lamps. A is the most significant bit, C the least significant bit.

The lamp logic needs to respond to the six codes out of the A to D. For ABC=000, no motion, no lamps light. For the five codes (001 to 101) lamps L1, L1&L2, L1&L2&L3, up to all lamps will light, as speed, voltage, and the A to D code (ABC) increases. We do not care about the response to input codes (110, 111) because these codes will never come out of the A to D due to the limiting in the tachometer block. We need to design five logic circuits to drive the five lamps.

Since, none of the lamps light for ABC=000 out of the A to D, enter a 0 in all K–maps for cell ABC=000. Since we don't care about the never to be encountered codes (110, 111), enter asterisks into those two cells in all five K–maps. Lamp L5 will only light for code ABC=101. Enter a 1 in that cell and five 0s into the remaining empty cells of L5 K–map.

L4 will light initially for code ABC=100, and will remain illuminated for any code greater, ABC=101, because all lamps below L5 will light when L5 lights. Enter 1s into cells 100 and 101 of the L4 map so that it will light for those codes. Four 0's fill the remaining L4 cells

L3 will initially light for code ABC=011. It will also light whenever L5 and L4 illuminate. Enter three 1s into cells 011, 100, 101 for L3 map. Fill three 0s into the remaining L3 cells. L2 lights før ABC=010 and codes greater. Fill 1s into cells 010, 011, 100, 101, and two 0s in the remaining cells. The only time L1 is not lighted is for no motion. There is already a 0 in cell ABC=000. All the other five cells receive 1s.

Group the 1's, using don't cares whenever a larger group results. The L1 map shows three product terms, corresponding to three groups of 4–cells. We used both don't cares in two of the groups and one don't care on the third group. The don't cares allowed us to form groups of four.

In a similar manner, the L2 and L4 maps both produce groups of 4–cells with the aid of the don't care cells. The L4 reduction is striking in that the L4 lamp is controlled by the most significant bit from the A to D converter, L5=A. No logic gates are required for lamp L4. In the L3 and L5 maps, single cells form groups of two with don't care cells.

In all five maps, the reduced Boolean equation is less complex than without the don't cares.

The gate diagram for the circuit is above. The outputs of the five K–map equations drive inverters. Note that the L1 OR gate is not a 3–input gate but a 2–input gate having inputs (A+B), C, outputting A+B+C The open collector inverters, 7406, are desirable for driving LEDs, though, not part of the K–map logic design. The output of an open collecter gate or inverter is open circuited at the collector internal to the integrated circuit package so that all collector current may flow through an external load. An active high into any of the inverters pulls the output low, drawing current through the LED and the current limiting resistor. The LEDs would likely be part of a solid state relay driving 120VAC lamps for a museum exhibit, not shown here.

Larger 5 & 6–Variable Karnaugh Maps

Larger Karnaugh maps reduce larger logic designs. How large is large enough? That depends on the number of inputs, fan–ins, to the logic circuit under consideration. One of the large programmable logic companies has an answer.

Altera's own data, extracted from its library of customer designs, supports the value of heterogeneity. By examining logic cones, mapping them onto LUT–based nodes and sorting them by the number of inputs that would be best at each node, Altera found that the distribution of fan–ins was nearly flat between two and six inputs, with a nice peak at five. The answer is no more than six inputs for most all designs, and five inputs for the average logic design. The five variable Karnaugh map follows. The older version of the five variable K–map, a Gray Code map or reflection map, is shown above. The top (and side for a 6–variable map) of the map is numbered in full Gray code. The Gray code reflects about the middle of the code. This style map is found in older texts. The newer preferred style is below.

The overlay version of the Karnaugh map, shown above, is simply two (four for a 6–variable map) identical maps except for the most significant bit of the 3–bit address across the top. If we look at the top of the map, we will see that the numbering is different from the previous Gray code map. If we ignore the most significant digit of the 3–digit numbers, the sequence 00, 01, 11, 10 is at the heading of both sub maps of the overlay map. The sequence of eight 3–digit numbers is not Gray code. Though the sequence of four of the least significant two bits is.

Let's put our 5–variable Karnaugh Map to use. Design a circuit which has a 5–bit binary input (A, B, C, D, E), with A being the MSB (Most Significant Bit). It must produce an output logic High for any prime number detected in the input data.

We show the solution above on the older Gray code (reflection) map for reference. The prime numbers are (1,2,3,5,7,11,13, 17,19,23,29,31). Plot a 1 in each corresponding cell. Then, proceed with grouping of the cells. Finish by writing the simplified result. Note that 4–cell group A'B'E consists of two pairs of cell on both sides of the mirror line. The same is true of the 2–cell group AB'DE. It is a group of 2–cells by being reflected about the mirror line. When using this version of the K–map look for mirror images in the other half of the map.

Out = A'B'E + B'C'E + A'C'DE + A'CD'E + ABCE + AB'DE + A'B'C'D

Below we show the more common version of the 5–variable map, the overlay map. If we compare the patterns in the two maps, some of the cells in the right half of the map are moved around since the addressing across the top of the map is different. We also need to take a different approach at spotting commonality between the two halves of the map. Overlay one half of the map atop the other half. Any overlap from the top map to the lower map is a potential group. The figure below shows that group AB'DE is composed of two stacked cells. Group A'B'E consists of two stacked pairs of cells.

For the A'B'E group of 4–cells ABCDE = 00xx1 for the group. That is A,B,E are the same 001 respectively for the group. And, CD=xx that is it varies, no commonality in CD=xx for the group of 4–cells. Since ABCDE = 00xx1, the group of 4–cells is covered by A'B'XXE = A'B'E.

The above 5–variable overlay map is shown stacked. An example of a six variable Karnaugh map follows. We have mentally stacked the four sub maps to see the group of 4–cells corresponding to Out = C'F'

A magnitude comparator (used to illustrate a 6–variable K–map) compares two binary numbers, indicating if they are equal, greater than, or less than each other on three respective outputs. A three bit magnitude comparator has two inputs A2A1A0 and B2B1B0 An integrated circuit magnitude comparator (7485) would actually have four inputs, But, the

Karnaugh map below needs to be kept to a reasonable size. We will only solve for the A>B output. Below, a 6–variable Karnaugh map aids simplification of the logic for a 3–bit magnitude comparator. This is an overlay type of map.

The binary address code across the top and down the left side of the map is not a full 3–bit Gray code. Though the 2–bit address codes of the four sub maps is Gray code. Find redundant expressions by stacking the four sub maps atop one another (shown above). There could be cells common to all four maps, though not in the example below. It does have cells common to pairs of sub maps.

The A>B output above is ABC>XYZ on the map below.

Where ever ABC is greater than XYZ, a 1 is plotted. In the first line ABC=000 cannot be greater than any of the values of XYZ. No 1s in this line. In the second line, ABC=001, only the first cell ABCXYZ= 001000 is ABC greater than XYZ. A single 1 is entered in the first cell of the second line. The fourth line, ABC=010, has a pair of 1s. The third line, ABC=011 has three 1s. Thus, the map is filled with 1s in any cells where ABC is greater than XXZ.

In grouping cells, form groups with adjacent sub maps if possible. All but one group of 16–cells involves cells from pairs of the sub maps. Look for the following groups:

- 1 Group of 16–Cells
- 2 Groups of 8–Cells
- 4 Groups of 4–Cells

One group of 8–cells is composed of a group of 4–cells in the upper sub map overlaying a similar group in the lower left map. The second group of 8–cells is composed of a similar group of 4–cells in the right sub map overlaying the same group of 4–cells in the lower left map.

The four groups of 4–cells are shown on the Karnaugh map above with the associated product terms. Along with the product terms for the two groups of 8–cells and the group of 16–cells, the final Sum–Of–Products reduction is shown, all seven terms. Counting the 1s in the map, there is a total of 16+6+6=28 ones. Before the K–map logic reduction there would have been 28 product terms in our SOP output, each with 6–inputs. The Karnaugh map yielded seven product terms of four or less inputs. This is really what Karnaugh maps are all about! The wiring diagram is not shown. However, here is the parts list for the 3–bit magnitude comparator for ABC>XYZ using 4 TTL logic family parts:

- 1 ea 7410 triple 3–input NAND gate AX', ABY', BX'Y'
- 2 ea 7420 dual 4–input NAND gate ABCZ', ACY'Z', BCX'Z', CX'Y'Z'
- 1 ea 7430 8–input NAND gate for output of 7–P–terms

Chapter 6

Multivibrators and Counters

DIGITAL LOGIC WITH FEEDBACK

With simple gate and combinational logic circuits, there is a definite output state for any given input state. Take the truth table of an OR gate, for instance:

For each of the four possible combinations of input states (0–0, 0–1, 1–0, and 1–1), there is one, definite, unambiguous output state. Whether we're dealing with a multitude of cascaded gates or a single gate, that output state is determined by the truth table(s) for the gate(s) in the circuit, and nothing else.

However, if we alter this gate circuit so as to give signal feedback from the output to one of the inputs, strange things begin to happen:

We know that if A is 1, the output must be 1, as well. Such is the nature of an OR gate: any "high" (1) input forces the output "high" (1). If A is "low" (0), however, we cannot guarantee the logic level or state of the output in our truth table.

Since the output feeds back to one of the OR gate's inputs, and we know that any 1 input to an OR gates makes the output 1, this circuit will "latch" in the 1 output state after any time that A is 1. When A is 0, the output could be either 0 or 1, depending on the circuit's prior state! The proper way to complete the above truth table would be to insert the word latch in place of the question mark, showing that the output maintains its last state when A is 0.

Any digital circuit employing feedback is called a multivibrator. The example we just explored with the OR gate was a very simple example of what is called a bistable multivibrator. It is called "bistable" because it can hold stable in one of two possible output states, either 0 or 1. There are also monostable multivibrators, which have only one stable output state (that other state being momentary), which we'll explore later; and astable multivibrators, which have no stable state (oscillating back and forth between an output of 0 and 1). A very simple astable multivibrator is an inverter with the output fed directly back to the input:

When the input is 0, the output switches to 1. That 1 output gets fed back to the input as a 1. When the input is 1, the output switches to 0. That 0 output gets fed back to the input as a 0, and the cycle repeats itself. The result is a high frequency (several megahertz) oscillator, if implemented with a solid–state (semiconductor) inverter gate:

If implemented with relay logic, the resulting oscillator will be considerably slower, cycling at a frequency well within the audio range. The buzzer or vibrator circuit thus formed was used extensively in early radio circuitry, as a way to convert steady, low–voltage DC power into pulsating DC power which could then be stepped up in voltage through a transformer to produce the high voltage necessary for operating the vacuum tube amplifiers. Henry Ford's engineers also employed the buzzer/transformer circuit to create continuous high voltage for operating the spark plugs on Model T automobile engines:

Borrowing terminology from the old mechanical buzzer (vibrator) circuits, solid–state circuit engineers referred to any circuit with two or more vibrators linked together as a multivibrator. The astable multivibrator mentioned previously, with only one "vibrator," is more commonly implemented with multiple gates, as we'll see later.

The most interesting and widely used multivibrators are of the bistable variety, so we'll explore them in detail now.

THE S–R LATCH

A bistable multivibrator has two stable states, as indicated by the prefix bi in its name. Typically, one state is referred to as set and the other as reset. The simplest bistable device, therefore, is known as a set–reset, or S–R, latch. To create an S–R latch, we can wire two NOR gates in such a way that the output of one feeds back to the input of another, and vice versa, like this:

The Q and not–Q outputs are supposed to be in opposite states. It is "supposed to" because making both the S and R inputs equal to 1 results in both Q and not–Q being 0. For this reason, having both S and R equal to 1 is called an invalid or illegal state for the S–R multivibrator. Otherwise, making S=1 and R=0 "sets" the multivibrator so that Q=1 and not–Q=0. Conversely, making R=1 and S=0 "resets" the multivibrator in the opposite state. When S and R are both equal to 0, the multivibrator's outputs "latch" in their prior states. Note how the same multivibrator function can be implemented in ladder logic, with the same results:

By definition, a condition of Q=1 and not–Q=0 is set. A condition of Q=0 and not–Q=1 is reset. These terms are universal in describing the output states of any multivibrator circuit.

The astute observer will note that the initial power–up condition of either the gate or ladder variety of S–R latch is such that both gates (coils) start in the de–energized mode. As such, one would expect that the circuit will start up in an invalid condition, with both Q and not–Q outputs being in the same state.

Actually, this is true! However, the invalid condition is unstable with both S and R inputs inactive, and the circuit will quickly stabilize in either the set or reset condition because one gate (or relay) is bound to react a little faster than the other. If both gates (or coils) were precisely identical, they would oscillate between high and low like an astable multivibrator upon power–up without ever reaching a point of stability! Fortunately for cases like this, such a precise match of components is a rare possibility.

It must be noted that although an astable (continually oscillating) condition would be extremely rare, there will most likely be a cycle or two of oscillation in the above circuit, and the final state of the circuit (set or reset) after power–up would be unpredictable. The root of the problem is a race condition between the two relays CR1 and CR2.

A race condition occurs when two mutually–exclusive events are simultaneously initiated through different circuit elements by a single cause. In this case, the circuit elements are relays CR1 and CR2, and their de–energized states are mutually exclusive due to the normally–closed interlocking contacts. If one relay coil is de–energized, its normally–closed contact will keep the other coil energized, thus maintaining the circuit in one of two states (set or reset).

Interlocking prevents both relays from latching. However, if both relay coils start in their de–energized states (such as after the whole circuit has been de–energized and is then powered up) both relays will "race" to become latched on as they receive power (the "single cause") through the normally–closed contact of the other relay. One of those relays will inevitably reach that condition before the other, thus opening its normally–closed interlocking contact and de–energizing the other relay coil. Which relay "wins" this race is dependent on the physical characteristics of the relays and not the circuit design, so the designer cannot ensure which state the circuit will fall into after power–up.

Race conditions should be avoided in circuit design primarily for the unpredictability that will be created. One way to avoid such a condition is to insert a time–delay relay into the circuit to disable one of the competing relays for a short time, giving the other one a clear advantage. In other words, by purposely slowing down the de–energization of one relay, we ensure that the other relay will always "win" and the race results will always be predictable.

Here is an example of how a time–delay relay might be applied to the above circuit to avoid the race condition.

When the circuit powers up, time–delay relay contact TD1 in the fifth rung down will delay closing for 1 second. Having that contact open for 1 second prevents relay CR2 from energizing through contact CR1 in its normally–closed state after power–up. Therefore, relay CR1 will be allowed to energize first (with a 1–second head start), thus opening the normally–closed CR1 contact in the fifth rung, preventing CR2 from being energized without the S input going active. The end result is that the circuit powers up cleanly and predictably in the reset state with S= 0 and R = 0.

It should be mentioned that race conditions are not restricted to relay circuits. Solid–state logic gate circuits may also suffer from the ill effects of race conditions if improperly designed. Complex computer programs, for that matter, may also incur race problems if improperly designed. Race problems are a possibility for any sequential system, and may not be discovered until some time after initial testing of the system. They can be very difficult problems to detect and eliminate.

A practical application of an S–R latch circuit might be for starting and stopping a motor, using normally–open, momentary pushbutton switch contacts for both start (S) and stop (R) switches, then energizing a motor contactor with either a CR1 or CR2 contact (or using a contactor in place of CR1 or CR2). Normally, a much simpler ladder logic circuit is employed, such as this.

In the above motor start/stop circuit, the CR1 contact in parallel with the start switch contact is referred to as a "seal–in" contact, because it "seals" or latches control relay CR1 in the energized state after the start switch has been released.

To break the "seal," or to "unlatch" or "reset" the circuit, the stop pushbutton is pressed, which de–energizes CR1 and restores the seal–in contact to its normally open status. Notice, however, that this circuit performs much the same function as the S–R latch. Also note that this circuit has no inherent instability problem (if even a remote possibility) as does the double–relay S–R latch design.

In semiconductor form, S–R latches come in prepackaged units so that you don't have to build them from individual gates. They are symbolized as such.

THE GATED S–R LATCH

It is sometimes useful in logic circuits to have a multivibrator which changes state only when certain conditions are met, regardless of its S and R input states. The conditional input is called the enable, and is symbolized by the letter E. Study the following example to see how this works.

When the E = 0, the outputs of the two AND gates are forced to 0, regardless of the states of either S or R. Consequently, the circuit behaves as though S and R were both 0, latching the Q and not–Q outputs in their last states. Only when the enable input is activated (1) will the latch respond to the S and R inputs. Note the identical function in ladder logic.

A practical application of this might be the same motor control circuit (with two normally–open pushbutton switches for start and stop), except with the addition of a master lockout input (E) that disables both pushbuttons from having control over the motor when its low (0).

Once again, these multivibrator circuits are available as prepackaged semiconductor devices, and are symbolized as such: It is also common to see the enable input designated by the letters "EN" instead of just "E".

The D Latch

Since the enable input on a gated S–R latch provides a way to latch the Q and not–Q outputs without regard to the status of S or R, we can eliminate one of those inputs to create a multivibrator latch circuit with no "illegal" input states. Such a circuit is called a D latch, and its internal logic looks like this.

Note that the R input has been replaced with the complement (inversion) of the old S input, and the S input has been renamed to D. As with the gated S–R latch, the D latch will not respond to a signal input if the enable input is 0 — it simply stays latched in its last state. When the enable input is 1, however, the Q output follows the D input.

Since the R input of the S–R circuitry has been done away with, this latch has no "invalid" or "illegal" state. Q and not–Q are always opposite of one another. If the above diagram is confusing at all, the next diagram should make the concept simpler.

Like both the S–R and gated S–R latches, the D latch circuit may be found as its own prepackaged circuit, complete with a standard symbol.

The D latch is nothing more than a gated S–R latch with an inverter added to make R the complement (inverse) of S. Let's explore the ladder logic equivalent of a D latch, modified from the basic ladder diagram of an S–R latch: An application for the D latch is a 1–bit memory circuit. You can "write" (store) a 0 or 1 bit in this latch circuit by making the enable input high (1) and setting D to whatever you want the stored bit to be. When the enable input is made low (0), the latch ignores the status of the D input and merrily holds the stored bit value, outputting at the stored value at Q, and its inverse on output not–Q.

EDGE–TRIGGERED LATCHES: FLIP–FLOPS

So far, we've studied both S–R and D latch circuits with an enable inputs. The latch responds to the data inputs (S–R or D) only when the enable input is activated. In many digital applications, however, it is desirable to limit the responsiveness of a latch circuit to a very short period of time instead of the entire duration that the enabling input is activated. One method of enabling a multivibrator circuit is called edge triggering, where the circuit's data inputs have control only during the time that the enable input is transitioning from one state to another. Let's compare timing diagrams for a normal D latch versus one that is edge–triggered.

In the first timing diagram, the outputs respond to input D whenever the enable (E) input is high, for however long it remains high. When the enable signal falls back to a low state, the circuit remains latched. In the second timing diagram, we note a distinctly different response in the circuit output(s): it only responds to the D input during that brief moment of time when the enable signal changes, or transitions, from low to high. This is known as positive edge–triggering.

There is such a thing as negative edge triggering as well, and it produces the following response to the same input signals.

Whenever we enable a multivibrator circuit on the transitional edge of a square–wave enable signal, we call it a flip–flop instead of a latch. Consequently, and edge–triggered S–R circuit is more properly known as an S–R flip–flop, and an edge–triggered D circuit as a D flip–flop. The enable signal is renamed to be the clock signal. Also, we refer to the data inputs (S, R, and D, respectively) of these flip–flops as synchronous inputs, because they have effect only at the time of the clock pulse edge (transition), thereby synchronizing any output changes with that clock pulse, rather than at the whim of the data inputs.

But, how do we actually accomplish this edge–triggering? To create a "gated" S–R latch from a regular S–R latch is easy enough with a couple of AND gates, but how do we implement logic that only pays attention to the rising or falling edge of a changing digital signal? What we need is a digital circuit that outputs a brief pulse whenever the input is activated for an arbitrary period of time, and we can use the output of this circuit to briefly enable the latch. We're getting a little ahead of ourselves here, but this is actually a kind of monostable multivibrator, which for now we'll call a pulse detector.

The duration of each output pulse is set by components in the pulse circuit itself. In ladder logic, this can be accomplished quite easily through the use of a time–delay relay with a very short delay time.

Implementing this timing function with semiconductor components is actually quite easy, as it exploits the inherent time delay within every logic gate (known as propagation delay). What we do is take an input signal and split it up two ways, then place a gate or a series of gates in one of those signal paths just to delay it a bit, then have both the original signal and its delayed counterpart enter into a two–input gate that outputs a high signal for the brief moment of time that the delayed signal has not yet caught up to the low–to–high change in the non–delayed signal. An example circuit for producing a clock pulse on a low–to–high input signal transition is shown here.

This circuit may be converted into a negative–edge pulse detector circuit with only a change of the final gate from AND to NOR: Now that we know how a pulse detector can be made, we can show it attached to the enable input of a latch to turn it into a flip–flop. In this case, the circuit is a S–R flip–flop: Only when the clock signal (C) is transitioning from low to high is the circuit responsive to the S and R inputs. For any other condition of the clock signal ("x") the circuit will be latched.

A ladder logic version of the S–R flip–flop is shown here.

Relay contact CR3 in the ladder diagram takes the place of the old E contact in the S–R latch circuit, and is closed only during the short time that both C is closed and time–delay contact TR1 is closed. In either case (gate or ladder circuit), we see that the inputs S and R have no effect unless C is transitioning from a low (0) to a high (1) state. Otherwise, the flip–flop's outputs latch in their previous states.

It is important to note that the invalid state for the S–R flip–flop is maintained only for the short period of time that the pulse detector circuit allows the latch to be enabled. After that brief time period has elapsed, the outputs will latch into either the set or the reset state. Once again, the problem of a race condition manifests itself. With no enable signal, an invalid output state cannot be maintained.

However, the valid "latched" states of the multivibrator — set and reset — are mutually exclusive to one another. Therefore, the two gates of the multivibrator circuit will "race" each other for supremacy, and whichever one attains a high output state first will "win." The block symbols for flip–flops are slightly different from that of their respective latch counterparts.

The triangle symbol next to the clock inputs tells us that these are edge–triggered devices, and consequently that these are flip–flops rather than latches. The symbols above are positive edge–triggered: that is, they "clock" on the rising edge (low–to–high transition) of the clock signal. Negative edge–triggered devices are symbolized with a bubble on the clock input line: Both of the above flip–flops will "clock" on the falling edge (high–to–low transition) of the clock signal.

THE J–K FLIP–FLOP

Another variation on a theme of bistable multivibrators is the J–K flip–flop. Essentially, this is a modified version of an S–R flip–flop with no "invalid" or "illegal" output state. Look closely at the following diagram to see how this is accomplished.

What used to be the S and R inputs are now called the J and K inputs, respectively. The old two–input AND gates have been replaced with 3–input AND gates, and the third input of each gate receives feedback from the Q and not–Q outputs. What this does for us is permit the J input to have effect only when the circuit is reset, and permit the K input to have effect only when the circuit is set. In other words, the two inputs are interlocked, to use a relay logic term, so that they cannot both be activated simultaneously. If the circuit is "set," the J input is inhibited by the 0 status of not–Q through the lower AND gate; if the circuit is "reset," the K input is inhibited by the 0 status of Q through the upper AND gate.

When both J and K inputs are 1, however, something unique happens. Because of the selective inhibiting action of those 3–input AND gates, a "set" state inhibits input J so that the flip–flop acts as if J=0 while K=1 when in fact both are 1. On the next clock pulse, the outputs will switch ("toggle") from set (Q=1 and not–Q=0) to reset (Q=0 and not–Q=1). Conversely, a "reset" state inhibits input K so that the flip–flop acts as if J=1 and K=0 when in fact both are 1. The next clock pulse toggles the circuit again from reset to set. See if you can follow this logical sequence with the ladder logic equivalent of the J–K flip–flop.

The end result is that the S–R flip–flop's "invalid" state is eliminated (along with the race condition it engendered) and we get a useful feature as a bonus: the ability to toggle between the two (bistable) output states with every transition of the clock input signal.

There is no such thing as a J–K latch, only J–K flip–flops. Without the edge–triggering of the clock input, the circuit would continuously toggle between its two output states when both J and K were held high (1), making it an astable device instead of a bistable device in that circumstance. If we want to preserve bistable operation for all combinations of input states, we must use edge–triggering so that it toggles only when we tell it to, one step (clock pulse) at a time.

The block symbol for a J–K flip–flop is a whole lot less frightening than its internal circuitry, and just like the S–R and D flip–flops, J–K flip–flops come in two clock varieties (negative and positive edge–triggered).

Asynchronous Flip–flop Inputs

The normal data inputs to a flip flop (D, S and R, or J and K) are referred to as synchronous inputs because they have effect on the outputs (Q and not–Q) only in step, or in sync, with the clock signal transitions. These extra inputs that are brought to our attention are called asynchronous because they can set or reset the flip–flop regardless of the status of the clock signal. Typically, they're called preset and clear.

When the preset input is activated, the flip–flop will be set (Q=1, not–Q=0) regardless of any of the synchronous inputs or the clock. When the clear input is activated, the flip–flop will be reset (Q=0, not–Q=1), regardless of any of the synchronous inputs or the clock. So, what happens if both preset and clear inputs are activated? Surprise, surprise: we get an invalid state on the output, where Q and not–Q go to the same state, the same as our old friend, the S–R latch! Preset and clear inputs find use when multiple flip–flops are ganged together to perform a function on a multi–bit binary word, and a single line is needed to set or reset them all at once.

Asynchronous inputs, just like synchronous inputs, can be engineered to be active–high or active–low. If they're active–low, there will be an inverting bubble at that input lead on the block symbol, just like the negative edge–trigger clock inputs. Sometimes the designations "PRE" and "CLR" will be shown with inversion bars above them, to further denote the negative logic of these inputs.

Monostable Multivibrators

We've already seen one example of a monostable multivibrator in use: the pulse detector used within the circuitry of flip–flops, to enable the latch portion for a brief time when the clock input signal transitions from either low to high or high to low. The pulse detector is classified as a monostable multivibrator because it has only one stable state. By stable, we mean a state of output where the device is able to latch or hold to forever, without external prodding.

A latch or flip–flop, being a bistable device, can hold in either the "set" or "reset" state for an indefinite period of time. Once its set or reset, it will continue to latch in that state unless prompted to change by an external input. A monostable device, on the other hand, is only able to hold in one particular state indefinitely. Its other state can only be held momentarily when triggered by an external input.

A mechanical analogy of a monostable device would be a momentary contact pushbutton switch, which spring–returns to its normal (stable) position when pressure is removed from its button actuator. Likewise, a standard wall (toggle) switch, such as the type used to turn lights on and off in a house, is a bistable device. It can latch in one of two modes: on or off. All monostable multivibrators are timed devices. That is, their unstable output state will hold only for a certain minimum amount of time before returning to its stable state.

With semiconductor monostable circuits, this timing function is typically accomplished through the use of resistors and capacitors, making use of the exponential charging rates of RC circuits. A comparator is often used to compare the voltage across the charging (or discharging) capacitor with a steady reference voltage, and the on/off output of the comparator used for a logic signal.

With ladder logic, time delays are accomplished with time–delay relays, which can be constructed with semiconductor/RC circuits like that just mentioned, or mechanical delay devices which impede the immediate motion of the relay's armature. Note the design and operation of the pulse detector circuit in ladder logic.

No matter how long the input signal stays high (1), the output remains high for just 1 second of time, then returns to its normal (stable) low state. For some applications, it is necessary to have a monostable device that outputs a longer pulse than the input pulse which triggers it. Consider the following ladder logic circuit.

When the input contact closes, TD1 contact immediately closes, and stays closed for 10 seconds after the input contact opens. No matter how short the input pulse is, the output stays high (1) for exactly 10 seconds after the input drops low again. This kind of monostable multivibrator is called a one–shot. More specifically, it is a retriggerable one–shot, because the timing begins after the input drops to a low state, meaning that multiple input pulses within 10 seconds of each other will maintain a continuous high output.

One application for a retriggerable one–shot is that of a single mechanical contact debouncer. As you can see from the above timing diagram, the output will remain high despite "bouncing" of the input signal from a mechanical switch. Of course, in a real–life switch debouncer circuit, you'd probably want to use a time delay of much shorter duration than 10 seconds, as you only need to "debounce" pulses that are in the millisecond range. What if we only wanted a 10 second timed pulse output from a relay logic circuit, regardless of how many input pulses we received or how long–lived they may be? In that case, we'd have to couple a pulse–detector circuit to the retriggerable one–shot time delay circuit, like this:

Time delay relay TD1 provides an "on" pulse to time delay relay coil TD2 for an arbitrarily short moment (in this circuit, for at least 0.5 second each time the input contact is actuated). As soon as TD2 is energized, the normally–closed, timed–closed TD2 contact in series with it prevents coil TD2 from being re–energized as long as its timing out (10 seconds).

This effectively makes it unresponsive to any more actuations of the input switch during that 10 second period. Only after TD2 times out does the normally–closed, timed–closed TD2 contact in series with it allow coil TD2 to be energized again. This type of one–shot is called a nonretriggerable one–shot. One–shot multivibrators of both the retriggerable and nonretriggerable variety find wide application in industry for siren actuation and machine sequencing, where an intermittent input signal produces an output signal of a set time.

COUNTERS

BINARY COUNT SEQUENCE

If we examine a four–bit binary count sequence from 0000 to 1111, a definite pattern will be evident in the "oscillations" of the bits between 0 and 1.

Note how the least significant bit (LSB) toggles between 0 and 1 for every step in the count sequence, while each succeeding bit toggles at one–half the frequency of the one before it. The most significant bit (MSB) only toggles once during the entire sixteen–step count sequence: at the transition between 7 (0111) and 8 (1000).

If we wanted to design a digital circuit to "count" in four–bit binary, all we would have to do is design a series of frequency divider circuits, each circuit dividing the frequency of a square–wave pulse by a factor of2:

J–K flip–flops are ideally suited for this task, because they have the ability to "toggle" their output state at the command of a clock pulse when both J and K inputs are made "high" (1).

If we consider the two signals (A and B) in this circuit to represent two bits of a binary number, signal A being the LSB and signal B being the MSB, we see that the count sequence is backward: from 11 to 10 to 01 to 00 and back again to 11. Although it might not be counting in the direction we might have assumed, at least it counts!

The following sections explore different types of counter circuits, all made with J–K flip–flops, and all based on the exploitation of that flip–flop's toggle mode of operation.

Asynchronous Counters

In the previous section, we saw a circuit using one J–K flip–flop that counted backward in a two–bit binary sequence, from 11 to 10 to 01 to 00. Since it would be desirable to have a circuit that could count forward and not just backward, it would be worthwhile to examine a forward count sequence again and look for more patterns that might indicate how to build such a circuit.

Since we know that binary count sequences follow a pattern of octave (factor of 2) frequency division, and that J–K flip–flop multivibrators set up for the "toggle" mode are capable of performing this type of frequency division, we can envision a circuit made up of several J–K flip–flops, cascaded to produce four bits of output. The main problem facing us is to determine how to connect these flip–flops together so that they toggle at the right times to produce the proper binary sequence. Examine the following binary count sequence, paying attention to patterns preceding the "toggling" of a bit between 0 and 1.

Note that each bit in this four–bit sequence toggles when the bit before it (the bit having a lesser significance, or place–weight), toggles in a particular direction: from 1 to 0. Small arrows indicate those points in the sequence where a bit toggles, the head of the arrow pointing to the previous bit transitioning from a "high" (1) state to a "low" (0) state.

Starting with four J–K flip–flops connected in such a way to always be in the "toggle" mode, we need to determine how to connect the clock inputs in such a way so that each succeeding bit toggles when the bit before it transitions from 1 to 0. The Q outputs of each flip–flop will serve as the respective binary bits of the final, four–bit count.

If we used flip–flops with negative–edge triggering (bubble symbols on the clock inputs), we could simply connect the clock input of each flip–flop to the Q output of the flip–flop before it, so that when the bit before it changes from a 1 to a 0, the "falling edge" of that signal would "clock" the next flip–flop to toggle the next bit.

This circuit would yield the following output waveforms, when "clocked" by a repetitive source of pulses from an oscillator.

The first flip–flop (the one with the Q0 output), has a positive–edge triggered clock input, so it toggles with each rising edge of the clock signal. Notice how the clock signal in this example has a duty cycle less than 50%. I've shown the signal in this manner for the purpose of demonstrating how the clock signal need not be symmetrical to obtain reliable, "clean" output bits in our four–bit binary sequence. In the very first flip–flop circuit, the clock signal itself as one of the output bits.

This is a bad practice in counter design, though, because it necessitates the use of a square wave signal with a 50% duty cycle ("high" time = "low" time) in order to obtain a count sequence where each and every step pauses for the same amount of time. Using one J–K flip–flop for each output bit, however, relieves us of the necessity of having a symmetrical clock signal, allowing the use of practically any variety of high/low waveform to increment the count sequence.

As indicated by all the other arrows in the pulse diagram, each succeeding output bit is toggled by the action of the preceding bit transitioning from "high" (1) to "low" (0). This is the pattern necessary to generate an "up" count sequence.

A less obvious solution for generating an "up" sequence using positive–edge triggered flip–flops is to "clock" each flip–flop using the Q' output of the preceding flip–flop rather than the Q output.

Since the Q' output will always be the exact opposite state of the Q output on a J–K flip–flop (no invalid states with this type of flip–flop), a high–to–low transition on the Q output will be accompanied by a low–to–high transition on the Q' output. In other words, each time the Q output of a flip–flop transitions from 1 to 0, the Q' output of the same flip–flop will transition from 0 to 1, providing the positive–going clock pulse we would need to toggle a positive–edge triggered flip–flop at the right moment.

One way we could expand the capabilities of either of these two counter circuits is to regard the Q' outputs as another set of four binary bits. If we examine the pulse diagram for such a circuit, we see that the Q' outputs generate a down–counting sequence, while the Q outputs generate an up–counting sequence.

Unfortunately, all of the counter circuits shown thusfar share a common problem: the ripple effect. This effect is seen in certain types of binary adder and data conversion circuits, and is due to accumulative propagation delays between cascaded gates. When the Q output of a flip–flop transitions from 1 to 0, it commands the next flip–flop to toggle. If the next flip–flop toggle is a transition from 1 to 0, it will command the flip–flop after it to toggle as well, and so on.

However, since there is always some small amount of propagation delay between the command to toggle (the clock pulse) and the actual toggle response (Q and Q' outputs changing states), any subsequent flip–flops to be toggled will toggle some time after the first flip–flop has toggled. Thus, when multiple bits toggle in a binary count sequence, they will not all toggle at exactly the same time.

As you can see, the more bits that toggle with a given clock pulse, the more severe the accumulated delay time from LSB to MSB. When a clock pulse occurs at such a transition point (say, on the transition from 0111 to 1000), the output bits will "ripple" in sequence from LSB to MSB, as each succeeding bit toggles and commands the next bit to toggle as well, with a small amount of propagation delay between each bit toggle. If we take a close–up look at this effect during the transition from 0111 to 1000, we can see that there will be false output counts generated in the brief time period that the "ripple" effect takes place.

Instead of cleanly transitioning from a "0111" output to a "1000" output, the counter circuit will very quickly ripple from 0111 to 0110 to 0100 to 0000 to 1000, or from 7 to 6 to 4 to 0 and then to 8. This behaviour earns the counter circuit the name of ripple counter, or asynchronous counter.

In many applications, this effect is tolerable, since the ripple happens very, very quickly (the width of the delays has been exaggerated here as an aid to understanding the effects). If all we wanted to do was drive a set of light–emitting diodes (LEDs) with the counter's outputs, for example, this brief ripple would be of no consequence at all. However, if we wished to use this counter to drive the "select" inputs of a multiplexer, index a memory pointer in a microprocessor (computer) circuit, or perform some other task where false outputs could cause spurious errors, it would not be acceptable. There is a way to use this type of counter circuit in applications sensitive to false, ripple–generated outputs, and it involves a principle known as strobing.

Most decoder and multiplexer circuits are equipped with at least one input called the "enable." The output(s) of such a circuit will be active only when the enable input is made active. We can use this enable input to strobe the circuit receiving the ripple counter's output so that it is disabled (and thus not responding to the counter output) during the brief period of time in which the counter outputs might be rippling, and enabled only when sufficient time has passed since the last clock pulse that all rippling will have ceased. In most cases, the strobing signal can be the same clock pulse that drives the counter circuit.

With an active–low Enable input, the receiving circuit will respond to the binary count of the four–bit counter circuit only when the clock signal is "low." As soon as the clock pulse goes "high," the receiving circuit stops responding to the counter circuit's output. Since the counter circuit is positive–edge triggered (as determined by the first flip–flop clock input), all the counting action takes place on the low–to–high transition of the clock signal, meaning that the receiving circuit will become disabled just before any toggling occurs on the counter circuit's four output bits.

The receiving circuit will not become enabled until the clock signal returns to a low state, which should be a long enough time after all rippling has ceased to be "safe" to allow the new count to have effect on the receiving circuit.

The crucial parameter here is the clock signal's "high" time: it must be at least as long as the maximum expected ripple period of the counter circuit. If not, the clock signal will prematurely enable the receiving circuit, while some rippling is still taking place.

Another disadvantage of the asynchronous, or ripple, counter circuit is limited speed. While all gate circuits are limited in terms of maximum signal frequency, the design of asynchronous counter circuits compounds this problem by making propagation delays additive. Thus, even if strobing is used in the receiving circuit, an asynchronous counter circuit cannot be clocked at any frequency higher than that which allows the greatest possible accumulated propagation delay to elapse well before the next pulse.

The solution to this problem is a counter circuit that avoids ripple altogether. Such a counter circuit would eliminate the need to design a "strobing" feature into whatever digital circuits use the counter output as an input, and would also enjoy a much greater operating speed than its asynchronous equivalent. This design of counter circuit is the subject of the next section.

SYNCHRONOUS COUNTERS

A synchronous counter, in contrast to an asynchronous counter, is one whose output bits change state simultaneously, with no ripple. The only way we can build such a counter circuit from J–K flip–flops is to connect all the clock inputs together, so that each and every flip–flop receives the exact same clock pulse at the exact same time.

Now, the question is, what do we do with the J and K inputs? We know that we still have to maintain the same divide–by–two frequency pattern in order to count in a binary sequence, and that this pattern is best achieved utilizing the "toggle" mode of the flip–flop, so the fact that the J and K inputs must both be (at times) "high" is clear. However, if we simply connect all the J and K inputs to the positive rail of the power supply as we did in the asynchronous circuit, this would clearly not work because all the flip–flops would toggle at the same time: with each and every clock pulse!

Let's examine the four–bit binary counting sequence again, and see if there are any other patterns that predict the toggling of a bit. Asynchronous counter circuit design is based on the fact that each bit toggle happens at the same time that the preceding bit toggles from a "high" to a "low" (from 1 to 0). Since we cannot clock the toggling of a bit based on the toggling of a previous bit in a synchronous counter circuit (to do so would create a ripple effect) we must find some other pattern in the counting sequence that can be used to trigger a bit toggle.

Examining the four–bit binary count sequence, another predictive pattern can be seen. Notice that just before a bit toggles, all preceding bits are "high".

This pattern is also something we can exploit in designing a counter circuit. If we enable each J–K flip–flop to toggle based on whether or not all preceding flip–flop outputs (Q) are "high," we can obtain the same counting sequence as the asynchronous circuit without the ripple effect, since each flip–flop in this circuit will be clocked at exactly the same time:

The result is a four–bit synchronous "up" counter. Each of the higher–order flip–flops are made ready to toggle (both J and K inputs "high") if the Q outputs of all previous flip–flops are "high." Otherwise, the J and K inputs for that flip–flop will both be "low," placing it into the "latch" mode where it will maintain its present output state at the next clock pulse. Since the first (LSB) flip–flop needs to toggle at every clock pulse, its J and K inputs are connected to Vcc or Vdd, where they will be "high" all the time. The next flip–flop need only "recognize" that the first flip–flop's Q output is high to be made ready to toggle, so no AND gate is needed. However, the remaining flip–flops should be made ready to toggle only when all lower–order output bits are "high," thus the need for AND gates.

To make a synchronous "down" counter, we need to build the circuit to recognize the appropriate bit patterns predicting each toggle state while counting down. Not surprisingly, when we examine the four–bit binary count sequence, we see that all preceding bits are "low" prior to a toggle (following the sequence from bottom to top).

Since each J–K flip–flop comes equipped with a Q' output as well as a Q output, we can use the Q' outputs to enable the toggle mode on each succeeding flip–flop, being that each Q' will be "high" every time that the respective Q is "low".

Taking this idea one step further, we can build a counter circuit with selectable between "up" and "down" count modes by having dual lines of AND gates detecting the appropriate bit conditions for an "up" and a "down" counting sequence, respectively, then use OR gates to combine the AND gate outputs to the J and K inputs of each succeeding flip–flop.

This circuit isn't as complex as it might first appear. The Up/Down control input line simply enables either the upper string or lower string of AND gates to pass the Q/Q' outputs to the succeeding stages of flip–flops. If the Up/Down control line is "high," the top AND gates become enabled, and the circuit functions exactly the same as the first ("up") synchronous counter circuit shown in this section. If the Up/Down control line is made "low," the bottom AND gates become enabled, and the circuit functions identically to the second ("down" counter) circuit shown in this section.

To illustrate, here is a diagram showing the circuit in the "up" counting mode (all disabled circuitry shown in grey rather than black).

Here, shown in the "down" counting mode, with the same grey coloring representing disabled circuitry.

Up/down counter circuits are very useful devices. A common application is in machine motion control, where devices called rotary shaft encoders convert mechanical rotation into a series of electrical pulses, these pulses "clocking" a counter circuit to track total motion.

As the machine moves, it turns the encoder shaft, making and breaking the light beam between LED and phototransistor, thereby generating clock pulses to increment the counter circuit. Thus, the counter integrates, or accumulates, total motion of the shaft, serving as an electronic indication of how far the machine has moved.

If all we care about is tracking total motion, and do not care to account for changes in the direction of motion, this arrangement will suffice. However, if we wish the counter to increment with one direction of motion and decrement with the reverse direction of motion, we must use an up/down counter, and an encoder/decoding circuit having the ability to discriminate between different directions.

If we re–design the encoder to have two sets of LED/phototransistor pairs, those pairs aligned such that their square–wave output signals are 90o out of phase with each other, we have what is known as a quadrature output encoder (the word "quadrature" simply refers to a 90o angular separation). A phase detection circuit may be made from a D–type flip–flop, to distinguish a clockwise pulse sequence from a counter–clockwise pulse sequence.

When the encoder rotates clockwise, the "D" input signal square–wave will lead the "C" input square–wave, meaning that the "D" input will already be "high" when the "C" transitions from "low" to "high," thus setting the D–type flip–flop (making the Q output "high") with every clock pulse. A "high" Q output places the counter into the "Up" count mode, and any clock pulses received by the clock from the encoder (from either LED) will increment it.

Conversely, when the encoder reverses rotation, the "D" input will lag behind the "C" input waveform, meaning that it will be "low" when the "C" waveform transitions from "low" to "high," forcing the D–type flip–flop into the reset state (making the Q output "low") with every clock pulse. This "low" signal commands the counter circuit to decrement with every clock pulse from the encoder.

This circuit, or something very much like it, is at the heart of every position–measuring circuit based on a pulse encoder sensor. Such applications are very common in robotics, CNC machine tool control, and other applications involving the measurement of reversible, mechanical motion.

Chapter 7

Shift Registers

Shift registers, like counters, are a form of sequential logic. Sequential logic, unlike combinational logic is not only affected by the present inputs, but also, by the prior history. In other words, sequential logic remembers past events. Shift registers produce a discrete delay of a digital signal or waveform. A waveform synchronized to a clock, a repeating square wave, is delayed by "*n*" discrete clock times, where "n" is the number of shift register stages. Thus, a four stage shift register delays "data in" by four clocks to "data out". The stages in a shift register are delay stages, typically type "D" Flip–Flops or type "JK" Flip–flops.

Formerly, very long (several hundred stages) shift registers served as digital memory. This obsolete application is reminiscent of the acoustic mercury delay lines used as early computer memory.

Serial data transmission, over a distance of meters to kilometers, uses shift registers to convert parallel data to serial form. Serial data communications replaces many slow parallel data wires with a single serial high speed circuit.

Serial data over shorter distances of tens of centimeters, uses shift registers to get data into and out of microprocessors. Numerous peripherals, including analog to digital converters, digital to analog converters, display drivers, and memory, use shift registers to reduce the amount of wiring in circuit boards.

Some specialized counter circuits actually use shift registers to generate repeating waveforms. Longer shift registers, with the help of feedback generate patterns so long that they look like random noise, pseudo–noise.

Basic shift registers are classified by structure according to the following types:

- Serial–in/serial–out
- Parallel–in/serial–out
- Serial–in/parallel–out
- Universal parallel–in/parallel–out
- Ring counter

Above we show a block diagram of a serial–in/serial–out shift register, which is 4–stages long. Data at the input will be delayed by four clock periods from the input to the output of the shift register.

Data at "data in", above, will be present at the Stage A output after the first clock pulse. After the second pulse stage A data is transfered to stage B output, and "data in" is transfered to stage A output. After the third clock, stage C is replaced by stage B; stage B is replaced by stage A; and stage A is replaced by "data in". After the fourth clock, the data originally present at "data in" is at stage D, "output". The "first in" data is "first out" as it is shifted from "data in" to "data out".

Data is loaded into all stages at once of a parallel–in/serial–out shift register. The data is then shifted out via "data out" by clock pulses. Since a 4– stage shift register is shown above, four clock pulses are required to shift out all of the data.

In the diagram above, stage D data will be present at the "data out" up until the first clock pulse; stage C data will be present at "data out" between the first clock and the second clock pulse; stage B data will be present between the second clock and the third clock; and stage A data will be present between the third and the fourth clock. After the fourth clock pulse and thereafter, successive bits of "data in" should appear at "data out" of the shift register after a delay of four clock pulses.

If four switches were connected to DA through DD, the status could be read into a microprocessor using only one data pin and a clock pin. Since adding more switches would require no additional pins, this approach looks attractive for many inputs.

Above, four data bits will be shifted in from "data in" by four clock pulses and be available at QA through QD for driving external circuitry such as LEDs, lamps, relay drivers, and horns.

After the first clock, the data at "data in" appears at QA. After the second clock, The old QA data appears at QB; QA receives next data from "data in". After the third clock, QB data is at QC. After the fourth clock, QC data is at QD. This stage contains the data first present at "data in". The shift register should now contain four data bits.

A parallel–in/laralel–out shift register combines the function of the parallel–in, serial–out shift register with the function of the serial–in, parallel–out shift register to yields the universal shift register. The "do anything" shifter comes at a price– the increased number of I/O (Input/ Output) pins may reduce the number of stages which can be packaged.

Data presented at DA through DD is parallel loaded into the registers. This data at QA through QD may be shifted by the number of pulses presented at the clock input. The shifted data is available at QA through QD. The "mode" input, which may be more than one input, controls parallel loading of data from DA through DD, shifting of data, and the direction of shifting. There are shift registers which will shift data either left or right.

If the serial output of a shift register is connected to the serial input, data can be perpetually shifted around the ring as long as clock pulses are present. If the output is inverted before being fed back, we do not have to worry about loading the initial data into the "ring counter".

SERIAL–IN/SERIAL–OUT SHIFT REGISTER

Serial–in, serial–out shift registers delay data by one clock time for each stage. They will store a bit of data for each register. A serial–in, serial–out shift register may be one to 64 bits in length, longer if registers or packages are cascaded.

Below is a single stage shift register receiving data which is not synchronized to the register clock. The "data in" at the D pin of the type D FF (Flip–Flop) does not change levels when the clock changes for low to high. We may want to synchronize the data to a system wide clock in a circuit board to improve the reliability of a digital logic circuit.

The obvious point (as compared to the figure below) illustrated above is that whatever "data in" is present at the D pin of a type D FF is transfered from D to output Q at clock time. Since our example shift register uses positive edge sensitive storage elements, the output Q follows the D input when the clock transitions from low to high as shown by the up arrows.

There is no doubt what logic level is present at clock time because the data is stable well before and after the clock edge. This is seldom the case in multi–stage shift registers. But, this was an easy example to start with. We are only concerned with the positive, low to high, clock edge. The falling edge can be ignored. It is very easy to see Q follow D at clock time above. Compare this to the diagram below where the "data in" appears to change with the positive clock edge.

Since "data in" appears to changes at clock time t1 above, what does the type D FF see at clock time? The short over simplified answer is that it sees the data that was present at D prior to the clock. That is what is transfered to Q at clock time t1. The correct waveform is QC. At t1 Q goes to a zero if it is not already zero. The D register does not see a one until time t2, at which time Q goes high.

Since data, above, present at D is clocked to Q at clock time, and Q cannot change until the next clock time, the D FF delays data by one clock period, provided that the data is already synchronized to the clock. The QA waveform is the same as "data in" with a one clock period delay.

A more detailed look at what the input of the type D Flip–Flop sees at clock time follows. Refer to the figure below. Since "data in" appears to changes at clock time (above), we need further information to determine what the D FF sees. If the "data in" is from another shift register stage, another same type D FF, we can draw some conclusions based on data sheet information. Manufacturers of digital logic make available information about their parts in data sheets, formerly only available in a collection called a data book. Data books are still available; though, the manufacturer's web site is the modern source.

The following data was extracted from the CD4006b data sheet for operation at 5VDC, which serves as an example to illustrate timing.

- tS = 100ns
- tH = 60ns
- tP = 200–400ns typ/max

tS is the setup time, the time data must be present before clock time. In this case data must be present at D 100ns prior to the clock. Furthermore, the data must be held for hold time tH=60ns after clock time. These two conditions must be met to reliably clock data from D to Q of the Flip–Flop.

There is no problem meeting the setup time of 60ns as the data at D has been there for the whole previous clock period if it comes from another shift register stage. For example, at a clock frequency of 1 Mhz, the clock period is 1000 μs, plenty of time. Data will actually be present for 1000μs prior to the clock, which is much greater than the minimum required tS of 60ns. The hold time tH=60ns is met because D connected to Q of another stage cannot change any faster than the propagation delay of the previous stage tP=200ns. Hold time is met as long as the propagation delay of the previous D FF is greater than the hold time. Data at D driven by another stage Q will not change any faster than 200ns for the CD4006b.

To summarize, output Q follows input D at nearly clock time if Flip–Flops are cascaded into a multi–stage shift register. Three type D Flip–Flops are cascaded Q to D and the clocks paralleled to form a three stage shift register above. Type JK FFs cascaded Q to J, Q' to K with clocks in parallel to yield an alternate form of the shift register above.

A serial–in/serial–out shift register has a clock input, a data input, and a data output from the last stage. In general, the other stage outputs are not available Otherwise, it would be a serial–in, parallel–out shift register. The waveforms below are applicable to either one of the preceding two versions of the serial–in, serial–out shift register. The three pairs of arrows show that a three stage shift register temporarily stores 3–bits of data and delays it by three clock periods from input to output.

At clock time t1 a "data in" of 0 is clocked from D to Q of all three stages. In particular, D of stage A sees a logic 0, which is clocked to QA where it remains until time t2. At clock time t2 a "data in" of 1 is clocked from D to QA. At stages B and C, a 0, fed from preceding stages is clocked to QB and QC. At clock time t3 a "data in" of 0 is clocked from D to QA. QA goes low and stays low for the remaining clocks due to "data in" being 0. QB goes high at t3 due to a 1 from the previous stage. QC is still low after t3 due to a low from the previous stage. QC finally goes high at clock t4 due to the high fed to D from the previous stage QB. All earlier stages have 0s shifted into them. And, after the next clock pulse at t5, all logic 1s will have been shifted out, replaced by 0s

Serial–In/Serial–Out Devices

We will take a closer look at the following parts available as integrated circuits, courtesy of Texas Instruments. For complete device data sheets follow the links.

- CD4006b 18–bit serial–in/ serial–out shift register
- CD4031b 64–bit serial–in/ serial–out shift register
- CD4517b dual 64–bit serial–in/ serial–out shift register

The following serial–in/ serial–out shift registers are 4000 series CMOS (Complementary Metal Oxide Semiconductor) family parts. As such, They will accept a VDD, positive power supply of 3–Volts to 15–Volts. The VSS pin is grounded. The maximum frequency of the shift clock, which varies with VDD, is a few megahertz. See the full data sheet for details.

The 18–bit CD4006b consists of two stages of 4–bits and two more stages of 5–bits with a an output tap at 4–bits. Thus, the 5–bit stages could be used as 4–bit shift registers. To get a full 18–bit shift register the output of one shift register must be cascaded to the input of another and so on until all stages create a single shift register.

A CD4031 64–bit serial–in/ serial–out shift register is shown below. A number of pins are not connected (nc). Both Q and Q' are available from the 64th stage, actually Q64 and Q'64. There is also a Q64 "delayed" from a half stage which is delayed by half a clock cycle. A major feature is a data selector which is at the data input to the shift register.

The "mode control" selects between two inputs: data 1 and data 2. If "mode control" is high, data will be selected from "data 2" for input to the shift register. In the case of "mode control" being logic low, the "data 1" is selected. Examples of this are shown in the two figures below.

The "data 2" above is wired to the Q64 output of the shift register. With "mode control" high, the Q64 output is routed back to the shifter data input D. Data will recirculate from output to input. The data will repeat every 64 clock pulses. The question that arises is how did this data pattern get into the shift register in the first place?

With "mode control" low, the CD4031 "data 1" is selected for input to the shifter. The output, Q64, is not recirculated because the lower data selector gate is disabled. By disabled we mean that the logic low "mode select" inverted twice to a low at the lower NAND gate prevents it for passing any signal on the lower pin (data 2) to the gate output. Thus, it is disabled.

A CD4517b dual 64–bit shift register is shown above. Note the taps at the 16th, 32nd, and 48th stages. That means that shift registers of those lengths can be configured from one of the 64–bit shifters. Of course, the 64–bit shifters may be cascaded to yield an 80–bit, 96–bit, 112–bit, or 128–bit shift register. The clock CLA and CLB need to be paralleled when cascading the two shifters. WEB and WEB are grounded for normal shifting operations. The data inputs to the shift registers A and B are DA and DB respectively.

Suppose that we require a 16–bit shift register. Can this be configured with the CD4517b? How about a 64–shift register from the same part?

Above we show A CD4517b wired as a 16–bit shift register for section B. The clock for section B is CLB. The data is clocked in at CLB. And the data delayed by 16–clocks is picked of off Q16B. WEB, the write enable, is grounded.

Above we also show the same CD4517b wired as a 64–bit shift register for the independent section A. The clock for section A is CLA. The data enters at CLA. The data delayed by 64–clock pulses is picked up from Q64A. WEA, the write enable for section A, is grounded.

PARALLEL–IN, SERIAL–OUT SHIFT REGISTER

Parallel–in/ serial–out shift registers do everything that the previous serial–in/ serial–out shift registers do plus input data to all stages simultaneously. The parallel–in/ serial–out shift register stores data, shifts it on a clock by clock basis, and delays it by the number of stages times the clock period. In addition, parallel–in/ serial–out really means that we can load data in parallel into all stages before any shifting ever begins.

This is a way to convert data from a parallel format to a serial format. By parallel format we mean that the data bits are present simultaneously on individual wires, one for each data bit. By serial format we mean that the data bits are presented sequentially in time on a single wire or circuit as in the case of the "data out" on the block diagram below.

Below we take a close look at the internal details of a 3–stage parallel–in/ serial–out shift register. A stage consists of a type D Flip–Flop for storage, and an AND–OR selector to determine whether data will load in parallel, or shift stored data to the right. In general, these elements will be replicated for the number of stages required. We show three stages due to space limitations. Four, eight or sixteen bits is normal for real parts.

Above we show the parallel load path when SHIFT/LD' is logic low. The upper NAND gates serving DA DB DC are enabled, passing data to the D inputs of type D Flip–Flops QA QB DC respectively. At the next positive going clock edge, the data will be clocked from D to Q of the three FFs. Three bits of data will load into QA QB DC at the same time.

The type of parallel load just described, where the data loads on a clock pulse is known as synchronous load because the loading of data is synchronized to the clock. This needs to be differentiated from asynchronous load where loading is controlled by the preset and clear pins of the Flip–Flops which does not require the clock. Only one of these load methods is used within an individual device, the synchronous load being more common in newer devices.

The shift path is shown above when SHIFT/LD' is logic high. The lower AND gates of the pairs feeding the OR gate are enabled giving us a shift register connection of SI to DA, QA to DB, QB to DC, QC to SO. Clock pulses will cause data to be right shifted out to SO on successive pulses.

The waveforms below show both parallel loading of three bits of data and serial shifting of this data. Parallel data at DA DB DC is converted to serial data at SO.

What we previously described with words for parallel loading and shifting is now set down as waveforms above. As an example we present 101 to the parallel inputs DAA DBB DCC. Next, the SHIFT/LD' goes low enabling loading of data as opposed to shifting of data. It needs to be low a short time before and after the clock pulse due to setup and hold requirements. It is considerably wider than it has to be. Though, with synchronous logic it is convenient to make it wide. We could have made the active low SHIFT/LD' almost two clocks wide, low almost a clock before t1 and back high just before t3. The important factor is that it needs to be low around clock time t1 to enable parallel loading of the data by the clock.

Note that at t1 the data 101 at DA DB DC is clocked from D to Q of the Flip–Flops as shown at QA QB QC at time t1. This is the parallel loading of the data synchronous with the clock.

Now that the data is loaded, we may shift it provided that SHIFT/LD' is high to enable shifting, which it is prior to t2. At t2 the data 0 at QC is shifted out of SO which is the same as the QC waveform. It is either shifted into another integrated circuit, or lost if there is nothing connected to SO. The data at QB, a 0 is shifted to QC. The 1 at QA is shifted into QB. With "data in" a 0, QA becomes 0. After t2, QA QB QC = 010.

After t3, QA QB QC = 001. This 1, which was originally present at QA after t1, is now present at SO and QC. The last data bit is shifted out to an external integrated circuit if it exists. After t4 all data from the parallel load is gone. At clock t5 we show the shifting in of a data 1 present on the SI, serial input.

Why provide SI and SO pins on a shift register? These connections allow us to cascade shift register stages to provide large shifters than available in a single IC (Integrated Circuit) package. They also allow serial connections to and from other ICs like microprocessors.

Parallel–In/Serial–Out Devices

Let's take a closer look at parallel–in/ serial–out shift registers available as integrated circuits, courtesy of Texas Instruments. For complete device data sheets follow these the links.

- SN74ALS166 parallel–in/ serial–out 8–bit shift register, synchronous load
- SN74ALS165 parallel–in/ serial–out 8–bit shift register, asynchronous load
- CD4014B parallel–in/ serial–out 8–bit shift register, synchronous load
- SN74LS647 parallel–in/ serial–out 16–bit shift register, synchronous load

The SN74ALS166 shown above is the closest match of an actual part to the previous parallel–in/ serial out shifter figures. First of all, there are 8–stages. We only show three. All 8–stages are shown on the data sheet available at the link above. The manufacturer labels the data inputs A, B, C, and so on to H. The SHIFT/LOAD control is called SH/LD'. It is abbreviated from our previous terminology, but works the same: parallel load if low, shift if high. The shift input (serial data in) is SER on the ALS166 instead of SI. The clock CLK is controlled by an inhibit signal, CLKINH. If CLKINH is high, the clock is inhibited, or disabled. Otherwise, this "real part" is the same as what we have looked at in detail.

Above is the ANSI (American National Standards Institute) symbol for the SN74ALS166 as provided on the data sheet. Once we know how the part operates, it is convenient to hide the details within a symbol. There are many general forms of symbols. The advantage of the ANSI symbol is that the labels provide hints about how the part operates.

The large notched block at the top of the '74ASL166 is the control section of the ANSI symbol. There is a reset indicted by R. There are three control signals: M1 (Shift), M2 (Load), and C3/1 (arrow) (inhibited clock). The clock has two functions. First, C3 for shifting parallel data wherever a prefix of 3 appears. Second, whenever M1 is asserted, as indicated by the 1 of C3/1 (arrow), the data is shifted as indicated by the right pointing arrow. The slash (/) is a separator between these two functions. The 8–

shift stages, as indicated by title SRG8, are identified by the external inputs A, B, C, to H.

The internal 2, 3D indicates that data, D, is controlled by M2 and C3 clock. In this case, we can conclude that the parallel data is loaded synchronously with the clock C3. The upper stage at A is a wider block than the others to accommodate the input SER. The legend 1, 3D implies that SER is controlled by M1 and C3 clock. Thus, we expect to clock in data at SER when shifting as opposed to parallel loading.

The ANSI/IEEE basic gate rectangular symbols are provided above for comparison to the more familiar shape symbols so that we may decipher the meaning of the symbology associated with the CLKINH and CLK pins on the previous ANSI SN74ALS166 symbol. The CLK and CLKINH feed an OR gate on the SN74ALS166 ANSI symbol. OR is indicated by => on the rectangular inset symbol.

The long triangle at the output indicates a clock. If there was a bubble with the arrow this would have indicated shift on negative clock edge (high to low). Since there is no bubble with the clock arrow, the register shifts on the positive (low to high transition) clock edge. The long arrow, after the legend C3/1 pointing right indicates shift right, which is down the symbol.

Part of the internal logic of the SN74ALS165 parallel–in/ serial–out, asynchronous load shift register is reproduced from the data sheet above. See the link at the beginning of this section the for the full diagram. We have not looked at asynchronous loading of data up to this point. First of all, the loading is accomplished by application of appropriate signals to the Set (preset) and Reset (clear) inputs of the Flip–Flops. The upper NAND gates feed the Set pins of the FFs and also cascades into the lower NAND gate feeding the Reset pins of the FFs. The lower NAND gate inverts the signal in going from the Set pin to the Reset pin.

First, SH/LD' must be pulled Low to enable the upper and lower NAND gates. If SH/LD' were at a logic high instead, the inverter feeding a logic low to all NAND gates would force a High out, releasing the "active low" Set and Reset pins of all FFs. There would be no possibility of loading the FFs.

With SH/LD' held Low, we can feed, for example, a data 1 to parallel input A, which inverts to a zero at the upper NAND gate output, setting FF QA to a 1. The 0 at the Set pin is fed to the lower NAND gate where it is inverted to a 1, releasing the Reset pin of QA. Thus, a data A=1 sets QA=1. Since none of this required the clock, the loading is asynchronous with respect to the clock. We use an asynchronous loading shift register if we cannot wait for a clock to parallel load data, or if it is inconvenient to generate a single clock pulse.

The only difference in feeding a data 0 to parallel input A is that it inverts to a 1 out of the upper gate releasing Set. This 1 at Set is inverted to a 0 at the lower gate, pulling Reset to a Low, which resets QA=0.

The ANSI symbol for the SN74ALS166 above has two internal controls C1 [LOAD] and C2 clock from the OR function of (CLKINH, CLK). SRG8 says 8–stage shifter. The arrow after C2 indicates shifting right or down. SER input is a function of the clock as indicated by internal label 2D. The parallel data inputs A, B, C to H are a function of C1 [LOAD], indicated by internal label 1D. C1 is asserted when sh/LD' =0 due to the half–arrow inverter at the input. Compare this to the control of the parallel data inputs by the clock of the previous synchronous ANSI SN75ALS166. Note the differences in the ANSI Data labels.

On the CD4014B above, M1 is asserted when LD/SH'=0. M2 is asserted when LD/SH'=1. Clock C3/1 is used for parallel loading data at 2, 3D when M2 is active as indicated by the 2,3 prefix labels. Pins P3 to P7 are understood to have the smae internal 2,3 prefix labels as P2 and P8. At SER, the 1,3D prefix implies that M1 and clock C3 are necessary to input serial data. Right shifting takes place when M1 active is as indicated by the 1 in C3/1 arrow.

The CD4021B is a similar part except for asynchronous parallel loading of data as implied by the lack of any 2 prefix in the data label 1D for pins P1, P2, to P8. Of course, prefix 2 in label 2D at input SER says that data is clocked into this pin. The OR gate inset shows that the clock is controlled by LD/SH'.

The above SN74LS674 internal label SRG 16 indicates 16–bit shift register. The MODE input to the control section at the top of the symbol is labeled 1,2 M3. Internal M3 is a function of input MODE and G1 and G2 as indicated by the 1,2 preceding M3.

The base label G indicates an AND function of any such G inputs. Input R/W' is internally labeled G1/2 EN. This is an enable EN (controlled by G1 AND G2) for tristate devices used elsewhere in the symbol. We note that CS' on (pin 1) is internal G2. Chip select CS' also is ANDed with the input CLK to give internal clock C4. The bubble within the clock arrow indicates that activity is on the negative (high to low transition) clock edge. The slash (/) is a separator implying two functions for the clock. Before the slash, C4 indicates control of anything with a prefix of 4. After the slash, the 3' (arrow) indicates shifting. The 3' of C4/3' implies shifting when M3 is de–asserted (MODE=0). The long arrow indicates shift right (down).

Moving down below the control section to the data section, we have external inputs P0–P15, pins (7–11, 13–23). The prefix 3,4 of internal label 3,4D indicates that M3 and the clock C4 control loading of parallel data. The D stands for Data. This label is assumed to apply to all the parallel inputs, though not explicitly written out. Locate the label 3',4D on the right of the P0 (pin7) stage. The complemented–3 indicates that M3=MODE=0 inputs (shifts) SER/Q15 (pin5) at clock time, (4 of 3',4D) corresponding to clock C4. In other words, with MODE=0, we shift data into Q0 from the serial input (pin 6). All other stages shift right (down) at clock time.

Moving to the bottom of the symbol, the triangle pointing right indicates a buffer between Q and the output pin. The Triangle pointing down indicates a tri–state device. We previously stated that the tristate is controlled by enable EN, which is actually G1 AND G2 from the control section. If R/W=0, the tri–state is disabled, and we can shift data into Q0 via SER (pin 6), a detail we omitted above. We actually need MODE=0, R/W'=0, CS'=0.

The internal logic of the SN74LS674 and a table summarizing the operation of the control signals is available in the link in the bullet list, top of section. If R/W'=1, the tristate is enabled, Q15 shifts out SER/Q15 (pin 6) and recirculates to the Q0 stage via the right hand wire to 3',4D. We have assumed that CS' was low giving us clock C4/3' and G2 to ENable the tri–state.

Practical Applications

An application of a parallel–in/ serial–out shift register is to read data into a microprocessor.

The Alarm above is controlled by a remote keypad. The alarm box supplies +5V and ground to the remote keypad to power it. The alarm reads the remote keypad every few tens of milliseconds by sending shift clocks to the keypad which returns serial data showing the status of the keys via a parallel–in/ serial–out shift register. Thus, we read nine key switches with four wires. How many wires would be required if we had to run a circuit for each of the nine keys?

A practical application of a parallel–in/ serial–out shift register is to read many switch closures into a microprocessor on just a few pins. Some low end microprocessors only have 6–I/O (Input/Output) pins available on an 8–pin package. Or, we may have used most of the pins on an 84–pin package. We may want to reduce the number of wires running around a circuit board, machine, vehicle, or building. This will increase the reliability of our system. It has been reported that manufacturers who have reduced the number of wires in an automobile produce a more reliable product. In any event, only three microprocessor pins are required to read in 8–bits of data. We have chosen an asynchronous loading device, the CD4021B because it is easier to control the loading of data without having to generate a single parallel load clock.

The parallel data inputs of the shift register are pulled up to +5V with a resistor on each input. If all switches are open, all 1s will be loaded into the shift register when the microprocessor moves the LD/SH' line from low to high, then back low in anticipation of shifting. Any switch closures will apply logic 0s to the corresponding parallel inputs. The data pattern at P1–P7 will be parallel loaded by the LD/SH'=1 generated by the microprocessor software.

The microprocessor generates shift pulses and reads a data bit for each of the 8–bits. This process may be performed totally with software, or larger microprocessors may have one or more serial interfaces to do the task more quickly with hardware. With LD/SH'=0, the microprocessor generates a 0 to 1 transition on the Shift clock line, then reads a data bit on the Serial data in line. This is repeated for all 8–bits.

The SER line of the shift register may be driven by another identical CD4021B circuit if more switch contacts need to be read. In which case, the microprocessor generates 16–shift pulses. More likely, it will be driven by something else compatible with this serial data format, for example, an analog to digital converter, a temperature sensor, a keyboard scanner, a serial read–only memory. As for the switch closures, they may be limit switches on the carriage of a machine, an over–temperature sensor, a magnetic reed switch, a door or window switch, an air or water pressure switch, or a solid state optical interrupter.

SERIAL–IN, PARALLEL–OUT SHIFT REGISTER

A serial–in/parallel–out shift register is similar to the serial–in/ serial–out shift register in that it shifts data into internal storage elements and shifts data out at the serial–out, data–out, pin. It is different in that it makes all the internal stages available as outputs. Therefore, a serial–in/parallel–out shift register converts data from serial format to parallel format. If four data bits are shifted in by four clock pulses via a single wire at data–in, below, the data becomes available simultaneously on the four Outputs QA to QD after the fourth clock pulse.

The practical application of the serial–in/parallel–out shift register is to convert data from serial format on a single wire to parallel format on multiple wires. Perhaps, we will illuminate four LEDs (Light Emitting Diodes) with the four outputs (QA QB QC QD).

The above details of the serial–in/parallel–out shift register are fairly simple. It looks like a serial–in/ serial–out shift register with taps added to each stage output. Serial data shifts in at SI (Serial Input). After a number of clocks equal to the number of stages, the first data bit in appears at SO (QD) in the above figure. In general, there is no SO pin. The last stage (QD above) serves as SO and is cascaded to the next package if it exists.

If a serial–in/parallel–out shift register is so similar to a serial–in/ serial–out shift register, why do manufacturers bother to offer both types? Why not just offer the serial–in/parallel–out shift register? They actually only offer the serial–in/parallel–out shift register, as long as it has no more than 8–bits. Note that serial–in/ serial–out shift registers come in gigger than 8–bit lengths of 18 to to 64–bits. It is not practical to offer a 64–bit serial–in/parallel–out shift register requiring that many output pins. See waveforms below for above shift register.

The shift register has been cleared prior to any data by CLR', an active low signal, which clears all type D Flip–Flops within the shift register. Note the serial data 1011 pattern presented at the SI input. This data is synchronized with the clock CLK. This would be the case if it is being shifted in from something like another shift register, for example, a parallel–in/ serial–out shift register (not shown here).

On the first clock at t1, the data 1 at SI is shifted from D to Q of the first shift register stage. After t2 this first data bit is at QB. After t3 it is at QC. After t4 it is at QD. Four clock pulses have shifted the first data bit all the way to the last stage QD. The second data bit a 0 is at QC after the 4th clock. The third data bit a 1 is at QB. The fourth data bit another 1 is at QA. Thus, the serial data input pattern 1011 is contained in (QD QC QB QA). It is now available on the four outputs.

It will available on the four outputs from just after clock t4 to just before t5. This parallel data must be used or stored between these two times, or it will be lost due to shifting out the QD stage on following clocks t5 to t8.

Serial–In/Parallel–Out Devices

Let's take a closer look at Serial–in/ parallel–out shift registers available as integrated circuits, courtesy of Texas Instruments. For complete device data sheets follow the links.

- SN74ALS164A serial–in/ parallel–out 8–bit shift register
- SN74AHC594 serial–in/ parallel–out 8–bit shift register with output register
- SN74AHC595 serial–in/ parallel–out 8–bit shift register with output register
- CD4094 serial–in/ parallel–out 8–bit shift register with output register

The 74ALS164A is almost identical to our prior diagram with the exception of the two serial inputs A and B. The unused input should be pulled high to enable the other input. We do not show all the stages above. However, all the outputs are shown on the ANSI symbol below, along with the pin numbers.

The CLK input to the control section of the above ANSI symbol has two internal functions C1, control of anything with a prefix of 1. This would be clocking in of data at 1D. The second function, the arrow after after the slash (/) is right (down) shifting of data within the shift register. The eight outputs are available to the right of the eight registers below the control section. The first stage is wider than the others to accommodate the A&B input.

The above internal logic diagram is adapted from the TI (Texas Instruments) data sheet for the 74AHC594. The type "D" FFs in the top row comprise a serial–in/ parallel–out shift register. This section works like the previously described devices. The outputs (QA' QB' to QH') of the shift register half of the device feed the type "D" FFs in the lower half in parallel. QH' (pin 9) is shifted out to any optional cascaded device package.

A single positive clock edge at RCLK will transfer the data from D to Q of the lower FFs. All 8–bits transfer in parallel to the output register (a collection of storage elements). The purpose of the output register is to maintain a constant data output while new data is being shifted into the upper shift register section. This is necessary if the outputs drive relays, valves, motors, solenoids, horns, or buzzers. This feature may not be necessary when driving LEDs as long as flicker during shifting is not a problem.

Note that the 74AHC594 has separate clocks for the shift register (SRCLK) and the output register (RCLK). Also, the shifter may be cleared by SRCLR and, the output register by RCLR. It desirable to put the outputs in a known state at power–on, in particular, if driving relays, motors, etc. The waveforms below illustrate shifting and latching of data.

The above waveforms show shifting of 4–bits of data into the first four stages of 74AHC594, then the parallel transfer to the output register. In actual fact, the 74AHC594 is an 8–bit shift register, and it would take 8–clocks to shift in 8–bits of data, which would be the normal mode of operation. However, the 4–bits we show saves space and adequately illustrates the operation.

We clear the shift register half a clock prior to t0 with SRCLR'=0. SRCLR' must be released back high prior to shifting. Just prior to t0 the output register is cleared by RCLR'=0. It, too, is released (RCLR'=1).

Serial data 1011 is presented at the SI pin between clocks t0 and t4. It is shifted in by clocks t1 t2 t3 t4 appearing at internal shift stages QA' QB' QC' QD'. This data is present at these stages between t4 and t5. After t5 the desired data (1011) will be unavailable on these internal shifter stages. Between t4 and t5 we apply a positive going RCLK transferring data 1011 to register outputs QA QB QC QD. This data will be frozen here as more data (0s) shifts in during the succeeding SRCLKs (t5 to t8). There will not be a change in data here until another RCLK is applied. The 74AHC595 is identical to the '594 except that the RCLR' is replaced by an OE' enabling a tri–state buffer at the output of each of the eight output register bits. Though the output register cannot be cleared, the outputs may be disconnected by OE'=1.

This would allow external pull–up or pull–down resistors to force any relay, solenoid, or valve drivers to a known state during a system power–up. Once the system is powered–up and, say, a microprocessor has shifted and latched data into the '595, the output enable could be asserted (OE'=0) to drive the relays, solenoids, and valves with valid data, but, not before that time. Above are the proposed ANSI symbols for these devices. C3 clocks data into the serial input (external SER) as indicate by the 3 prefix of 2,3D. The arrow after C3/ indicates shifting right (down) of the shift register, the 8–stages to the left of the '595symbol below the control section. The 2 prefix of 2,3D and 2D indicates that these stages can be reset by R2 (external SRCLR').

The 1 prefix of 1,4D on the '594 indicates that R1 (external RCLR') may reset the output register, which is to the right of the shift register section. The '595, which has an EN at external OE' cannot reset the output register. But, the EN enables tristate (inverted triangle) output buffers. The right pointing triangle of both the '594 and'595 indicates internal buffering. Both the '594 and'595 output registers are clocked by C4 as indicated by 4 of 1,4D and 4D respectively.

The CD4094B is a 3 to 15VDC capable latching shift register alternative to the previous 74AHC594 devices. CLOCK, C1, shifts data in at SERIAL IN as implied by the 1 prefix of 1D. It is also the clock of the right shifting shift register (left half of the symbol body) as indicated by the/(right–arrow) of C1/(arrow) at the CLOCK input.

STROBE, C2 is the clock for the 8–bit output register to the right of the symbol body. The 2 of 2D indicates that C2 is the clock for the output register. The inverted triangle in the output latch indicates that the output is tristated, being enabled by EN3. The 3 preceding the inverted triangle and the 3 of EN3 are often omitted, as any enable (EN) is understood to control the tristate outputs. QS and QS' are non–latched outputs of the shift register stage. QS could be cascaded to SERIAL IN of a succeeding device.

Practical Applications

A real–world application of the serial–in/ parallel–out shift register is to output data from a microprocessor to a remote panel indicator. Or, another remote output device which accepts serial format data.

The figure "Alarm with remote key pad" is repeated here from the parallel–in/ serial–out section with the addition of the remote display.

Thus, we can display, for example, the status of the alarm loops connected to the main alarm box. If the Alarm detects an open window, it can send serial data to the remote display to let us know. Both the keypad and the display would likely be contained within the same remote enclosure, separate from the main alarm box. However, we will only look at the display panel in this section.

If the display were on the same board as the Alarm, we could just run eight wires to the eight LEDs along with two wires for power and ground. These eight wires are much less desirable on a long run to a remote panel. Using shift registers, we only need to run five wires– clock, serial data, a strobe, power, and ground. If the panel were just a few inches away from the main board, it might still be desirable to cut down on the number of wires in a connecting cable to improve reliability.

Also, we sometimes use up most of the available pins on a microprocessor and need to use serial techniques to expand the number of outputs. Some integrated circuit output devices, such as Digital to Analog converters contain serial–in/ parallel–out shift registers to receive data from microprocessors. The techniques illustrated here are applicable to those parts.

We have chosen the 74AHC594 serial–in/ parallel–out shift register with output register; though, it requires an extra pin, RCLK, to parallel load the shifted–in data to the output pins. This extra pin prevents the outputs from changing while data is shifting in. This is not much of a problem for LEDs. But, it would be a problem if driving relays, valves, motors, etc.

Code executed within the microprocessor would start with 8–bits of data to be output. One bit would be output on the "Serial data out" pin, driving SER of the remote 74AHC594. Next, the microprocessor generates a low to high transition on "Shift clock", driving SRCLK of the '595 shift register. This positive clock shifts the data bit at SER from "D" to "Q" of the first shift register stage.

This has no effect on the QA LED at this time because of the internal 8–bit output register between the shift register and the output pins (QA to QH). Finally, "Shift clock" is pulled back low by the microprocessor. This completes the shifting of one bit into the '595.

The above procedure is repeated seven more times to complete the shifting of 8–bits of data from the microprocessor into the 74AHC594 serial–in/ parallel–out shift register. To transfer the 8–bits of data within the internal '595 shift register to the output requires that the microprocessor generate a low to high transition on RCLK, the output register clock. This applies new data to the LEDs. The RCLK needs to be pulled back low in anticipation of the next 8–bit transfer of data.

The data present at the output of the '595 will remain until the process in the above two paragraphs is repeated for a new 8–bits of data. In particular, new data can be shifted into the '595 internal shift register without affecting the LEDs.

The LEDs will only be updated with new data with the application of the RCLK rising edge. What if we need to drive more than eight LEDs? Simply cascade another 74AHC594 SER pin to the QH' of the existing shifter. Parallel the SRCLK and RCLK pins. The microprocessor would need to transfer 16–bits of data with 16–clocks before generating an RCLK feeding both devices.

The discrete LED indicators, which we show, could be 7–segment LEDs. Though, there are LSI (Large Scale Integration) devices capable of driving several 7–segment digits. This device accepts data from a microprocessor in a serial format, driving more LED segments than it has pins by by multiplexing the LEDs. For example, see link below for MAX6955

PARALLEL–IN, PARALLEL–OUT, UNIVERSAL SHIFT REGISTER

The purpose of the parallel–in/ parallel–out shift register is to take in parallel data, shift it, then output it. A universal shift register is a do–everything device in addition to the parallel–in/ parallel–out function.

Above we apply four bit of data to a parallel–in/ parallel–out shift register at DA DB DC DD. The mode control, which may be multiple inputs, controls parallel loading vs shifting. The mode control may also control the direction of shifting in some real devices. The data will be shifted one bit position for each clock pulse.

The shifted data is available at the outputs QA QB QC QD. The "data in" and "data out" are provided for cascading of multiple stages. Though, above, we can only cascade data for right shifting. We could accommodate cascading of left–shift data by adding a pair of left pointing signals, "data in" and "data out", above.

The internal details of a right shifting parallel–in/ parallel–out shift register are shown below. The tri–state buffers are not strictly necessary to the parallel–in/ parallel–out shift register, but are part of the real–world device shown below.

The 74LS395 so closely matches our concept of a hypothetical right shifting parallel–in/ parallel–out shift register that we use an overly simplified version of the data sheet details above. See the link to the full data sheet more more details, later in this chapter.

LD/SH' controls the AND–OR multiplexer at the data input to the FF's. If LD/SH'=1, the upper four AND gates are enabled allowing application of parallel inputs DA DB DC DD to the four FF data inputs.

Note the inverter bubble at the clock input of the four FFs. This indicates that the 74LS395 clocks data on the negative going clock, which is the high to low transition.

The four bits of data will be clocked in parallel from DA DB DC DD to QA QB QC QD at the next negative going clock. In this "real part", OC' must be low if the data needs to be available at the actual output pins as opposed to only on the internal FFs. The previously loaded data may be shifted right by one bit position if LD/SH'=0 for the succeeding negative going clock edges. Four clocks would shift the data entirely out of our 4–bit shift register. The data would be lost unless our device was cascaded from QD' to SER of another device.

Above, a data pattern is presented to inputs DA DB DC DD. The pattern is loaded to QA QB QC QD. Then it is shifted one bit to the right. The incoming data is indicated by X, meaning the we do no know what it is. If the input (SER) were grounded, for example, we would know what data (0) was shifted in. Also shown, is right shifting by two positions, requiring two clocks.

The above figure serves as a reference for the hardware involved in right shifting of data. It is too simple to even bother with this figure, except for comparison to more complex figures to follow. Right shifting of data is provided above for reference to the previous right shifter.

If we need to shift left, the FFs need to be rewired. Compare to the previous right shifter. Also, SI and SO have been reversed. SI shifts to QC. QC shifts to QB. QB shifts to QA. QA leaves on the SO connection, where it could cascade to another shifter SI. This left shift sequence is backwards from the right shift sequence.

Above we shift the same data pattern left by one bit.

There is no market for it. Nobody manufactures a shift–left part. A "real device" which shifts one direction can be wired externally to shift the other direction. Or, should we say there is no left or right in the context of a device which shifts in only one direction. However, there is a market for a device which will shift left or right on command by a control line. Of course, left and right are valid in that context.

What we have above is a hypothetical shift register capable of shifting either direction under the control of L'/R. It is setup with L'/R=1 to shift the normal direction, right. L'/R=1 enables the multiplexer AND gates labeled R.

This allows data to follow the path illustrated by the arrows, when a clock is applied. Data shifts in at SR, to QA, to QB, to QC, where it leaves at SR cascade. This pin could drive SR of another device to the right. What if we change L'/R to L'/R=0?

With L'/R=0, the multiplexer AND gates labeled L are enabled, yielding a path, shown by the arrows, the same as the above "shift left" figure. Data shifts in at SL, to QC, to QB, to QA, where it leaves at SL cascade. This pin could drive SL of another device to the left.

The prime virtue of the above two figures illustrating the "shift left/ right register" is simplicity. The operation of the left right control L'/R=0 is easy to follow. A commercial part needs the parallel data loading implied by the section title. This appears in the figure below.

Now that we can shift both left and right via L'/R, let us add SH/LD', shift/ load, and the AND gates labeled "load" to provide for parallel loading of data from inputs DA DB DC. When SH/LD'=0, AND gates R and L are disabled, AND gates "load" are enabled to pass data DA DB DC to the FF data inputs. the next clock CLK will clock the data to QA QB QC. As long as the same data is present it will be re–loaded on succeeding clocks. However, data present for only one clock will be lost from the outputs when it is no longer present on the data inputs. One solution is to load the data on one clock, then proceed to shift on the next four clocks. This problem is remedied in the 74ALS299 by the addition of another AND gate to the multiplexer.

If SH/LD' is changed to SH/LD'=1, the AND gates labeled "load" are disabled, allowing the left/ right control L'/R to set the direction of shift on the L or R AND gates. Shifting is as in the previous figures.

The only thing needed to produce a viable integrated device is to add the fourth AND gate to the multiplexer as alluded for the 74ALS299. This is shown in the next section for that part.

Parallel–In/Parallel–Out and Universal Devices

Let's take a closer look at Serial–in/ parallel–out shift registers available as integrated circuits, courtesy of Texas Instruments. For complete device data sheets, follow the links.

- SN74LS395A parallel–in/ parallel–out 4–bit shift register
- SN74ALS299 parallel–in/ parallel–out 8–bit universal shift register

We have already looked at the internal details of the SN74LS395A, see above previous figure, 74LS395 parallel–in/ parallel–out shift register with tri–state output. Directly above is the ANSI symbol for the 74LS395.

Why only 4–bits, as indicated by SRG4 above? Having both parallel inputs, and parallel outputs, in addition to control and power pins, does not allow for any more I/O (Input/Output) bits in a 16–pin DIP (Dual Inline Package).

R indicates that the shift register stages are reset by input CLR' (active low– inverting half arrow at input) of the control section at the top of the symbol. OC', when low, (invert arrow again) will enable (EN4) the four tristate output buffers (QA QB QC QD) in the data section. Load/shift' (LD/SH') at pin (7) corresponds to internals M1 (load) and M2 (shift). Look for prefixes of 1 and 2 in the rest of the symbol to ascertain what is controlled by these.

The negative edge sensitive clock (indicated by the invert arrow at pin–10) C3/2has two functions. First, the 3 of C3/2 affects any input having a prefix of 3, say 2,3D or 1,3D in the data section. This would be parallel load at A, B, C, D attributed to M1 and C3 for 1,3D. Second, 2 of C3/2–right–arrow indicates data clocking wherever 2 appears in a prefix (2,3D at pin–2). Thus we have clocking of data at SER into QA with mode 2. The right arrow after C3/2 accounts for shifting at internal shift register stages QA QB QC QD.

The right pointing triangles indicate buffering; the inverted triangle indicates tri–state, controlled by the EN4. Note, all the 4s in the symbol associated with the EN are frequently omitted. Stages QB QC are understood to have the same attributes as QD. QD' cascades to the next package's SER to the right.

The table above, condensed from the data '299 data sheet, summarizes the operation of the 74ALS299 universal shift/ storage register.

Follow the '299 link above for full details. The Multiplexer gates R, L, load operate as in the previous "shift left/ right register" figures. The difference is that the mode inputs S1 and S0 select shift left, shift right, and load with mode set to S1 S0 = to 01, 10, and 11respectively, enabling multiplexer gates L, R, and load respectively. See table. A minor difference is the parallel load path from the tri–state outputs. Actually the tri–state buffers are (must be) disabled by S1 S0 = 11 to float the I/O bus for use as inputs.

A bus is a collection of similar signals. The inputs are applied to A, B through H (same pins as QA, QB, through QH) and routed to the load gate in the multiplexers, and on the the D inputs of the FFs. Data is parallel load on a clock pulse.

The one new multiplexer gate is the AND gate labeled hold, enabled by S1 S0 = 00. The hold gate enables a path from the Q output of the FF back to the hold gate, to the D input of the same FF. The result is that with mode S1 S0 = 00, the output is continuously re–loaded with each new clock pulse. Thus, data is held. This is summarized in the table.

To read data from outputs QA, QB, through QH, the tri–state buffers must be enabled by OE2', OE1' =00 and mode =S1 S0 = 00, 01, or 10. That is, mode is anything except load. See second table.

Right shift data from a package to the left, shifts in on the SR input. Any data shifted out to the right from stage QH cascades to the right via

QH'. This output is unaffected by the tri–state buffers. The shift right sequence for S1 S0 = 10 is:

SR > QA > QB > QC > QD > QE > QF > QG > QH (QH')

Left shift data from a package to the right shifts in on the SL input. Any data shifted out to the left from stage QA cascades to the left via QA', also unaffected by the tri–state buffers. The shift left sequence for S1 S0 = 01 is:

(QA') QA < QB < QC < QD < QE < QF < QG < QH (QSL')

Shifting may take place with the tri–state buffers disabled by one of OE2' or OE1' = 1. Though, the register contents outputs will not be accessible. See table.

The "clean" ANSI symbol for the SN74ALS299 parallel–in/ parallel–out 8–bit universal shift register with tri–state output is shown for reference above.

The annotated version of the ANSI symbol is shown to clarify the terminology contained therein. Note that the ANSI mode (S0 S1) is reversed from the order (S1 S0) used in the previous table. That reverses the decimal mode numbers (1 & 2). In any event, we are in complete agreement with the official data sheet, copying this inconsistency.

Practical Applications

The Alarm with remote keypad block diagram is repeated below. Previously, we built the keypad reader and the remote display as separate units. Now we will combine both the keypad and display into a single unit using a universal shift register. Though separate in the diagram, the Keypad and Display are both contained within the same remote enclosure.

We will parallel load the keyboard data into the shift register on a single clock pulse, then shift it out to the main alarm box. At the same time, we will shift LED data from the main alarm to the remote shift register to illuminate the LEDs. We will be simultaneously shifting keyboard data out and LED data into the shift register.

Eight LEDs and current limiting resistors are connected to the eight I/O pins of the 74ALS299 universal shift register. The LEDS can only be driven during Mode 3 with S1=0 S0=0. The OE1' and OE2' tristate enables are grounded to permenantly enable the tristate outputs during modes 0, 1, 2. That will cause the LEDS to light (flicker) during shifting. If this were a problem the EN1' and EN2' could be ungrounded and paralleled with S1 and S0 respectively to only enable the tristate buffers and light the LEDS during hold, mode 3. Let's keep it simple for this example.

During parallel loading, S0=1 inverted to a 0, enables the octal tristate buffers to ground the switch wipers. The upper, open, switch contacts are pulled up to logic high by the resister–LED combination at the eight inputs. Any switch closure will short the input low. We parallel load the switch data into the '299 at clock t0 when both S0 and S1 are high. See waveforms below.

Once S0 goes low, eight clocks (t0 tot8) shift switch closure data out of the '299 via the Qh' pin. At the same time, new LED data is shifted in at SR of the 299 by the same eight clocks. The LED data replaces the switch closure data as shifting proceeds.

After the 8th shift clock, t8, S1 goes low to yield hold mode (S1 S0 = 00). The data in the shift register remains the same even if there are more clocks, for example, T9, t10, etc. Where do the waveforms come from? They could be generated by a microprocessor if the clock rate were not over 100 kHz, in which case, it would be inconvenient to generate any clocks after t8. If the clock was in the megahertz range, the clock would run continuously. The clock, S1 and S0 would be generated by digital logic, not shown here.

RING COUNTERS

If the output of a shift register is fed back to the input. a ring counter results. The data pattern contained within the shift register will recirculate as long as clock pulses are applied. For example, the data pattern will repeat every four clock pulses in the figure below. However, we must load a data pattern. All 0's or all 1's doesn't count. Is a continuous logic level from such a condition useful?

We make provisions for loading data into the parallel–in/ serial–out shift register configured as a ring counter below. Any random pattern may be loaded. The most generally useful pattern is a single 1.

Loading binary 1000 into the ring counter, above, prior to shifting yields a viewable pattern. The data pattern for a single stage repeats every four clock pulses in our 4–stage example. The waveforms for all four stages look the same, except for the one clock time delay from one stage to the next. See figure below. The circuit above is a divide by 4 counter. Comparing the clock input to any one of the outputs, shows a frequency ratio of 4:1. How may stages would we need for a divide by 10 ring counter? Ten stages would recirculate the 1 every 10 clock pulses.

An alternate method of initializing the ring counter to 1000 is shown above. The shift waveforms are identical to those above, repeating every fourth clock pulse. The requirement for initialization is a disadvantage of the ring counter over a conventional counter.

At a minimum, it must be initialized at power–up since there is no way to predict what state flip–flops will power up in. In theory, initialization should never be required again. In actual practice, the flip–flops could eventually be corrupted by noise, destroying the data pattern.

A "self correcting" counter, like a conventional synchronous binary counter would be more reliable.

The above binary synchronous counter needs only two stages, but requires decoder gates. The ring counter had more stages, but was self decoding, saving the decode gates above. Another disadvantage of the ring counter is that it is not "self starting". If we need the decoded outputs, the ring counter looks attractive, in particular, if most of the logic is in a single shift register package. If not, the conventional binary counter is less complex without the decoder. The waveforms decoded from the synchronous binary counter are identical to the previous ring counter waveforms. The counter sequence is (QA QB) = (00 01 10 11).

Johnson Counters

The switch–tail ring counter, also know as the Johnson counter, overcomes some of the limitations of the ring counter. Like a ring counter a Johnson counter is a shift register fed back on its' self. It requires half the stages of a comparable ring counter for a given division ratio. If the complement output of a ring counter is fed back to the input instead of the true output, a Johnson counter results. The difference between a ring counter and a Johnson counter is which output of the last stage is fed back (Q or Q'). Carefully compare the feedback connection below to the previous ring counter.

This "reversed" feedback connection has a profound effect upon the behaviour of the otherwise similar circuits. Recirculating a single 1 around a ring counter divides the input clock by a factor equal to the number of stages. Whereas, a Johnson counter divides by a factor equal to twice the number of stages. For example, a 4–stage ring counter divides by 4. A 4–stage Johnson counter divides by 8.

Start a Johnson counter by clearing all stages to 0s before the first clock. This is often done at power–up time. Referring to the figure below, the first clock shifts three 0s from (QA QB QC) to the right into (QB QC QD). The 1 at QD' (the complement of Q) is shifted back into QA. Thus, we start shifting 1s to the right, replacing the 0s. Where a ring counter recirculated a single 1, the 4–stage Johnson counter recirculates four 0s then four 1s for an 8–bit pattern, then repeats.

The above waveforms illustrates that multi–phase square waves are generated by a Johnson counter. The 4–stage unit above generates four overlapping phases of 50% duty cycle. How many stages would be required to generate a set of three phase waveforms? For example, a three stage Johnson counter, driven by a 360 Hertz clock would generate three 120o phased square waves at 60 Hertz.

The outputs of the flop–flops in a Johnson counter are easy to decode to a single state. Below for example, the eight states of a 4–stage Johnson counter are decoded by no more than a two input gate for each of the states. In our example, eight of the two input gates decode the states for our example Johnson counter.

No matter how long the Johnson counter, only 2–input decoder gates are needed. Note, we could have used uninverted inputs to the AND gates by changing the gate inputs from true to inverted at the FFs, Q to Q', (and vice versa). However, we are trying to make the diagram above match the data sheet for the CD4022B, as closely as practical.

Above, our four phased square waves QA to QD are decoded to eight signals (G0 to G7) active during one clock period out of a complete 8–clock cycle. For example, G0 is active high when both QA and QD are low. Thus, pairs of the various register outputs define each of the eight states of our Johnson counter example.

Above is the more complete internal diagram of the CD4022B Johnson counter. See the manufacturers' data sheet for minor details omitted. The major new addition to the diagram as compared to previous figures is the disallowed state detector composed of the two NOR gates. Take a look at the inset state table. There are 8–permissible states as listed in the table. Since our shifter has four flip–flops, there are a total of 16–states, of which there are 8–disallowed states. That would be the ones not listed in the table.

In theory, we will not get into any of the disallowed states as long as the shift register is RESET before first use. However, in the "real world" after many days of continuous operation due to unforeseen noise, power line disturbances, near lightning strikes, etc, the Johnson counter could get into one of the disallowed states. For high reliability applications, we need to plan for this slim possibility. More serious is the case where the circuit is not cleared at power–up. In this case there is no way to know which of the 16–states the circuit will power up in. Once in a disallowed state, the Johnson counter will not return to any of the permissible states without intervention. That is the purpose of the NOR gates.

Examine the table for the sequence (QA QB QC) = (010). Nowhere does this sequence appear in the table of allowed states. Therefore (010) is disallowed. It should never occur. If it does, the Johnson counter is in a disallowed state, which it needs to exit to any allowed state. Suppose that (QA QB QC) = (010). The second NOR gate will replace QB = 1 with a 0 at the D input to FF QC. In other words, the offending 010 is replaced by 000. And 000, which does appear in the table, will be shifted right. There are may triple–0 sequences in the table. This is how the NOR gates get the Johnson counter out of a disallowed state to an allowed state.

Not all disallowed states contain a 010 sequence. However, after a few clocks, this sequence will appear so that any disallowed states will eventually be escaped. If the circuit is powered–up without a RESET, the outputs will be unpredictable for a few clocks until an allowed state is reached. If this is a problem for a particular application, be sure to RESET on power–up.

Johnson Counter Devices

A pair of integrated circuit Johnson counter devices with the output states decoded is available. We have already looked at the CD4017 internal logic in the discussion of Johnson counters. The 4000 series devices can operate from 3V to 15V power supplies. The the 74HC' part, designed for a TTL compatiblity, can operate from a 2V to 6V supply, count faster, and has greater output drive capability. For complete device data sheets, follow the links.

- CD4017 Johnson counter with 10 decoded outputs
- CD4022 Johnson counter with 8 decoded outputs
- 74HC4017 Johnson counter, 10 decoded outputs

The ANSI symbols for the modulo–10 (divide by 10) and modulo–8 Johnson counters are shown above. The symbol takes on the characteristics of a counter rather than a shift register derivative, which it is. Waveforms for the CD4022 modulo–8 and operation were shown previously. The CD4017B/ 74HC4017 decade counter is a 5–stage Johnson counter with ten decoded outputs. The operation and waveforms are similar to the CD4017. In fact, the CD4017 and CD4022 are both detailed on the same data sheet. See above links. The 74HC4017 is a more modern version of the decade counter.

These devices are used where decoded outputs are needed instead of the binary or BCD (Binary Coded Decimal) outputs found on normal counters. By decoded, we mean one line out of the ten lines is active at a time for the '4017 in place of the four bit BCD code out of conventional counters. See previous waveforms for 1–of–8 decoding for the '4022 Octal Johnson counter.

Practical Applications

The above Johnson counter shifts a lighted LED each fifth of a second around the ring of ten. Note that the 74HC4017 is used instead of the '40017 because the former part has more current drive capability. From the data sheet, (at the link above) operating at VCC= 5V, the VOH= 4.6V at 4ma. In other words, the outputs can supply 4 ma at 4.6 V to drive the LEDs. Keep in mind that LEDs are normally driven with 10 to 20 ma of current. Though, they are visible down to 1 ma. This simple circuit illustrates an application of the 'HC4017. Need a bright display for an exhibit? Then, use inverting buffers to drive the cathodes of the LEDs pulled up to the power supply by lower value anode resistors.

The 555 timer, serving as an astable multivibrator, generates a clock frequency determined by R1 R2 C1. This drives the 74HC4017 a step per clock as indicated by a single LED illuminated on the ring. Note, if the 555 does not reliably drive the clock pin of the '4015, run it through a single buffer stage between the 555 and the '4017. A variable R2 could change the step rate. The value of decoupling capacitor C2 is not critical. A similar capacitor should be applied across the power and ground pins of the '4017.

The Johnson counter above generates 3–phase square waves, phased 60o apart with respect to (QA QB QC). However, we need 120o phased waveforms of power applications. Choosing P1=QA P2=QC P3=QB' yields the 120o phasing desired. See figure below. If these (P1 P2 P3) are low–pass filtered to sine waves and amplified, this could be the beginnings of a 3–phase power supply.

For example, do you need to drive a small 3–phase 400 Hz aircraft motor? Then, feed 6x 400Hz to the above circuit CLOCK. Note that all these waveforms are 50% duty cycle. The circuit below produces 3–phase nonoverlapping, less than 50% duty cycle, waveforms for driving 3–phase stepper motors.

Above we decode the overlapping outputs QA QB QC to non–overlapping outputs P0 P1 P2. These waveforms drive a 3–phase stepper motor after suitable amplification from the milliamp level to the fractional amp level using the ULN2003 drivers shown above, or the discrete component Darlington pair driver shown in the circuit which follow.

Not counting the motor driver, this circuit requires three IC (Integrated Circuit) packages: two dual type "D" FF packages and a quad NAND gate. A single CD4017, above, generates the required 3–phase stepper waveforms in the circuit above by clearing the Johnson counter at count 3. Count 3 persists for less than a microsecond before it clears its' self. The other counts (Q0=G0 Q1=G1 Q2=G2) remain for a full clock period each.

The Darlington bipolar transistor drivers shown above are a substitute for the internal circuitry of the ULN2003. The design of drivers is beyond the scope of this digital electronics chapter. Either driver may be used with either waveform generator circuit.

The above waceforms make the most sense in the context of the internal logic of the CD4017 shown earlier in this section. Though, the AND gating equations for the internal decoder are shown. The signals QA QB QC are Johnson counter direct shift register outputs not available on pin–outs. The QD waveform shows resetting of the '4017 every three clocks. Q0 Q1 Q2, etc. are decoded outputs which actually are available at output pins.

Above we generate waveforms for driving a unipolar stepper motor, which only requires one polarity of driving signal. That is, we do not have to reverse the polarity of the drive to the windings. This simplifies the power driver between the '4017 and the motor. Darlington pairs from a prior diagram may be substituted for the ULN3003.

Once again, the CD4017B generates the required waveforms with a reset after the teminal count. The decoded outputs Q0 Q1 Q2 Q3 sucessively drive the stepper motor windings, with Q4 reseting the counter at the end of each group of four pulses.

Chapter 8

Digital–Analog Conversion

Connecting digital circuitry to sensor devices is simple if the sensor devices are inherently digital themselves. Switches, relays, and encoders are easily interfaced with gate circuits due to the on/off nature of their signals. However, when analog devices are involved, interfacing becomes much more complex. What is needed is a way to electronically translate analog signals into digital (binary) quantities, and vice versa. An analog–to–digital converter, or ADC, performs the former task while a digital–to–analog converter, or DAC, performs the latter.

An ADC inputs an analog electrical signal such as voltage or current and outputs a binary number. In block diagram form, it can be represented as such:

A DAC, on the other hand, inputs a binary number and outputs an analog voltage or current signal. In block diagram form, it looks like this: Together, they are often used in digital systems to provide complete interface with analog sensors and output devices for control systems such as those used in automotive engine controls:

It is much easier to convert a digital signal into an analog signal than it is to do the reverse. Therefore, we will begin with DAC circuitry and then move to ADC circuitry.

THE R/2NR DAC

This DAC circuit, otherwise known as the binary–weighted–input DAC, is a variation on the inverting summer op–amp circuit. If you recall, the classic inverting summer circuit is an operational amplifier using negative feedback for controlled gain, with several voltage inputs and one voltage output. The output voltage is the inverted (opposite polarity) sum of all input voltages:

For a simple inverting summer circuit, all resistors must be of equal value. If any of the input resistors were different, the input voltages would have different degrees of effect on the output, and the output voltage would not be a true sum.

Let's consider, however, intentionally setting the input resistors at different values. Suppose we were to set the input resistor values at multiple powers of two: R, 2R, and 4R, instead of all the same value R:

Starting from V1 and going through V3, this would give each input voltage exactly half the effect on the output as the voltage before it. In other words, input voltage V1 has a 1:1 effect on the output voltage (gain of 1), while input voltage V2 has half that much effect on the output (a gain of 1/2), and V3 half of that (a gain of 1/4).

These ratios are were not arbitrarily chosen: they are the same ratios corresponding to place weights in the binary numeration system. If we drive the inputs of this circuit with digital gates so that each input is either 0 volts or full supply voltage, the output voltage will be an analog representation of the binary value of these three bits. If we chart the output voltages for all eight combinations of binary bits (000 through 111) input to this circuit, we will get the following progression of voltages:

Binary	*Output voltage*
000	0.00 V
001	–1.25 V
010	–2.50 V
011	–3.75 V
100	–5.00 V
101	–6.25 V
110	–7.50 V
111	–8.75 V

Note that with each step in the binary count sequence, there results a 1.25 volt change in the output. This circuit is very easy to simulate using SPICE. In the following simulation, the DAC circuit with a binary input of 110 (note the first node numbers for resistors R1, R2, and R3: a node number of "1" connects it to the positive side of a 5 volt battery, and a node number of "0" connects it to ground). The output voltage appears on node 6 in the simulation:

Binary–weighted dac v1 1 0 dc 5 rbogus 1 0 99k r1 1 5 1k r2 1 5 2k r3 0 5 4k rfeedbk 5 6 1k e1 6 0 5 0 999k end node voltage (1) 5.0000	node voltage (5) 0.0000	node voltage (6) –7.5000

We can adjust resistors values in this circuit to obtain output voltages directly corresponding to the binary input. For example, by making the feedback resistor 800 ohms instead of 1 k, the DAC will output –1 volt for the binary input 001, –4 volts for the binary input 100, –7 volts for the binary input 111, and so on.

(with feedback resistor set at 800 ohms)	
Binary	*Output voltage*
000	0.00 V
001	–1.00 V
010	–2.00 V
011	–3.00 V
100	–4.00 V
101	–5.00 V
110	–6.00 V
111	–7.00 V

If we wish to expand the resolution of this DAC (add more bits to the input), all we need to do is add more input resistors, holding to the same power–of–two sequence of values:

It should be noted that all logic gates must output exactly the same voltages when in the "high" state. If one gate is outputting +5.02 volts for a "high" while another is outputting only +4.86 volts, the analog output of the DAC will be adversely affected. Likewise, all "low" voltage levels should be identical between gates, ideally 0.00 volts exactly. It is recommended that CMOS output gates are used, and that input/feedback resistor values are chosen so as to minimize the amount of current each gate has to source or sink.

The R/2R DAC

An alternative to the binary–weighted–input DAC is the so–called R/2R DAC, which uses fewer unique resistor values. A disadvantage of the former DAC design was its requirement of several different precise input resistor values: one unique value per binary input bit. Manufacture may be simplified if there are fewer different resistor values to purchase, stock, and sort prior to assembly. Of course, we could take our last DAC circuit and modify it to use a single input resistance value, by connecting multiple resistors together in series:

Unfortunately, this approach merely substitutes one type of complexity for another: volume of components over diversity of component values. There is, however, a more efficient design methodology.

By constructing a different kind of resistor network on the input of our summing circuit, we can achieve the same kind of binary weighting with only two kinds of resistor values, and with only a modest increase in resistor count. This "ladder" network looks like this:

Mathematically analyzing this ladder network is a bit more complex than for the previous circuit, where each input resistor provided an easily–calculated gain for that bit. For those who are interested in pursuing the intricacies of this circuit further, you may opt to use Thevenin's theorem for each binary input (remember to consider the effects of the virtual ground), and/or use a simulation programme like SPICE to determine circuit response. Either way, you should obtain the following table of figures:

Binary	Output voltage
000	0.00 V
001	–1.25 V
010	–2.50 V
011	–3.75 V
100	–5.00 V
101	–6.25 V
110	–7.50 V
111	–8.75 V

As was the case with the binary–weighted DAC design, we can modify the value of the feedback resistor to obtain any "span" desired. For example, if we're using +5 volts for a "high" voltage level and 0 volts for a "low" voltage level, we can obtain an analog output directly corresponding to the binary input (011 = –3 volts, 101 = –5 volts, 111 = –7 volts, etc.) by using a feedback resistance with a value of 1.6R instead of 2R.

Flash ADC

Also called the parallel A/D converter, this circuit is the simplest to understand. It is formed of a series of comparators, each one comparing the input signal to a unique reference voltage. The comparator outputs connect to the inputs of a priority encoder circuit, which then produces a binary output. The following illustration shows a 3–bit flash ADC circuit:

Vref is a stable reference voltage provided by a precision voltage regulator as part of the converter circuit, not shown in the schematic. As the analog input voltage exceeds the reference voltage at each comparator, the comparator outputs will sequentially saturate to a high state. The priority encoder generates a binary number based on the highest–order active input, ignoring all other active inputs. When operated, the flash ADC produces an output that looks something like this:

For this particular application, a regular priority encoder with all its inherent complexity isn't necessary. Due to the nature of the sequential comparator output states (each comparator saturating "high" in sequence from lowest to highest), the same "highest–order–input selection" effect may be realized through a set of Exclusive–OR gates, allowing the use of a simpler, non–priority encoder:

And, of course, the encoder circuit itself can be made from a matrix of diodes, demonstrating just how simply this converter design may be constructed: Not only is the flash converter the simplest in terms of operational theory, but it is the most efficient of the ADC technologies in terms of speed, being limited only in comparator and gate propagation delays. Unfortunately, it is the most component–intensive for any given number of output bits.

This three–bit flash ADC requires eight comparators. A four–bit version would require 16 comparators. With each additional output bit, the number of required comparators doubles. Considering that eight bits is generally considered the minimum necessary for any practical ADC (256 comparators needed!), the flash methodology quickly shows its weakness.

An additional advantage of the flash converter, often overlooked, is the ability for it to produce a non–linear output. With equal–value resistors in the reference voltage divider network, each successive binary count represents the same amount of analog signal increase, providing a proportional response. For special applications, however, the resistor values in the divider network may be made non–equal. This gives the ADC a custom, nonlinear response to the analog input signal. No other ADC design is able to grant this signal–conditioning behaviour with just a few component value changes.

DIGITAL RAMP ADC

Also known as the stairstep–ramp, or simply counter A/D converter, this is also fairly easy to understand but unfortunately suffers from several limitations.

The basic idea is to connect the output of a free–running binary counter to the input of a DAC, then compare the analog output of the DAC with the analog input signal to be digitized and use the comparator's output to tell the counter when to stop counting and reset. The following schematic shows the basic idea:

As the counter counts up with each clock pulse, the DAC outputs a slightly higher (more positive) voltage. This voltage is compared against the input voltage by the comparator. If the input voltage is greater than the DAC output, the comparator's output will be high and the counter will continue counting normally. Eventually, though, the DAC output will exceed the input voltage, causing the comparator's output to go low. This will cause two things to happen: first, the high–to–low transition of the comparator's output will cause the shift register to "load" whatever binary count is being output by the counter, thus updating the ADC circuit's output; secondly, the counter will receive a low signal on the active–low LOAD input, causing it to reset to 00000000 on the next clock pulse.

The effect of this circuit is to produce a DAC output that ramps up to whatever level the analog input signal is at, output the binary number corresponding to that level, and start over again. Plotted over time, it looks like this:

Note how the time between updates (new digital output values) changes depending on how high the input voltage is. For low signal levels, the updates are rather close–spaced. For higher signal levels, they are spaced further apart in time:

For many ADC applications, this variation in update frequency (sample time) would not be acceptable. This, and the fact that the circuit's need to count all the way from 0 at the beginning of each count cycle makes for relatively slow sampling of the analog signal, places the digital–ramp ADC at a disadvantage to other counter strategies.

SUCCESSIVE APPROXIMATION ADC

One method of addressing the digital ramp ADC's shortcomings is the so–called successive–approximation ADC. The only change in this design is a very special counter circuit known as a successive–approximation register. Instead of counting up in binary sequence, this register counts by trying all values of bits starting with the most–significant bit and finishing at the least–significant bit. Throughout the count process, the register monitors the comparator's output to see if the binary count is less than or greater than the analog signal input, adjusting the bit values accordingly.

The way the register counts is identical to the "trial–and–fit" method of decimal–to–binary conversion, whereby different values of bits are tried from MSB to LSB to get a binary number that equals the original decimal number. The advantage to this counting strategy is much faster results: the DAC output converges on the analog signal input in much larger steps than with the 0–to–full count sequence of a regular counter.

Without showing the inner workings of the successive–approximation register (SAR), the circuit looks like this:

It should be noted that the SAR is generally capable of outputting the binary number in serial (one bit at a time) format, thus eliminating the need for a shift register. Plotted over time, the operation of a successive–approximation ADC looks like this:

Note how the updates for this ADC occur at regular intervals, unlike the digital ramp ADC circuit.

Tracking ADC

A third variation on the counter–DAC–based converter theme is, in my estimation, the most elegant. Instead of a regular "up" counter driving the DAC, this circuit uses an up/down counter. The counter is continuously clocked, and the up/down control line is driven by the output of the comparator. So, when the analog input signal exceeds the DAC output, the counter goes into the "count up" mode. When the DAC output exceeds the analog input, the counter switches into the "count down" mode. Either way, the DAC output always counts in the proper direction to track the input signal.

Notice how no shift register is needed to buffer the binary count at the end of a cycle. Since the counter's output continuously tracks the input (rather than counting to meet the input and then resetting back to zero), the binary output is legitimately updated with every clock pulse.

An advantage of this converter circuit is speed, since the counter never has to reset. Note the behaviour of this circuit.

Note the much faster update time than any of the other "counting" ADC circuits. Also note how at the very beginning of the plot where the counter had to "catch up" with the analog signal, the rate of change for the output was identical to that of the first counting ADC. Also, with no shift register in this circuit, the binary output would actually ramp up rather than jump from zero to an accurate count as it did with the counter and successive approximation ADC circuits.

Perhaps the greatest drawback to this ADC design is the fact that the binary output is never stable: it always switches between counts with every clock pulse, even with a perfectly stable analog input signal. This phenomenon is informally known as bit bobble, and it can be problematic in some digital systems.

This tendency can be overcome, though, through the creative use of a shift register. For example, the counter's output may be latched through a parallel–in/parallel–out shift register only when the output changes by two or more steps. Building a circuit to detect two or more successive counts in the same direction takes a little ingenuity, but is worth the effort.

Slope (Integrating) ADC

So far, we've only been able to escape the sheer volume of components in the flash converter by using a DAC as part of our ADC circuitry. However, this is not our only option. It is possible to avoid using a DAC if we substitute an analog ramping circuit and a digital counter with precise timing. The is the basic idea behind the so–called single–slope, or integrating ADC. Instead of using a DAC with a ramped output, we use an op–amp circuit called an integrator to generate a sawtooth waveform which is then compared against the analog input by a comparator. The time it takes for the sawtooth waveform to exceed the input signal voltage level is measured by means of a digital counter clocked with a precise–frequency square wave (usually from a crystal oscillator). The basic schematic diagram is shown here.

The IGFET capacitor–discharging transistor scheme shown here is a bit oversimplified. In reality, a latching circuit timed with the clock signal would most likely have to be connected to the IGFET gate to ensure full discharge of the capacitor when the comparator's output goes high. The basic idea, however, is evident in this diagram. When the comparator output is low (input voltage greater than integrator output), the integrator is allowed to charge the capacitor in a linear fashion. Meanwhile, the counter is counting up at a rate fixed by the precision clock frequency.

The time it takes for the capacitor to charge up to the same voltage level as the input depends on the input signal level and the combination of –Vref, R, and C. When the capacitor reaches that voltage level, the comparator output goes high, loading the counter's output into the shift register for a final output. The IGFET is triggered "on" by the comparator's high output, discharging the capacitor back to zero volts. When the integrator output voltage falls to zero, the comparator output switches back to a low state, clearing the counter and enabling the integrator to ramp up voltage again.

This ADC circuit behaves very much like the digital ramp ADC, except that the comparator reference voltage is a smooth sawtooth waveform rather than a "stairstep".

The single–slope ADC suffers all the disadvantages of the digital ramp ADC, with the added drawback of calibration drift. The accurate correspondence of this ADC's output with its input is dependent on the voltage slope of the integrator being matched to the counting rate of the counter (the clock frequency).

With the digital ramp ADC, the clock frequency had no effect on conversion accuracy, only on update time. In this circuit, since the rate of integration and the rate of count are independent of each other, variation between the two is inevitable as it ages, and will result in a loss of accuracy. The only good thing to say about this circuit is that it avoids the use of a DAC, which reduces circuit complexity.

An answer to this calibration drift dilemma is found in a design variation called the dual–slope converter. In the dual–slope converter, an integrator circuit is driven positive and negative in alternating cycles to ramp down and then up, rather than being reset to 0 volts at the end of every cycle.

In one direction of ramping, the integrator is driven by the positive analog input signal (producing a negative, variable rate of output voltage change, or output slope) for a fixed amount of time, as measured by a counter with a precision frequency clock.

Then, in the other direction, with a fixed reference voltage (producing a fixed rate of output voltage change) with time measured by the same counter. The counter stops counting when the integrator's output reaches the same voltage as it was when it started the fixed–time portion of the cycle. The amount of time it takes for the integrator's capacitor to discharge back to its original output voltage, as measured by the magnitude accrued by the counter, becomes the digital output of the ADC circuit.

The dual–slope method can be thought of analogously in terms of a rotary spring such as that used in a mechanical clock mechanism. Imagine we were building a mechanism to measure the rotary speed of a shaft. Thus, shaft speed is our "input signal" to be measured by this device. The measurement cycle begins with the spring in a relaxed state. The spring is then turned, or "wound up," by the rotating shaft (input signal) for a fixed amount of time.

This places the spring in a certain amount of tension proportional to the shaft speed: a greater shaft speed corresponds to a faster rate of winding. and a greater amount of spring tension accumulated over that period of time. After that, the spring is uncoupled from the shaft and allowed to unwind at a fixed rate, the time for it to unwind back to a relaxed state measured by a timer device. The amount of time it takes for the spring to unwind at that fixed rate will be directly proportional to the speed at which it was wound (input signal magnitude) during the fixed–time portion of the cycle.

This technique of analog–to–digital conversion escapes the calibration drift problem of the single–slope ADC because both the integrator's integration coefficient (or "gain") and the counter's rate of speed are in effect during the entire "winding" and "unwinding" cycle portions. If the counter's clock speed were to suddenly increase, this would shorten the fixed time period where the integrator "winds up" (resulting in a lesser voltage accumulated by the integrator), but it would also mean that it would count faster during the period of time when the integrator was allowed to "unwind" at a fixed rate.

The proportion that the counter is counting faster will be the same proportion as the integrator's accumulated voltage is diminished from before the clock speed change. Thus, the clock speed error would cancel itself out and the digital output would be exactly what it should be.

Another important advantage of this method is that the input signal becomes averaged as it drives the integrator during the fixed–time portion of the cycle. Any changes in the analog signal during that period of time have a cumulative effect on the digital output at the end of that cycle. Other ADC strategies merely "capture" the analog signal level at a single point in time every cycle.

If the analog signal is "noisy" (contains significant levels of spurious voltage spikes/dips), one of the other ADC converter technologies may occasionally convert a spike or dip because it captures the signal repeatedly at a single point in time. A dual–slope ADC, on the other hand, averages together all the spikes and dips within the integration period, thus providing an output with greater noise immunity. Dual–slope ADCs are used in applications demanding high accuracy.

DELTA–SIGMA ADC

One of the more advanced ADC technologies is the so–called delta–sigma. In mathematics and physics, the capital Greek letter delta (δ) represents difference or change, while the capital letter sigma (Σ) represents summation: the adding of multiple terms together. Sometimes this converter is referred to by the same Greek letters in reverse order: sigma–delta.

In a converter, the analog input voltage signal is connected to the input of an integrator, producing a voltage rate–of–change, or slope, at the output corresponding to input magnitude. This ramping voltage is then compared against ground potential (0 volts) by a comparator. The comparator acts as a sort of 1–bit ADC, producing 1 bit of output ("high" or "low") depending on whether the integrator output is positive or negative.

The comparator's output is then latched through a D–type flip–flop clocked at a high frequency, and fed back to another input channel on the integrator, to drive the integrator in the direction of a 0 volt output. The basic circuit looks like this:

The leftmost op–amp is the (summing) integrator. The next op–amp the integrator feeds into is the comparator, or 1–bit ADC. Next comes the D–type flip–flop, which latches the comparator's output at every clock pulse, sending either a "high" or "low" signal to the next comparator at the top of the circuit.

This final comparator is necessary to convert the single–polarity 0V/ 5V logic level output voltage of the flip–flop into a +V/ –V voltage signal to be fed back to the integrator.

If the integrator output is positive, the first comparator will output a "high" signal to the D input of the flip–flop. At the next clock pulse, this "high" signal will be output from the Q line into the noninverting input of the last comparator.

This last comparator, seeing an input voltage greater than the threshold voltage of 1/2 +V, saturates in a positive direction, sending a full +V signal to the other input of the integrator. This +V feedback signal tends to drive the integrator output in a negative direction. If that output voltage ever becomes negative, the feedback loop will send a corrective signal (–V) back around to the top input of the integrator to drive it in a positive direction. This is the delta–sigma concept in action: the first comparator senses a difference between the integrator output and zero volts. The integrator sums the comparator's output with the analog input signal.

Functionally, this results in a serial stream of bits output by the flip–flop. If the analog input is zero volts, the integrator will have no tendency to ramp either positive or negative, except in response to the feedback voltage.

In this scenario, the flip–flop output will continually oscillate between "high" and "low," as the feedback system "hunts" back and forth, trying to maintain the integrator output at zero volts.

If, however, we apply a negative analog input voltage, the integrator will have a tendency to ramp its output in a positive direction. Feedback can only add to the integrator's ramping by a fixed voltage over a fixed time, and so the bit stream output by the flip–flop will not be quite the same.

By applying a larger (negative) analog input signal to the integrator, we force its output to ramp more steeply in the positive direction. Thus, the feedback system has to output more 1's than before to bring the integrator output back to zero volts:

As the analog input signal increases in magnitude, so does the occurrence of 1's in the digital output of the flip–flop:

A parallel binary number output is obtained from this circuit by averaging the serial stream of bits together. For example, a counter circuit could be designed to collect the total number of 1's output by the flip–flop in a given number of clock pulses. This count would then be indicative of the analog input voltage.

Variations on this theme exist, employing multiple integrator stages and/or comparator circuits outputting more than 1 bit, but one concept common to all converters is that of oversampling.

Oversampling is when multiple samples of an analog signal are taken by an ADC (in this case, a 1–bit ADC), and those digitized samples are averaged. The end result is an effective increase in the number of bits resolved from the signal. In other words, an oversampled 1–bit ADC can do the same job as an 8–bit ADC with one–time sampling, albeit at a slower rate.

PRACTICAL CONSIDERATIONS OF ADC CIRCUITS

Perhaps the most important consideration of an ADC is its resolution. Resolution is the number of binary bits output by the converter. Because ADC circuits take in an analog signal, which is continuously variable, and resolve it into one of many discrete steps, it is important to know how many of these steps there are in total.

For example, an ADC with a 10–bit output can represent up to 1024 (210) unique conditions of signal measurement. Over the range of measurement from 0% to 100%, there will be exactly 1024 unique binary numbers output by the converter (from 0000000000 to 1111111111, inclusive). An 11–bit ADC will have twice as many states to its output (2048, or 211), representing twice as many unique conditions of signal measurement between 0% and 100%.

Resolution is very important in data acquisition systems (circuits designed to interpret and record physical measurements in electronic form). Suppose we were measuring the height of water in a 40–foot tall storage tank using an instrument with a 10–bit ADC. 0 feet of water in the tank corresponds to 0% of measurement, while 40 feet of water in the tank corresponds to 100% of measurement.

Because the ADC is fixed at 10 bits of binary data output, it will interpret any given tank level as one out of 1024 possible states. To determine how much physical water level will be represented in each step of the ADC, we need to divide the 40 feet of measurement span by the number of steps in the 0–to–1024 range of possibilities, which is 1023 (one less than 1024). Doing this, we obtain a figure of 0.039101 feet per step. This equates to 0.46921 inches per step, a little less than half an inch of water level represented for every binary count of the ADC.

This step value of 0.039101 feet (0.46921 inches) represents the smallest amount of tank level change detectable by the instrument. Admittedly, this is a small amount, less than 0.1% of the overall measurement span of 40 feet. However, for some applications it may not be fine enough. Suppose we needed this instrument to be able to indicate tank level changes down to one–tenth of an inch. In order to achieve this degree of resolution and still maintain a measurement span of 40 feet, we would need an instrument with more than ten ADC bits.

To determine how many ADC bits are necessary, we need to first determine how many 1/10 inch steps there are in 40 feet. The answer to this is 40/(0.1/12), or 4800 1/10 inch steps in 40 feet. Thus, we need enough bits to provide at least 4800 discrete steps in a binary counting sequence.

10 bits gave us 1023 steps, and we knew this by calculating 2 to the power of 10 (210 = 1024) and then subtracting one. Following the same mathematical procedure, 211–1 = 2047, 212–1 = 4095, and 213–1 = 8191. 12 bits falls shy of the amount needed for 4800 steps, while 13 bits is more than enough. Therefore, we need an instrument with at least 13 bits of resolution.

Another important consideration of ADC circuitry is its sample frequency, or conversion rate. This is simply the speed at which the converter outputs a new binary number. Like resolution, this consideration is linked to the specific application of the ADC. If the converter is being used to measure slow–changing signals such as level in a water storage tank, it could probably have a very slow sample frequency and still perform adequately. Conversely, if it is being used to digitize an audio frequency signal cycling at several thousand times per second, the converter needs to be considerably faster.

Consider the following illustration of ADC conversion rate versus signal type, typical of a successive–approximation ADC with regular sample intervals.

Here, for this slow–changing signal, the sample rate is more than adequate to capture its general trend. But consider this example with the same sample time.

When the sample period is too long (too slow), substantial details of the analog signal will be missed. Notice how, especially in the latter portions of the analog signal, the digital output utterly fails to reproduce the true shape. Even in the first section of the analog waveform, the digital reproduction deviates substantially from the true shape of the wave.

It is imperative that an ADC's sample time is fast enough to capture essential changes in the analog waveform. In data acquisition terminology, the highest–frequency waveform that an ADC can theoretically capture is the so–called Nyquist frequency, equal to one–half of the ADC's sample frequency. Therefore, if an ADC circuit has a sample frequency of 5000 Hz, the highest–frequency waveform it can successfully resolve will be the Nyquist frequency of 2500 Hz.

If an ADC is subjected to an analog input signal whose frequency exceeds the Nyquist frequency for that ADC, the converter will output a digitized signal of falsely low frequency. This phenomenon is known as aliasing. Observe the following illustration to see how aliasing occurs.

Note how the period of the output waveform is much longer (slower) than that of the input waveform, and how the two waveform shapes aren't even similar.

It should be understood that the Nyquist frequency is an absolute maximum frequency limit for an ADC, and does not represent the highest practical frequency measurable. To be safe, one shouldn't expect an ADC to successfully resolve any frequency greater than one–fifth to one–tenth of its sample frequency.

A practical means of preventing aliasing is to place a low–pass filter before the input of the ADC, to block any signal frequencies greater than the practical limit. This way, the ADC circuitry will be prevented from seeing any excessive frequencies and thus will not try to digitize them. It is generally considered better that such frequencies go unconverted than to have them be "aliased" and appear in the output as false signals.

Yet another measure of ADC performance is something called step recovery. This is a measure of how quickly an ADC changes its output to match a large, sudden change in the analog input. In some converter technologies especially, step recovery is a serious limitation. One example is the tracking converter, which has a typically fast update period but a disproportionately slow step recovery.

An ideal ADC has a great many bits for very fine resolution, samples at lightning–fast speeds, and recovers from steps instantly. It also, unfortunately, doesn't exist in the real world.

Of course, any of these traits may be improved through additional circuit complexity, either in terms of increased component count and/or special circuit designs made to run at higher clock speeds. Different ADC technologies, though, have different strengths. Here is a summary of them ranked from best to worst.

Chapter 9

Amplitude Modulation

LINEAR AMPLITUDE MODULATION

The amplitude of the carrier $x_c(t)$ is proportional to the message signal $m(t)$.

Double Side Band Modulation (DSB)

DSB is also called amplitude modulation—suppressed carrier (AM-SC).

Description

$$x_c(t) = A_c m(t) \cos 2\pi f_c t$$

$$x_c(f) = \frac{A_c}{2}[M(f + f_c) + M(f - f_c)]$$

Test Tone

$$m(t) = A_m \cos 2\pi f_m t\,.$$

$$\begin{aligned} x_c(t) &= A_m \cos(2\pi f_m t) A_m \cos(2\pi f_c t) \\ &= \frac{A_c A_m}{2} \cos[2\pi(f_c - f_m)t] \\ &+ \frac{A_c A_m}{2} \cos[2\pi(f_c + f_m)t] \end{aligned}$$

$$\begin{aligned} X_c(f) &= \frac{A_c A_m}{4}[\delta(f + f_c + f_m) + \delta(f + f_c - f_m) \\ &+ \delta(f - (f_c + f_m)) + \delta(f - (f_c - f_m))] \end{aligned}$$

Carrier Power

$$\begin{aligned} \langle x_c^2(t) \rangle &= \langle A_c^2 m^2(t) \cos^2(2\pi f_c t) \rangle \\ &= \lim_{T \to \infty} \frac{1}{2T} \int_{-T}^{T} A_c^2 m^2(t) \cos^2(2\pi f_c t) dt \\ &= \lim_{T \to \infty} \frac{1}{2T} \int_{-T}^{T} \left[\frac{A^2}{2} m^2(t) + \frac{A^2}{2} \cos 4\pi f_c t \right] dt \\ &= \lim_{T \to \infty} \frac{1}{2T} \int_{-T}^{T} \frac{A^2}{2} m^2(t) dt \end{aligned}$$

by the Riemann-Lebesque Lemma

$$= \frac{A_c^2}{2}\left\langle m^2(t)\right\rangle.$$

DSB Bandwidth

Using the modulation theorem, it is seen that the bandwidth occupied by $X_c(f)$ is twice that of $M(f)$.

$$B = 2W.$$

Generation of DSB

DSB signal is generated by the multiplication of the carrier by the message signal. The circuit which performs this operation is often referred to as a *mixer*.

Amplitude Modulation—Total Carrier (AM-TC)

AM-TC is also refered to DSB-TC.

AM-TC Description

$$x_c(t) = A_c[A + m(t)]\cos 2\pi f_c t)$$
$$= A_c^f[1 + am_n(t)]\cos 2\pi f_c t$$

where

$$m_n(t) = \frac{m(t)}{|\min\{m(t)\}|}$$

so that min $\{mn(t)\} = -1$ and

$$a = \frac{|\min\{m(t)\}}{A}$$

is the *modulation index*. The modulation index must satisfy $a \leq 1$ for no distortion.

$$X_c(f) = \frac{A_c'}{2}[aM_n(f + f_c) + \delta(f + f_c) + aM_n(f - f_c) + \delta(f - f_c)]$$

Test Tone

Let $m(t) = A_m \cos 2\pi f_m t$.

$$\min\{m(t) = -A_m$$

$$mn(t) = \frac{m(t)}{|\min\{m(t)\}|}$$
$$= \cos 2\pi f_m t$$

$$x_c(t) = A_c'[1 + a\cos(2\pi f_m t)]\cos(2\pi f_c t)$$
$$= A_c' \cos(2\pi f_c t) + \frac{aA_c'}{2}\cos[2\pi(f_c - f_m)t]$$
$$+ \frac{aA_c'}{2}\cos[2\pi(f_c + f_m)t]$$

$$X_c(f) = \frac{A_c'}{2}\Big[\delta(f + f_c) + \delta(f - f_c) + \frac{a}{2}\delta(f + f_c + f_m)$$
$$+ \frac{a}{2}\delta(f + f_c - f_m)$$
$$+ \frac{a}{2}\delta(f - (f_c + f_m)) + \frac{a}{2}\delta(f - (f_c - f_m))\Big]$$

Carrier Power

$$\langle x_c^2(t)\rangle = \langle (A_c')^2 [1 + am_n(t)]^2 \cos^2(2\pi f_c t)\rangle$$
$$= \frac{(A_c')^2}{2}\left[1 + a^2\langle m_n^2(t)\rangle\right]$$
$$= \frac{(A_c A)^2}{2} + A_c^2\langle m^2(t)\rangle$$

The *efficiency* is defined as the percentage of the total carrier power that conveys information. Only the sidebands convey information. Thus,

$$E = \frac{(A_c'a)^2 / 2\langle m_n^2(t)\rangle}{\langle x_c^2(t)\rangle} \times 100\%$$

$$= \frac{a^2\langle m_n^2(t)\rangle}{1 + a^2\langle m_n^2(t)\rangle} \times 100\%$$

so that the carrier power is

$$\langle x_c^2(t)\rangle = \frac{A_c^2\langle m^2(t)\rangle}{2E}$$

Clearly $0 \le E \le 50\%$.

AM-TC Bandwidth

The carrier spectrum of AM-TC is identical to that of DSB except for the impulse at $f = f_c$ which represents the carrier. Thus

$$B = 2W.$$

AM-TC GENERATION

SSB DESCRIPTION

$$x_c(t) = z\frac{1}{2}A_c m(t)\cos 2\pi f_c t \pm \frac{1}{2}A_c \hat{m}(t)\sin 2\pi f_c t$$
$$X_c(f) = \frac{A_c}{4}[M(f + f_c)\cdot\{1 \pm \text{sgn}(f + f_c)\}$$
$$+ M(f - f_c)\cdot\{1 \mp \text{sgn}(f - f_c)\}]$$

Test Tone

Let $m(t) = A_m \cos 2\pi f_m t$.

$$x_c(t) = \frac{A_c A_m}{2} \cos(2\pi f_m t)\cos(2\pi f_c t)$$
$$\pm \frac{A_c A_m}{2} \sin 2\pi f_m t \sin 2\pi f_c t$$
$$= \frac{A_c A_m}{2} \cos[2\pi(f_c + f_m)t]$$
$$X_c(f) = \frac{A_c A_m}{4}[\delta(f + f_c + f_m) + \delta(f - (f_c + f_m))]$$

Carrier Power

$$\langle x_c^2(t)\rangle = \left\langle\left[\frac{1}{2}A_c m(t)\cos 2\pi f_c t \pm \frac{1}{2}A_c \hat{m}(t)\sin 2\pi f_c t\right]^2\right\rangle$$
$$= \frac{A_c^2}{4}\langle m^2(t)\rangle.$$

SSB Bandwidth

The bandwidth of SSB is

$$B = W$$

which is half that required for DSB or AM-TC.

Coherent Demodulation

Coherent Demodulation is accomplished by remodulating using a local oscillator (LO) which is at the same frequency and in phase with the original carrier.

Ideal Coherent Demodulation

Let $x_q(t) = x_c(t) = A(t)\cos 2\pi f_c t + B(t)\sin 2\pi f_c t$

where

$$A(t) = \begin{cases} A_c m(t) & \text{for DSB} \\ A_c'[1 + a m_n(t)] & \text{for AM-TC} \\ \dfrac{\Lambda_\alpha}{2} m(t) & \text{for SSB} \end{cases}$$

and

$$B(t) = \begin{cases} 0 & \text{for DSB} \\ 0 & \text{for AM-TC} \\ \pm\dfrac{\Lambda_\alpha}{2}\hat{m}(t) & \text{for SSB} \end{cases}$$

Let the LO output be cos $(2\pi f_c\, t)$. Then

$$d(t) = [A(t)\cos(2\pi f_c t) + B(t)\sin 2\pi f_c t]\cos(2\pi f_c t)$$

$$= \frac{A(t)}{2} + \frac{A(t)}{2}\cos 2\pi 2 f_c t + \frac{B(t)}{2}\sin 2\pi 2 f_c t$$

$$y_D(t) = \frac{A(t)}{2}$$

$$= \begin{cases} \frac{\Lambda_\alpha}{2} m(t) & \text{for DSB} \\ \frac{\Lambda'_c}{2_c}\, [1 + am_n(t)] & \text{for AM-TC} \\ \frac{\Lambda_\alpha}{4} m(t) & \text{for SSB} \end{cases}$$

For AM-TC, the DC component of y_D(t) is removed to yield

$$\frac{A'_c}{2} am_n(t) = \frac{A_c}{2} m(t)$$

Effect of Lo Offset

Now let the Lo output be $\cos[2\pi f_c t + \theta(t)]$. Then

$$d(t) = [A(t)\cos(2\pi f_c t) + B(t)\sin(2\pi f_c t)]\cos(2\pi f_c t + \theta(t))$$

$$= \frac{A(t)}{2}\cos\theta(t) + \frac{A(t)}{2}\cos[2\pi 2 f_c t + \theta(t)]$$

$$- \frac{B(t)}{2}\sin\theta(t) + \frac{B(t)}{2}\sin[2\pi 2 f_c t + \theta(t)]$$

$$y_D(t) = \frac{A(t)}{2}\sin\theta(t) - \frac{B(t)}{2}\sin\theta(t)$$

$$= \begin{cases} \frac{\Lambda_c}{2} m(t)\cos\theta(t) & \text{for DSB} \\ \frac{\Lambda'_c}{2}[1 + am_n(t)]\cos\theta(t) & \text{for AM-TC} \\ \frac{\Lambda_c}{4} m(t)\cos\theta(t) \mp \frac{\Lambda_c}{4} m(t)\sin\theta(t) & \text{for SSB} \end{cases}$$

If $\theta(t) = \theta$ which is a phase offset, then the effect is simple attenuation for DSB modulation and phase distortion for SSB.

If $\theta(t)\ 2\pi\Delta\, ft$ where Δf is a slight frequency offset, then distortion is introduced which is called "warble" for DSB. For SSB, the spectrum of the information signal is translated in frequency from baseband by Δf Hz which sounds like the "Donald Duck" effect.

Pilot Tone is the most common method to generate coherent carrier phase reference at the receiver.

Non-coherent Demodulation

The simplest form of non-coherent demodulation is envelope detection.

Envelope Detection

For AM-TC, a technique that does not require a coherent carrier reference can be used if sufficient carrier power is transmitted. This method is called *envelope detection.*

The *envelope* $e(t)$ of the general signal $x(t)$ is defined mathematically as the magnitude of $x(t)+j\hat{x}(t)$. In this case

$$\begin{aligned} e(t) &= |A(t)\cos(2\pi f_c t) + jH\{A(t)\cos(2\pi f_c t)\}| \\ &= |A(t)\cos(2\pi f_c t) + jA(t)\sin(2\pi f_c t)| \\ &= |A(t)[\cos(2\pi f_c t) + j\sin(2\pi f_c t)]| \\ &= |A(t)e^{j2\pi f_c t}| \\ &= |A(t)| \end{aligned}$$

which is unambiguous as long as $A(t) \geq 0$.

An envelope detector produces an output $e(t)$ when the input is $x_c(t)$ and can be realized using a simple diode with an RC network.

Interference

The interference modeled as a sinusoid at a frequency slightly different than that of the carrier. The received signal is

$$\begin{aligned} x_r(t) &= x_c(t) + A_i \cos 2\pi f_i t \\ &= A(t)\cos 2\pi f_c t + A_i \cos 2\pi f_i t \end{aligned}$$

Coherent Demodulation

$$\begin{aligned} y(t) &= x_r(t)\cos 2\pi f_c t \\ &= [A(t)\cos 2\pi f_c t + A_i \cos 2\pi f_i]\cos 2\pi f_c t \\ &= \frac{1}{2}A(t) + \frac{1}{2}A(t)\cos 2\pi 2 f_c t \\ &+ \frac{1}{2}A_i \cos[2\pi(f_i - f_c)t] + \frac{1}{2}A_i \cos[2\pi(f_i + f_c)t] \end{aligned}$$

$$y_D(t) = \frac{1}{2}A(t) + \frac{1}{2}A_i \cos[2\pi(f_i - f_c)t]$$

DSB (AM-SC)

$$y_D(t) = \frac{1}{2}A_c[1 + am_n(t)] + \frac{1}{2}A_i \cos[2\pi(f_i - f_c)t]$$

The signal and interference powers are

$$S = \frac{A_c^2 \langle m^2(t) \rangle}{4}$$

$$= \frac{\langle x_c^2(t) \rangle}{2}$$

$$I = \frac{A_i^2}{8}$$

so that the signal-to-interference ratio is

$$S/I = \frac{2A_c^2 \langle m^2(t) \rangle}{A_i^2}$$

$$= \frac{2\langle x_c^2(t) \rangle}{A_i^2/2)}$$

$$= 2(C/I)$$

where C/I is the carrier-to-interference ratio.

DSB-TC

$$y_D(t) = \frac{1}{2}A(t) + \frac{1}{2}A_i \cos[2\pi(f_i - f_c)t]$$

The signal and interference powers are

$$S = \frac{(A_c'\alpha)^2 \langle m_n^2(t) \rangle}{4}$$

$$= \frac{A_c^2 \langle m^2(t) \rangle}{4}$$

$$= \frac{2E\langle x_c^2(t) \rangle}{4}$$

$$I = \frac{A_i^2}{8}$$

so that the signal-to-interference ratio is

$$S/I = \frac{2A_c^2 \langle m^2(t) \rangle}{A_i^2}$$

$$= \frac{2E\langle x_c^2(t) \rangle}{A_i^2/2}$$

$$= 2E(C/I)$$

where C/I is the carrier-to-interference ratio.

Envelope Detection

The received signal is expressed as

$$x_r(t) = A(t)\cos 2\pi f_c t + A_i \cos[2\pi(f_i - f_c + f_c t]$$

$$= A(t)\cos 2\pi f_c t + A_i \cos[2\pi(f_i - f_c t]\cos[2\pi f_c t]$$
$$- A_i \sin[2\pi(f_i - f_c)\sin[2\pi f_c t]$$
$$= \{A(t) + A_i \cos[2\pi(f_i - f_c)t]\}\cos(2\pi f_c t)$$
$$-\{A_i \sin[2\pi(f_i - f_c)t]\}\sin(2\pi f_c t)$$
$$= e(t)\cos[2\pi f_c t + \theta(t)]$$

where

$$e(t) = \sqrt{\{A(t) + A_i \cos[2\pi(f_i - f_c)t]\}^2 + \{A_i \sin[2\pi(f_i - f_c)t\}^2}$$

$$\theta(t) = \tan^{-1}\left\{\frac{A_i \sin[2\pi(f_i - f_c)t]}{A(t) + A_i \cos[2\pi(f_i - f_c)t}\right\}$$

Clearly, the envelope is $e(t)$ which may be expressed as

$$e(t) = \{A(t) + A_i \cos[2\pi(f_i - f_c)t]\}\sqrt{1 + \left\{\frac{A_i \sin[2\pi(f_i - f_c)t]}{A(t) + A_i \cos[2\pi(f_i - f_c)t]}\right\}^2}$$

$$\cong \{A(t) + A_i \cos[2\pi(f_i - f_c)t]\}\left(1 + \frac{1}{2}\left\{\frac{A_i \sin[2\pi(f_i - f_c)t]}{A(t) + A_i \cos[2\pi(f_i - f_c)t}\right\}^2\right)$$

$$\cong \{A(t) + A_i \cos[2\pi(f_i - f_c)t]\}$$

This is exactly the result for coherent demodulation. Note that the approximation used are valid only when

$$A_c >> A_i$$

which is the case when the signal power is much stronger than the interference power.

Comparison of Linear Modulation Systems

1	DSB	AM-TC	SSB
$x_c(t)$	(3.1)	(3.7)	(3.19)
$X_c(f)$	(3.2)	(3.11)	(3.20)
Test Tone $x_c(t)$	(3.3)	(3.12)	(3.21)
Test Tone $X_c(f)$	(3.4)	(3.14)	(3.22)
$\langle x_c^2(t)\rangle$	$\frac{A_c^2}{2}\langle m^2(t)\rangle$	$\frac{A_c^2}{2E}\langle m^2(t)\rangle$	$\frac{A_c^2}{4}\langle m^2(t)\rangle$
Band width	2W	2W	W
Generation	Simple	Simple	Not so simple
Demodulation	Coherent	Coherent Envelope Detector	Coherent
S/I Ratio	2C/I	2EC/	

ANGLE MODULATION

GENERALIZED ANGLE MODULATION

The angle of the carrier $x_c(t) = A_c \cos[2\pi f_c t + \phi(t)]$ is $2\pi f_c t + \phi(t)$.

There are two main characteristics of the angle: the *instantaneous phase* of the carrier is

$$\theta_i(t) = 2\pi f_c t + \phi(t)$$

and the *instantaneous frequency* of the carrier which is

$$f_i(t) = \frac{1}{2\pi}\frac{d}{dt}\theta_i(t) = f_c + \frac{1}{2\pi}\frac{d\phi(t)}{dt}$$

The first term f_c is the carrier frequency and the second term represents a change in the frequency from f_c. It is called the instantaneous *frequency deviation.*

FREQUENCY MODULATION (FM)

The instantaneous frequency deviation is proportional to the message signal $m(t)$.

$$\frac{1}{2\pi}\frac{d\phi(t)}{dt} = f_d m(t).$$

f_d is called the *frequency deviation constant*. Integrating both sides the instantaneous phase:

$$\phi(t) = 2\pi f_d \int^t m(\tau)d\tau.$$

The lower limit on the integral is not usually specified since an initial condition is not included.

Description of FM

$$x_c(t) = A_c \cos\left[2\pi f_c t + 2\pi f_d \int^t m(\tau)d\tau\right]$$

Since $x_c(t)$ is not a linear function of $m(t)$, it is, in general, not possible to express $X_c(f)$ in terms of .

Test Tone

$$m(t) = A_m \cos 2\pi f_m t\,.$$

$$x_c(t) = A_m \cos[2\pi f_c t + 2\pi f_d \int^t A_m \cos 2\pi f_m \tau d\tau$$

$$= A_c \cos\left[2\pi f_c t + A_m \frac{f_d}{f_m}\sin 2\pi f_m \tau\right]$$

$$= A_c \cos[2\pi f_c t + \beta \sin 2\pi f_m \tau]$$

$$= R\left\{A_c e^{j(2\pi f_c t + \beta \sin 2\pi f_m t)}\right\}$$
$$= R\left\{A_c e^{j2\pi f_c t} e^{j\beta \sin 2\pi f_m t}\right\}$$

The factor

$$\beta = \frac{A_m f_d}{f_m} = \frac{\text{peak frequency deviation}}{\text{max frequency of } m(t)}$$

is called the modulation index. The function $e^{j\beta \sin 2\pi f_m t}$ is periodic with period $T_0 = 1/f_m$. Thus, it may be expanded into a Fourier Series:

$$e^{j\beta \sin 2\pi f_m t} = \sum_{n=-\infty}^{\infty} C_n e^{j2\pi n f_m t}$$

where

$$C_n = \frac{1}{T_0}\int_{-T_0/2}^{T_0/2} e^{j\beta \sin 2\pi f_m t} e^{-j2\pi n f_m t}\, dt$$
$$= \frac{1}{T_0}\int_{-T_0/2}^{T_0/2} e^{-j(2\pi n f_m t - \beta \sin 2\pi f_m t)}\, dt$$
$$= \frac{1}{2\pi}\int_{-\pi}^{\pi} e^{-j(nx - \beta \sin x)}\, dx$$
$$= J_n(\beta)$$

which is the nth order Bessel function of the first kind. (β is called the "argument".) Thus

$$e^{j\beta \sin 2\pi f_m t} = \sum_{n=-\infty}^{\infty} J_n(\beta) e^{j2\pi n f_m t}$$

and

Carrier Power

$$\left\langle x_c^2(t)\right\rangle = \left\langle A_c^2 \cos^2[2\pi f_c t + \phi(t)]\right\rangle$$
$$= \frac{A_c^2}{2}.$$

This can also be determined for the case of sinusoidal modulation by using Parseval's Theorem. The power spectral density of $x_c(t)$ is

$$S_{x_c}(f) = \sum_{n=-\infty}^{\infty} \frac{A_c^2 J_n^2(\beta)}{4}\delta(f + f_c + nf_m) + \sum_{n=-\infty}^{\infty} \frac{A_c^2 J_n^2(\beta)}{4}\delta(f - f_c - nf_m).$$

By Parseval's Theorem,

$$\left\langle x_c^2(t)\right\rangle = \int_{-\infty}^{\infty} S_{x_c}(f)\, df$$
$$= \sum_{n=-\infty}^{\infty} \frac{A_c^2 J_n^2(\beta)}{4} + \sum_{n=-\infty}^{\infty} \frac{A_c^2 J_n^2(\beta)}{4}$$

$$= \sum_{n=-\infty}^{\infty} \frac{A_c^2 J_n^2(\beta)}{2}$$

$$= \frac{A_c^2}{2} \sum_{n=-\infty}^{\infty} J_n^2(\beta)$$

$$= \frac{A_c^2}{2}.$$

$$x_c(t) - R\left\{A_c e^{j2\pi f_c t} \sum_{n=-\infty}^{\infty} J_n(\beta) e^{j2\pi n f_m t}\right\}$$

$$= R\left\{A_c \sum_{n=-\infty}^{\infty} J_n(\beta) e^{j2\pi(f_c + nf_m)t}\right\}$$

$$= A_c \sum_{n=\infty}^{\infty} J_n(\beta) \cos[2\pi(f_c + nf_m)t]$$

$$X_c(f) = \sum_{n=\infty}^{\infty} \frac{A_c J_n(\beta)}{2} [\delta(f + f_c + nf_m) + \delta(f - f_c - nf_m)].$$

FM Bandwidth

For arbitrary $m(t)$, the bandwidth is virtually impossible to determine exactly. For sinusoidal modulation, the bandwidth is theoretically infinite, but for practical purposes, B_{98} is used. B_{98} is determined by the value of k for which

$$0.98 = \frac{\frac{A_c^2}{2} \sum_{n=-k}^{k} J_n^2(\beta)}{\frac{A_c^2}{2}}$$

$$= \sum_{n=-k}^{k} J_n^2(\beta)$$

$$= J_0^2(\beta) + 2\sum_{n=1}^{k} J_n^2(\beta)$$

so that

$$B = 2kf_m.$$

Table reveals $k = \beta + 1$. Thus,

$$B_{98} = 2(\beta + 1)f_m.$$

This rule of thumb is called *Carsons's Rule* in honor of John Carson, a radio engineer who first observed this in the 1940's. For arbitrary $m(t)$, experimental results have shown that the same rule of thumb works well:

$$B = 2(D + 1)\,W$$

where

$$D \frac{\text{peak frequency devation}}{\text{bandwidth of } m(t)} = \frac{f_d[\max\{|m(t)|\}]}{W}$$

FM Generation

1. *VCO:* A *Voltage Controled Oscillator* (VCO) is an oscillator whose output frequency is proportional to the input voltage. It really is a frequency modulator. Typically, these devices are not able to produce large frequency deviations.
2. *Indirect Modulation:* Narrow Band Frequency Modulation (NBFM) is FM where D *(or* β) $\ll 1$. In this case

$$\begin{aligned} x_c(t) &= A_c \cos[2\pi f_c t + \phi(t)] \\ &= A_c \cos(\phi(t))\cos(2\pi f_c t) - A_c \sin(\phi(t))\sin(2\pi f_c t) \end{aligned}$$

Since D (or β) $\ll 1$, $\phi(t) \ll 1$ so that

$$\cos \phi(t) \approx 1$$

$$\sin \phi(t) \approx \phi(t)$$

and

$$x_c(t) \approx A_c \cos 2\pi f_c t + A_c \phi(t) \sin 2\pi f_c t.$$

This is almost like AM-TC where

$$x_c(t) = A_c' \cos 2\pi f_c t + A_c' a m_n(t) \cos 2\pi f_c t.$$

Note the differences between NBFM and AM-TC.

The bandwidth occupied by NBFM modulated carrier is seen to be 2W. Carson's rule also gives this result for small D (or β).

em Wide Band Frequency Modulation (WBFM) is FM where D (or β) $\gg 1$. WBFM is usually generated by using a frequency multiplier to perform narrow band to wideband conversion. A $\times$ N frequency multiplier multiplies the angle of a sinusoid by N. (Compare this operation to that of a mixer which performs a linear translation of the carrier frequency but does not effect the instantaneous phase or frequency deviation).

Demodulation (FM Discriminator)

There are four basic types of FM discriminators:

1. *Ideal FM Discriminator:* The ideal FM discriminator consists of a differentiator followed by an envelope detector. In this case let $x_r(t) = x_c(t)$ so that

$$x_r(t) = A_c \cos\left[2\pi f_c t + 2\pi f_d \int m(\tau)d\tau\right]$$

Thus,

$$e(t) = \frac{d}{dt}x_r(t)$$

$$= -A_c\{2\pi f_c + 2\pi f_d m(t)\} \sin\left[2\pi f_c t + 2\pi f_d \int^t m(\tau)d\tau\right]$$

$$y_D(t) = |A_c\{2\pi f_c + 2\pi f_d m(t)\}|$$

$$= A_c\{2\pi f_c + 2\pi f_d m(t)\}$$

if $f_c < f_d \min\{m(t)\}$ which is almost always the case. Removing the DC component yields

$$y_D(t) = A_c 2\pi f_d m(t).$$

If the amplitude of the carrier is perturbed by noise or other interference so that

$$x_r(t) = A_c(t)\cos\left[2\pi f_c t + 2\pi f_d \int^t m(\tau)d\tau\right]$$

then the discriminator output is

$$y_D(t) = A_c(t)2\pi f_d m(t) + 2\pi f_c A(t).$$

The carrier amplitude variations cause distortion at the output. This distortion can be removed by passing $x_r(t)$ through a *limiter* prior to the differentiator . The output of the limiter is square wave given by

$$s(t) = K\text{sgn}(m(t)).$$

The limiter output must then be converted to a sinusoid by passing it through a band-pass filter with center frequency f_c and sufficient bandwidth to pass the varying fundamental. The result is a constant amplitude sinusoid which is differentiated and passed through the envelope detector to produce the desired signal.

Time-Delay/Phase-Shift Demodulator

The time derivative of $x(t)$ is defined by the following limit:

$$\frac{dx(t)}{dt} = \lim_{\tau \to 0} \frac{x(t) - x(t-\tau)}{\tau}.$$

For small τ

$$x(t) - x(t-\tau) \approx \tau \frac{dx(t)}{dt}$$

so that the differentiation process may be approximated by time delay and subtraction operation.

A Phase shift demodulator uses a linear phase shift network (or delay line) to produce the delayed verion of the modulated carrier.

The phase-shift network has a group delay t_1 and a carrier t_0 delay designed so that

$$2\pi f_c t_0 = \frac{\pi}{2}$$

Let the output of the bandpass filter be

$$K\cos[2\pi f_c t + \phi(t)]$$

The output of the phase shift network is thus

$$K\cos[2\pi f_c(t - t_1)] = K\sin[2\pi f_c t + \phi(t - t_1)]$$

The low pass filter output of the product is

$$y_D(t) = \frac{K}{2}\sin[\phi(t) - \phi(t - t_1)].$$

Now if t_1 is small and that the change is $\phi(t)$ is very small during t_1 seconds,

$$y_D(t) \approx \phi(t) - \phi(t - t_1)$$

$$\approx t_1 \frac{d}{dt}\phi(t)$$

$$= t_1 2\pi f_d m(t).$$

Since the phase-shift network produces a quadrature version of the modulated carrier, this demodulator is often called a *quadrature detector.*

Zero Crossing Detector

All the message information is contained in the frequency of the carrier not in the amplitude (that is why the limiter is able to remove all amplitude information from the carrier without destroying any of the information content of the carrier). The frequency of the carrier can be measured by observing the zero crossings of the carrier.

The square-wave FM signal from the hard limiter triggers a monostable pulse generator which produces a short pulse of duration at each positive (or negative) zero crossing of the FM square wave. The monostable output $v(t)$ is a pulse train with period

$$T_m = \frac{1}{f_c + f_d m(t)}.$$

During any interval of T seconds where

$$W \ll \frac{1}{T} \ll f_c,$$

there are $T[f_c + f_d m(t)]$ pulses. Continually integrating $v(t)$ over this T second interval yields

$$y_D(t) = \int_{t-T}^{t} v\tau d\tau$$
$$= T[f_c + f_d m(t)]\tau$$
$$= (T\tau f_d)m(t) \text{ afer DC block}$$

PLL Discriminator

Figure: Phase-Shift (Delay-Line) FM Demodulator.

$$x_c(t) = A_c \cos[2\pi f_c t \mid \phi(t)]$$

Figure: Zero-Crossing FM Demodulator.

Interference in Angle Modulation

Let the modulated carrier be given by

$$\phi(t) = \begin{cases} 2\pi f_d \int^t m(\tau)d\tau & \text{for FM} \\ k_p m(t) & \text{for PM} \end{cases}$$

where

$$A_i \cos 2\pi f_i t$$

The interference signal is a sinusoid given by

$$x_r(t) = x_c(t) + A_i \cos 2\pi f_i t$$
$$= A_c \cos[2\pi f_c t + \phi(t)] + A_i \cos 2\pi f_i t$$

so that the received signal is

$$C = \frac{A_c^2}{2}\cdot$$
$$I = \frac{A_i^2}{2}$$

Clearly, for both FM and PM, the carrier and interference powers are

$$C/I = \frac{A_c^2}{A_i^2}.$$

so that the carrier-to-interference ratio is

$$x_r(t) = A_c \cos[2\pi f_c t + \phi(t)] + A_i \cos[2\pi f_i t - 2\pi f_c t - \phi(t) + 2\pi f_c t + \phi(t)]$$
$$= A_c \cos[2\pi f_c t + \phi(t)] + A_i \cos[2\pi f_i t - f_c t - \phi(t)] \cos[2\pi f_c t + \phi(t)]$$
$$- A_i \sin[2\pi (f_i + f_c)t - \phi(t)] \sin[2\pi f_c t + \phi(t)]$$
$$= \{A_c + A_i \cos[2\pi (f_i - f_c)t - \phi(t)]\} \cos[2\pi f_c t + \phi(t)]$$
$$- A_i \sin[2\pi (f_i - f_c)t - \phi(t)] \sin[2\pi f_c t + \phi(t)]$$
$$= R(t) \cos[2\pi f_c t + \phi(t)] + \theta(t)]$$

FM Interference

The signal-to-interference ratio is derived for the ideal FM discriminator. The received signal is expressed as,

$$R(t) = \sqrt{\{A_c + A_i \cos[2\pi(f_i - f_c)t - \phi(t)]\}^2 + \{A_i + \sin[2\pi(f_i - f_c)t - \phi(t)]\}^2}$$

$$\theta(t) = -\tan^{-1}\left\{\frac{A_i \sin[2\pi(f_i - f_c)t - \phi(t)]}{A_c + A_i \cos[2\pi(f_i - f_c)t - \phi(t)]}\right\}$$

where

$$x_r(t) = K \cos[2\pi fct + \phi(t) + \theta(t)].$$

After passing through the hard-limiter, the received signal is expressed as

$$\tan^{-1} x = x - \frac{1}{3}x^3 + \frac{1}{5}x^5 - \cdots$$

$$\approx x$$

Using

$$A_c < A_i$$

$$\theta(t) \approx \frac{A_i \sin[2\pi(f_i - f_c)t - \phi(t)]}{A_c + A_i \cos[2\pi(f_i - f_c)t - \phi(t)]}$$

$$\approx \frac{A_i \sin[2\pi(f_i - f_c)t - \phi(t)]}{A_c}$$

for small x, it is seen that for

$$e(t) = -K\left[2\pi f_c + \frac{d}{dt}\phi(t) + \frac{d}{dt}\theta(t)\right]\sin\left[2\pi f_c t + \phi(t) + \theta(t)\right]$$

$$y_D(t) = K\frac{d}{dt}\phi(t) + K\frac{d}{dt}\theta(t)$$

$$= K\frac{d}{dt}2\pi f_d \int^t m(\tau)d\tau + K\frac{d}{dt}\left\{\frac{A_i \sin[2\pi(f_i - f_c)t - \phi(t)]}{A_c}\right\}$$

$$= 2\pi K f_d m(t) + \frac{A_i}{A_c}\frac{d}{dt}\sin[2\pi(f_i - f_c)t - \phi(t)]$$

The outputs of the differentiator and envelope detector are

$$S = 4\pi^2 K^2 f_d^2 \left\langle m^2(t)\right\rangle.$$

The first term represents the signal the power of which is

$m = 0$

The second term represents a combination of the signal and the interference at the discriminator output.

The interference power is determined by observing the power of the interference signal in the presence of an unmodulated carrer. Setting $\phi(t) = 0$, it is seen that $y_D(t)$ and interference component of is

$$\frac{d}{dt}\theta(t) = K\frac{A_i}{A_c}\frac{d}{dt}\sin[2\pi(f_i - f_c)t]$$

$$= K\frac{A_i}{A_c}2\pi(f_i - f_c)\cos[2\pi(f_i - f_c)t]$$

$$I = \frac{2\pi^2 K^2 A_i^2 (f_i - f_c)^2}{A_c^2}$$

which is a sinusoid with a frequency dependent amplitude. The interfernece power is

$$S/I = \frac{2A_c^2 f_d^2 \langle m^2(t)\rangle}{A_i^2 (f_i - f_c)^2}$$

$$= \frac{2f_d^2 \langle m^2(t)\rangle}{(f_i - f_c)^2}\cdot C/I$$

and the signal-to-interference ratio is

$$y_{D\Gamma M}(t) = \int^t y_{DFM}(t)$$

$$= K\phi(t) + K\theta(t)$$

$$\approx Kk_p m(t) + \frac{A_i K}{A_c}\sin[2\pi(f_i - f_c)t - \phi(t)].$$

PM Interference

The PM demodulator is effectively an ideal FM demodulator followed by an integrator. Thus

$$S = K^2 k_p^2 \langle m^2(t)\rangle.$$

The signal power is

$\phi(t) = 0$

The interference power is determined by calculating the power of the demodulator output when the input is an unmodulated carrer. With

$$y_{D\Gamma M}(t) = \frac{A_i K}{A_c} \sin[2\pi(f_i - f_c)t]$$

$$I = \frac{A_i^2 K^2}{2A_c^2}$$

$$S/I = \frac{2A_c^2 f_d^2 \langle m^2(t) \rangle}{A_i^2}$$

$$= 2k_p^2 \langle m^2(t) \rangle (C/I)$$

The signal-to-interference ratio is

$$\phi(t) = k_p m(t).$$

Phase Modulation (PM)

The instantaneous phase deviation is proportional to the message signal k_p

$$x_c(t) = A_c \cos[2\pi f_c t + k_p m(t)]$$

The parameter is called the phase deviation constant.

PM Description

$$m(t) = A_m \cos 2\pi f_m t$$

Test Tone

$$x_c(t) = A_c \cos[2\pi f_c t + k_p A_m \cos 2\pi f_m t]$$

$$= A_c \cos[2\pi f_c t + \beta \cos 2\pi f_m t]$$

$$= \Re\{A_c e^{j2\pi f_c t} e^{j\beta \cos 2\pi f_m t}\}$$

$$\beta = k_p A_m$$

where

$$e^{j\beta \cos 2\pi f_m t}$$

is the maximum phase deviation. The term

$$T_0 = \frac{1}{f_m}.$$

is periodic in t with period

$$e^{j\beta \cos 2\pi f_m t}$$

$$= \sum_{n=-\infty}^{\infty} C_n e^{jn2\pi f_m t}$$

This periodic term may be expressed as

$$C_n = \frac{1}{T_0}\int_{-\frac{3T_0}{4}}^{\frac{T}{4}} e^{j\beta\cos 2\pi f_m t} e^{-jn2\pi f_m t}\,dt$$

$$= \frac{1}{2\pi}\int_{-\frac{3\pi}{2}}^{\frac{\pi}{2}} e^{j\beta\cos z} e^{-jnz}\,dz$$

$$= \frac{1}{2\pi}\int_{-\frac{3\pi}{2}}^{\frac{\pi}{2}} e^{j\beta\sin(z+\pi/2)} e^{-jn(z+\pi/2)} e^{jn\pi/2}\,dz$$

$$= e^{jn\pi/2}\frac{1}{2\pi}\int_{-\pi}^{\pi} e^{j\beta\sin x} e^{-jnx}\,dx$$

$$= e^{jn\pi/2} J_n(\beta)$$

$$= (j)^n J_n(\beta).$$

where

$$e^{j\beta\cos 2\pi f_m t} = \sum_{n=-\infty}^{\infty} (j)^n J_n(\beta) e^{jn2\pi f_m t}$$

Thus

$$x_c(t) = \Re\left\{A_c e^{j2\pi f_c t}\sum_{n=-\infty}^{\infty} e^{jn\pi/2} J_n(\beta) e^{jn2\pi f_m t}\right\}$$

$$= \Re\left\{A\sum_{n=-\infty}^{\infty} J_n(\beta) e^{j2\pi(f_c+nf_m)t+n\pi/2}\right\}$$

=

$$A_c\left\{A_c\sum_{n=-\infty}^{\infty} J_n(\beta)\cos[2\pi(f_c+nf_m)t+n\pi/2]\right\}$$

$$X_c(f) = \sum_{n=-\infty}^{\infty}\frac{A_c J_n(\beta)}{2}\{e^{-\frac{n\pi}{2}}\delta(f+f_c+nf_m)+e^{\frac{n\pi}{2}}\delta(f-f_c-nf_m)\}$$

and

$$\left\langle x_c^2(t)\right\rangle = \left\langle A_c^2\cos^2[2\pi f_c t + k_p m(t)]\right\rangle$$

$$= \frac{A_c^2}{2}$$

Carrier Power

$x_c(t)$

The case of sinusoidal modulation by using Parseval's Theorem. The power spectral density of is

$$Sx_c(f) = \sum_{n=-\infty}^{\infty} \frac{A_c^2 J_n^2(\beta)}{4} \delta(f + f_c + nf_m)$$

$$+ \sum_{n=-\infty}^{\infty} \frac{A_c^2 J_n^2(\beta)}{4} \delta(f + f_c + nf_m)$$

$$\langle x_c^2(t) \rangle = \int_{-\infty}^{\infty} S_{x_c}(f)\, df$$

$$= \sum_{n=-\infty}^{\infty} \frac{A_c^2 J_n^2(\beta)}{4} + \sum_{n=-\infty}^{\infty} \frac{A_c^2 J_n^2(\beta)}{4}$$

$$= \sum_{n=-\infty}^{\infty} \frac{A_c^2 J_n^2(\beta)}{2}$$

$$= \frac{A_c^2}{2} \sum_{n=-\infty}^{\infty} J_n^2(\beta)$$

$$= \frac{A_c^2}{2}$$

$m\ (t)$

Thus by Parseval's Theorem,

PM Bandwidth

Just as in the case for FM, the power spectral density and bandwidth are impossible to determine for arbitrary B_{98}. For sinusoidal modulation Carson's rule is used to determine $B_{98} = 2(\beta + 1) f_m$. Thus

$$\beta = k_p A_m$$

where β

is the maximum phase deviation.

Note that this definition of b is different than that for the FM case. f_m is not a function of $m(t)$. Extending these results to the case of arbitrary $B = 2(D_p + 1)W$, it is seen that

$$D_p = \text{maximum phase deviation} = kp \max \{|m(t)|\}$$

where

$$\begin{aligned} x_r(t) &= x_c(t) + A_c \cos 2\pi f_i t \\ &= A_c \cos [2\pi f_c t + \phi(t)] \end{aligned}$$

Interference

Let the received signal be

$$\phi(t) = m_p m(t)$$

where

$$C/I = \frac{A_c^2}{A_i^2}$$

Clearly, the carrier-to-interference ratio is

$$\begin{aligned} y_{DΓM}(t) &= \int^t y_{DFM}(t) \\ &= K\phi(t) - K\theta(t) \\ &\approx K k_p m(t) - \frac{A_i K}{A_c} \sin[2\pi(f_i - f_c)t - \phi(t)] \end{aligned}$$

The PM demodulator is an FM demodulator followed by an integrator. Thus

$$S = K^2 k_p^2 \langle m^2(t) \rangle.$$

The signal power is

$$\phi(t) = 0$$

The interference power is determined by calculating the power of the demodulator output when the input is an unmodulated carrer. With

$$y_{DΓM}(t) = -\frac{A_i K}{A_c} \sin[2\pi(f_i - f_c)t]$$

$$I = \frac{A_i^2 K^2}{2A_c^2}$$

$$S/I = \frac{2A_c^2 k_p^2 \langle m^2(t) \rangle}{A_i^2}$$

$$= 2k_p^2 \langle m^2(t) \rangle (C/I)$$

The signal-to-interference ratio is

$$m(t) = u(t)$$

FREQUENCY DIVISION MULTIPLEXING AND COMMERICAL BROADCASTING

FREQUENCY DIVISION MULTIPLEXING

Commercial FM Broadcasting

Characteristic	*FCC Standard*
Assigned bandwidth	6 Mhz
Video carrier frequency	1.25 ± 0.001 MHz above lower boundary of channel
Audio carrier frequecy	4.25 ± 0.001 MHz above video carrier frequency
Chrominance subcarrier frequency	3.759545 Mhz 10 Hz above the video carrier frequency
Video modulation type	VSB
Audio modulation type	FM with peak frequency deviation = 25 kHz
Audio frequency response	50 Hz to 15 kHz following a 75 μsec pre-emphasis cureve

Commercial Broadcast TV

Characteristic	*A Service (Nonwire Line)*	*B Service (Wire Line)*
Cell base station	869-880	880-890
Transmit bands (MHz)	890-891.5	891.5-894
Mobile station	824-835	835-845
Transmit bands (MHz)	845-846.5	846.5-849
Maximum transmit power(W)	3	3
Cell radius (km)	2-20	2-20
Channel bandwidth (kHz)	30	30
Voice modulation type	FM	FM
Control signal	FSK	FSK
	8 kHz frequency deviation 10 kbits/sec Manchester line code	8 kHz frequency deviation 10 kbits/sec Manchester line code

Cellular Telephone

Cellular Telephone: AMPS (Advanced Mobile Phone System) Standard.

AT&T FDM Hierarchy

$$r(t) = \sum_{i=1}^{N} x_{ci}(t)$$

Heterodyne Receivers

There are two basic methods for demodulating FDM signals. The first is the Variable Tuned Filter (VTF). In this method, the center frequency of the variable band-pass filter is changed to pass only the desired signal and reject all others. The requirements of such a filter are severe. Approximations to the ideal requirements result in rather poor performance.

The second method is the super-heterodyne receiver and is by far the more common method used. The super-heterodyne receiver employs a band-pass filter at a fixed center frequency (called the intermediate frequency or IF) and a variable local oscillator to frequency translate the desired signal into the pass band of the band-pass filter. The wide-band variable band-pass filter is necessary only to reject the signals centered at the image frequencies.

To understand *image frequencies* consider the following FDM system consisting of N signals:

$$x_{ci}(t) = A_i(t) \cos[2\pi f_i t + \phi_i(t)]$$

where

$$x_{ci}(t)$$

Suppose the desired signal the message portion of $x_{ci}(t)$. The superheterodyne receiver must perform a two step process:

Step 1: Frequency translate f_i from F_{IF} to $r(t)$.

Step 2: BPF the translated signal and demodulate.

Step 1 is achieved by mixing cos $2\pi f_{\text{LO}} t$ with a local oscillator f_{LO}. There are two possibilities for:

$$f_{\text{LO}} = \begin{cases} f_{IF} + f_i & \text{high side tuning} \\ f_{IF} - f_i & \text{low side tuning} \end{cases}$$

$$r(t) = A_i(t)\cos[2\pi f_i t + \phi_i(t)]$$
$$+ B(t)\cos[2\pi f_i + 2f_{IF})t + \theta(t)]$$

For high side tuning, let

The mixer output $x_r(t)$ and the band-pass filter output are given by

$$d(t) = r(t) \cos 2\pi\,(I_{\text{IF}} + f_i)t$$

$$= \frac{A_i(t)}{2} \cos[2\pi(f_{IF} + 2f_i)t + \phi_i(t)]$$

$$+\frac{A_i(t)}{2}\cos[2\pi(f_{IF}t-\phi_i(t)]$$

$$=\frac{B(t)}{2}\cos[2\pi(f_{IF}+2f_i)t+\theta(t)]$$

$$+\frac{B(t)}{2}\cos[2\pi(f_{IF}t+\theta(t)]$$

$$x_r(t)=\frac{A_i(t)}{2}\cos[2\pi(f_{IF}+2f_i)t+\phi_i(t)]$$

$$+\frac{B(t)}{2}\cos[2\pi(f_{IF}t+\theta(t)].$$

are given by

$$f_i+2f_{IF}$$

The input to the demodulator consists of two signals superimposed on each other so that the demodulator will not be able distinguish between the two. The unwanted signal is centered at. Since this undesired signal signal is also mixed $r(t) = A_i(t)\cos[2\pi f_i t + \phi_i(t)] + B(t)\cos[2\pi(fi - 2fIF)\,t + \theta\,(t)$ to the passband of the band-pass filter, it is termed the image frequency.

The mixer output $x_r(t)$ and the band-pass filter output

$d(t) = r(t)\cos 2\pi(f_{IF} - fi)t$

$$=\frac{A_i(t)}{2}\cos[2\pi(f_{IF}t+\phi_i(t)] + \frac{A_i(t)}{2}\cos[2\pi(2f_i-f_{IF})t+\phi_i(t)]$$

$$=\frac{B(t)}{2}\cos[2\pi(2f_i-3f_{IF})t+\theta(t)] + \frac{B(t)}{2}\cos[2\pi f_{IF}t-\theta(t)]$$

$$x_r(t)=\frac{A_i(t)}{2}\cos[2\pi(f_{IF}+f_i)t+\phi_i(t)] + \frac{B(t)}{2}\cos[2\pi f_{IF}t-\theta(t)]$$

In this case, the unwanted signal is centered at the image frequencey.

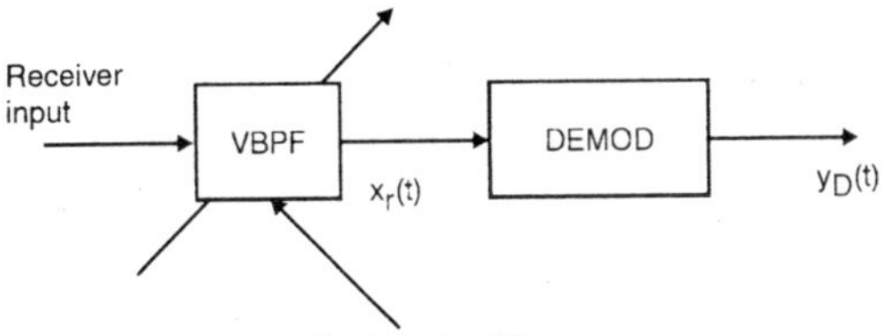

Predetection Filter

A wide-band variable band pass filter is used to reject the image frequencies prior to mixing to the intermediate frequency. The requirements on this filter are not severe so that physical realization is practical.

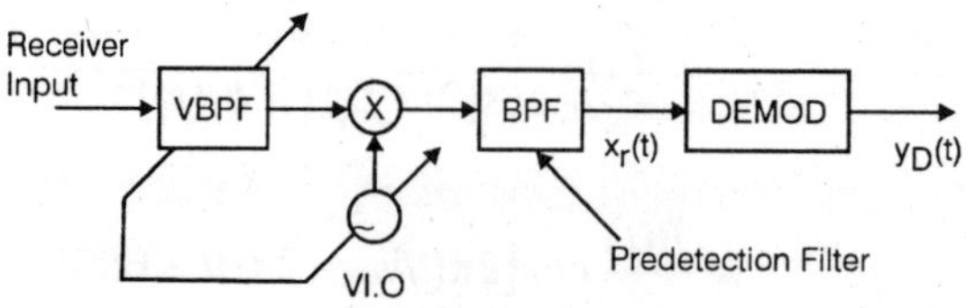

Fig. Ideal VTF Receiver

NOISE IN MODULATION SYSTEMS

For the purposes of noise calculations, both the VTF and the Heterodyne receiver systems are equivalent to the common feature which they share: A bandpass filter followed by a demodulator.

The band-pass filter is used to isolate the desired signal and is typically called the "predetection filter." The predetection filter precedes the demodulator and needs to have a bandwidth wide enough to pass the desired signal without causing distortion but as narrow as possible to reduce the noise passed to the demodulator.

The output of the predetection filter, , is a combination of the modulated carrier and narrow band noise:
where $n(t)$ is the channel attenuation and

$$Sn(f) = \frac{N_0}{2} \quad \text{for } | f - f_c | \leq B$$

is narrow band white Gaussian random process with power spectral density

$$xr(t) = \alpha \ddot{E}(t) \cos (2\pi f_c t | \theta) | n(t)$$

where B is the bandwidth of the predetection filter.

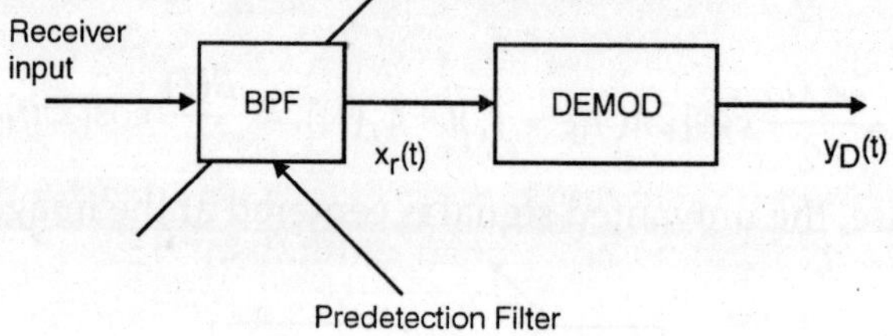

Fig. Receiver System Model for Noise Calculations

NOISE IN DSB SYSTEMS

The required bandwidth of the predetection filter is 2W. The output of the predetection filter is

$$A(t) = \begin{cases} A_c m(t) & \text{for DSB-SC} \\ A_c^t [1 + am_n(t)] & \text{for DSB-TC} \end{cases}$$

where is an arbitrary phase angle induced by the channel and

$$\frac{\langle \alpha^2 A^2(t) \rangle}{2} = \begin{cases} \dfrac{\alpha^2 \Lambda_c^2}{2} \langle m^2(t) \rangle & \text{for DSB-SC} \\ \dfrac{\alpha^2 \Lambda_c^2 \langle m^2(t) \rangle}{2E} & \text{for DSB-TC} \end{cases}$$

Carrier to Noise Ratio (CNR)

The carrier power C is

$$N = \langle n^2(t) \rangle$$

$$= 2\int_0^{\infty} S_n(f)df$$

$$= 2\int_{f_c-W}^{f_c+W} \frac{N_0}{2} df$$

$$= 2N_0W.$$

The noise power is

$$\text{CNR} = \begin{cases} \dfrac{\alpha^2 \Lambda_c^2 \langle m^2(t) \rangle}{4N_0W} & \text{for DSB-SC} \\ \dfrac{\alpha^2 \Lambda_c^2 \langle m^2(t) \rangle}{4EN_0W} & \text{for DSB-TC} \end{cases}$$

The CNR = C/N and is given by

SNR: Coherent Demodulation

The band limited noise f_c at the output of the predetection filter may be expanded into quadrature components about so that

$$x_r(t) = \alpha A(t) \cos(2\pi f_c t + \theta) + n_c(t) \cos(2\pi f_c t + \theta) - n_s(t) \sin(2\pi f_c t + \theta).$$

$$d(t) = \frac{\alpha A(t)}{2} + \frac{\alpha A(t)}{2} \cos(4\pi f_c t + 2\theta)$$

$$+ \frac{n_c(t)}{2} + \frac{n_c(t)}{2} \cos(4\pi f_c t + 2\theta)$$

$$- \frac{n_s(t)}{2} \cos(4\pi f_c t + 2\theta)$$

$$y_D(t) = \frac{\alpha A(t)}{2} + \frac{n_c(t)}{2}$$

Thus

$$S = \frac{\alpha^2 A_c^2}{4}\langle m^2(t)\rangle.$$

In both cases, the signal power is

$$N = \frac{1}{4}\langle n_c^2(t)\rangle$$

$$= \frac{1}{2}\int_0^{\infty} S_{nc}(f)\,df$$

$$= \frac{1}{2}\int_0^{W} N_0\,df$$

$$= \frac{N_0 W}{2}.$$

The noise power at the detector output is

$$\text{SNR} = \frac{\alpha^2 A_c^2\langle m^2(t)\rangle}{2N_0 W}\begin{cases} 2(\text{CNR}) & \text{for DSB-SC} \\ 2E(\text{CNR}) & \text{for DSB-TC} \end{cases}$$

The signal to noise ratio SNR = and is given by

$$x_r(t) = \alpha A(t)\cos(2\pi f_c t + \theta) + n_c(t)\cos(2\pi f_c t + \theta) - n_s(t)\sin(2\pi f_c t + \theta)$$
$$= [\alpha A(t) + n_c(t)]\cos(2\pi f_c t + \theta) - n_c(t)\sin(2\pi f_c t + \theta)$$
$$= \sqrt{[\alpha A(t) + n_c(t)]^2 + n_s^2(t)}\cos(2\pi f_c t + \theta - \theta(t))$$

SNR: Envelope Detection [sh]

In this case, the output of the predetection filter is expressed as

$$\theta(t) = \tan^{-1}\frac{n_s(t)}{\alpha A(t) + n_c(t)}$$

where

$$e(t) = \left|\sqrt{[\alpha A(t) + n_c(t)]^2 + n_s^2(t)}\right|$$
$$\approx \alpha A(t) + n_c(t)$$

The output of the envelope detector is

$$\alpha A(t) + n_c(t) \gg n_s(t)$$

$$S = \alpha^2 A_c^2 \langle m^2(t) \rangle$$

$$N = 2N_0 W$$

when (i.e. the CNR is high). Thus the signal and noise powers are

$$\text{SNR} = \frac{\alpha^2 A_c^2}{2N_0 W}\langle m^2(t) \rangle.$$

and

$$x_r(t) = \alpha \frac{A_c}{2} m(t) \cos(2\pi f_c t + \theta)$$

$$\pm \alpha \frac{A_c}{2} \hat{m}(t) \sin(2\pi f_c t + \theta) + n(t).$$

NOISE IN SSB SYSTEMS

The predetection filter has a required bandwidth of W.

CNR

Let the output of the predetection filter be

$$C = \alpha^2 \frac{A_c}{4} \langle m^2(t) \rangle$$

$$N = \langle n^2(t) \rangle$$

$$= \int_0^{\infty} S_n(f)\, df$$

$$= 2\int_{f_c}^{f_c+W} \frac{N_0}{2}\, df = N_0 W.$$

The carrier power and noise powers are

$$\text{CNR} = \frac{\alpha^2 A_c^2}{4N_0 W}\langle m^2(t) \rangle.$$

Thus, the CNR = is given by

SNR [sh]

The noise at the predetection filter output may expanded into quadrature components about so that

$$x_r(t) = \alpha \frac{\alpha A_c}{2} m(t) \cos(2\pi f_c t + \theta) \pm \frac{\alpha A_c}{2} \hat{m}(t) \sin(2\pi f_c t + \theta).$$

$$+ n_c(t) \cos(2\pi f_c t + \theta) - n_s(t) \sin(2\pi f_c t + \theta)$$

$$d(t) = \frac{\alpha A_c}{2} m(t) + \frac{\alpha A_c}{2} m(t)\cos(4\pi f_c t + 2\theta)$$

$$\pm \frac{\alpha A_c}{4} \hat{m}(t)\sin(4\pi f_c t + 2\theta)$$

$$+ \frac{n_c(t)}{2} + \frac{n_c(t)}{2}\cos(4\pi f_c t + 2\theta) - \frac{n_c(t)}{2}\sin(4\pi f_c t + 2\theta)$$

$$y_D(t) = \frac{\alpha A_c}{4} m(t) + \frac{n_c(t)}{2}.$$

The signal power and noise powers are

$$S = \frac{\alpha^2 A_c^2}{16}\langle m^2(t)\rangle$$

$$N = \frac{1}{4}\langle n^2(t)\rangle$$

$$= \frac{1}{2}\int_0^{\infty} S_{nc}(f)\,df$$

$$= \frac{1}{2}\int_0^{W} \frac{N_0}{2}\,df$$

$$= \frac{N_0 W}{4}.$$

and the signal to noise ratio SNR = is

$$\text{SNR} = \frac{\alpha^2 A_c^2}{4N_0 W}\langle m^2(t)\rangle = \text{CNR},.$$

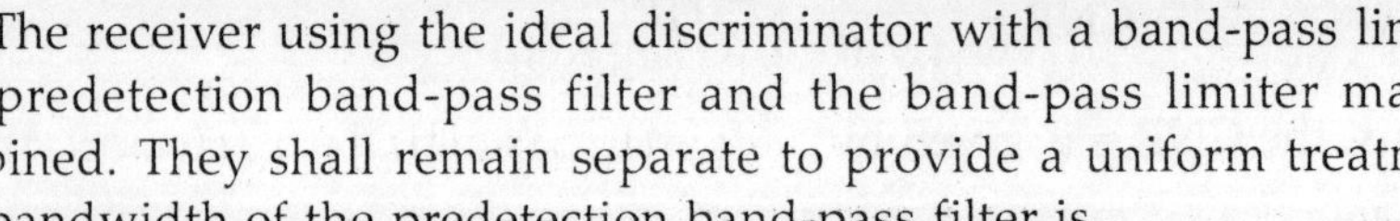

Fig. Ideal FM Differentiator Discriminator

NOISE IN FM SYSTEMS

The receiver using the ideal discriminator with a band-pass limiter. The predetection band-pass filter and the band-pass limiter may be combined. They shall remain separate to provide a uniform treatment. The bandwidth of the predetection band-pass filter is

$$x_r(t) = \alpha A_c \cos[2\pi f_c t + \phi(t) + \theta] + n(t)$$

CNR

The output of the predetection filter is

$$\phi(t) = 2\pi f_d \int m(\tau)\,d\tau$$

where

$n(t)$ and

$$C = \frac{\alpha^2 A_c^2}{2}$$

$$N = \langle n^2(t) \rangle$$

$$= 2\int_0^{\infty} S_n(f)\,df$$

$$= 2\int_{f_c+(D+1)W}^{f_c+(D+1)W} \frac{N_0}{2}\,df$$

$$= 2(D+1)\,W\,N_0.$$

is band limited white Gaussian random process. The carrier power and noise powers are

$$\text{CNR} = \frac{\alpha^2 A_c^2}{4(D+1)WN_0}.$$

The CNR is f_c

SNR [sh]

The noise at the output of the predetection filter may be expanded about so that

$$x_r(t) = \alpha A_c \cos(2\pi f_c t + \phi(t) + \theta] + n_c(t)\cos(2\pi f_c t + \theta) - n_s(t)\sin(2\pi f_c t + \theta)$$

$$= \alpha A_c \cos(2\pi f_c t + \phi(t) + \theta] + n_c(t)\cos(2\pi f_c t + \phi(t) + \theta - \phi(t)]$$
$$- n_c(t)\sin(2\pi f_c t + \phi(t) + \theta - \phi(t)]$$

$$= \alpha A_c \cos(2\pi f_c t + \phi(t) + \theta] + n_c(t)\cos(2\pi f_c t + \phi(t) + \theta]\cos[\phi(t)]$$
$$- n_c(t)\sin(2\pi f_c t + \phi(t) + \theta - \phi(t)]$$
$$+ n_s(t)\cos(2\pi f_c t + \phi(t) + \theta]\sin[\phi(t)]$$

$$= (\alpha A_c + n_c(t)]\cos[\phi(t)] + n_s(t)\sin[\phi(t)]\cos[2\pi f_c t + \phi(t) + \theta]$$
$$+ (n_c(t)\sin[\phi(t)] - n_s(t)\cos[\phi(t)]\sin[2\pi f_c t + \phi(t) + \theta]$$

$$= R(r)\cos[2\pi f_c t + \phi(t) + \theta - \theta(t)]$$

and

$$R(t) = \sqrt{(\alpha A_c + n_c(t)\cos[\phi(t)] + n_s(t)\sin[\phi(t)])^2 + (n_c(t)\sin[\phi(t)] - n_s(t)\cos[\phi(t)])^2}$$

where

$$\theta(t) = \tan^{-1}\frac{n_c(t)\sin[\phi(t)] - n_s(t)\cos[\phi(t)]}{\alpha A_c + n_c(t)\cos[\phi(t)] + n_s(t)\sin[\phi(t)]}$$

$$\approx \tan^{-1}\frac{n_c(t)\sin[\phi(t)] - n_s(t)\cos[\phi(t)]}{\alpha A_c}$$

$$\approx \frac{n_c(t)\sin[\phi(t)] - n_s(t)\cos[\phi(t)]}{\alpha A_c}$$

and $\alpha A_c \gg n_c(t)$

for low noise levels where $\alpha A_c \gg n_c(t)$ and most of the time (e.g. high CNR). Thus

$$x_r(t) \approx R(t)\left[2\pi f_c t + \phi(t) + \theta - \frac{n_c(t)\sin[\phi(t)] - n_s(t)\cos[\phi(t)]}{\alpha A_c}\right]$$

The output of the bandpass limiter is

$$d(t) = -V_0\left\{2\pi f_c + \frac{d\phi(t)}{dt} - \frac{1}{\alpha A_c}\frac{d}{dt}\left(n_c(t)\sin[\phi(t)] - n_s(t)\cos[\phi(t)]\right)\right\}$$

$$\times \sin\left[2\pi f_c t + \phi(t) + \theta - \frac{n_c(t)\sin[\phi(t)] - n_s(t)\cos[\phi(t)]}{\alpha A_c}\right]$$

The output of the differentiator is

$$y_D(t) = V_0\frac{d}{dt}\left\{2\pi f_d \int^t m(\tau)d\tau\right\} - 2\frac{V_0}{\alpha A_c}\frac{d}{dt}\{n_c(t)\sin[\phi(t)] - n_s(t)\cos[\phi(t)]\}$$

$$= V_0 2\pi f_d m(t) - \frac{V_0}{\alpha A_c}\frac{d}{dt}\{n_c(t)\sin[\phi(t)] - n_s(t)\cos[\phi(t)]\}$$

The output of envelope detector (with the DC term removed) is

$$S = \left\langle [V_0 2\pi f_d m(t)]^2 \right\rangle$$

$$= 4\pi^2 f_d^2 V_0^2 \left\langle m^2(t) \right\rangle$$

The first term represents the signal and the second term represents a combination of the signal and the noise. The signal power is

$$y_D(t)$$

The noise component of $n_D(t)$, $m(t) = 0$, is determined by observing the discriminator output when the input is an unmodulated carrier accompanied by noise. This is accomplished by the setting $\phi(t) = 0$. This forces

$$n_D(t) = \frac{V_0}{\alpha A_c}\frac{d}{dt}n_s(t).$$

as well. The resulting noise output is

$$S_{nD}(f) = |H(f)|^2 S_{ns}(f)$$

$$= \frac{V_0^2}{\alpha^2 A_c^2}|j2\pi f|^2 N_0$$

$$= \frac{4\pi^2 V_0^2 N_0}{\alpha^2 A_c^2} f^2$$

is determined by viewing the differentiation operation as a filter and using the relation

$$N = \int_{-W}^{W} S_{nD}(f)df$$

$$= \int_{-W}^{W} \frac{4\pi^2 V_0^2 N_0}{\alpha^2 A_c^2} f^2 df$$

$$= \frac{8\pi^2 V_0^2 N_0 W^3}{3\alpha^2 A_c^2}$$

The power spectral density of the noise is not flat, but rather quadratic in f. The higher frequencies of the message signal are affected by noise more than the lower frequencies. The noise power is

$$\text{SNR} = \int_{-W}^{W} \frac{3}{2} \frac{\alpha^2 A_c^2 f_d^2 \langle m^2(t)\rangle}{N_0 W^2}$$

$$= \frac{3}{2}\left(\frac{f_d}{W}\right)^2 \langle m^2(t)\rangle$$

$$\alpha^2 A^2_{\overline{cN_0W}} = 6D^2(D+1)\langle m_n^2(t)\rangle \frac{\alpha^2 \Lambda_c^2}{4N_0(D+1)W}$$

$$= 6D^2(D+1)\langle m_n^2(t)\rangle \text{CRN}.$$

so that the SNR is

$$\alpha A_c$$

The approximations used to derive the SNR are good only when the noise levels are low compared to *T*. When this is not the case, the performance of the FM discriminator is poor. The point at which this occurs is called the *threshold* and is usually given by CNR f_d^2. Typical values are 10 to 12 dB for the differentiator discriminator and about 8 dB for the best PLL discriminator.

Above threshold, the SNR increases as D^2 (or what is equivalent with *T*). This implies that the SNR performance actually increases as the RF bandwidth occupied by the modulated carrier increases. Thus, with FM, there is a tradeoff between RF bandwidth and SNR.

This does not imply, however, that the SNR can be increased to any arbitrary value by simply increasing the frequency deviation constant and thus the RF bandwidth. The CNR is a decreasing function of the frequency deviation ratio (and thus the frequency deviation constant). Increasing the frequency deviation constant too much will cause the CNR to fall below threshold (CNR).

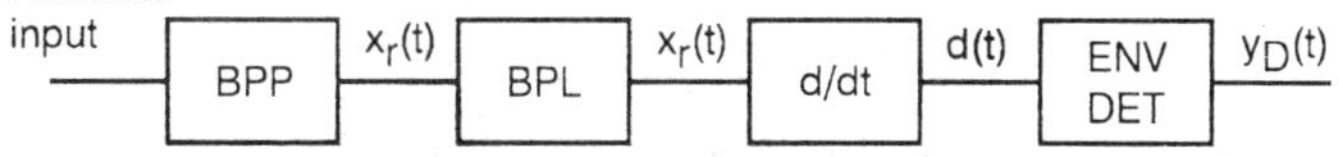

Noise in PM Systems

$$xr(t) = \Lambda_c \cos[2\pi f_c t \,|\, \phi(t) \,|\, \theta \,|\, n(t)$$

The PM demodulator is an FM discriminator followed by an integrator. The analysis of the preceding section may be used to compute the CNR and SNR performance of the ideal PM demodulator.

The received signal is

$$f(t) = k_p m(t)$$

where

$$\text{CNR} = \frac{\alpha^2 A_c^2}{4(D+1)W N_0}$$

CNR

The CNR is identical to the CNR in the FM case:

$$D = k_p \max\{|m(t)|\}$$

except where D now represents the *peak phase deviation* given by

$$e(t) = V_0 \frac{d\phi(t)}{dt} - \frac{V_0}{\alpha A_c}\frac{d}{dt}\{n_c(t)\sin[\phi(t)] - n_s(t)\cos[\phi(t)]\}$$

$$= V_0 k_p \frac{dm(t)}{dt} - \frac{V_0}{\alpha A_c}\frac{d}{dt}\{n_c(t)\sin[\phi(t)] - n_s(t)\cos[\phi(t)]\}$$

SNR

From the analysis of noise in the FM system, the output of the envelope detector (with the DC term removed) is

$$y_D(t) = \int^t e(\tau)\, d\tau$$

$$= \int^t V_0 k_p \frac{dm(\tau)}{d\tau} d\tau$$

$$= -\int^t -\frac{V_0}{\alpha A_c}\frac{d}{d\tau}\{n_c(\tau)\sin[\phi(\tau)] - n_s(\tau)\cos[\phi(\tau)]\}\, d\tau$$

$$= V_0 k_p m(t) - \frac{V_0}{\alpha A_c} n_c(t)\sin[\phi(t)] + \frac{V_0}{\alpha A_c} n_s(t)\cos[\phi(t)]$$

The demodulator output is then

$$S = V_0 k_p^2 \langle m^2(t) \rangle.$$

The signal power is seen to be

$$m(t) = 0$$

The noise power is again determined by setting and calculating the power at the demodulator output. In this case the noise output is

$$n_D(t) = \frac{V_0}{\alpha A_c} n_s(t)$$

and the noise power is determined from the power spectral density of

$$N = \frac{V_0^2}{\alpha^2 A_c^2} \langle n_s^2(t) \rangle$$

$$= 2\frac{V_0^2}{\alpha^2 A_c^2} \int_0^\infty S_{ns}(f)\,df$$

$$= 2\frac{V_0^2}{\alpha^2 A_c^2} \int_0^W N_0(f)\,df$$

$$= \frac{2V_0^2 N_0 W}{\alpha^2 A_c^2}.$$

Thus the SNR is

$$\text{SNR} = \frac{\alpha^2 A_c^2 k_p^2 \langle m^2(t) \rangle}{2N_0 W}$$

$$= \frac{\alpha^2 A_c^2 k_p^2 (\max\{|m(t)|\})^2 \langle m^2(t) \rangle}{2N_0 W}$$

$$= \frac{\alpha^2 A_c^2 D^2 \langle m^2(t) \rangle}{2N_0 W} \times \frac{2(D+1)}{2(D+1)}$$

$$= 2D^2(D+1)\langle m^2(t) \rangle \frac{\alpha^2 A_c^2}{4(D+1)W N_0}$$

$$= 2D^2(D+1)\langle m^2(t) \rangle \text{ CNR}.$$

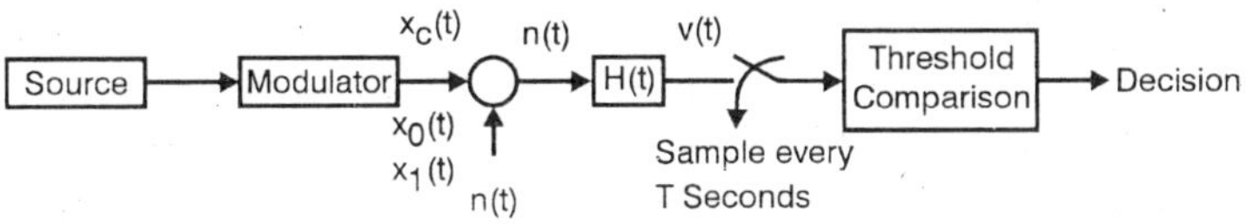

Chapter 10

Digital Communication

In the design of large and complex digital systems, it is often necessary to have one device communicate digital information to and from other devices. One advantage of digital information is that it tends to be far more resistant to transmitted and interpreted errors than information symbolized in an analog medium.

This accounts for the clarity of digitally–encoded telephone connections, compact audio disks, and for much of the enthusiasm in the engineering community for digital communications technology. However, digital communication has its own unique pitfalls, and there are multitudes of different and incompatible ways in which it can be sent. Hopefully, this chapter will enlighten you as to the basics of digital communication, its advantages, disadvantages, and practical considerations.

Suppose we are given the task of remotely monitoring the level of a water storage tank. Our job is to design a system to measure the level of water in the tank and send this information to a distant location so that other people may monitor it. Measuring the tank's level is quite easy, and can be accomplished with a number of different types of instruments, such as float switches, pressure transmitters, ultrasonic level detectors, capacitance probes, strain gauges, or radar level detectors.

For the sake of this illustration, we will use an analog level–measuring device with an output signal of 4–20 mA. 4 mA represents a tank level of 0%, 20 mA represents a tank level of 100%, and anything in between 4 and 20 mA represents a tank level proportionately between 0% and 100%. If we wanted to, we could simply send this 4–20 milliamp analog current signal to the remote monitoring location by means of a pair of copper wires, where it would drive a panel meter of some sort, the scale of which was calibrated to reflect the depth of water in the tank, in whatever units of measurement preferred.

This analog communication system would be simple and robust. For many applications, it would suffice for our needs perfectly. But, it is not the only way to get the job done. For the purposes of exploring digital techniques, we'll explore other methods of monitoring this hypothetical tank, even though the analog method just described might be the most practical.

The analog system, as simple as it may be, does have its limitations. One of them is the problem of analog signal interference. Since the tank's water level is symbolized by the magnitude of DC current in the circuit, any "noise" in this signal will be interpreted as a change in the water level. With no noise, a plot of the current signal over time for a steady tank level of 50% would look like this.

If the wires of this circuit are arranged too close to wires carrying 60 Hz AC power, for example, inductive and capacitive coupling may create a false "noise" signal to be introduced into this otherwise DC circuit. Although the low impedance of a 4–20 mA loop means that small noise voltages are significantly loaded (and thereby attenuated by the inefficiency of the capacitive/inductive coupling formed by the power wires), such noise can be significant enough to cause measurement problems.

The above example is a bit exaggerated, but the concept should be clear: any electrical noise introduced into an analog measurement system will be interpreted as changes in the measured quantity. One way to combat this problem is to symbolize the tank's water level by means of a digital signal instead of an analog signal. We can do this really crudely by replacing the analog transmitter device with a set of water level switches mounted at different heights on the tank.

Each of these switches is wired to close a circuit, sending current to individual lamps mounted on a panel at the monitoring location. As each switch closed, its respective lamp would light, and whoever looked at the panel would see a 5–lamp representation of the tank's level.

Being that each lamp circuit is digital in nature — either 100% on or 100% off — electrical interference from other wires along the run have much less effect on the accuracy of measurement at the monitoring end than in the case of the analog signal.

A huge amount of interference would be required to cause an "off" signal to be interpreted as an "on" signal, or vice versa. Relative resistance to electrical interference is an advantage enjoyed by all forms of digital communication over analog.

Now that we know digital signals are far more resistant to error induced by "noise," let's improve on this tank level measurement system. For instance, we could increase the resolution of this tank gauging system by adding more switches, for more precise determination of water level. Suppose we install 16 switches along the tank's height instead of five. This would significantly improve our measurement resolution, but at the expense of greatly increasing the quantity of wires needing to be strung between the tank and the monitoring location. One way to reduce this wiring expense would be to use a priority encoder to take the 16 switches and generate a binary number which represented the same information:

Now, only 4 wires (plus any ground and power wires necessary) are needed to communicate the information, as opposed to 16 wires (plus any ground and power wires). At the monitoring location, we would need some kind of display device that could accept the 4–bit binary data and generate an easy–to–read display for a person to view. A decoder, wired to accept the 4–bit data as its input and light 1–of–16 output lamps, could be used for this task, or we could use a 4–bit decoder/driver circuit to drive some kind of numerical digit display.

Still, a resolution of 1/16 tank height may not be good enough for our application. To better resolve the water level, we need more bits in our binary output. We could add still more switches, but this gets impractical rather quickly.

A better option would be to re–attach our original analog transmitter to the tank and electronically convert its 4–20 milliamp analog output into a binary number with far more bits than would be practical using a set of discrete level switches.

Since the electrical noise we're trying to avoid is encountered along the long run of wire from the tank to the monitoring location, this A/D conversion can take place at the tank (where we have a "clean" 4–20 mA signal). There are a variety of methods to convert an analog signal to digital, but we'll skip an in–depth discussion of those techniques and concentrate on the digital signal communication itself.

The type of digital information being sent from our tank instrumentation to the monitoring instrumentation is referred to as parallel digital data. That is, each binary bit is being sent along its own dedicated wire, so that all bits arrive at their destination simultaneously. This obviously necessitates the use of at least one wire per bit to communicate with the monitoring location.

We could further reduce our wiring needs by sending the binary data along a single channel (one wire + ground), so that each bit is communicated one at a time. This type of information is referred to as serial digital data.

We could use a multiplexer or a shift register to take the parallel data from the A/D converter (at the tank transmitter), and convert it to serial data. At the receiving end (the monitoring location) we could use a demultiplexer or another shift register to convert the serial data to parallel again for use in the display circuitry.

The exact details of how the mux/demux or shift register pairs are maintained in synchronization is, like A/D conversion, a topic for another lesson. Fortunately, there are digital IC chips called UARTs (Universal Asynchronous Receiver–Transmitters) that handle all these details on their own and make the designer's life much simpler. For now, we must continue to focus our attention on the matter at hand: how to communicate the digital information from the tank to the monitoring location.

NETWORKS AND BUSSES

This collection of wires that is kept refered to between the tank and the monitoring location can be called a bus or a network. The distinction between these two terms is more semantic than technical, and the two may be used interchangeably for all practical purposes. In my experience, the term "bus" is usually used in reference to a set of wires connecting digital components within the enclosure of a computer device, and "network" is for something that is physically more widespread.

In recent years, however, the word "bus" has gained popularity in describing networks that specialize in interconnecting discrete instrumentation sensors over long distances ("Fieldbus" and "Profibus" are two examples).

In either case, we are making reference to the means by which two or more digital devices are connected together so that data can be communicated between them.

Names like "Fieldbus" or "Profibus" encompass not only the physical wiring of the bus or network, but also the specified voltage levels for communication, their timing sequences (especially for serial data transmission), connector pinout specifications, and all other distinguishing technical features of the network. In other words, when we speak of a certain type of bus or network by name, we're actually speaking of a communications standard, roughly analogous to the rules and vocabulary of a written language.

For example, before two or more people can become pen–pals, they must be able to write to one another in a common format. To merely have a mail system that is able to deliver their letters to each other is not enough. If they agree to write to each other in French, they agree to hold to the conventions of character set, vocabulary, spelling, and grammar that is specified by the standard of the French language.

Likewise, if we connect two Profibus devices together, they will be able to communicate with each other only because the Profibus standard has specified such important details as voltage levels, timing sequences, etc. Simply having a set of wires strung between multiple devices is not enough to construct a working system (especially if the devices were built by different manufacturers!).

To illustrate in detail, let's design our own bus standard. Taking the crude water tank measurement system with five switches to detect varying levels of water, and using (at least) five wires to conduct the signals to their destination, we can lay the foundation for the mighty BogusBus.

The physical wiring for the BogusBus consists of seven wires between the transmitter device (switches) and the receiver device (lamps). The transmitter consists of all components and wiring connections to the left of the leftmost connectors (the "—>>—" symbols). Each connector symbol represents a complementary male and female element.

The bus wiring consists of the seven wires between the connector pairs. Finally, the receiver and all of its constituent wiring lies to the right of the rightmost connectors. Five of the network wires (labeled 1 through 5) carry the data while two of those wires (labeled +V and –V) provide connections for DC power supplies. There is a standard for the 7–pin connector plugs, as well. The pin layout is asymmetrical to prevent "backward" connection.

In order for manufacturers to receive the awe–inspiring "BogusBus–compliant" certification on their products, they would have to comply with the specifications set by the designers of BogusBus (most likely another company, which designed the bus for a specific task and ended up marketing it for a wide variety of purposes).

For instance, all devices must be able to use the 24 Volt DC supply power of BogusBus: the switch contacts in the transmitter must be rated for switching that DC voltage, the lamps must definitely be rated for being powered by that voltage, and the connectors must be able to handle it all.

Wiring, of course, must be in compliance with that same standard: lamps 1 through 5, for example, must be wired to the appropriate pins so that when LS4 of Manufacturer XYZ's transmitter closes, lamp 4 of Manufacturer ABC's receiver lights up, and so on.

Since both transmitter and receiver contain DC power supplies rated at an output of 24 Volts, all transmitter/receiver combinations (from all certified manufacturers) must have power supplies that can be safely wired in parallel. Consider what could happen if Manufacturer XYZ made a transmitter with the negative (–) side of their 24VDC power supply attached to earth ground and Manufacturer ABC made a receiver with the positive (+) side of their 24VDC power supply attached to earth ground. If both earth grounds are relatively "solid" (that is, a low resistance between them, such as might be the case if the two grounds were made on the metal structure of an industrial building), the two power supplies would short–circuit each other!

BogusBus, of course, is a completely hypothetical and very impractical example of a digital network. It has incredibly poor data resolution, requires substantial wiring to connect devices, and communicates in only a single direction (from transmitter to receiver). It does, however, suffice as a tutorial example of what a network is and some of the considerations associated with network selection and operation.

There are many types of buses and networks that you might come across in your profession. Each one has its own applications, advantages, and disadvantages. It is worthwhile to associate yourself with some of the "alphabet soup" that is used to label the various designs:

Short–Distance Busses

PC/AT Bus used in early IBM–compatible computers to connect peripheral devices such as disk drive and sound cards to the motherboard of the computer.

PCI Another bus used in personal computers, but not limited to IBM–compatibles. Much faster than PC/AT. Typical data transfer rate of 100 Mbytes/second (32 bit) and 200 Mbytes/second (64 bit).

PCMCIA A bus designed to connect peripherals to laptop and notebook sized personal computers. Has a very small physical "footprint," but is considerably slower than other popular PC buses.

VME A high–performance bus (co–designed by Motorola, and based on Motorola's earlier Versa–Bus standard) for constructing versatile industrial and military computers, where multiple memory, peripheral, and even microprocessor cards could be plugged in to a passive "rack" or "card cage" to facilitate custom system designs. Typical data transfer rate of 50 Mbytes/second (64 bits wide).

VXI Actually an expansion of the VME bus, VXI (VME eXtension for Instrumentation) includes the standard VME bus along with connectors for analog signals between cards in the rack.

S–100 Sometimes called the Altair bus, this bus standard was the product of a conference in 1976, intended to serve as an interface to the Intel 8080 microprocessor chip. Similar in philosophy to the VME, where multiple function cards could be plugged in to a passive "rack," facilitating the construction of custom systems.

MC6800 The Motorola equivalent of the Intel–centric S–100 bus, designed to interface peripheral devices to the popular Motorola 6800 microprocessor chip.

STD Stands for Simple–To–Design, and is yet another passive "rack" similar to the PC/AT bus, and lends itself well toward designs based on IBM–compatible hardware. Designed by Pro–Log, it is 8 bits wide (parallel), accommodating relatively small (4.5 inch by 6.5 inch) circuit cards. Multibus I and II Another bus intended for the flexible design of custom computer systems, designed by Intel. 16 bits wide (parallel).

CompactPCI An industrial adaptation of the personal computer PCI standard, designed as a higher–performance alternative to the older VME bus. At a bus clock speed of 66 MHz, data transfer rates are 200 Mbytes/second (32 bit) or 400 Mbytes/sec (64 bit).

Microchannel Yet another bus, this one designed by IBM for their ill–fated PS/2 series of computers, intended for the interfacing of PC motherboards to peripheral devices.

IDE A bus used primarily for connecting personal computer hard disk drives with the appropriate peripheral cards. Widely used in today's personal computers for hard drive and CD–ROM drive interfacing.

SCSI An alternative (technically superior to IDE) bus used for personal computer disk drives. SCSI stands for Small Computer System Interface. Used in some IBM–compatible PC's, as well as Macintosh (Apple), and many mini and mainframe business computers. Used to interface hard drives, CD–ROM drives, floppy disk drives, printers, scanners, modems, and a host of other peripheral devices. Speeds up to 1.5 Mbytes per second for the original standard.

GPIB (IEEE 488) General Purpose Interface Bus, also known as HPIB or IEEE 488, which was intended for the interfacing of electronic test equipment such as oscilloscopes and multimeters to personal computers. 8 bit wide address/data "path" with 8 additional lines for communications control.

Centronics parallel Widely used on personal computers for interfacing printer and plotter devices. Sometimes used to interface with other peripheral devices, such as external ZIP (100 Mbyte floppy) disk drives and tape drives.

USB Universal Serial Bus, which is intended to interconnect many external peripheral devices (such as keyboards, modems, mice, etc.) to personal computers.

Long used on Macintosh PC's, it is now being installed as new equipment on IBM–compatible machines.

FireWire (IEEE 1394) A high–speed serial network capable of operating at 100, 200, or 400 Mbps with versatile features such as "hot swapping" (adding or removing devices with the power on) and flexible topology. Designed for high–performance personal computer interfacing.

Bluetooth A radio–based communications network designed for office linking of computer devices. Provisions for data security designed into this network standard.

Extended–Distance Networks

20 mA current loop Not to be confused with the common instrumentation 4–20 mA analog standard, this is a digital communications

network based on interrupting a 20 mA (or sometimes 60 mA) current loop to represent binary data. Although the low impedance gives good noise immunity, it is susceptible to wiring faults (such as breaks) which would fail the entire network.

RS–232C The most common serial network used in computer systems, often used to link peripheral devices such as printers and mice to a personal computer. Limited in speed and distance (typically 45 feet and 20 kbps, although higher speeds can be run with shorter distances). I've been able to run RS–232 reliably at speeds in excess of 100 kbps, but this was using a cable only 6 feet long! RS–232C is often referred to simply as RS–232 (no "C").

RS–422A/RS–485 Two serial networks designed to overcome some of the distance and versatility limitations of RS–232C. Used widely in industry to link serial devices together in electrically "noisy" plant environments. Much greater distance and speed limitations than RS–232C, typically over half a mile and at speeds approaching 10 Mbps.

Ethernet (IEEE 802.3) A high–speed network which links computers and some types of peripheral devices together. "Normal" Ethernet runs at a speed of 10 million bits/second, and "Fast" Ethernet runs at 100 million bits/second. The slower (10 Mbps) Ethernet has been implemented in a variety of means on copper wire (thick coax = "10BASE5", thin coax = "10BASE2", twisted–pair = "10BASE–T"), radio, and on optical fibre ("10BASE–F"). The Fast Ethernet has also been implemented on a few different means (twisted–pair, 2 pair = 100BASE–TX; twisted–pair, 4 pair = 100BASE–T4; optical fibre = 100BASE–FX).

Token ring Another high–speed network linking computer devices together, using a philosophy of communication that is much different from Ethernet, allowing for more precise response times from individual network devices, and greater immunity to network wiring damage.

FDDI A very high–speed network exclusively implemented on fibre–optic cabling.

Modbus/Modbus Plus Originally implemented by the Modicon corporation, a large maker of Programmable Logic Controllers (PLCs) for linking remote I/O (Input/Output) racks with a PLC processor. Still quite popular.

Profibus Originally implemented by the Siemens corporation, another large maker of PLC equipment.

Foundation Fieldbus A high–performance bus expressly designed to allow multiple process instruments (transmitters, controllers, valve positioners) to communicate with host computers and with each other. May ultimately displace the 4–20 mA analog signal as the standard means of interconnecting process control instrumentation in the future.

DATA FLOW

Buses and networks are designed to allow communication to occur between individual devices that are interconnected. The flow of information, or data, between nodes can take a variety of forms:

With simplex communication, all data flow is unidirectional: from the designated transmitter to the designated receiver. BogusBus is an example of simplex communication, where the transmitter sent information to the remote monitoring location, but no information is ever sent back to the water tank. If all we want to do is send information one–way, then simplex is just fine. Most applications, however, demand more:

With duplex communication, the flow of information is bidirectional for each device. Duplex can be further divided into two sub–categories:

Half–duplex communication may be likened to two tin cans on the ends of a single taut string: Either can may be used to transmit or receive, but not at the same time.

Full–duplex communication is more like a true telephone, where two people can talk at the same time and hear one another simultaneously, the mouthpiece of one phone transmitting the the earpiece of the other, and vice versa. Full–duplex is often facilitated through the use of two separate channels or networks, with an individual set of wires for each direction of communication. It is sometimes accomplished by means of multiple–frequency carrier waves, especially in radio links, where one frequency is reserved for each direction of communication.

ELECTRICAL SIGNAL TYPES

With BogusBus, our signals were very simple and straightforward: each signal wire (1 through 5) carried a single bit of digital data, 0 Volts representing "off" and 24 Volts DC representing "on." Because all the bits arrived at their destination simultaneously, we would call BogusBus a parallel network technology.

If we were to improve the performance of BogusBus by adding binary encoding (to the transmitter end) and decoding (to the receiver end), so that more steps of resolution were available with fewer wires, it would still be a parallel network. If, however, we were to add a parallel–to–serial converter at the transmitter end and a serial–to–parallel converter at the receiver end, we would have something quite different.

It is primarily with the use of serial technology that we are forced to invent clever ways to transmit data bits. Because serial data requires us to send all data bits through the same wiring channel from transmitter to receiver, it necessitates a potentially high frequency signal on the network wiring. Consider the following illustration: a modified BogusBus system is communicating digital data in parallel, binary–encoded form. Instead of 5 discrete bits like the original BogusBus, we're sending 8 bits from transmitter to receiver.

The A/D converter on the transmitter side generates a new output every second. That makes for 8 bits per second of data being sent to the receiver. For the sake of illustration, let's say that the transmitter is bouncing between an output of 10101010 and 10101011 every update (once per second).

Since only the least significant bit (Bit 1) is changing, the frequency on that wire (to ground) is only 1/2 Hertz. In fact, no matter what numbers are being generated by the A/D converter between updates, the frequency on any wire in this modified BogusBus network cannot exceed 1/2 Hertz, because that's how fast the A/D updates its digital output. 1/2 Hertz is pretty slow, and should present no problems for our network wiring.

On the other hand, if we used an 8–bit serial network, all data bits must appear on the single channel in sequence. And these bits must be output by the transmitter within the 1–second window of time between A/D converter updates. Therefore, the alternating digital output of 10101010 and 10101011 (once per second) would look something like this:

The frequency of our BogusBus signal is now approximately 4 Hertz instead of 1/2 Hertz, an eightfold increase! While 4 Hertz is still fairly slow, and does not constitute an engineering problem, you should be able to appreciate what might happen if we were transmitting 32 or 64 bits of data per update, along with the other bits necessary for parity checking and signal synchronization, at an update rate of thousands of times per second! Serial data network frequencies start to enter the radio range, and simple wires begin to act as antennas, pairs of wires as transmission lines, with all their associated quirks due to inductive and capacitive reactances.

What is worse, the signals that we're trying to communicate along a serial network are of a square–wave shape, being binary bits of information. Square waves are peculiar things, being mathematically equivalent to an infinite series of sine waves of diminishing amplitude and increasing frequency.

A simple square wave at 10 kHz is actually "seen" by the capacitance and inductance of the network as a series of multiple sine–wave frequencies which extend into the hundreds of kHz at significant amplitudes. What we receive at the other end of a long 2–conductor network won't look like a clean square wave anymore, even under the best of conditions!

When engineers speak of network bandwidth, they're referring to the practical frequency limit of a network medium. In serial communication, bandwidth is a product of data volume (binary bits per transmitted "word") and data speed ("words" per second). The standard measure of network bandwidth is bits per second, or bps. An obsolete unit of bandwidth known as the baud is sometimes falsely equated with bits per second, but is actually the measure of signal level changes per second. Many serial network standards use multiple voltage or current level changes to represent a single bit, and so for these applications bps and baud are not equivalent.

The general BogusBus design, where all bits are voltages referenced to a common "ground" connection, is the worst–case situation for high–frequency square wave data communication.

Everything will work well for short distances, where inductive and capacitive effects can be held to a minimum, but for long distances this method will surely be problematic:

A robust alternative to the common ground signal method is the differential voltage method, where each bit is represented by the difference of voltage between a ground–isolated pair of wires, instead of a voltage between one wire and a common ground.

This tends to limit the capacitive and inductive effects imposed upon each signal and the tendency for the signals to be corrupted due to outside electrical interference, thereby significantly improving the practical distance of a serial network: The triangular amplifier symbols represent differential amplifiers, which output a voltage signal between two wires, neither one electrically common with ground.

Having eliminated any relation between the voltage signal and ground, the only significant capacitance imposed on the signal voltage is that existing between the two signal wires.

Capacitance between a signal wire and a grounded conductor is of much less effect, because the capacitive path between the two signal wires via a ground connection is two capacitances in series (from signal wire #1 to ground, then from ground to signal wire #2), and series capacitance values are always less than any of the individual capacitances.

Furthermore, any "noise" voltage induced between the signal wires and earth ground by an external source will be ignored, because that noise voltage will likely be induced on both signal wires in equal measure, and the receiving amplifier only responds to the differential voltage between the two signal wires, rather than the voltage between any one of them and earth ground.

RS–232C is a prime example of a ground–referenced serial network, while RS–422A is a prime example of a differential voltage serial network. RS–232C finds popular application in office environments where there is little electrical interference and wiring distances are short. RS–422A is more widely used in industrial applications where longer wiring distances and greater potential for electrical interference from AC power wiring exists.

However, a large part of the problem with digital network signals is the square–wave nature of such voltages, as was previously mentioned. If only we could avoid square waves all together, we could avoid many of their inherent difficulties in long, high–frequency networks.

One way of doing this is to modulate a sine wave voltage signal with our digital data. "Modulation" means that magnitude of one signal has control over some aspect of another signal. Radio technology has incorporated modulation for decades now, in allowing an audio–frequency voltage signal to control either the amplitude (AM) or frequency (FM) of a much higher frequency "carrier" voltage, which is then send to the antenna for transmission.

The frequency–modulation (FM) technique has found more use in digital networks than amplitude–modulation (AM), except that its referred to as Frequency Shift Keying (FSK). With simple FSK, sine waves of two distinct frequencies are used to represent the two binary states, 1 and 0:

Due to the practical problems of getting the low/high frequency sine waves to begin and end at the zero crossover points for any given combination of 0's and 1's, a variation of FSK called phase–continuous FSK is sometimes used, where the consecutive combination of a low/high frequency represents one binary state and the combination of a high/low frequency represents the other. This also makes for a situation where each bit, whether it be 0 or 1, takes exactly the same amount of time to transmit along the network.

With sine wave signal voltages, many of the problems encountered with square wave digital signals are minimized, although the circuitry required to modulate (and demodulate) the network signals is more complex and expensive.

OPTICAL DATA COMMUNICATION

A modern alternative to sending (binary) digital information via electric voltage signals is to use optical (light) signals. Electrical signals from digital circuits (high/low voltages) may be converted into discrete optical signals (light or no light) with LEDs or solid–state lasers. Likewise, light signals can be translated back into electrical form through the use of photodiodes or phototransistors for introduction into the inputs of gate circuits.

Transmitting digital information in optical form may be done in open air, simply by aiming a laser at a photodetector at a remote distance, but interference with the beam in the form of temperature inversion layers, dust, rain, fog, and other obstructions can present significant engineering problems: One way to avoid the problems of open–air optical data transmission is to send the light pulses down an ultra–pure glass fibre.

Glass fibers will "conduct" a beam of light much as a copper wire will conduct electrons, with the advantage of completely avoiding all the associated problems of inductance, capacitance, and external interference plaguing electrical signals. Optical fibers keep the light beam contained within the fibre core by a phenomenon known as total internal reflectance.

An optical fibre is composed of two layers of ultra–pure glass, each layer made of glass with a slightly different refractive index, or capacity to "bend" light. With one type of glass concentrically layered around a central glass core, light introduced into the central core cannot escape outside the fibre, but is confined to travel within the core.

These layers of glass are very thin, the outer "cladding" typically 125 microns (1 micron = 1 millionth of a meter, or 10–6 meter) in diameter. This thinness gives the fibre considerable flexibility. To protect the fibre from physical damage, it is usually given a thin plastic coating, placed inside of a plastic tube, wrapped with kevlar fibers for tensile strength, and given an outer sheath of plastic similar to electrical wire insulation. Like electrical wires, optical fibers are often bundled together within the same sheath to form a single cable.

Optical fibers exceed the data–handling performance of copper wire in almost every regard. They are totally immune to electromagnetic interference and have very high bandwidths. However, they are not without certain weaknesses.

One weakness of optical fibre is a phenomenon known as microbending. This is where the fibre is bend around too small of a radius, causing light to escape the inner core, through the cladding:

Not only does microbending lead to diminished signal strength due to the lost light, but it also constitutes a security weakness in that a light sensor intentionally placed on the outside of a sharp bend could intercept digital data transmitted over the fibre.

Another problem unique to optical fibre is signal distortion due to multiple light paths, or modes, having different distances over the length of the fibre. When light is emitted by a source, the photons (light particles) do not all travel the exact same path. This fact is patently obvious in any source of light not conforming to a straight beam, but is true even in devices such as lasers.

If the optical fibre core is large enough in diameter, it will support multiple pathways for photons to travel, each of these pathways having a slightly different length from one end of the fibre to the other. This type of optical fibre is called multimode fibre.

A light pulse emitted by the LED taking a shorter path through the fibre will arrive at the detector sooner than light pulses taking longer paths. The result is distortion of the square–wave's rising and falling edges, called pulse stretching. This problem becomes worse as the overall fibre length is increased.

However, if the fibre core is made small enough (around 5 microns in diameter), light modes are restricted to a single pathway with one length. Fibre so designed to permit only a single mode of light is known as single–mode fibre. Because single–mode fibre escapes the problem of pulse stretching experienced in long cables, it is the fibre of choice for long–distance (several miles or more) networks. The drawback, of course, is that with only one mode of light, single–mode fibers do not conduct as as much light as multimode fibers. Over long distances, this exacerbates the need for "repeater" units to boost light power.

NETWORK TOPOLOGY

If we want to connect two digital devices with a network, we would have a kind of network known as "point–to–point".

For the sake of simplicity, the network wiring is symbolized as a single line between the two devices. In actuality, it may be a twisted pair of wires, a coaxial cable, an optical fibre, or even a seven–conductor BogusBus. Right now, we're merely focusing on the "shape" of the network, technically known as its topology.

If we want to include more devices (sometimes called nodes) on this network, we have several options of network configuration to choose from:

Many network standards dictate the type of topology which is used, while others are more versatile. Ethernet, for example, is commonly implemented in a "bus" topology but can also be implemented in a "star" or "ring" topology with the appropriate interconnecting equipment. Other networks, such as RS–232C, are almost exclusively point–to–point; and token ring (as you might have guessed) is implemented solely in a ring topology. Different topologies have different pros and cons associated with them.

Point–To–Point

Bus

Very simple to install and maintain. Nodes can be easily added or removed with minimal wiring changes. On the other hand, the one bus network must handle all communication signals from all nodes. This is known as broadcast networking, and is analogous to a group of people talking to each other over a single telephone connection, where only one person can talk at a time (limiting data exchange rates), and everyone can hear everyone else when they talk (which can be a data security issue). Also, a break in the bus wiring can lead to nodes being isolated in groups.

Star

With devices known as "gateways" at branching points in the network, data flow can be restricted between nodes, allowing for private communication between specific groups of nodes. This addresses some of the speed and security issues of the simple bus topology. However, those branches could easily be cut off from the rest of the "star" network if one of the gateways were to fail. Can also be implemented with "switches" to connect individual nodes to a larger network on demand. Such a switched network is similar to the standard telephone system.

Ring

This topology provides the best reliability with the least amount of wiring. Since each node has two connection points to the ring, a single break in any part of the ring doesn't affect the integrity of the network. The devices, however, must be designed with this topology in mind. Also, the network must be interrupted to install or remove nodes. As with bus topology, ring networks are broadcast by nature.

As you might suspect, two or more ring topologies may be combined to give the "best of both worlds" in a particular application. Quite often, industrial networks end up in this fashion over time, simply from engineers and technicians joining multiple networks together for the benefit of plant–wide information access.

NETWORK PROTOCOLS

Aside from the issues of the physical network (signal types and voltage levels, connector pinouts, cabling, topology, etc.), there needs to be a standardized way in which communication is arbitrated between multiple nodes in a network, even if its as simple as a two–node, point–to–point system.

When a node "talks" on the network, it is generating a signal on the network wiring, be it high and low DC voltage levels, some kind of modulated AC carrier wave signal, or even pulses of light in a fibre. Nodes that "listen" are simply measuring that applied signal on the network (from the transmitting node) and passively monitoring it. If two or more nodes "talk" at the same time, however, their output signals may clash (imagine two logic gates trying to apply opposite signal voltages to a single line on a bus!), corrupting the transmitted data.

The standardized method by which nodes are allowed to transmit to the bus or network wiring is called a protocol. There are many different protocols for arbitrating the use of a common network between multiple nodes, and I'll cover just a few here.

However, its good to be aware of these few, and to understand why some work better for some purposes than others. Usually, a specific protocol is associated with a standardized type of network. This is merely another "layer" to the set of standards which are specified under the titles of various networks.

The International Standards Organization (ISO) has specified a general architecture of network specifications in their DIS7498 model (applicable to most any digital network). Consisting of seven "layers," this outline attempts to categorize all levels of abstraction necessary to communicate digital data.

- *Level 1:* Physical Specifies electrical and mechanical details of communication: wire type, connector design, signal types and levels.
- *Level 2:* Data link Defines formats of messages, how data is to be addressed, and error detection/correction techniques.
- *Level 3:* Network Establishes procedures for encapsulation of data into "packets" for transmission and reception.
- *Level 4:* Transport Among other things, the transport layer defines how complete data files are to be handled over a network.
- *Level 5:* Session Organizes data transfer in terms of beginning and end of a specific transmission. Analogous to job control on a multitasking computer operating system.
- *Level 6:* Presentation Includes definitions for character sets, terminal control, and graphics commands so that abstract data can be readily encoded and decoded between communicating devices.
- *Level 7:* Application The end–user standards for generating and/or interpreting communicated data in its final form. In other words, the actual computer programs using the communicated data.

Some established network protocols only cover one or a few of the DIS7498 levels. For example, the widely used RS–232C serial communications protocol really only addresses the first ("physical") layer of this seven–layer model. Other protocols, such as the X–windows graphical client/server system developed at MIT for distributed graphic–user–interface computer systems, cover all seven layers.

Different protocols may use the same physical layer standard. An example of this is the RS–422A and RS–485 protocols, both of which use the same differential–voltage transmitter and receiver circuitry, using the same voltage levels to denote binary 1's and 0's. On a physical level, these two communication protocols are identical. However, on a more abstract level the protocols are different: RS–422A is point–to–point only, while RS–485 supports a bus topology "multidrop" with up to 32 addressable nodes. Perhaps the simplest type of protocol is the one where there is only one transmitter, and all the other nodes are merely receivers. Such is the case for BogusBus, where a single transmitter generates the voltage signals impressed on the network wiring, and one or more receiver units (with 5 lamps each) light up in accord with the transmitter's output. This is always the case with a simplex network: there's only one talker, and everyone else listens!

When we have multiple transmitting nodes, we must orchestrate their transmissions in such a way that they don't conflict with one another. Nodes shouldn't be allowed to talk when another node is talking, so we give each node the ability to "listen" and to refrain from talking until the network is silent. This basic approach is called Carrier Sense Multiple Access (CSMA), and there exists a few variations on this theme. Please note that CSMA is not a standardized protocol in itself, but rather a methodology that certain protocols follow.

One variation is to simply let any node begin to talk as soon as the network is silent. This is analogous to a group of people meeting at a round table: anyone has the ability to start talking, so long as they don't interrupt anyone else. As soon as the last person stops talking, the next person waiting to talk will begin.

So, what happens when two or more people start talking at once? In a network, the simultaneous transmission of two or more nodes is called a collision. With CSMA/CD (CSMA/Collision Detection), the nodes that collide simply reset themselves with a random delay timer circuit, and the first one to finish its time delay tries to talk again. This is the basic protocol for the popular Ethernet network.

Another variation of CSMA is CSMA/BA (CSMA/Bitwise Arbitration), where colliding nodes refer to pre–set priority numbers which dictate which one has permission to speak first. In other words, each node has a "rank" which settles any dispute over who gets to start talking first after a collision occurs, much like a group of people where dignitaries and common citizens are mixed. If a collision occurs, the dignitary is generally allowed to speak first and the common person waits afterward.

In either of the two examples above (CSMA/CD and CSMA/BA), we assumed that any node could initiate a conversation so long as the network was silent. This is referred to as the "unsolicited" mode of communication. There is a variation called "solicited" mode for either CSMA/CD or CSMA/BA where the initial transmission is only allowed to occur when a designated master node requests (solicits) a reply. Collision detection (CD) or bitwise arbitration (BA) applies only to post–collision arbitration as multiple nodes respond to the master device's request.

An entirely different strategy for node communication is the Master/

Slave protocol, where a single master device allots time slots for all the other nodes on the network to transmit, and schedules these time slots so that multiple nodes cannot collide. The master device addresses each node by name, one at a time, letting that node talk for a certain amount of time. When it is finished, the master addresses the next node, and so on, and so on.

Yet another strategy is the Token–Passing protocol, where each node gets a turn to talk (one at a time), and then grants permission for the next node to talk when its done. Permission to talk is passed around from node to node as each one hands off the "token" to the next in sequential order. The token itself is not a physical thing: it is a series of binary 1's and 0's broadcast on the network, carrying a specific address of the next node permitted to talk. Although token–passing protocol is often associated with ring–topology networks, it is not restricted to any topology in particular. And when this protocol is implemented in a ring network, the sequence of token passing does not have to follow the physical connection sequence of the ring.

Just as with topologies, multiple protocols may be joined together over different segments of a heterogeneous network, for maximum benefit. For instance, a dedicated Master/Slave network connecting instruments together on the manufacturing plant floor may be linked through a gateway device to an Ethernet network which links multiple desktop computer workstations together, one of those computer workstations acting as a gateway to link the data to an FDDI fibre network back to the plant's mainframe computer. Each network type, topology, and protocol serves different needs and applications best, but through gateway devices, they can all share the same data.

It is also possible to blend multiple protocol strategies into a new hybrid within a single network type. Such is the case for Foundation Fieldbus, which combines Master/Slave with a form of token–passing. A Link Active Scheduler (LAS) device sends scheduled "Compel Data" (CD) commands to query slave devices on the Fieldbus for time–critical information. In this regard, Fieldbus is a Master/Slave protocol. However, when there's time between CD queries, the LAS sends out "tokens" to each of the other devices on the Fieldbus, one at a time, giving them opportunity to transmit any unscheduled data.

When those devices are done transmitting their information, they return the token back to the LAS. The LAS also probes for new devices on the Fieldbus with a "Probe Node" (PN) message, which is expected to produce a "Probe Response" (PR) back to the LAS.

The responses of devices back to the LAS, whether by PR message or returned token, dictate their standing on a "Live List" database which the

LAS maintains. Proper operation of the LAS device is absolutely critical to the functioning of the Fieldbus, so there are provisions for redundant LAS operation by assigning "Link Master" status to some of the nodes, empowering them to become alternate Link Active Schedulers if the operating LAS fails. Other data communications protocols exist, but these are the most popular.

The opportunity to work on an old (circa 1975) industrial control system made by Honeywell where a master device called the Highway Traffic Director, or HTD, arbitrated all network communications. What made this network interesting is that the signal sent from the HTD to all slave devices for permitting transmission was not communicated on the network wiring itself, but rather on sets of individual twisted–pair cables connecting the HTD with each slave device.

Devices on the network were then divided into two categories: those nodes connected to the HTD which were allowed to initiate transmission, and those nodes not connected to the HTD which could only transmit in response to a query sent by one of the former nodes. Primitive and slow are the only fitting adjectives for this communication network scheme, but it functioned adequately for its time.

PRACTICAL CONSIDERATIONS

A principal consideration for industrial control networks, where the monitoring and control of real–life processes must often occur quickly and at set times, is the guaranteed maximum communication time from one node to another. If you're controlling the position of a nuclear reactor coolant valve with a digital network, you need to be able to guarantee that the valve's network node will receive the proper positioning signals from the control computer at the right times. If not, very bad things could happen!

The ability for a network to guarantee data "throughput" is called determinism. A deterministic network has a guaranteed maximum time delay for data transfer from node to node, whereas a non–deterministic network does not. The preeminent example of a non–deterministic network is Ethernet, where the nodes rely on random time–delay circuits to reset and re–attempt transmission after a collision.

Being that a node's transmission of data could be delayed indefinitely from a long series of re–sets and re–tries after repeated collisions, there is no guarantee that its data will ever get sent out to the network. Realistically though, the odds are so astronomically great that such a thing would happen that it is of little practical concern in a lightly–loaded network.

Another important consideration, especially for industrial control networks, is network fault tolerance: that is, how susceptible is a particular network's signaling, topology, and/or protocol to failures? We've already briefly discussed some of the issues surrounding topology, but protocol impacts reliability just as much.

For example, a Master/Slave network, while being extremely deterministic (a good thing for critical controls), is entirely dependent upon the master node to keep everything going (generally a bad thing for critical controls). If the master node fails for any reason, none of the other nodes will be able to transmit any data at all, because they'll never receive their alloted time slot permissions to do so, and the whole system will fail.

A similar issue surrounds token–passing systems: what happens if the node holding the token were to fail before passing the token on to the next node? Some token–passing systems address this possibility by having a few designated nodes generate a new token if the network is silent for too long.

This works fine if a node holding the token dies, but it causes problems if part of a network falls silent because a cable connection comes undone: the portion of the network that falls silent generates its own token after awhile, and you essentially are left with two smaller networks with one token that's getting passed around each of them to sustain communication. Trouble occurs, however, if that cable connection gets plugged back in: those two segmented networks are joined in to one again, and now there's two tokens being passed around one network, resulting in nodes' transmissions colliding!

There is no "perfect network" for all applications. The task of the engineer and technician is to know the application and know the operations of the network(s) available. Only then can efficient system design and maintenance become a reality.

DIGITAL STORAGE (MEMORY)

DIGITAL

Although many textbooks provide good introductions to digital memory technology. While many of these memory designs are obsolete, their foundational principles are still quite interesting and educational, and may even find re–application in the memory technologies of the future. The basic goal of digital memory is to provide a means to store and access binary data: sequences of 1's and 0's. The digital storage of information holds advantages over analog techniques much the same as digital communication of information holds advantages over analog communication.

This is not to say that digital data storage is unequivocally superior to analog, but it does address some of the more common problems associated with analog techniques and thus finds immense popularity in both consumer and industrial applications. Digital data storage also complements digital computation technology well, and thus finds natural application in the world of computers.

The most evident advantage of digital data storage is the resistance to corruption. Suppose that we were going to store a piece of data regarding the magnitude of a voltage signal by means of magnetizing a small chunk of magnetic material. Since many magnetic materials retain their strength of magnetization very well over time, this would be a logical media candidate for long–term storage of this particular data (in fact, this is precisely how audio and video tape technology works: thin plastic tape is impregnated with particles of iron–oxide material, which can be magnetized or demagnetized via the application of a magnetic field from an electromagnet coil.

The data is then retrieved from the tape by moving the magnetized tape past another coil of wire, the magnetized spots on the tape inducing voltage in that coil, reproducing the voltage waveform initially used to magnetize the tape).

If we represent an analog signal by the strength of magnetization on spots of the tape, the storage of data on the tape will be susceptible to the smallest degree of degradation of that magnetization.

As the tape ages and the magnetization fades, the analog signal magnitude represented on the tape will appear to be less than what it was when we first recorded the data. Also, if any spurious magnetic fields happen to alter the magnetization on the tape, even if its only by a small amount, that altering of field strength will be interpreted upon re–play as an altering (or corruption) of the signal that was recorded. Since analog signals have infinite resolution, the smallest degree of change will have an impact on the integrity of the data storage.

If we were to use that same tape and store the data in binary digital form, however, the strength of magnetization on the tape would fall into two discrete levels: "high" and "low," with no valid in–between states. As the tape aged or was exposed to spurious magnetic fields, those same locations on the tape would experience slight alteration of magnetic field strength, but unless the alterations were extreme, no data corruption would occur upon re–play of the tape.

By reducing the resolution of the signal impressed upon the magnetic tape, we've gained significant immunity to the kind of degradation and "noise" typically plaguing stored analog data. On the other hand, our data resolution would be limited to the scanning rate and the number of bits output by the A/D converter which interpreted the original analog signal, so the reproduction wouldn't necessarily be "better" than with analog, merely more rugged. With the advanced technology of modern A/D's, though, the tradeoff is acceptable for most applications.

Also, by encoding different types of data into specific binary number schemes, digital storage allows us to archive a wide variety of information that is often difficult to encode in analog form. Text, for example, is represented quite easily with the binary ASCII code, seven bits for each character, including punctuation marks, spaces, and carriage returns.

A wider range of text is encoded using the Unicode standard, in like manner. Any kind of numerical data can be represented using binary notation on digital media, and any kind of information that can be encoded in numerical form (which almost any kind can!) is storable, too. Techniques such as parity and checksum error detection can be employed to further guard against data corruption, in ways that analog does not lend itself to.

DIGITAL MEMORY TERMS AND CONCEPTS

When we store information in some kind of circuit or device, we not only need some way to store and retrieve it, but also to locate precisely where in the device that it is. Most, if not all, memory devices can be thought of as a series of mail boxes, folders in a file cabinet, or some other metaphor where information can be located in a variety of places. When we refer to the actual information being stored in the memory device, we usually refer to it as the data. The location of this data within the storage device is typically called the address, in a manner reminiscent of the postal service.

With some types of memory devices, the address in which certain data is stored can be called up by means of parallel data lines in a digital circuit (we'll discuss this in more detail later in this lesson). With other types of devices, data is addressed in terms of an actual physical location on the surface of some type of media (the tracks and sectors of circular computer disks, for instance).

However, some memory devices such as magnetic tapes have a one–dimensional type of data addressing: if you want to play your favorite song in the middle of a cassette tape album, you have to fast–forward to that spot in the tape, arriving at the proper spot by means of trial–and–error, judging the approximate area by means of a counter that keeps track of tape position, and/or by the amount of time it takes to get there from the beginning of the tape.

The access of data from a storage device falls roughly into two categories: random access and sequential access. Random access means that you can quickly and precisely address a specific data location within the device, and non–random simply means that you cannot. A vinyl record platter is an example of a random–access device: to skip to any song, you just position the stylus arm at whatever location on the record that you want (compact audio disks so the same thing, only they do it automatically for you). Cassette tape, on the other hand, is sequential. You have to wait to go past the other songs in sequence before you can access or address the song that you want to skip to. The process of storing a piece of data to a memory device is called writing, and the process of retrieving data is called reading. Memory devices allowing both reading and writing are equipped with a way to distinguish between the two tasks, so that no mistake is made by the user (writing new information to a device when all you wanted to do is see what was stored there). Some devices do not allow for the writing of new data, and are purchased "pre–written" from the manufacturer.

Such is the case for vinyl records and compact audio disks, and this is typically referred to in the digital world as read–only memory, or ROM. Cassette audio and video tape, on the other hand, can be re–recorded (re–written) or purchased blank and recorded fresh by the user. This is often called read–write memory.

Another distinction to be made for any particular memory technology is its volatility, or data storage permanence without power. Many electronic memory devices store binary data by means of circuits that are either latched in a "high" or "low" state, and this latching effect holds only as long as electric power is maintained to those circuits. Such memory would be properly referred to as volatile. Storage media such as magnetized disk or tape is nonvolatile, because no source of power is needed to maintain data storage.

This is often confusing for new students of computer technology, because the volatile electronic memory typically used for the construction of computer devices is commonly and distinctly referred to as RAM (Random Access Memory).

While RAM memory is typically randomly–accessed, so is virtually every other kind of memory device in the computer! What "RAM" really refers to is the volatility of the memory, and not its mode of access. Nonvolatile memory integrated circuits in personal computers are commonly (and properly) referred to as ROM (Read–Only Memory), but their data contents are accessed randomly, just like the volatile memory circuits!

Finally, there needs to be a way to denote how much data can be stored by any particular memory device. This, fortunately for us, is very simple and straightforward: just count up the number of bits (or bytes, 1 byte = 8 bits) of total data storage space. Due to the high capacity of modern data storage devices, metric prefixes are generally affixed to the unit of bytes in order to represent storage space: 1.6 Gigabytes is equal to 1.6

billion bytes, or 12.8 billion bits, of data storage capacity. The only caveat here is to be aware of rounded numbers. Because the storage mechanisms of many random–access memory devices are typically arranged so that the number of "cells" in which bits of data can be stored appears in binary progression (powers of 2), a "one kilobyte" memory device most likely contains 1024 (2 to the power of 10) locations for data bytes rather than exactly 1000.

A "64 kbyte" memory device actually holds 65,536 bytes of data (2 to the 16th power), and should probably be called a "66 Kbyte" device to be more precise. When we round numbers in our base–10 system, we fall out of step with the round equivalents in the base–2 system.

MODERN NONMECHANICAL MEMORY

Now we can proceed to studying specific types of digital storage devices. These are not necessarily the newest technologies, as one might suspect, although they will most likely replace moving–part technologies in the future. A very simple type of electronic memory is the bistable multivibrator. Capable of storing a single bit of data, it is volatile (requiring power to maintain its memory) and very fast. The D–latch is probably the simplest implementation of a bistable multivibrator for memory usage, the D input serving as the data "write" input, the Q output serving as the "read" output, and the enable input serving as the read/write control line:

If we desire more than one bit's worth of storage (and we probably do), we'll have to have many latches arranged in some kind of an array where we can selectively address which one (or which set) we're reading from or writing to. Using a pair of tristate buffers, we can connect both the data write input and the data read output to a common data bus line, and enable those buffers to either connect the Q output to the data line (READ), connect the D input to the data line (WRITE), or keep both buffers in the High–Z state to disconnect D and Q from the data line (unaddressed mode). One memory "cell" would look like this, internally.

When the address enable input is 0, both tristate buffers will be placed in high–Z mode, and the latch will be disconnected from the data input/ output (bus) line. Only when the address enable input is active (1) will the latch be connected to the data bus. Every latch circuit, of course, will be enabled with a different "address enable" (AE) input line, which will come from a 1–of–n output decoder.

In the above circuit, 16 memory cells are individually addressed with a 4–bit binary code input into the decoder. If a cell is not addressed, it will be disconnected from the 1–bit data bus by its internal tristate buffers: consequently, data cannot be either written or read through the bus to or from that cell. Only the cell circuit that is addressed by the 4–bit decoder input will be accessible through the data bus. This simple memory circuit is random–access and volatile. Technically, it is known as a static RAM. Its total memory capacity is 16 bits. Since it contains 16 addresses and has a data bus that is 1 bit wide, it would be designated as a 16 x 1 bit static RAM circuit. As you can see, it takes an incredible number of gates (and multiple transistors per gate!) to construct a practical static RAM circuit.

This makes the static RAM a relatively low–density device, with less capacity than most other types of RAM technology per unit IC chip space. Because each cell circuit consumes a certain amount of power, the overall power consumption for a large array of cells can be quite high. Early static RAM banks in personal computers consumed a fair amount of power and generated a lot of heat, too. CMOS IC technology has made it possible to lower the specific power consumption of static RAM circuits, but low storage density is still an issue.

To address this, engineers turned to the capacitor instead of the bistable multivibrator as a means of storing binary data. A tiny capacitor could serve as a memory cell, complete with a single MOSFET transistor for connecting it to the data bus for charging (writing a 1), discharging (writing a 0), or reading.

Unfortunately, such tiny capacitors have very small capacitances, and their charge tends to "leak" away through any circuit impedances quite rapidly. To combat this tendency, engineers designed circuits internal to the RAM memory chip which would periodically read all cells and recharge (or "refresh") the capacitors as needed. Although this added to the complexity of the circuit, it still required far less componentry than a RAM built of multivibrators.

They called this type of memory circuit a dynamic RAM, because of its need of periodic refreshing.

Recent advances in IC chip manufacturing has led to the introduction of flash memory, which works on a capacitive storage principle like the dynamic RAM, but uses the insulated gate of a MOSFET as the capacitor itself. Before the advent of transistors (especially the MOSFET), engineers had to implement digital circuitry with gates constructed from vacuum tubes. As you can imagine, the enormous comparative size and power consumption of a vacuum tube as compared to a transistor made memory circuits like static and dynamic RAM a practical impossibility. Other, rather ingenious, techniques to store digital data without the use of moving parts were developed.

HISTORICAL, NONMECHANICAL MEMORY TECHNOLOGIES

Perhaps the most ingenious technique was that of the delay line. A delay line is any kind of device which delays the propagation of a pulse or wave signal. If you've ever heard a sound echo back and forth through a canyon or cave, you've experienced an audio delay line: the noise wave travels at the speed of sound, bouncing off of walls and reversing direction of travel. The delay line "stores" data on a very temporary basis if the signal is not strengthened periodically, but the very fact that it stores data at all is a phenomenon exploitable for memory technology.

Early computer delay lines used long tubes filled with liquid mercury, which was used as the physical medium through which sound waves traveled along the length of the tube. An electrical/sound transducer was mounted at each end, one to create sound waves from electrical impulses, and the other to generate electrical impulses from sound waves. A stream of serial binary data was sent to the transmitting transducer as a voltage signal.

The sequence of sound waves would travel from left to right through the mercury in the tube and be received by the transducer at the other end. The receiving transducer would receive the pulses in the same order as they were transmitted.

A feedback circuit connected to the receiving transducer would drive the transmitting transducer again, sending the same sequence of pulses through the tube as sound waves, storing the data as long as the feedback circuit continued to function. The delay line functioned like a first–in–first–out (FIFO) shift register, and external feedback turned that shift register behaviour into a ring counter, cycling the bits around indefinitely.

The delay line concept suffered numerous limitations from the materials and technology that were then available. The EDVAC computer of the early 1950's used 128 mercury–filled tubes, each one about 5 feet long and storing a maximum of 384 bits.

Temperature changes would affect the speed of sound in the mercury, thus skewing the time delay in each tube and causing timing problems. Later designs replaced the liquid mercury medium with solid rods of glass, quartz, or special metal that delayed torsional (twisting) waves rather than longitudinal (lengthwise) waves, and operated at much higher frequencies.

One such delay line used a special nickel–iron–titanium wire (chosen for its good temperature stability) about 95 feet in length, coiled to reduce the overall package size. The total delay time from one end of the wire to the other was about 9.8 milliseconds, and the highest practical clock frequency was 1 MHz.

This meant that approximately 9800 bits of data could be stored in the delay line wire at any given time. Given different means of delaying signals which wouldn't be so susceptible to environmental variables (such as serial pulses of light within a long optical fibre), this approach might someday find re–application.

Another approach experimented with by early computer engineers was the use of a cathode ray tube (CRT), the type commonly used for oscilloscope, radar, and television viewscreens, to store binary data. Normally, the focused and directed electron beam in a CRT would be used to make bits of phosphor chemical on the inside of the tube glow, thus producing a viewable image on the screen.

In this application, however, the desired result was the creation of an electric charge on the glass of the screen by the impact of the electron beam, which would then be detected by a metal grid placed directly in front of the CRT. Like the delay line, the so–called Williams Tube memory needed to be periodically refreshed with external circuitry to retain its data. Unlike the delay line mechanisms, it was virtually immune to the environmental factors of temperature and vibration.

The IBM model 701 computer sported a Williams Tube memory with 4 Kilobyte capacity and a bad habit of "overcharging" bits on the tube screen with successive re–writes so that false "1" states might overflow to adjacent spots on the screen.

The next major advance in computer memory came when engineers turned to magnetic materials as a means of storing binary data. It was discovered that certain compounds of iron, namely "ferrite," possessed hysteresis curves that were almost square:

Shown on a graph with the strength of the applied magnetic field on the horizontal axis (field intensity), and the actual magnetization (orientation of electron spins in the ferrite material) on the vertical axis (flux density), ferrite won't become magnetized one direction until the applied field exceeds a critical threshold value. Once that critical value is exceeded, the electrons in the ferrite "snap" into magnetic alignment and the ferrite becomes magnetized. If the applied field is then turned off, the ferrite maintains full magnetism.

To magnetize the ferrite in the other direction (polarity), the applied magnetic field must exceed the critical value in the opposite direction. Once that critical value is exceeded, the electrons in the ferrite "snap" into magnetic alignment in the opposite direction. Once again, if the applied field is then turned off, the ferrite maintains full magnetism. To put it simply, the magnetization of a piece of ferrite is "bistable."

Exploiting this strange property of ferrite, we can use this natural magnetic "latch" to store a binary bit of data. To set or reset this "latch," we can use electric current through a wire or coil to generate the necessary magnetic field, which will then be applied to the ferrite.

Jay Forrester of MIT applied this principle in inventing the magnetic "core" memory, which became the dominant computer memory technology during the 1970's.

A grid of wires, electrically insulated from one another, crossed through the centre of many ferrite rings, each of which being called a "core." As DC current moved through any wire from the power supply to ground, a circular magnetic field was generated around that energized wire. The resistor values were set so that the amount of current at the regulated power supply voltage would produce slightly more than 1/2 the critical magnetic field strength needed to magnetize any one of the ferrite rings.

Therefore, if column #4 wire was energized, all the cores on that column would be subjected to the magnetic field from that one wire, but it would not be strong enough to change the magnetization of any of those cores. However, if column #4 wire and row #5 wire were both energized, the core at that intersection of column #4 and row #5 would be subjected to a sum of those two magnetic fields: a magnitude strong enough to "set" or "reset" the magnetization of that core. In other words, each core was addressed by the intersection of row and column.

The distinction between "set" and "reset" was the direction of the core's magnetic polarity, and that bit value of data would be determined by the polarity of the voltages (with respect to ground) that the row and column wires would be energized with.

The following photograph shows a core memory board from a Data General brand, "Nova" model computer, circa late 1960's or early 1970's. It had a total storage capacity of 4 kbytes (that's kilobytes, not megabytes!). A ball–point pen is shown for size comparison.

The electronic components seen around the periphery of this board are used for "driving" the column and row wires with current, and also to read the status of a core. A close–up photograph reveals the ring–shaped cores, through which the matrix wires thread. Again, a ball–point pen is shown for size comparison.

A core memory board of later design (circa 1971) is shown in the next photograph. Its cores are much smaller and more densely packed, giving more memory storage capacity than the former board (8 kbytes instead of 4 kbytes).

And, another close–up of the cores: Writing data to core memory was easy enough, but reading that data was a bit of a trick. To facilitate this essential function, a "read" wire was threaded through all the cores in a memory matrix, one end of it being grounded and the other end connected to an amplifier circuit.

A pulse of voltage would be generated on this "read" wire if the addressed core changed states (from 0 to 1, or 1 to 0). In other words, to read a core's value, you had to write either a 1 or a 0 to that core and monitor the voltage induced on the read wire to see if the core changed.

Obviously, if the core's state was changed, you would have to re–set it back to its original state, or else the data would have been lost.

This process is known as a destructive read, because data may be changed (destroyed) as it is read. Thus, refreshing is necessary with core memory, although not in every case (that is, in the case of the core's state not changing when either a 1 or a 0 was written to it).

One major advantage of core memory over delay lines and Williams Tubes was nonvolatility. The ferrite cores maintained their magnetization indefinitely, with no power or refreshing required. It was also relatively easy to build, denser, and physically more rugged than any of its predecessors.

Core memory was used from the 1960's until the late 1970's in many computer systems, including the computers used for the Apollo space programme, CNC machine tool control computers, business ("mainframe") computers, and industrial control systems. Despite the fact that core memory is long obsolete, the term "core" is still used sometimes with reference to a computer's RAM memory.

All the while that delay lines, Williams Tube, and core memory technologies were being invented, the simple static RAM was being improved with smaller active component (vacuum tube or transistor) technology. Static RAM was never totally eclipsed by its competitors: even the old ENIAC computer of the 1950's used vacuum tube ring–counter circuitry for data registers and computation. Eventually though, smaller and smaller scale IC chip manufacturing technology gave transistors the practical edge over other technologies, and core memory became a museum piece in the 1980's.

One last attempt at a magnetic memory better than core was the bubble memory. Bubble memory took advantage of a peculiar phenomenon in a mineral called garnet, which, when arranged in a thin film and exposed to a constant magnetic field perpendicular to the film, supported tiny regions of oppositely–magnetized "bubbles" that could be nudged along the film by prodding with other external magnetic fields.

"Tracks" could be laid on the garnet to focus the movement of the bubbles by depositing magnetic material on the surface of the film. A continuous track was formed on the garnet which gave the bubbles a long loop in which to travel, and motive force was applied to the bubbles with a pair of wire coils wrapped around the garnet and energized with a 2–phase voltage.

Bubbles could be created or destroyed with a tiny coil of wire strategically placed in the bubbles' path.

The presence of a bubble represented a binary "1" and the absence of a bubble represented a binary "0." Data could be read and written in this chain of moving magnetic bubbles as they passed by the tiny coil of wire, much the same as the read/write "head" in a cassette tape player, reading the magnetization of the tape as it moves. Like core memory, bubble memory was nonvolatile: a permanent magnet supplied the necessary background field needed to support the bubbles when the power was turned off.

Unlike core memory, however, bubble memory had phenomenal storage density: millions of bits could be stored on a chip of garnet only a couple of square inches in size. What killed bubble memory as a viable alternative to static and dynamic RAM was its slow, sequential data access. Being nothing more than an incredibly long serial shift register (ring counter), access to any particular portion of data in the serial string could be quite slow compared to other memory technologies.

An electrostatic equivalent of the bubble memory is the Charge–Coupled Device (CCD) memory, an adaptation of the CCD devices used in digital photography. Like bubble memory, the bits are serially shifted along channels on the substrate material by clock pulses. Unlike bubble memory, the electrostatic charges decay and must be refreshed. CCD memory is therefore volatile, with high storage density and sequential access. Interesting, isn't it? The old Williams Tube memory was adapted from CRT viewing technology, and CCD memory from video recording technology.

Read–Only Memory

Read–only memory (ROM) is similar in design to static or dynamic RAM circuits, except that the "latching" mechanism is made for one–time (or limited) operation. The simplest type of ROM is that which uses tiny "fuses" which can be selectively blown or left alone to represent the two binary states. Obviously, once one of the little fuses is blown, it cannot be made whole again, so the writing of such ROM circuits is one–time only. Because it can be written (programmed) once, these circuits are sometimes referred to as PROMs (Programmable Read–Only Memory).

However, not all writing methods are as permanent as blown fuses. If a transistor latch can be made which is resettable only with significant effort, a memory device that's something of a cross between a RAM and a ROM can be built. Such a device is given a rather oxymoronic name: the EPROM (Erasable Programmable Read–Only Memory). EPROMs come in two basic varieties.

Electrically–erasable (EEPROM) and Ultraviolet–erasable (UV/EPROM). Both types of EPROMs use capacitive charge MOSFET devices to latch on or off. UV/EPROMs are "cleared" by long–term exposure to ultraviolet light. They are easy to identify: they have a transparent glass window which exposes the silicon chip material to light. Once programmed, you must cover that glass window with tape to prevent ambient light from degrading the data over time.

EPROMs are often programmed using higher signal voltages than what is used during "read–only" mode.

Memory with Moving Parts: "Drives"

The earliest forms of digital data storage involving moving parts was that of the punched paper card. Joseph Marie Jacquard invented a weaving loom in 1780 which automatically followed weaving instructions set by carefully placed holes in paper cards.

This same technology was adapted to electronic computers in the 1950's, with the cards being read mechanically (metal–to–metal contact through the holes), pneumatically (air blown through the holes, the presence of a hole sensed by air nozzle backpressure), or optically (light shining through the holes).

An improvement over paper cards is the paper tape, still used in some industrial environments (notably the CNC machine tool industry), where data storage and speed demands are low and ruggedness is highly valued. Instead of wood–fibre paper, mylar material is often used, with optical reading of the tape being the most popular method.

Magnetic tape (very similar to audio or video cassette tape) was the next logical improvement in storage media. It is still widely used today, as a means to store "backup" data for archiving and emergency restoration for other, faster methods of data storage.

Like paper tape, magnetic tape is sequential access, rather than random access. In early home computer systems, regular audio cassette tape was used to store data in modulated form, the binary 1's and 0's represented by different frequencies (similar to FSK data communication). Access speed was terribly slow (if you were reading ASCII text from the tape, you could almost keep up with the pace of the letters appearing on the computer's screen!), but it was cheap and fairly reliable.

Tape suffered the disadvantage of being sequential access. To address this weak point, magnetic storage "drives" with disk– or drum–shaped media were built. An electric motor provided constant–speed motion. A movable read/write coil (also known as a "head") was provided which could be positioned via servo–motors to various locations on the height of the drum or the radius of the disk, giving access that is almost random (you might still have to wait for the drum or disk to rotate to the proper position once the read/write coil has reached the right location).

The disk shape lent itself best to portable media, and thus the floppy disk was born. Floppy disks (so–called because the magnetic media is thin and flexible) were originally made in 8–inch diameter formats. Later, the 5–1/4 inch variety was introduced, which was made practical by advances in media particle density.

All things being equal, a larger disk has more space upon which to write data. However, storage density can be improved by making the little grains of iron–oxide material on the disk substrate smaller. Today, the 3–1/2 inch floppy disk is the preeminent format, with a capacity of 1.44 Mbytes (2.88 Mbytes on SCSI drives). Other portable drive formats are becoming popular, with IoMega's 100 Mbyte "ZIP" and 1 Gbyte "JAZ" disks appearing as original equipment on some personal computers.

Still, floppy drives have the disadvantage of being exposed to harsh environments, being constantly removed from the drive mechanism which reads, writes, and spins the media. The first disks were enclosed units, sealed from all dust and other particulate matter, and were definitely not portable. Keeping the media in an enclosed environment allowed engineers to avoid dust altogether, as well as spurious magnetic fields. This, in turn, allowed for much closer spacing between the head and the magnetic material, resulting in a much tighter–focused magnetic field to write data to the magnetic material.

The following photograph shows a hard disk drive "platter" of approximately 30 Mbytes storage capacity. A ball–point pen has been set near the bottom of the platter for size reference.

Modern disk drives use multiple platters made of hard material (hence the name, "hard drive") with multiple read/write heads for every platter. The gap between head and platter is much smaller than the diameter of a human hair. If the hermetically–sealed environment inside a hard disk drive is contaminated with outside air, the hard drive will be rendered useless. Dust will lodge between the heads and the platters, causing damage to the surface of the media.

Here is a hard drive with four platters, although the angle of the shot only allows viewing of the top platter. This unit is complete with drive motor, read/write heads, and associated electronics. It has a storage capacity of 340 Mbytes, and is about the same length as the ball–point pen shown in the previous photograph.

While it is inevitable that non–moving–part technology will replace mechanical drives in the future, current state–of–the–art electromechanical drives continue to rival "solid–state" nonvolatile memory devices in storage density, and at a lower cost. In 1998, a 250 Mbyte hard drive was announced that was approximately the size of a quarter (smaller than the metal platter hub in the centre of the last hard disk photograph)! In any case, storage density and reliability will undoubtedly continue to improve.

An incentive for digital data storage technology advancement was the advent of digitally encoded music. A joint venture between Sony and Phillips resulted in the release of the "compact audio disc" (CD) to the public in the late 1980's.

This technology is a read–only type, the media being a transparent plastic disc backed by a thin film of aluminum. Binary bits are encoded as pits in the plastic which vary the path length of a low–power laser beam. Data is read by the low–power laser (the beam of which can be focused more precisely than normal light) reflecting off the aluminum to a photocell receiver. The advantages of CDs over magnetic tape are legion. Being digital, the information is highly resistant to corruption. Being non–contact in operation, there is no wear incurred through playing. Being optical, they are immune to magnetic fields (which can easily corrupt data on magnetic tape or disks). It is possible to purchase CD "burner" drives which contain the high–power laser necessary to write to a blank disc.

Following on the heels of the music industry, the video entertainment industry has leveraged the technology of optical storage with the introduction of the Digital Video Disc, or DVD. Using a similar–sized plastic disc as the music CD, a DVD employs closer spacing of pits to achieve much greater storage density. This increased density allows feature–length movies to be encoded on DVD media, complete with trivia information about the movie, director's notes, and so on.

Much effort is being directed toward the development of a practical read/write optical disc (CD–W). Success has been found in using chemical substances whose colour may be changed through exposure to bright laser light, then "read" by lower–intensity light. These optical discs are immediately identified by their characteristically colored surfaces, as opposed to the silver–colored underside of a standard CD.

PRINCIPLES OF DIGITAL COMPUTING

A BINARY ADDER

Suppose we wanted to build a device that could add two binary bits together. Such a device is known as a half–adder, and its gate circuit looks like this: The Σ symbol represents the "sum" output of the half–adder, the sum's least significant bit (LSB). Cout represents the "carry" output of the half–adder, the sum's most significant bit (MSB).

If we were to implement this same function in ladder (relay) logic, it would look like this:

Either circuit is capable of adding two binary digits together. The mathematical "rules" of how to add bits together are intrinsic to the hard–wired logic of the circuits. If we wanted to perform a different arithmetic operation with binary bits, such as multiplication, we would have to construct another circuit. The above circuit designs will only perform one function: add two binary bits together. To make them do something else would take re–wiring, and perhaps different componentry.

In this sense, digital arithmetic circuits aren't much different from analog arithmetic (operational amplifier) circuits: they do exactly what they're wired to do, no more and no less. We are not, however, restricted to designing digital computer circuits in this manner. It is possible to embed the mathematical "rules" for any arithmetic operation in the form of digital data rather than in hard–wired connections between gates. The result is unparalleled flexibility in operation, giving rise to a whole new kind of digital device: the programmable computer.

While this chapter is by no means exhaustive, it provides what we believe is a unique and interesting look at the nature of programmable computer devices, starting with two devices often overlooked in introductory textbooks: look–up table memories and finite–state machines.

Look–Up Tables

Having learned about digital memory devices in the last chapter, we know that it is possible to store binary data within solid–state devices. Those storage "cells" within solid–state memory devices are easily addressed by driving the "address" lines of the device with the proper binary value(s). Suppose we had a ROM memory circuit written, or programmed, with certain data, such that the address lines of the ROM served as inputs and the data lines of the ROM served as outputs, generating the characteristic response of a particular logic function. Theoretically, we could programme this ROM chip to emulate whatever logic function we wanted without having to alter any wire connections or gates.

Consider the following example of a 4 × 2 bit ROM memory (a very small memory!) programmed with the functionality of a half adder:

If this ROM has been written with the above data (representing a half–adder's truth table), driving the A and B address inputs will cause the respective memory cells in the ROM chip to be enabled, thus outputting the corresponding data as the Sum and Cout bits.

Unlike the half–adder circuit built of gates or relays, this device can be set up to perform any logic function at all with two inputs and two outputs, not just the half–adder function. To change the logic function, all we would need to do is write a different table of data to another ROM chip. We could even use an EPROM chip which could be re–written at will, giving the ultimate flexibility in function.

It is vitally important to recognize the significance of this principle as applied to digital circuitry. Whereas the half–adder built from gates or relays processes the input bits to arrive at a specific output, the ROM simply remembers what the outputs should be for any given combination of inputs.

This is not much different from the "times tables" memorized in grade school: rather than having to calculate the product of 5 times 6 (5 + 5 + 5 + 5 + 5 + 5 = 30), school–children are taught to remember that 5 × 6 = 30, and then expected to recall this product from memory as needed. Likewise, rather than the logic function depending on the functional arrangement of hard–wired gates or relays (hardware), it depends solely on the data written into the memory (software).

Such a simple application, with definite outputs for every input, is called a look–up table, because the memory device simply "looks up" what the output(s) should to be for any given combination of inputs states.

This application of a memory device to perform logical functions is significant for several reasons:

- Software is much easier to change than hardware.
- Software can be archived on various kinds of memory media (disk, tape), thus providing an easy way to document and manipulate the function in a "virtual" form; hardware can only be "archived" abstractly in the form of some kind of graphical drawing.
- Software can be copied from one memory device (such as the EPROM chip) to another, allowing the ability for one device to "learn" its function from another device.
- Software such as the logic function example can be designed to perform functions that would be extremely difficult to emulate with discrete logic gates (or relays!).

The usefulness of a look–up table becomes more and more evident with increasing complexity of function. Suppose we wanted to build a 4–bit adder circuit using a ROM. We'd require a ROM with 8 address lines (two 4–bit numbers to be added together), plus 4 data lines (for the signed output).

With 256 addressable memory locations in this ROM chip, we would have a fair amount of programming to do, telling it what binary output to generate for each and every combination of binary inputs. We would also run the risk of making a mistake in our programming and have it output an incorrect sum, if we weren't careful. However, the flexibility of being able to configure this function (or any function) through software alone generally outweighs that costs.

Consider some of the advanced functions we could implement with the above "adder." We know that when we add two sets of numbers in 2's complement signed notation, we risk having the answer overflow. For instance, if we try to add 0111 (decimal 7) to 0110 (decimal 6) with only a 4–bit number field, the answer we'll get is 1001 (decimal –7) instead of the correct value, 13 (7 + 6), which cannot be expressed using 4 signed bits.

If we wanted to, we could avoid the strange answers given in overflow conditions by programming this look–up table circuit to output something else in conditions where we know overflow will occur (that is, in any case where the real sum would exceed +7 or –8). One alternative might be to programme the ROM to output the quantity 0111 (the maximum positive value that can be represented with 4 signed bits), or any other value that we determined to be more appropriate for the application than the typical overflowed "error" value that a regular adder circuit would output. It's all up to the programmer to decide what he or she wants this circuit to do, because we are no longer limited by the constraints of logic gate functions.

The possibilities don't stop at customized logic functions, either. By adding more address lines to the 256 × 4 ROM chip, we can expand the look–up table to include multiple functions:

With two more address lines, the ROM chip will have 4 times as many addresses as before (1024 instead of 256). This ROM could be programmed so that when A8 and A9 were both low, the output data represented the sum of the two 4–bit binary numbers input on address lines A0 through A7, just as we had with the previous 256 × 4 ROM circuit. For the addresses A8=1 and A9=0, it could be programmed to output the difference (subtraction) between the first 4–bit binary number (A0 through A3) and the second binary number (A4 through A7).

For the addresses A8=0 and A9=1, we could programme the ROM to output the difference (subtraction) of the two numbers in reverse order (second – first rather than first – second), and finally, for the addresses A8=1 and A9=1, the ROM could be programmed to compare the two inputs and output an indication of equality or inequality. What we will have then is a device that can perform four different arithmetical operations on 4–bit binary numbers, all by "looking up" the answers programmed into it.

If we had used a ROM chip with more than two additional address lines, we could programme it with a wider variety of functions to perform on the two 4–bit inputs. There are a number of operations peculiar to binary data (such as parity check or Exclusive–ORing of bits) that we might find useful to have programmed in such a look–up table.

Devices such as this, which can perform a variety of arithmetical tasks as dictated by a binary input code, are known as Arithmetic Logic Units (ALUs), and they comprise one of the essential components of computer technology. Although modern ALUs are more often constructed from very complex combinational logic (gate) circuits for reasons of speed, it should be comforting to know that the exact same functionality may be duplicated with a "dumb" ROM chip programmed with the appropriate look–up table(s).

In fact, this exact approach was used by IBM engineers in 1959 with the development of the IBM 1401 and 1620 computers, which used look–up tables to perform addition, rather than binary adder circuitry. The machine was fondly known as the "CADET," which stood for "Can't Add, Doesn't Even Try."

A very common application for look–up table ROMs is in control systems where a custom mathematical function needs to be represented. Such an application is found in computer–controlled fuel injection systems for automobile engines, where the proper air/fuel mixture ratio for efficient and clean operation changes with several environmental and operational variables. Tests performed on engines in research laboratories determine what these ideal ratios are for varying conditions of engine load, ambient air temperature, and barometric air pressure.

The variables are measured with sensor transducers, their analog outputs converted to digital signals with A/D circuitry, and those parallel digital signals used as address inputs to a high–capacity ROM chip programmed to output the optimum digital value for air/fuel ratio for any of these given conditions.

Sometimes, ROMs are used to provide one–dimensional look–up table functions, for "correcting" digitized signal values so that they more accurately represent their real–world significance. An example of such a device is a thermocouple transmitter, which measures the millivoltage signal generated by a junction of dissimilar metals and outputs a signal which is supposed to directly correspond to that junction temperature. Unfortunately, thermocouple junctions do not have perfectly linear temperature/voltage responses, and so the raw voltage signal is not perfectly proportional to temperature.

By digitizing the voltage signal (A/D conversion) and sending that digital value to the address of a ROM programmed with the necessary correction values, the ROM's programming could eliminate some of the nonlinearity of the thermocouple's temperature–to–millivoltage relationship, so that the final output of the device would be more accurate. The popular instrumentation term for such a look–up table is a digital characterizer.

Another application for look–up tables is in special code translation. A 128 × 8 ROM, for instance, could be used to translate 7–bit ASCII code to 8–bit EBCDIC code:

Again, all that is required is for the ROM chip to be properly programmed with the necessary data so that each valid ASCII input will produce a corresponding EBCDIC output code.

FINITE–STATE MACHINES

Feedback is a fascinating engineering principle. It can turn a rather simple device or process into something substantially more complex. We've seen the effects of feedback intentionally integrated into circuit designs with some rather astounding effects:

- Comparator + negative feedback ⟶ controllable–gain amplifier
- Comparator + positive feedback ⟶ comparator with hysteresis
- Combinational logic + positive feedback ⟶ multivibrator

  In the field of process instrumentation, feedback is used to transform a simple measurement system into something capable of control:
- Measurement system + negative feedback ⟶ closed–loop control system

Feedback, both positive and negative, has the tendency to add whole new dynamics to the operation of a device or system. Sometimes, these new dynamics find useful application, while other times they are merely interesting.

With look–up tables programmed into memory devices, feedback from the data outputs back to the address inputs creates a whole new type of device: the Finite State Machine, or FSM:

The above circuit illustrates the basic idea: the data stored at each address becomes the next storage location that the ROM gets addressed to. The result is a specific sequence of binary numbers (following the sequence programmed into the ROM) at the output, over time.

To avoid signal timing problems, though, we need to connect the data outputs back to the address inputs through a 4–bit D–type flip–flop, so that the sequence takes place step by step to the beat of a controlled clock pulse:

An analogy for the workings of such a device might be an array of post–office boxes, each one with an identifying number on the door (the address), and each one containing a piece of paper with the address of another P.O. box written on it (the data). A person, opening the first P.O. box, would find in it the address of the next P.O. box to open. By storing a particular pattern of addresses in the P.O. boxes, we can dictate the sequence in which each box gets opened, and therefore the sequence of which paper gets read.

Having 16 addressable memory locations in the ROM, this Finite State

Machine would have 16 different stable "states" in which it could latch. In each of those states, the identity of the next state would be programmed in to the ROM, awaiting the signal of the next clock pulse to be fed back to the ROM as an address.

One useful application of such an FSM would be to generate an arbitrary count sequence, such as Gray Code:

Address	→ Data	Gray Code	Count Sequence:
0000	→ 0001	0	0000
0001	→ 0011	1	0001
0010	→ 0110	2	0011
0011	→ 0010	3	0010
0100	→ 1100	4	0110
0101	→ 0100	5	0111
0110	→ 0111	6	0101
0111	→ 0101	7	0100
1000	→ 0000	8	1100
1001	→ 1000	9	1101
1010	→ 1011	10	1111
1011	→ 1001	11	1110
1100	→ 1101	12	1010
1101	→ 1111	13	1011
1110	→ 1010	14	1001
1111	→ 1110	15	1000

Try to follow the Gray Code count sequence as the FSM would do it: starting at 0000, follow the data stored at that address (0001) to the next address, and so on (0011), and so on (0010), and so on (0110), etc. The result, for the programme table shown, is that the sequence of addressing jumps around from address to address in what looks like a haphazard fashion, but when you check each address that is accessed, you will find that it follows the correct order for 4–bit Gray code. When the FSM arrives at its last programmed state (address 1000), the data stored there is 0000, which starts the whole sequence over again at address 0000 in step with the next clock pulse.

We could expand on the capabilities of the above circuit by using a ROM with more address lines, and adding more programming data:

Now, just like the look–up table adder circuit that we turned into an Arithmetic Logic Unit (+, –, x,/ functions) by utilizing more address lines as "function control" inputs, this FSM counter can be used to generate more than one count sequence, a different sequence programmed for the four feedback bits (A0 through A3) for each of the two function control line input combinations (A4 = 0 or 1).

Address	Data	Address	Data
00000 →	0001	10000	→ 0001
00001 →	0010	10001	→ 0011
00010 →	0011	10010	→ 0110
00011 →	0100	10011	→ 0010
00100 →	0101	10100	→ 1100
00101 →	0110	10101	→ 0100
00110 →	0111	10110	→ 0111
00111 →	1000	10111	→ 0101
01000 →	1001	11000	→ 0000
01001 →	1010	11001	→ 1000
01010 →	1011	11010	→ 1011
01011 →	1100	11011	→ 1001
01100 →	1101	11100	→ 1101
01101 →	1110	11101	→ 1111
01110 →	1111	11110	→ 1010
01111 →	0000	1111	→ 1110

If A4 is 0, the FSM counts in binary; if A4 is 1, the FSM counts in Gray Code. In either case, the counting sequence is arbitrary: determined by the whim of the programmer. For that matter, the counting sequence doesn't even have to have 16 steps, as the programmer may decide to have the sequence recycle to 0000 at any one of the steps at all. It is a completely flexible counting device, the behaviour strictly determined by the software (programming) in the ROM.

We can expand on the capabilities of the FSM even more by utilizing a ROM chip with additional address input and data output lines. Take the following circuit, for example:

Here, the D0 through D3 data outputs are used exclusively for feedback to the A0 through A3 address lines. Date output lines D4 through D7 can be programmed to output something other than the FSM's "state" value. Being that four data output bits are being fed back to four address bits, this is still a 16–state device. However, having the output data come from other data output lines gives the programmer more freedom to configure functions than before. In other words, this device can do far more than just count!

The programmed output of this FSM is dependent not only upon the state of the feedback address lines (A0 through A3), but also the states of the input lines (A4 through A7). The D–type flip/flop's clock signal input does not have to come from a pulse generator, either. To make things more interesting, the flip/flop could be wired up to clock on some external event, so that the FSM goes to the next state only when an input signal tells it to.

Now we have a device that better fulfills the meaning of the word "programmable." The data written to the ROM is a programme in the truest sense: the outputs follow a pre–established order based on the inputs to the device and which "step" the device is on in its sequence. This is very close to the operating design of the Turing Machine, a theoretical computing device invented by Alan Turing, mathematically proven to be able to solve any known arithmetic problem, given enough memory capacity.

MICROPROCESSORS

Early computer science pioneers such as Alan Turing and John Von Neumann postulated that for a computing device to be really useful, it not only had to be able to generate specific outputs as dictated by programmed instructions, but it also had to be able to write data to memory, and be able to act on that data later. Both the programme steps and the processed data were to reside in a common memory "pool," thus giving way to the label of the stored–programme computer.

Turing's theoretical machine utilized a sequential–access tape, which would store data for a control circuit to read, the control circuit re–writing data to the tape and/or moving the tape to a new position to read more data. Modern computers use random–access memory devices instead of sequential–access tapes to accomplish essentially the same thing, except with greater capability.

A helpful illustration is that of early automatic machine tool control technology. Called open–loop, or sometimes just NC (numerical control), these control systems would direct the motion of a machine tool such as a lathe or a mill by following instructions programmed as holes in paper tape. The tape would be run one direction through a "read" mechanism, and the machine would blindly follow the instructions on the tape without regard to any other conditions. While these devices eliminated the burden of having to have a human machinist direct every motion of the machine tool, it was limited in usefulness.

Because the machine was blind to the real world, only following the instructions written on the tape, it could not compensate for changing conditions such as expansion of the metal or wear of the mechanisms. Also, the tape programmer had to be acutely aware of the sequence of previous instructions in the machine's programme to avoid troublesome circumstances (such as telling the machine tool to move the drill bit laterally while it is still inserted into a hole in the work), since the device had no memory other than the tape itself, which was read–only.

Upgrading from a simple tape reader to a Finite State control design gave the device a sort of memory that could be used to keep track of what it had already done (through feedback of some of the data bits to the address bits), so at least the programmer could decide to have the circuit remember "states" that the machine tool could be in (such as "coolant on," or tool position). However, there was still room for improvement.

The ultimate approach is to have the programme give instructions which would include the writing of new data to a read/write (RAM) memory, which the programme could easily recall and process. This way, the control system could record what it had done, and any sensor–detectable process changes, much in the same way that a human machinist might jot down notes or measurements on a scratch–pad for future reference in his or her work. This is what is referred to as CNC, or Closed–loop Numerical Control.

Engineers and computer scientists looked forward to the possibility of building digital devices that could modify their own programming, much the same as the human brain adapts the strength of inter–neural connections depending on environmental experiences (that is why memory retention improves with repeated study, and behaviour is modified through consequential feedback). Only if the computer's programme were stored in the same writable memory "pool" as the data would this be practical.

It is interesting to note that the notion of a self–modifying programme is still considered to be on the cutting edge of computer science. Most computer programming relies on rather fixed sequences of instructions, with a separate field of data being the only information that gets altered.

To facilitate the stored–programme approach, we require a device that is much more complex than the simple FSM, although many of the same principles apply. First, we need read/write memory that can be easily accessed: this is easy enough to do. Static or dynamic RAM chips do the job well, and are inexpensive. Secondly, we need some form of logic to process the data stored in memory.

Because standard and Boolean arithmetic functions are so useful, we can use an Arithmetic Logic Unit (ALU) such as the look–up table ROM example explored earlier. Finally, we need a device that controls how and where data flows between the memory, the ALU, and the outside world. This so–called Control Unit is the most mysterious piece of the puzzle yet, being comprised of tri–state buffers (to direct data to and from buses) and decoding logic which interprets certain binary codes as instructions to carry out. Sample instructions might be something like: "add the number stored at memory address 0010 with the number stored at memory address 1101," or, "determine the parity of the data in memory address 0111." The choice of which binary codes represent which instructions for the Control Unit to decode is largely arbitrary, just as the choice of which binary codes to use in representing the letters of the alphabet in the ASCII standard was largely arbitrary. ASCII, however, is now an internationally recognized standard, whereas control unit instruction codes are almost always manufacturer–specific.

Putting these components together (read/write memory, ALU, and control unit) results in a digital device that is typically called a processor. If minimal memory is used, and all the necessary components are contained on a single integrated circuit, it is called a microprocessor. When combined with the necessary bus–control support circuitry, it is known as a Central Processing Unit, or CPU.

CPU operation is summed up in the so–called fetch/execute cycle. Fetch means to read an instruction from memory for the Control Unit to decode. A small binary counter in the CPU (known as the programme counter or instruction pointer) holds the address value where the next instruction is stored in main memory. The Control Unit sends this binary address value to the main memory's address lines, and the memory's data output is read by the Control Unit to send to another holding register.

If the fetched instruction requires reading more data from memory (for example, in adding two numbers together, we have to read both the numbers that are to be added from main memory or from some other source), the Control Unit appropriately addresses the location of the requested data and directs the data output to ALU registers. Next, the Control Unit would execute the instruction by signaling the ALU to do whatever was requested with the two numbers, and direct the result to another register called the accumulator. The instruction has now been "fetched" and "executed," so the Control Unit now increments the programme counter to step the next instruction, and the cycle repeats itself.

Microprocessor (CPU)	
** Programme counter ** (increments address value sent to external memory chip(s) to fetch the next instruction)	⟶ Address bus (to RAM memory)
** Control Unit ** (decodes instructions read from programme in memory, enables flow of data to and from ALU, internal registers, and external devices)	⟶ Control Bus (to all devices sharing address and/or data busses; arbitrates all bus communi–cations)
**Arithmetic Logic Unit (ALU) ** (performs all mathematical calculations and Boolean functions)	

Microprocessor (CPU)	
**Registers ** (small read/write memories for holding instruction codes, error codes, ALU data, etc; includes the "accumulator")	——→Data Bus (from RAM memory and other external devices)

As one might guess, carrying out even simple instructions is a tedious process. Several steps are necessary for the Control Unit to complete the simplest of mathematical procedures. This is especially true for arithmetic procedures such as exponents, which involve repeated executions ("iterations") of simpler functions.

Just imagine the sheer quantity of steps necessary within the CPU to update the bits of information for the graphic display on a flight simulator game! The only thing which makes such a tedious process practical is the fact that microprocessor circuits are able to repeat the fetch/execute cycle with great speed.

In some microprocessor designs, there are minimal programs stored within a special ROM memory internal to the device (called microcode) which handle all the sub–steps necessary to carry out more complex math operations.

This way, only a single instruction has to be read from the programme RAM to do the task, and the programmer doesn't have to deal with trying to tell the microprocessor how to do every minute step. In essence, its a processor inside of a processor; a programme running inside of a programme.

MICROPROCESSOR PROGRAMMING

The "vocabulary" of instructions which any particular microprocessor chip possesses is specific to that model of chip. An Intel 80386, for example, uses a completely different set of binary codes than a Motorola 68020, for designating equivalent functions. Unfortunately, there are no standards in place for microprocessor instructions. This makes programming at the very lowest level very confusing and specialized.

When a human programmer develops a set of instructions to directly tell a microprocessor how to do something (like automatically control the fuel injection rate to an engine), they're programming in the CPU's own "language." This language, which consists of the very same binary codes which the Control Unit inside the CPU chip decodes to perform tasks, is often referred to as machine language. While machine language software can be "worded" in binary notation, it is often written in hexadecimal form, because it is easier for human beings to work with. For example, I'll present just a few of the common instruction codes for the Intel 8080 micro–processor chip:

Hexadecimal	*Binary*	*Instruction description*
7B	01111011	Move contents of register A to register E
87	10000111	Add contents of register A to register D
1C	00011100	Increment the contents of register E by 1
D3	11010011	Output byte of data to data bus

Even with hexadecimal notation, these instructions can be easily confused and forgotten. For this purpose, another aid for programmers exists called assembly language. With assembly language, two to four letter mnemonic words are used in place of the actual hex or binary code for describing program steps. For example, the instruction 7B for the Intel 8080 would be "MOV A,E" in assembly language. The mnemonics, of course, are useless to the microprocessor, which can only understand binary codes, but it is an expedient way for programmers to manage the writing of their programs on paper or text editor (word processor).

There are even programs written for computers called assemblers which understand these mnemonics, translating them to the appropriate binary codes for a specified target microprocessor, so that the programmer can write a program in the computer's native language without ever having to deal with strange hex or tedious binary code notation.

Once a program is developed by a person, it must be written into memory before a microprocessor can execute it. If the program is to be stored in ROM (which some are), this can be done with a special machine called a ROM programmer, or (if you're masochistic), by plugging the ROM chip into a breadboard, powering it up with the appropriate voltages, and writing data by making the right wire connections to the address and data lines, one at a time, for each instruction.

If the program is to be stored in volatile memory, such as the operating computer's RAM memory, there may be a way to type it in by hand through that computer's keyboard (some computers have a mini–program stored in ROM which tells the microprocessor how to accept keystrokes from a keyboard and store them as commands in RAM), even if it is too dumb to do anything else.

Many "hobby" computer kits work like this. If the computer to be programmed is a fully–functional personal computer with an operating system, disk drives, and the whole works, you can simply command the assembler to store your finished program onto a disk for later retrieval. To "run" your program, you would simply type your program's filename at the prompt, press the Enter key, and the microprocessor's Program Counter register would be set to point to the location ("address") on the disk where the first instruction is stored, and your program would run from there.

Although programming in machine language or assembly language makes for fast and highly efficient programs, it takes a lot of time and skill to do so for anything but the simplest tasks, because each machine language instruction is so crude. The answer to this is to develop ways for programmers to write in "high level" languages, which can more efficiently express human thought.

Instead of typing in dozens of cryptic assembly language codes, a programmer writing in a high–level language would be able to write something like this ... Print "Hello, world!" and expect the computer to print "Hello, world!" with no further instruction on how to do so. This is a great idea, but how does a microprocessor understand such "human" thinking when its vocabulary is so limited?

The answer comes in two different forms: interpretation, or compilation. Just like two people speaking different languages, there has to be some way to transcend the language barrier in order for them to converse. A translator is needed to translate each person's words to the other person's language, one way at a time. For the microprocessor, this means another program, written by another programmer in machine language, which recognizes the ASCII character patterns of high–level commands such as Print (P–r–i–n–t) and can translate them into the necessary bite–size steps that the microprocessor can directly understand. If this translation is done during program execution, just like a translator intervening between two people in a live conversation, it is called "interpretation." On the other hand, if the entire program is translated to machine language in one fell swoop, like a translator recording a monologue on paper and then translating all the words at one sitting into a written document in the other language, the process is called "compilation."

Interpretation is simple, but makes for a slow–running program because the microprocessor has to continually translate the program between steps, and that takes time. Compilation takes time initially to translate the whole program into machine code, but the resulting machine code needs no translation after that and runs faster as a consequence. Programming languages such as BASIC and FORTH are interpreted. Languages such as C, C++, FORTRAN, and PASCAL are compiled. Compiled languages are generally considered to be the languages of choice for professional programmers, because of the efficiency of the final product.

Naturally, because machine language vocabularies vary widely from microprocessor to microprocessor, and since high–level languages are designed to be as universal as possible, the interpreting and compiling programs necessary for language translation must be microprocessor–specific. Development of these interpreters and compilers is a most impressive feat: the people who make these programs most definitely earn their keep, especially when you consider the work they must do to keep their software product current with the rapidly–changing microprocessor models appearing on the market!

To mitigate this difficulty, the trend–setting manufacturers of microprocessor chips (most notably, Intel and Motorola) try to design their new products to be backwardly compatible with their older products. For example, the entire instruction set for the Intel 80386 chip is contained within the latest Pentium IV chips, although the Pentium chips have additional instructions that the 80386 chips lack.

What this means is that machine–language programs (compilers, too) written for 80386 computers will run on the latest and greatest Intel Pentium IV CPU, but machine–language programs written specifically to take advantage of the Pentium's larger instruction set will not run on an 80386, because the older CPU simply doesn't have some of those instructions in its vocabulary: the Control Unit inside the 80386 cannot decode them.

Index

K

L

M

N

O

P